COMPANY LAW

BY

SINEAD MCGRATH

B.C.L., LL.M., B.L., Attorney at Law
(New York)

DUBLIN
THOMSON ROUND HALL
2003

Published in 2003 by
Round Hall Ltd.
43 Fitzwilliam Place
Dublin 2
Ireland

Typeset by
Devlin Typesetting, Dublin

Printed by
ColourBooks, Dublin

A CIP catalogue record for this book is available from the British Library

ISBN 1-85800-286-9

CONTENTS

Table of Cases ix
Table of Statutes xxx

1. Developments in Company Law

1.1 Companies in general 1
1.2 The Companies Acts 2
1.3 European developments 4
1.4 The Office of Director of Corporate Enforcement 10
1.5 The Company Law Review Group (the "CLRG") 15

2. Company Formation

2.1 Limited and unlimited companies 25
2.2 Private and public companies 27
2.3 Conversion of companies 30
2.5 Incorporation 36
2.6 Consequences of incorporation 41

3. Company Promoters

3.1 Promoters' duties 49
3.2 Breach of duties 51
3.3 Pre-incorporation contracts 52

4. Company Constitution

4.1 Memorandum of Association 55
4.2 Articles of Association 67
4.3 Section 25 contract 70
4.4 Public documents 71

5. Corporate Personality

5.1 The Salomon case 73
5.2 The effect of the corporate veil 75
5.3 Lifting the veil by statute 78
5.4 Lifting the veil by the court 85
5.5 The character of a company 93

6. Company Contracts

6.1 Contracts in breach of the objects of the company 95
6.2 Contracts in breach of the express ancillary powers of the company 99
6.3 Contracts without company authority 100
6.4 Contracts in breach of the company's internal rules 107

7. Company Directors

7.1 Appointment, removal and remuneration of directors 112
7.2 Register of directors 117
7.3 Meetings of directors 118
7.4 Disclosure of interests 119
7.5 Substantial property transactions 123
7.6 Prohibited transactions 124
7.7 Powers of directors 129
7.8 Directors' duties 129

8. Restriction and Disqualification

8.1 Restriction orders 139
8.2 Disqualification orders 146

9. Company Accounts, Auditors and Annual Returns

9.1 Company accounts 153
9.2 Company auditors 157
9.3 Annual returns 167

10. Reckless and Fraudulent Trading

10.1 Reckless and fraudulent trading 170
10.2 Reckless trading 171
10.3 Fraudulent trading 175

11. Insider Dealing

11.1 Unlawful dealings by connected persons 178
11.2 Unlawful dealings by unconnected persons 180
11.3 The company's right to deal 180
11.4 Civil liability for insider dealing 181
11.5 Criminal liability for insider dealing 181
11.6 Exempt transactions 182
11.7 Role of the stock exchange 183
11.8 Stabilisation of share price 184

12. Company Shares

12.1 Shares 186
12.2 Dividends 190
12.3 Shareholders' rights 193
12.4 Classes of shares 195
12.5 Share allotment 200
12.6 Disclosure of interests in shares 208

13. Company Membership
13.1 Membership 216
13.2 Share transfer and transmission 222
13.3 Shareholders' meetings 229

14. Shareholders' Remedies
14.1 The rule in Foss v. Harbottle 239
14.2 Section 205 of the Companies Act 1963 246

15. Capital Maintenance Rules
15.1 Redemption of shares 253
15.2 Acquisition by a company of its own shares 257
15.3 Assisting the purchase of a company's own shares 262
15.4 Capital reduction 268
15.5 Serious capital loss 270

16. Company Borrowing and Security
16.1 Security for loan capital 272
16.2 Debentures 272
16.3 Fixed charges 275
16.4 Floating charges 276
16.5 Fixed charges over book debts 280
16.6 Retention of title charges 284

17. Registration of Company Charges
17.1 Particulars of the charge 291
17.2 Registrable charges 292
17.3 Responsibility for compliance 295
17.4 Time frame for compliance 295
17.5 Certificate of registration and errors in registration 296
17.6 Effect of non-compliance 297
17.7 Late registration 297

18. Receivership
18.1 Appointment of a receiver 300
18.2 Effect of receivership 306
18.3 Duties of a receiver 307
18.4 Removal and resignation of a receiver 311

19. Company Investigations
19.1 Categories of investigations 313
19.2 Court investigations 314
19.3 Formal investigations of company membership 321

19.4 Informal investigations by the Director of Corporate Enforcement 323
19.5 Section 16 restrictions 324
19.6 Production of documents 325
19.7 Search warrants 331
19.8 Security of reports 331

20. Examinership
20.1 Petition 334
20.2 Accountant's report 336
20.3 Examiner 338
20.4 Hearing of the petition 341
20.5 Protection period 342
20.6 Powers of the examiner 346
20.7 Examiner's report 350

21. Voluntary winding up
21.1 Members' voluntary winding up 356
21.2 Creditors' voluntary winding up 358
21.3 Conversion: A members' winding up to a creditors' winding up 362
21.4 Conversion: A voluntary winding up to a court winding up 363
21.5 Duties of a voluntary liquidator 364
21.6 Powers of a voluntary liquidator 364
21.7 Liability of a liquidator 367
21.8 Company dissolution 368

22. Involuntary winding up
22.1 Petitioners 369
22.2 Grounds for a court winding up 373
22.3 Involuntary winding up procedure 377
22.4 The liquidator 379
22.5 Powers of the liquidator 381
22.6 Powers of the court 382
22.7 Cross-border insolvency 384
22.8 Company dissolution 385
22.9 Restoration to the company register 385

23. Disposition of Company Assets
23.1 Realisation of company assets 392
23.2 Distribution of company assets 404

Index 411

Table of Cases

Aberdeen Railway Company v. Blaikie Bros (1854) 1 Macq 461 .... 7.8.3
Adams v. Cape Industries plc [1990] B.C.L.C. 479 .... 5.4.1
Airlines Airspares Ltd v. Handley Page Ltd [1970] 1 All E.R. 29 .... 18.2.3(1)
Aktieselskabet Dansk Skibsfinansiering v Brothers et al (2001) 2 B.C.L.C. 324 .... 10.3
Al Levy (Holdings) Ltd, Re [1963] 2 All E.R. 85 .... 23.1.2(3)
Alexander v. Automatic Telephone Co [1900] 2 Ch. 56 .... 12.1.4
Alexander Hull & Company Ltd v. O'Carroll Kent & Company Ltd 89 [1955] ILTR 70 .... 18.1.3
Allen v. Gold Reefs of West Africa Ltd [1900] 1 Ch. 656 .... 4.2.2, 13.3.3
Allen v. Hyatt (1914) 30 T.L.R. 444 (PC) .... 7.8.4(1)
Allied Irish Bank Ltd v. Ardmore Studios International (1972) Ltd, unreported, High Court, May 30, 1973 .... 6.4.1
Allied Irish Coal Supplies Ltd v. Powell Duffryn International Fuels [1998] 2 I.R. 519 .... 5.4.4
Aluminum Industrie Vaasem BV v. Romalpa Aluminum Ltd [1976] 2 All E.R. 552 .... 16.6, 16.6.3
Aluminium Fabricators Ltd, Re [1984] I.L.R.M. 399 .... 10.3.1
Amalgamated Syndicates Ltd, Re [1901] 2 Ch. 181 .... 21.1.4
Amantiss Enterprises Ltd, Re [2000] 2 I.L.R.M. 177 .... 22.9.8
Andrabell Ltd, Re [1984] 3 All E.R. 407 .... 16.6.3
Angelis v. Algemene Bank Nederland (Ireland) Ltd, unreported, High Court, July 4, 1974 .... 18.1.3
Apthorpe (Surveyor of Taxes) v. Peter Schoenhofen Brewing Co Ltd (1899) 4 TC 41 .... 5.4.2
Ardmore Studios (Ireland) Ltd v. Lynch [1965] I.R. 1 .... 18.2.3(1)
Armagas Ltd v. Mundagas SA [1985] 3 All E.R. 795 .... 6.3.3
Armagh Shoes Ltd, Re [1982] NI 59 .... 16.5.1
Ashbury Railway Carriage and Iron Co Ltd v. Riche (1875) LR 7 HL 653 .... 4.1.4, 6.1
Ashclad Ltd (in liquidation), Re, unreported, High Court April 5, 2000 .... 5.3.6, 9.1.1

Ashmark Ltd Ltd (No. 1) (1990), Re .... 23.1.2(3)
Ashmark Ltd (No. 2), Re [1990] I.L.R.M. 455 .... 23.1.2(2)
Ashmark Ltd v. Allied Irish Bank plc
[1994] 1 I.L.R.M. 223 .... 23.1.2(2)
ASRS Establishment Ltd (in administrative receivership
and liquidation), Re [2000] 1 B.C.L.C. 727 .... 16.5.1
Assignees of Taylor (1869-70) I.R.CL 129 .... 23.1.3(2)
Associated Alloys Pty Ltd v. Metropolitan Engineering
& Fabrication Ltd, unreported, High Court (Australia),
May 11, 2000 .... 16.6.3
Athenaeum Life Assurance Society, Re, ex p. Eagle
Insurance Co., Re Co (1858) 4 K & J 549 .... 6.3.1
Atlantic Magnetics Ltd, Re (in receivership) [1993]
2 I.R. 561 .... 20, 20.3.1, 20.5
A-G. v. Great Eastern Railway (1880)
5 App Cas 473 .... 4.1.4(3)
A-G. v. Mersey Railway Co [1907] 1 Ch. 81 .... 4.1.4(4)
Autodata v. Gibbons [2000], unreported, July 13, 2000 .... 13.1.4
Badgerhill Properties Ltd v. Cottrell [1991] B.C.L.C. 805 .... 3.3.2
Bahiaa and San Francisco Railway Co., Re (1868)
LR 3 Q.B. 584 .... 12.1.2
Bairstow et al v. Queens Moat Houses plc [2001]
2 B.C.L.C. 531 .... 12.2.4
Bank of Ireland Finance Ltd v. Rockfield Ltd [1979]
I.R. 21 .... 6.1.1, 15.3.4
Bank of Ireland Finance Ltd v. DJ Daly Ltd
(in liquidation) [1978] I.R. 79 .... 17.2.1
Barclays Bank plc v. Stuart Landon Ltd & anor,
[2001] 2 B.C.L.C. 316 .... 17.7
Barned's Banking Co, Re; Peel's case (1867) 2 Ch. App 674 .... 2.4.3
Barnett, Hoares and Co v. Slough London Tramways Co
(1887) 18 Q.B.D. 815 .... 6.3.1
Bath Glass Ltd, Re [1988] B.C.L.C. 329 .... 8.2.6
Battle v. Irish Art Promotion Centre Ltd [1968] I.R. 252................. 5.2
Bede Steam Company Ltd, Re [1917] 1 Ch. 123......................... 13.2.4
Belfast Empire Theatre of Varieties, Re [1963] I.R. 41 .... 12.2.3
Bell Houses Ltd v. City Wall Properties Ltd [1996]
2 All E.R. 674.. 4.1.4(4)
Bellador Silk Ltd, Re [1965] 1 All E.R. 667 .... 14.2.1

Benfield Greig Group plc, Nugent and anor v. Benfield Greig Group plc et al [2000] 2 B.C.L.C. 488 .... 13.2.2
Betts & Co Ltd v. Macnaughton, Re [1910) 1 Ch. 430 .... 13.3.7
Biggerstaff v. Rowatt's Wharf Ltd (1896) 2 Ch. 93 .... 6.3.2
Birch v. Cropper, Re Bridge Water Navigation Co Ltd (1889) 14 App Cas 525 .... 12.4
Blenheim Leisure (Restaurants) Ltd (No. 2), Re [2000] B.C.C. 821 .... 22.9.8
Bloomenthal v. Ford [1897] A.C. 156 .... 12.1.2
Blue Note Enterprises Ltd, Re [2001] 2 B.C.L.C. 427 .... 22.9.8
Bond v. Barrow Haematite Steel Co [1902] 1 Ch. 353 .... 12.2.2
Bond Worth Ltd, Re [1980] Ch. 288 .... 16.6.2, 17.2.7
Borden (UK) v. Scottish Timber Products Ltd [1981] Ch. 35 .... 16.6.2
Borlands Trustee Company v. Steele [1901] 1 Ch. 279.............. 12.3.5
Boschoek Pty Co Ltd v. Fuke [1906] 1 Ch. 148 .... 6.3.1
Bradcrown Ltd; Official Receiver v. Ireland (2001) 1 B.C.L.C. 547 .... 8.2.6
Bradford Banking Co v. Briggs, Son & Co. (1886) 12 App Cas 29 .... 12.4.5
Bradman v. Trinity Estates plc [1989] B.C.L.C. 757 .... 13.3.3
Bratton Seymour Service Company Ltd v. Oxborough [1992] B.C.L.C. 693 .... 4.3
Brightlife Ltd, Re [1987] 2 W.L.R. 197 .... 16.4.2
Brook's Wharf and Bull Ltd v. Goodman Brothers [1937] 1 K.B. 534 .... 5.3.1
Brown & Gregory Ltd, Re [1904] 1 Ch. 627 .... 16.2.4
Brumark Investments Ltd, Re [2001] 2 B.C.L.C. 188 .... 16.5.2
Bryanston Finance Ltd v. DeVires (No. 2) [1976] Ch. 63 ...... 22.1.2(2)
Buchanan (Peter) Ltd v. McVey [1954] I.R. 89 .... 7.3
Bugle Press Ltd, Re [1961] Ch. 270 .... 5.4.1
Bula Ltd et al v. Crowley et al, unreported, High Court, February 1, 2002 .... 18.1.2
Bula Ltd, Re, unreported, Supreme Court, May 13, 1988; unreported, High Court, July 18, 1986 .... 22.1.2
Burton v. Palmer, unreported, Supreme Court (NSW Australia), December 17, 1980 .... 15.3.1
Business Communications Ltd v. Baxter & Parsons, unreported, High Court, July 21, 1995......... 8.1, 8.1.1, 8.1.3, 8.2.6

Butler Engineering Ltd, Re, unreported, High Court, March 1, 1996 Court 20.3.1
Byng v. London Life Association Ltd [Companies Act 1990] 1 Ch. 170 .... 4.3, 14.1.4
Campbell v. Rofe [1933] A.C. 91 .... 12.4
Cane v. Jones [1981] 1 W.L.R. 1451 .... 4.2.3
Caparo Industries plc v. Dickman (Companies Act 1990) B.C.L.C. 273 .... 9.2.8
Car Replacements Ltd, Re, unreported, High Court, December 15, 1999 .... 22.4.4
Carroll Group Distributors Ltd v. G & JF Bourke Ltd [1990] I.L.R.M. 285 .... 16.6.3
Carvill v. Irish Industrial Bank Ltd [1968] I.R. 325 .... 7.1.5
Casali v. Crisp [2001], unreported, Supreme Court (NSW Australia), October 3, 2001) .... 22.9.7(1)
Casey v. Bentley [1902] 1 I.R. 376 .... 13.2.5
Casey v. Intercontinental Bank [1979] I.R. 364 .... 18.3.2(2)
Castleholdings Investment Company Ltd, Re, unreported, High Court, November 8, 2001 .... 20.7.5
CB Readymix Ltd, Cahill (Official Liquidation) v. Grimes, unreported, Supreme Court, March 1, 2002 .... 8.2.6
CEM Connections Ltd, Re [2000] B.C.C. 917 .... 7.1.1
Centrebind Ltd, Re [1966] 3 All E.R. 889, [1967] W.L.R. 377 .... 21.6.3
Chalk v. Kahn & anor [2000] 2 B.C.L.C. 418 .... 16.5.1
Charitable Corporation v. Sutton (1742) 2 Atk 400 .... 7.8.2
Charterhouse Investment Trust Ltd v. Tempest Diesels Ltd [1986] B.C.L.C. 1 .... 15.3.1
Chestvale Properties Ltd v. Glackin [1993] 3 I.R. 35 .... 19.2.5(1)
City Equitable Fire Insurance Company Ltd, Re (1925) Ch. 407 .... 7.8.2
Cladrose Ltd, Re [1990] B.C.L.C. 204 .... 8.2.6
Clare Textiles Ltd, Re, unreported, High Court, February 1, 1993 .... 16.1
Clarke v. Workman [1920] 1 I.R. 107 .... 7.8.1
Clemens v. Clemens Bros Ltd [1976] 2 All E.R. 268 .... 4.2.2
Clough Mill Ltd v. Martin [1984] 3 All E.R. 982 .... 16.6.1, 16.6.2
Clubman Shirts [1983] I.L.R.M. 323 .... 14.2.4
CMS Dolphin Ltd v. Simonet and anor (2001) B.C.C. 679 .... 7.8.3

Cockburn v. Newbridge Sanitary Steam Laundry Ltd [1915] 1 I.R. 237 .... 14.1.3
Coleman v. Myers [1977] 2 N.Z.L.R. 225 .... 7.8.4(1)
Comet Food Machinery Co Ltd, Re (in liquidation) [1999] I.R. 485 .... 21.6.4
Compania Electrical de la Provencia de Buenos Aires Ltd, Re [1980] 3 Ch. 146 .... 12.2.3
Cook v. Deeks [1916] 1 A.C. 554 .... 14.1.5(1)
Corran Construction Co v. Bank of Ireland Finance Ltd [1976-7] I.L.R.M. 175 .... 23.1.3(2)
Costello Doors Ltd, Re, unreported, High Court, July 21, 1995 .... 8.1.2
Cotman v. Brougham [1918] A.C. 514 .... 4.1.4(2)
Coubrough v. James Panton & Co Ltd [1965] I.R. 272 .... 7.1.4
County Palatine Loan and Discount Co, Re, Cartmell's case (1874) 9 Ch. App 691 .... 6.3.1
Countyglen Ltd v. Carway, unreported, High Court, February 20, 1996 .... 19.8
Coutts & Co v. Stock [2000] 1 W.L.R. 906 .... 23.1.2(2)
Cox v. Dublin City Distillery Ltd (No 2) [1915] I.R. 345 .... 6.4.2(3)
Craven Textiles Engineers Ltd v. Batley Football Club Ltd [2001] 7.8.3
Crawley's Case (1869) 12.5.2
Creasey v. Breachwood Motors Ltd [1993] B.C.L.C. 480 .... 5.4.1
Crindle Investments v. Wymes [1998] 4 I.R. 567 .... 7.8.4(1)
Cripps (RA) & Son Ltd v. Wickenden [1973] 1 W.L.R. 944 .... 18.2.1
Crompton & Co Ltd, Re [1914] 1 Ch. 954 .... 16.4.2
Cuckmire Brick Co Ltd v. Mutual Finance Company Ltd [1971] Ch. 949 .... 18.3.2
Cummings v. Stewart [1911] 1 I.R. 236 .... 5.4.1
Cummins Ltd: Barton v. Bank of Ireland, Re [1939] I.R. 60 .... 6.2
Currencies Direct Ltd v. Ellis [2001] T.L.R. 654 .... 7.6.2
Cyclists' Touring Club, Re (1907) 1 Ch. 269 .... 4.1.4(5)
Daimler Co Ltd v. Continental Tyre & Rubber Co (Great Britain) Ltd [1916] 2 A.C. 307 .... 5.2, 5.5
Daly & Co, Re [1887-8] 19 LR I.R. 83 .... 23.1.3(2)
Daniel Murphy Ltd, Re [1964] I.R. 1 .... 23.1.5
David Payne & Company Ltd, Re [1904] 2 Ch. 608 .... 6.2
Davies v. R Bolton & Co [1894] 3 Ch. 678 .... 6.4.1

Dawson International plc v. Coets Paton plc [1989] B.C.L.C. 233 ... 7.8.4
De Beers Consolidated Mines Ltd v. Howe [1906] A.C. 45 ... 5.5
Dean v. Prince [1954] Ch. 409 ... 13.2.2
Deauville Communications Worldwide Ltd, Re, unreported, Supreme Court, March 15, 2002 ... 22.9.7
Demaglass Holdings Ltd, Re [2001] 2 B.C.L.C. 633 ... 22.1.2(1)
Dempsey v. Bank of Ireland, unreported, Supreme Court, December 6, 1985 ... 23.2.2(3)
Desmond v. Glackin (No. 2) [1993] 3 I.R. 67 ... 19.2.5(5)
Dey v. Pullinger Engineering Co (1921) 1 K.B. 77 ... 6.3.2
DHN Food Distributors Ltd v. Tower Hamlets LBC [1976] 3 All E.R. 462 ... 5.4.4
Dimbleby & Sons Ltd v. NUJ [1984] 1 W.L.R. 427 ... 5.3
Don Bluth Entertainment Ltd, Re [1994] 3 I.R. 141 ... 20.6.6
Donovan v. Landys Ltd [1963] I.R. 441 ... 10.2.1
Dorchester Finance Co Ltd v. Stebbing [1989] B.C.L.C. 498 ... 7.8.2
Double S Printers Ltd (in liquidation), Re [1999] B.C.C. 303 ... 16.5.1
Duomatic Ltd, Re [1969] 2 Ch. 365 ... 16.2.3
Dublin Co Co v. Elton Homes Ltd [1984] I.L.R.M. 297 ... 5.4.1
Dublin Co Co v. O'Riordan [1986] I.L.R.M. 104 ... 5.4.1
Dun Laoghaire Corporation v. Park Hill Developments Ltd & ors [1989] I.R. 447 ... 5.4.1
Dunleckney Ltd, Re, unreported, High Court, February 18, 1999 ... 8.1.2
Dunlop Pneumatic Tyre Co Ltd v. Selfridge & Co Ltd [1915] A.C. 847 ... 2.6.6(1)
Dunn v. MBS Distribution Ltd (1990) EAT/132/89 June 12, 1990 (UK) ... 6.3.3
Dunnes Stores (Ireland) Co v. Moloney [1999] I I.L.R.M. 119, [1999] 3 I.R. 542 ... 19.2.1, 19.2.3, 19.6.4
Dunnes Stores (Ireland) Co v. Ryan, unreported, High Court, Kinlen J., July 6, 1999 ... 19.6.1, 19.6.4
Dunnes Stores (Ireland) Co & Heffernan v. Ryan, unreported, Supreme Court, Keane C.J., February 8, 2000 ... 19.6.4
Dunnes Stores (Ireland) Co & Heffernan v. Ryan, unreported, High Court, Butler J., July 29, 2000 ... 19.6.4

Dunnes Stores (Ireland) Co & Heffernan v. Ryan, unreported, Supreme Court, Keane C.J., February 1, 2002 .... 19.6.4
Dunnes Stores (Ireland) Co & Heffernan v. Ryan, unreported, High Court, Kearns J., June 5, 2002 .... 19.6.4
Ebrahimi v. Westbourne Galleries Ltd [1973] A.C. 360 .... 22.2.5(1)
Edenfell Holdings Ltd, unreported, High Court, July 30, 1997 ....18.3.2, 18.3.2(1)
Edenpark Construction Ltd, Re [1994] 3 I.R. 126....................... 20.6.6
Edwards v. Haliwell [1950] 2 All E.R. 1064............ 4.3, 12.3.5, 14.1.4
Eley v. Positive Government Security Life Assurance Co Ltd (1876) 1 Ex D 88.. 4.3
Emma Silver Mining Company Co Ltd v. Lewis & Son (1879) 4 CPD 396 3
English & Scottish Mercantile Investment Co Ltd [1892] 2 Q.B. 700.. 16.4.3
Erlanger v. New Sombrero Phosphate Co [1878] 3 A.C. 1218 .... 3.1.1, 3.2.1
Estmanco (Kilner House) Ltd v. GLC [1982] 1 All E.R. 437 .... 14.1.5(1)
Evans v. Rival Granite Quarries Ltd [1910] 2 K.B. 979.............. 16.4.1
Evans v. Brunner, Mond & Co [1921] 1 Ch. 359 .... 4.1.4(3)
Exchange Banking Co, Re Flitcroft's case (1882) 21 Ch. D 519 .... 12.2.4, 15
Favon Investments Co Ltd, Re [1993] 1 I.R. 87 .... 21.3.3
Feighery v. Feighery & Co [1999] I I.R. 321................................ 7.1.4
Fireproof Doors Ltd, Re [1916] 2 Ch. 142 .... 6.4.1
Firestone Tyre and Public Company v. Llewellin [1957] 1 All E.R. 561 .... 5.4.2
Firth v. Stains (1897) 2 Q.B. 70 .... 3.3.1
Fisher v. St John's Opera House Co (1937) 4 DLR 337 .... 14.1.5(2)
Five Minute Car Wash Services Ltd, Re [1966] 1 All E.R. 242 .... 14.2.4
Flanagan v. Kelly, unreported, High Court, February 18, 1999 .... 14.1.7
Foamcrete (UK) Ltd v Thrust engineering Ltd [2002] B.C.C. 221.. 16.4.1
Foss v. Harbottle [1843] 2 Hare 461 .... 14, 14.1, 14.1.1, 14.1.2, 14.1.3, 14.1.4, 14.1.5(3), 14.1.6
Frederick Inns Ltd et al, Re [1994] 1 I.L.R.M. 387 (SC), [1991] I.L.R.M. 542 (HC).. 6.2, 7.8.4(2)

Freeman & Lockyer v. Buckhurst Park Properties (Mangal) Ltd [1964] 2 Q.B. 480 .... 6.3.3
Fulham Football Club Ltd v. Cabra Estates plc [1994] 1 B.C.L.C. 363 .... 7.8.1
G & S Doherty Ltd v. Doherty, unreported, Supreme Court, December 19, 1969 .... 4.2.2
Galeforce Pleating Co Ltd, Re [1999] 2 B.C.L.C. 704 .... 22.4.3
Galway and Salthill Tramways Co, Re [1918] 1 I.R. 62 .... 22.1.1
Gasco Ltd, Re, unreported, High Court, February 5, 2001 .... 8.1.2
Gencor ACP et al v. Dalby et al [2000] 2 B.C.L.C. 734 .... 7.8.3
General Rolling Stock Co Ltd, Re (1872) 7 Ch. App 646 .... 23.2.1
Gent, Gent-Davis v. Harris, Re (1889) 40 Ch. D 190 .... 18.1.3
George Whitechurch Ltd v. Cavanagh (1902) A.C. 117 .... 6.3.2
German Date Coffee Co, Re (1882) 2 Ch. D 169 .... 4.1.4, 6.1, 22.2.5(3)
Gilford Motor Company Ltd v. Horne [1933] Ch. 939 .... 5.4.1
Gilt Construction Ltd, Re, unreported, High Court, June 3, 1994 .... 21.4
Glackin v. Trustee Savings Bank [1993] 3 I.R. 55 .... 19.2.5(2)
Glouster County Bank v. Rudry Merthyr Steam and House Coal Colliery Co [1895] 1 Ch. 629 .... 6.4.1
Glover v. BLN Ltd [1973] I.R. 388 .... 7.1.5
Gluckstein v. Barnes [1990] A.C. 240 .... 3.1.1, 3.2.2
Goodman International, Re, unreported, High Court, January 28, 1991 .... 20.7.5
Gosling v. Gaskell (1897) A.C. 575 .... 18.1.5
Gray's Inn Construction Co Ltd, Re [1980] 1 All E.R. 814 .... 23.1.2(2), 23.1.2(3)
Great Wheel Poolgooth Ltd, Re (1883) 53 LJ Ch. 42 3
Greenhalgh Cinemas v. Arderne Cinemas Ltd [1950] 2 All E.R. 1120 (CA) 4.2.2
Greenhalgh Cinemas v. Arderne Cinemas Ltd [1946] 1 All E.R. 512 .... 12.4.6
Greenore Trading Company, Re [1980] I.L.R.M. 94 .... 14.2.4
Griffiths v. Secretary of State for Social Services [1974] Q.B. 468 .... 18.2.3(3)
Grove v. Advantage Healthcare (T 10) Ltd, unreported, High Court (English), November 19, 1999 .... 17.5
Guinness v. Land Corporation of Ireland [1882] 22 Ch. 349 .... 15.2

Guinness Ireland Group et al v. Kilkenny Brewing Co Ltd [1999] I.L.R.M. 531 ....
Guinness plc v. Saunders [1988] 2 All E.R. 940 .... 7.4.1
Gwembe Valley Development Co Ltd (in receivership) v. Koshy et al [2000] T.L.R. 81 .... 18.1.1
GWI Ltd, Re, unreported, High Court, November 16, 1988 .... 23.1.1
Hackney Pavilion Ltd, Re [1924] 1 Ch. 276 .... 13.2.4
Hafner: Olhausen v. Powderly, Re [1949] 1 All E.R. 167 .... 13.2.2, 13.2.4
Hardie v. Hanson (1960) CLR 451 .... 10.3.1
Hardoon v. Belilios [1901] A.C. 118 .... 13.1.5
Harmer (HR) Ltd, Re [1958] 3 All E.R. 689 .... 14.2.4
Hartley Baird Ltd, Re [1954] Ch. 143 .... 13.3.4
Haughey, Re [1971] I.R. 217 .... 19.2.5(4)
Haven Gold Mining Co., Re (1882) 20 Ch. D 151 .... 4.1.4(1)
Hefferon Kearns Ltd, Re (No. 2) [1993] 3 I.R. 191 .... 10.2.1, 10.2.2, 10.2.3, 10.2.4
Hely-Hutchinson v. Brayhead Ltd [1968] 1 Q.B. 549 .... 6.3.2
Hendy Lennox Ltd v. Grahame Puttick Ltd [1984] 1 W.L.R. 485 .... 16.6.2, 16.6.3
Hennessy v. National Agricultural and Industrial Development Association [1947] I.R. 159 .... 14.1.2
Heything v. Dupont [1964] 1 W.L.R. 843 .... 14.1.6
Hickman v. Kent & or Romney Marsh Sheepbreeders Association [1915] 1 Ch. 881 .... 4.3
Hilger Analytical Ltd v. Rank Precision Industries Ltd et al [1984] B.C.L.C. 301 .... 16.2.4
Hindle v. Cotton (John) Ltd (1919) 56 SLT 625 .... 7.8.1
HKN Invest OY v. Incotrade PVT et al [1993] 3 I.R. 152 .... 3.3.2
Hogg v. Cramphorn Ltd [1966] 3 All E.R. 420 .... 12.5.2
Holders Investment Trust, Re [1971] 2 All E.R. 289 .... 15.4.1
Holidair Ltd, Re [1994] 1 I.L.R.M. 481 .... 16.4.2, 16.5.1, 16.5.2, 20.5.2, 20.6.6
Holland et al v. Ms Gill et al, unreported, March 16, 1990) HC 7.3
Hollicourt (Contracts) Ltd v. Bank of Ireland [2001] 1 All E.R. 289 .... 23.1.2(2)
Holohan v. Friends Provident and Century Life Office [1966] I.R. 1 .... 18.3.2, 18.3.2(3)

Home and Colonial Insurance Company Ltd, Re (1930) 1 Ch. 102 .... 21.7
Hopkins v. Shannon Transport Systems Ltd, unreported, High Court, January 10, 1972 .... 3.1.1, 3.2.1
Horbury Bridge Co, Re (1879) 11 Ch. D 109 .... 13.3.8
Horgan v. Murray and Milton [1998] I.L.R.M. 110........ 14.1.5(3)
Horsely & Weight Ltd, Re [1982] 3 All E.R. 1045........ 4.1.4(1)
Hunting Lodges Ltd, Re [1985] I.L.R.M. 75 .... 7.8.5, 10.3.1
Huon Foam Pty Ltd, Re [2000] Supreme Court of Tasmania (TASSC) 99, July 21, 2000 .... 22.1.2(1)
Hutton v. West Cork Rly Co (1883) 23 Ch. 654 .... 4.1.4(3)
Hydrodam (Corby) Ltd, Re [1994] 2 B.C.L.C. 180 7
Igote Ltd v Badsey Ltd, unreported, Supreme Court, July 18, 2001 .... 12.2.1
Illingworth v. Houldsworth [1904] A.C. 355 .... 16.3, 16.4, 16.4.1
Imperial Hotel (Cork) Ltd, Re [1950] I.R. 115........ 12.4.2
Industrial Development Consultants v. Cooley [1972] 2 All E.R. 162........ 7.8.3
Industrial Services Company (Dublin) Ltd, Re [2001] 2 I.R. 118 .... 23.1.2, 23.1.2(2)
International Sales & Agencies Ltd & anor v. Marcus [1982] 3 All E.R. 551 .... 6.1.2
Introductions Ltd, Re; Introductions Ltd v. National Provincial Bank Ltd [1968] 2 All E.R. 1221) .... 4.1.4(2), 6.2
Introductions Ltd v. National Provincial Bank Ltd [1970] Ch. 199........ 4.1.4
Irish Oil & Cake Mills Ltd v. Donnelly, unreported, High Court, March 27, 1983 .... 18.3.1, 18.3.2
Irish Press plc v. Ingersoll Irish Publications Ltd (No. 1) [1994] 1 I.R. 176 .... 14.2.2, 14.2.4
Irish Press plc v. Ingersoll Irish Publications Ltd [1993] I.L.R.M. 747 (HC) 14.2.3
Irish Press plc v. Ingersoll Irish Publications Ltd [1995] 2 I.L.R.M. 270 (SC) 14.2.3
Irish Tourist Promotions Ltd, Re, unreported, High Court, April 22, 1974 .... 22.2.5(2)
Irvine v. Union Bank of Australia (1877) 2 App Cas 366 .... 6.4.2(2)
Jackson v. Munster Bank (1884-85) 13 LR (I.R.) 118........ 13.3.3
Jarvis plc et al v PriceWaterhouse Coopers [2001] B.C.C. 670 .... 9.2.4

Jermyn Street Turkish Baths Ltd, Re [1971] 3 All E.R. 184 .... 7.8.1, 12.5.2
JJ Harrison (Properties) Ltd v. Harrison [2002] 1 B.C.L.C. 162 .... 7.8
John Hood & Co. Ltd v. Magee (1918) 2 I.R. 34 .... 5.5
John Power & Son Sons Ltd, Re [1934] I.R. 412 .... 15.4.1
Johnson (B) & Co (Builders) Ltd, Re [1995] Ch. 634........ 18.2.3(1)
Jon Beauforte (London) Ltd, Re (1953) 1 All E.R. 634........ 6.1, 4.1.4
Jones v. Lipman [1962] 1 All E.R. 442 .... 5.4.1
Jowett (Angus) & Co v. Tailors' and Garment Western Union [1985] I.R.LR 376........ 18.2.3(3)
JSF Finance and Currency Exchange Co Ltd v. Akma Solutions Inc [2001] 2 B.C.L.C. 307 .... 22.1.2
Kaytech International plc, Re [1999] B.C.C. 390 7
Keenan Bros Ltd, Re [1985] I.R. 401 .... 16.5.1, 16.5.2
Kelly v. Haughey Boland & Co [1989] I.L.R.M. 373 .... 9.2.7
Kelly's Carpetdrome Ltd, Re, unreported, High Court, July 1, 1983 .... 10.3.1
Kelner v. Baxter (1966] LR 2 CP 174 .... 3.3.1
Kernohan Estates Ltd v. Boyd [1967] NI 27 .... 18.1.6
Kett v. Shannon & English [1987] I.L.R.M. 364........ 6.3.3
Keypak Homecare Ltd, Re [1990] B.C.L.C. 440........ 8.2.6
Killick and anor v. PricewaterhouseCoopers (a firm) [2001] 1 B.C.L.C. 65 .... 9.2.8
Kingston Cotton Mill Co (No. 2), Re [1896] 2 Ch. 279........ 9.2.8
Kinsella v. Alliance and Dublin Consumers Gas Co et al, unreported, High Court, October 5, 1982 .... 13.3.6, 13.3.8
Kinsella v. Russell Kinsella Property Ltd [1986] 4 N.S.W.L.R. 722 .... 7.8.4(2)
Kinsella v. Somers, unreported, High Court, November 22, 1999........ 18.3.1
Kushler (M) Ltd, Re [1943] Ch. 248 .... 23.1.3(2)
La Moselle Clothing Ltd (in liquidation) and Rosegem Ltd (in liquidation) v. Djarnel Soualhi, unreported, May 11, 1998 .... 8.1.1, 8.1.2, 8.2.6
Lac Minerals Ltd v. Chevron Mineral Corp of Ireland [1995] I.L.R.M. 161 .... 5.4.4
Lady Gwendolyn, The [1965] 3 W.L.R. 91 .... 2.6.6(2)
Lafayette Ltd, Re [1950] I.R. 100........ 12.4.2

Lagunas Nitrate Company v. Lagunas Nitrate Syndicate (1899) 2 Ch. 392 .... 3.1.1
Lakeglen Construction Co Ltd, Re [1980] I.R. 347 .... 16.5.1
Lambert Jones Estate Ltd v. Donnelly, unreported, High Court, November 5, 1982 .... 18.3.2(4)
Landhurst Leasing plc, Re [1999] 1 B.C.L.C. 287 .... 8.2.6
Lascomme Ltd v. United Dominions Trust (Ireland) Ltd [1994] I.L.R.M. 227 .... 18.2.2
Lee & Co (Dublin) Ltd v. Egan (Wholesale) Ltd, unreported, High Court, April 24, 1978 .... 4.3, 13.2.4
Lee v. Lee's Air Farming Company Ltd [1961] A.C. 12 .... 5.2
Leeds & Hanley Theatres of Varieties Ltd, Re (1902) 2 Ch. 809 .... 3.2.2
Leinster Contract Corpn, Re (1902) I.R. 349 .... 23.2.2(6), 12.5.5
Leitch (Wc) Bros Ltd, Re [1932] 2 Ch. 71 .... 10.3.1
Lennard's Carrying Co Ltd v. Asiatic Petroleum Co [1915] A.C. 705 .... 2.6.6(2), 2.6.6(3)
Levy v. Abercorris Company (1887) 33 Ch. 260 .... 16.2
Lewis v. Inland Revenue Commissioners et al [2000] T.L.R. 800 .... 23.2.2(7)
Linz v. Electric Wire Company of Palestine [1948] A.C. 371 .... 13.1.2
Littlewood Mail Order Stores Ltd v. I.R.C [1969] 3 All E.R. 855 .... 5.4.3
Liverpool & District Hospital v. AG [1981] All E.R. 994 .... 12.3.3
Lloyd v. Grace, Smith & Co [1912] A.C. 716 .... 12.1.2
Lombard & Ulster Banking Ltd v. Amurec Ltd [1978] 112 I.L.T.R. 1 .... 17.5
Lombard and Ulster Banking Ltd v. Bank of Ireland, unreported, High Court, June 2, 1987 .... 15.3.2, 15.3.4
Longman v. Bath Electric Tramways [1905] 1 Ch. 646 .... 13.2.1
Lummus Agricultural Services Ltd [1999] B.C.C. 953 .... 22.1.2(1)
Lyle & Scott Ltd v. Scotts' Trustees (1959) A.C. 763 .... 13.2.2
Lyons v. Curran [1993] I.L.R.M. 375 .... 19.2.5(1)
Macaura v. Northern Assurance Company [1925] A.C. 619 .... 5.2
MacDougall v. Gardiner (1875) 1 Ch. D 13 .... 14.1.4
Mackley's case (1875) 1 Ch. D 247 .... 13.1.1
Maclaine Watson & Company Ltd v. Department of Trade and Industry (1989) 3 All E.R. 1056 .... 5.2

Mahony v. East Holyford Mining Company (1875) LR 7 HL 869 .... 6.3.3
Maidstone Building Provisions Ltd, Re [1971] 3 All E.R. 363 .... 10.3.1
Mal Bower's Macquarie Electrical Centre Pty Ltd, Re [1974] 1 N.S.W.L.R. 254 .... 23.1.2(2)
Mann v. Goldstein [1968] 1 W.L.R. 1091 .... 22.1.2(2)
Mastertrade (Exports) Ltd et al v. Phelan et al, unreported, High Court, December 4, 2001 .... 5.4.1
McBirney & Co Ltd, Re, unreported, High Court, July 2, 1992 .... 23.1.2(3)
McGill and anor v. Bogue et al, unreported, Supreme Court, July 11, 2000 .... 15.3.1
McGilligan v. O'Grady [1999] 1 I.R. 346 .... 7.1.4, 22.2.5(1)
McGowan v. Gannon [1983] I.L.R.M. 516 .... 18.3.4
McKinnon v. Armstrong (1877) 2 App Cas 531 .... 23.2.2(3)
McSweeney v. Bourke, unreported, High Court, November 24, 1980 .... 2.6.6(2)
Mechanisations Eaglescliffe Ltd, Re [1964] 3 All E.R. 840 .... 17.5
Medforth v. Blake et al [1999] 2 All E.R. 97 .... 18.1.6
Mehigan v. Duignan [1997] 1 I.R. 340 .... 5.3.6, 9.1.1
Menier v. Hooper's Telegraph Works Ltd [1874] LR 9 Ch. App 350 .... 14.1.5(1)
Merchant Navy Supply Association Ltd, Re (1947) 177 LT 386 .... 12.3.3
Meridian Global Funds Management Asia Ltd v. Securities Commission (1995) 2 A.C. 500 .... 2.5.6(3)
MIG Trust Ltd, Re [1933] Ch. 542 .... 17.7
Millhouse Taverns Ltd, Re, unreported, High Court, April 3, 2000 .... 22.1.2(2)
Mills v. Shields (1950) 12.1.2
Money Markets International Stock Brokers Ltd v. Fanning et al, unreported, High Court, February 11, 2000 .... 22.6
Monolithic Building Company, Re [1915] 1 Ch. 643 .... 17.6
Moore v. Xnet Information Systems Ltd et al, unreported, High Court, February 8, 2002 .... 7.1.4
Moorgate Mercantile Holdings Ltd, Re [1980] 1 All E.R. 40 .... 13.3.3, 13.3.7
Morphites v. Bernasconi et al (2001) 2 B.C.L.C. 1 .... 10.3.1

Morris v. Banque Arabe et Internationale d'Investissment SA (No. 2) (2000) T.L.R. 749 .... 10.3.1
Moylan v. Irish Whiting Manufacturers Ltd, unreported, High Court, April 14, 1980 .... 14.1.6
Muckross Park Hotel Ltd, Re, unreported, The Irish Times, February 22, 2001 .... 13.3.1
Murph's Restaurants Ltd, Re [1979] I.L.R.M. 141 .... 7.1.4, 14.2.1, 14.2.3, 14.2.4, 22.2.5(1)
Musselwhite & anor v. CH Muselwhite & Son [1962] Ch. 964........ 13.2.3
Nash v. Lancegaye Safety Glass (Ireland) Ltd (1958) 92 I.L.T.R. 11 .... 7.8.1, 12.5.2
Nelson & Co v. Faber & Co [1903] 2 K.B. 367........ 18.2.1
NEW-AD Advertising Company Ltd, Re, unreported, High Court, July 1, 1997 .... 14.2.3
Newcastle Timber Ltd and Atwood Ltd, Re, unreported, High Court, October 16, 2001 .... 8.2.6
Newstead Inspector of Taxes v. Frost [1980] 1 W.L.R. 135........ 4.1.4
New British Iron Co., Re [1989] 1 Ch. 324........ 4.3
New Bullas Trading Ltd, Re (1994) B.C.C. 36........ 16.5.2
Nicholson v. Permakraft (NZ) Ltd [1985] 1 N.Z.L.R. 242........ 7.8.4(2)
Nicol's case (1885) 29 Ch. D 421........ 13.1.1
Nicoll v. Cutts [1985] B.C.L.C. 322 .... 18.2.3(3)
Nisbet v. Shepherd [1994] 1 B.C.L.C. 300 .... 5.3.1
NL Electrical Ltd, Re [1994] 1 B.C.L.C. 22........ 15.3.2
Norditrack (UK) Ltd, Re [1999] T.L.R. 782........ 21.1.1
North West Holdings Plaintiff, Re [2001] 1 B.C.L.C. 468........ 22.1.4
Northern Bank Finance Corporation v. Quinn and Achates Investment Co [1979] I.L.R.M. 221 .... 6.1.1
Northern Bank Finance Corporation v. Charlton [1979] I.R. 149 .... 3.2.1
Northern Counties Securities Ltd v. Jackson & Steeple Ltd [1974] 2 All E.R. 625 .... 5.2
Northside Motor Co Ltd, Re: Eddison v. Allied Irish Banks Ltd, unreported, High Court, July 24, 1985........ 15.3.2
Newdigate Colliery Ltd, Re (1912) 1 Ch. 468........ 18.2.3(1)
O'Gorman et al v. Kelleher et al, unreported, High Court, July 19, 1999 .... 13.2.3
O'Neill v. Ryan & ors [1993] I.L.R.M. 557 .... 14.1.6, 14.1.7, 5.2
Oakes v. Turquand [1867] LR 2 HL 325........ 13.1.2, 13.1.4

Oakthorpe Holdings Ltd, Re [1988] I.L.R.M. 62 .... 21.1.121.4
Official Receiver v. Vass and anor [1999] B.C.C. 516 .... 8.2.6
Old Bushmills Distillery Co., Re, ex p Brett,
[1879] I I.R. 488 .... 16.4
Old Silkstone Collieries, Re [1954] 1 All E.R. 68 .... 15.4.1
Oxford Society, Re (1887) 35 Ch. D 502 .... 7.1.5
Pageboy Couriers Ltd, Re [1993] I.L.R.M. 51 .... 22.1.2(2)
Panorama Developments (Guilford) Ltd v. Fidelis Furnishing
Fabrics Ltd [1971] 3 All E.R. 16 .... 6.3.1
Parke v. Daily News Ltd [1962] Ch. 927 .... 4.1.4(3), 7.8.4(3)
Parkes & Sons Ltd v. Hong Kong and Shanghai
Banking Corp [1990] I.L.R.M. 341
.... 6.2, 7.8.4(2), 23.1.3, 23.1.3(2),
Pat Ruth Ltd, Re [1981] I.L.R.M. 51 .... 23.1.2(2)
Patrick and Lyon Ltd, Re [1933] Ch. 786 .... 10.3.1
Pelling v. Families Need Fathers Ltd [2002]
2 All E.R. 440 .... 13.1.4, 16.4.1
Pender v. Lushington (1877) 6 Ch. D 70 .... 4.3, 14.1.4
Penrose v. Martyr (1858) EB & E 499 .... 4.1.3(4), 5.3.5
Percival v. Wright [1902] 2 Ch. 421 .... 7.8.4, 7.8.4(1)
Peso Silver Mines Ltd v. Cropper (1966) 58 DLR 1 .... 7.8.3
Peter's American Delicacy Co Ltd v. Heath (1938-9)
61 CLR 457 .... 4.2.2
Phelan v. Goodman and Taher, unreported, High Court,
December 4, 2001 .... 13.2.3
Phelan v. Goodman et al, unreported, High Court,
September 11, 2001 .... 13.2.2
Phonogram Ltd v. Lane [1981] 3 All E.R. 182 .... 3.3.2
Pioneer Seafood Ltd v. The Braer Corporation
[2000] B.C.C. 680 .... 21.7
PMPA Coaches Ltd, Re, unreported, High Court,
June 15, 1993 .... 23.1.2(1)
Potters Oil Ltd (No 2), Re [1986] B.C.L.C. 98 .... 18.1.1
Power Supermarkets Ltd v. Crumlin Investments
Ltd and Dunnes Stores et al, unreported, High Court,
June 22, 1981 .... 5.4.4
Primor plc v. Stokes Kennedy Crowley [1996] 2 I.R. 459 .... 8.1.3
Probets v. Glackin [1993] 3 I.R. 145 .... 19.2.5(1)
Profinance Trust SA v. Gladstone [2001] T.L.R. 501 .... 14.2.3

Prudential Assurance Co v. Newman Industries Ltd (No. 2) [1982] Ch. 204 .... 5.2, 14.1 14.1.2, 14.1.6, 14.1.7
R Ltd, Re [1989] I.R. 126 .... 14.2.2, 20.4
R v. Board of Trade, ex p. St Martin's Preserving Co Ltd [1965] 1 Q.B. 603 .... 19.2.3
R v. Lambeth (1839) 8 Ad & El 356 .... 13.3.8
R v. Registrar of Companies, ex p. Central Bank of India [1986] Q.B. 1114 .... 17.5
R v. P & O European Ferries (Dover) Ltd (1991) 93 Cr. App. R. 72 .... 2.6.6(4)
R (Cottingham) v. The Justices of Cork [1906] 2 I.R. 415 .... 2.6.6(3)
Rafsanjan Pistachio Producers Co-operative v. Reiss [1990] B.C.L.C. 352 .... 4.1.3(4)
Rakusens Ltd v. Baser Ambalaj Plastik Sanayi Ticaret Asi [2002] 1 B.C.L.C. 104 .... 2.3.6
Rama Corporation Ltd v. Proved Tin and General Investments Ltd [1952] 1 All E.R. 554 .... 6.4.2(1)
Rayfield v. Hands [1960] 1 Ch. 1 .... 4.3, 12.3.5
Read v. Astoria Garage (Streatham) Ltd (1952) Ch. 637 .... 7.1.5
Rearden v. Provincial Bank of Ireland [1896] I.R. 532 .... 13.1.5
Regal (Hastings) Ltd v. Gulliver [1942] 1 All E.R. 378 .... 7.8.3
Regentcrest plc (in liquidation) v. Cohen & anor, unreported, English High Court, June 6, 2001 .... 7.8.1
Resinoid & Mica Products Ltd, Re [Companies (Amendment) Act 1983] Ch. 132... 17.7
Revenue Commissioners v. Bank of Ireland (1925) 2 I.R. 90 .... 2.6.2
Rex Pet Foods Ltd v. Lamb Bros (Dublin) Ltd et al, unreported, High Court, December 5, 1985 .... 5.4.4
Roberts v. Coventry Corporation (1947) 1 All E.R. 308 .... 5.2
Robinson v. Forrest [1999] 1 I.R. 426 .... 8.1.4
Rolled Steel Products (Holdings) Ltd v. British Steel Corp et al [1985] 3 All E.R. 52 .... 1.6, 4.1.4(1), 4.1.4(3), 6.2
Roper v. Ward [1981] I.L.R.M. 408.. 4.2
Roundabout Ltd v. Beirne [1959] I.R. 423 .... 5.2, 5.4.1
Royal Bank of Canada v. W Got & Associates Electric Ltd [2002] 178 DLR (4th) 385 (SC)... 18.1.1
Royal British Bank v. Turquand (1856) 6 E & B 327.................... 6.4, 6.4.1, 6.4.2(1), 6.4.2(2), 6.4.2(3), 7.7

Ruben v. Great Fingall Consolidated Co (1906) A.C. 439 .... 6.4.1, 12.1.2
Ruby Property Company Ltd et al v. Raymond Kilty and anor, unreported, High Court, December 1, 1999 .... 18.3.2, 18.3.2(4)
RW Sharman Ltd, Re [1957] 1 All E.R. 737 .... 22.1.2(1)
Salomon v. Salomon & Company Ltd [1897] A.C. 22 .... 5, 5.2, 5.3, 5.4.2, 5.4.4, 5.5
Salton v. New Boston Cycle Co [1900] 1 Ch. 43 .... 18.1.5
Scott v. Scott [1943] All ER 582 .... 12.2.2
Scottish Co-operative Wholesale Society Ltd v. Meyer [1959] A.C. 324 .... 14.2.3, 14.2.4
Secretary of State for Trade and Industry v. Aurum Marketing Ltd et al [2000] T.L.R. 615 .... 22.1.4
Secretary of State for Trade and Industry v. Derverell and anor [2000] T.L.R. 34 7
Secretary of State for Trade and Industry v. Langridge [1991] 3 All E.R. 591 .... 8.2.2
Secretary of State for Trade and Industry v. Travel Time (UK) Ltd et al [2000] B.C.C. 792 .... 22.1.4
Selukwe Ltd, Re, unreported, High Court, December 20, 1991 .... 20.1.1
Sevenoaks Stationers (Retail) Ltd, Re [1990] 3 W.L.R. 1165 .... 8.2.2
Sewell's case (1868) 3 Ch. App 131 .... 13.1.4
SH & Co (Realisations) 1990 Ltd, Re [1993] B.C.L.C. 1309 .... 15.3.2
Shannonside Holdings Ltd, Re, unreported, High Court, May 20, 1993 .... 4.2.3, 17.5, 21.2.1
Shawinigan v. Vodkins [1961] 1 W.L.R. 1206 .... 10.2.1
Sheehan v. Carrier Air Conditioning Pty Ltd, unreported, High Court, August 12, 1997 .... 18.1.2
Shinkwin v. Quin-Con Ltd and Quinlan, unreported, Supreme Court, November 21, 2000 .... 5.2
Short v. Treasury Commissioners (Comrs [1948] A.C. 534 .... 5.2
Shrinkpak Ltd, Re, unreported, High Court, 20 December 1989 .... 22.2.5(4)
Shuttleworth v. Cox Brothers & Co. Co (Maidenhead) Ltd [1927] 2 K.B. 9 .... 4.2.2
Siebe Gorman & Co Ltd v. Barclay's Bank Ltd [1979] 2 Lloyd's Reports 142 .... 16.5.1

Simmon Box (Diamonds) Ltd, Re Ltd (2000) B.C.C. 275 .... 7.8.6
Simpson v. Westminster Palace Hotel Co. [1860] 8 HL Cas 712 .... 14.1.2
Sisk (John) & Son Ltd v. Flinn, unreported, High Court, July 18, 1994 .... 9.2.8
Skinner v. The City of London Marien Insurance Corp (1885) 14 Q.B.D 882 .... 13.2.3
SMC Electronics Ltd v. Akhter Computers Ltd et al [2001] 1 B.C.L.C. 433 .... 6.3.1
Smith & Fawcett Ltd, Re [1942] 2 All E.R. 542 .... 7.8.1, 13.2.4
Smith (Administrator of Cosslett (Contractors) Ltd) v. Bridgend County Borough Council [2002] 1 All E.R. 292 .... 17.6
Smith v. Croft (No. 2) [1988] Ch. 114 .... 14.1.2
Smith v. Croft (No. 3) [1987] B.C.L.C. 355 .... 14.1.5(3)
Smyth v. Darley (1849) 2 HL Cas 789 .... 12.3.2
Smith Howard Ltd v. Ampol Petroleum Ltd [1974] A.C. 821 .... 7.8.1
Smith, Stone and Knight Ltd v. Birmingham Corporation [1939] 4 All E.R. 116 .... 5.4.2
Smurfit Paribas Bank Ltd v. AAB Export Finance Ltd (No. 2) [1991] 2 I.R. 19 .... 23.1.5
Societe Generale de Paris .v. Walker (1885) 11 App Cas 20 .... 13.1.5
Somers v. James Allen (Ireland) Ltd [1984] I.L.R.M. 437 .... 16.6.2
South London Greyhound Racecourses Ltd v. Wake [1931] 1 Ch. 496 .... 6.4.1
Southern Cross Interiors Pty Ltd and another v. Deptuty Commissioner of Taxation [2001] NSWSC 621 .... 7.8.5
Spiller v. Mayo (Rhodesia) etc [1926] WN 78 .... 13.3.5
Springline Ltd, Re [1997] 1 I.R. 467 .... 20.6.6
Squash (Ireland) Ltd, Re, unreported, Supreme Court, February 8, 2001 .... 8.1.2
Standard Chartered Bank v. Walker (1982) 3 All E.R. 938 .... 18.3.2, 18.3.4
State (McInerney & Co Ltd) v. Dublin Co. Co., unreported, High Court, December 12, 1984 .... 5.4, 5.4.4
Station Motors Ltd, Re [1985] I.L.R.M. 756 .... 23.1.3(2)
Steamline Ltd (in voluntary liquidation), Re, unreported, High Court, June 24, 1998 .... 8.1.1, 8.1.2
Stewart's case (1886) 1 Ch. App 74 .... 13.1.4
Stonegate Securities Ltd v. Gregory (1980) Ch. 576 .... 22.1.2(2)

Sugar Distributors Ltd v. Monaghan Cash & Carry Ltd [1982] I.L.R.M. 399 .... 16.6.3
Supply of Ready Mixed Concrete (No. 2), Re [1995] 1 A.C. 456 .... 2.6.6(3)
Sykes' case (1872) LR 13 Eq 525 .... 12.1.4
Tangney v. The Clarence Hotels Company Ltd (1933) I.R. 51 .... 13.2.3, 13.2.4
Taylors Industrial Flooring Ltd v. M & H Plant Hire (Manchester) Ltd [1990] 2 B.C.L.C. 216 .... 22.2.4
Teck Corporation Ltd v. Millar (1972) 33 DLR 288 .... 12.5.2, 7.8.1
Telecom Eireann plc, Re, The Irish Times, June 29, 1999 .... 12.6.4
Telematic Ltd, Re [1994] 1 B.C.L.C. 90, ... 17.7
Telford Motors Ltd, Re, unreported, High Court, January 27, 1978 .... 17.7
Tempany v. Royal Liver Co. [1984] I.L.R.M. 273 .... 23.1.1
Tesco Supermarkets Ltd v. Nattrass Ltd [1972] A.C. 153 .... 2.6.6(3)
Thomas Gerrard & Sons Ltd [1968] Ch. 455 .... 9.2.8, 12.2.4
Thomas Williamson Ltd and anor v. Bailieborough Co-operative Agricultural Society Ltd, unreported, High Court, July 31, 1986 .... 6.2
Top Creative Ltd & anor v. St Albans District Council [1999] B.C.C. 999 .... 22.9.8
Torvale Group Ltd, Re [1999] 2 B.C.L.C. 605 .... 16.2.3
Tradalco Ltd; Bluzwed Metals Ltd v. Transworld Metals SA, Re, unreported, High Court, May 9, 2001 .... 22.2.5(2)
Trebanog Working Men's Club and Institute Ltd v. Macdonald [1940] 1 K.B. 576 .... 5.4.3
Trevor v. Whitworth (1887) 12 App Cas 409 .... 15.2, 15.4.3
Truck and Machinery Sales Ltd v. Marubeni Komatsu Ltd, unreported, Supreme Court, March 13, 1996 .... 22.1.2(2)
Truster AB v. Smallbone et al (No. 2) [2001] 3 All E.R. 987 .... 5.4.4
Tullow Engineering (Holding) Ltd, Re [1990] 1 I.R. 452 .... 16.4.1
Tuskar Resources plc, Re [2001] 1 I.R. 668 .... 20.1.1, 20.2, 20.3.1, 20.3.2, 20.4
Twycross v. Grant (1877) 2 CPD 469 3
Tyman's Ltd v. Craven [1952] 2 Q.B. 100 .... 22.9.8
Ulster Factors Ltd v. Entonglen Ltd (in liquidation) and George Moloney, unreported, High Court, February 21, 1997 .... 6.3.3

Ulster Investment Bank Ltd v. Euro Estates Ltd
[1982] I.L.R.M. 57 .... 6.4.1
Underwood (AL) Ltd v. Bank of Liverpool & Martins
[1924] All E.R. 230 .... 6.3.2, 6.4.2(3)
Union Hill Silver Co, Re (1870) 22 LT 400 .... 13.3.3
United Bars Ltd et al v. Revenue Commissioner [1991]
1 I.R. 396 .... 18.3.3
United States v. Milwaukee Refrigerator Transit Co
142 Fed 247 (1905) 5.4.1
Vehicle Buildings and Insulations Ltd, Re [1986]
I.L.R.M. 239 .... 22.2.5(2)
Vehicle Imports Ltd, Re, unreported, High Court,
November 23, 2000 .... 8.1.2
Verit Hotel & Leisure (Ireland) Ltd, Re [2000] 8.1.3
Via Net Works Ltd, Re, unreported, Supreme Court,
April 23, 2002 .... 14.2.1
Victoria Housing Estates Ltd v. Ashpurton Estates Ltd
(1983) Ch. 110 .... 17.7
W J Hickey Ltd, Re [1988] I.R. 126 .... 16.6.3
Walker v. Wimbourne [1976] 50 A.L.J.R. 446 .... 7.8.4(2)
Wallersteiner v. Moir (No. 2) [1975] Q.B. 373 .... 14.1.5(3)
Wallersteiner v. Moir [1974] 3 All E.R. 217 .... 15.3.1
Ward v. Dublin North City Milling Company Ltd
[1919] 1 I.R. 5 .... 12.1.4, 12.2.3
Webb v. Earle [1875] LR 20 Eq 556 .... 12.4.2
Welch v. Bowmaker (Ireland) Ltd [1980] I.R. 251 .... 16.4, 16.4.3
West Cumberland Iron and Steel Company Ltd, Re
(1889) 40 Ch. D 361 .... 21.1.1
Westport Construction Company Ltd, unreported, High Court,
September 1, 1996 .... 20.3.1
Westwinds Holdings Co Ltd, Re, unreported, High Court,
May 21, 1974 .... 14.2.1, 14.2.4
Whaley Bridge Calico Printing Co Ltd v. Green & Smith
(1879) 5 Q.B.D 109 .... 3.1
White v. Bristol Aeroplane Co Ltd (1953) Ch. 65 .... 12.4.6
Wiggins and anor v Rigby et al, unreported,
Supreme Court Victoria, August 10, 2000 .... 2.6.6
Will v. United Lankat Plantations Co [1914] A.C. 11 .... 12.4.2
Williams Group Tullamore Ltd, Re [1985] I.R. 613 .... 14.2.4, 14.2.5

Wilson (Inspector of Taxes) v. Dunnes Stores (Cork) Ltd, unreported, High Court, January 22, 1976 .... 12.2.3
Wilson v. Jones (1866) LR 1 Exch 193 .... 5.2
Wilson v. Kelland [1910] 2 Ch. 306 .... 16.4.3
Wilson v. West Hartlepool Rly Co (1865) 2 De G J & Sm 475 .... 6.3.4
Wiltshire Iron Co., Re (1868) 3 Ch. App 443 .... 23.1.2(3)
WMG (Toughening) Ltd, Re, unreported, High Court, April 6, 2001 .... 22.1.2(1), 22.2.4
Wogans (Drogheda) Ltd (No. 2), Re, unreported, High Court, May 7, 1992 .... 20.1.1, 20.4, 20.7.5
Wogans (Drogheda) Ltd (No. 3), Re, unreported, High Court, February 9, 1993 .... 20.4
Wogan's (Drogheda) Ltd, Re, unreported, Supreme Court, April 10, 1993 .... 16.4.2, 16.5.1
Wood v. Odessa Waterworks Company [1889] 42 Ch. D 636 .... 12.2.2
Woodruffes (Musical Instruments) Ltd, Re [1986] Ch. 366 .... 16.4.2
Yenidje Tobacco Co., Re [1916] 2 Ch. 462 .... 22.2.5(2)
Yorkshire Woolcombers Association Ltd, Re [1903] 2 Ch. 284 .... 16.4

Table of Statutes

pre 1922

Limited Partners Act 1907 .... 1.1
Partnership Act 1890 .... 7.6.2
s. 1(1) 1.1

post 1922

Bankruptcy Act 1988
s. 44(1) 13.2.6
s. 136(2) .... 23.2.2(5)
Charities Acts 1961 .... 7.4.2, 12.6.2
Companies (Amendment) (No. 2) Act 1999 .... 1.2.5, 7.2, 20.5,
.... 20.5.3, 20.7.4
Pt II 1.2.5, 20
Pt III 1.2.5
s. 5 .... 20.3, 20.3.1
s. 6 .... 20.1
s. 7 .... 20.2
s. 9 .... 20.2
s. 10 .... 20.4
s. 11 .... 20.2
s. 12 .... 20.3.2
s. 13 .... 20.1.1
s. 14 .... 20.5
s. 14(b)(ii) 20.6.8
s. 15 .... 20.6.7
s. 16 .... 18.1.4, 20.5.2, 20.5.5
s. 17 .... 20.5.2
s. 18 .... 20.5.2, 20.6.5
s. 19 .... 20.6.2
s. 21 .... 20.2.2
s. 22 .... 20.7.2
s. 23 .... 20.7.4
s. 24 .... 20.7.5
s. 25 .... 20.5.3
s. 28 .... 20.6.6, 23.2.2(7)
s. 32 .... 9.2.9

Companies (Amendment) (No. 2) Act 1999— *contd.*
s. 32(3) 9.2.9
s. 33 .... 9.2.9
s. 34 .... 9.2.9
s. 35 .... 9.2.9
s. 42(1) 1.3.2, 2.4.1
s. 42(2) 2.4.1
s. 43 .... 7.1.2
s. 43(3) 7.1.2
s. 43(9) 7.1.2
s. 43(11) 7.1.2
s. 44 .... 7.1.2, 7.1.3
s. 44(8) 7.1.2
s. 45 .... 7.1.3
s. 45(15) 22.9.5
s. 46 .... 22.9.1, 22.9.2, 22.9.7(1)
Companies (Amendment) Act 1977 .... 1.2.1
Companies (Amendment) Act 1982 .... 1.2.1
s. 3 .... 7.1.1
s. 3A 2.4.2
s. 3A(1) 8.2.1
s. 4 .... 2.4.6
s. 11 .... 22.9.3, 22.9.4
s. 12 .... 8.2.3, 22.9, 22.9.1, 22.9.6, 22.9.7(1), 22.9.7(2), 22.9.8
s. 12(1) 22.9.1
s. 12(3) 22.9.1
s. 12A .... 22.9, 22.9.2, 22.9.6, 22.9.7(1), 22.9.7(2)
s. 12A(3) .... 22.9.2, 22.9.7(2)
s. 12B(1) 22.9.6
s. 12B(2) 22.9.6
s. 12B(3) .... 22.9.7(1)
s. 12B(4) .... 22.9.7(1)
s. 12B(7) .... 22.9.7(1)
s. 12C .... 22.9.7(2)
s. 15 .... 21.2.2(2)

Companies (Amendment) Act 1983 .... 1.2.1, 1.3.1, 2.2.3, 22.2.7
s. 2 .... 2.2.3
s. 3(6).......... 2.4.2
s. 5(2).......... 2.2.3, 4.1.6
s. 5(4).......... 2.4.3
s. 6 16
s. 6(1).......... 2.4.5
s. 6(6).......... 2.4.5
s. 6(8).......... 2.4.5
s. 7 .... 2.2.3
s. 9 .... 2.3.1
s. 9(1)(a) 2.3.1
s. 9(1)(b) 2.3.1
s. 10 .... 2.3.1
s. 10(1).......... 2.3.1
s. 10(1)(a) 2.3.1
s. 10(1)(b) 2.3.1
s. 10(1)(c) 2.3.1
s. 10(1)(d) 2.3.1
s. 12 .... 2.2.3
s. 12(9).......... 22.2.8
s. 13 .... 2.2.3
s. 14 .... 2.3.2
s. 14(5).......... 2.3.2
s. 15 .... 2.3.2, 15.4.2
s. 15(2).......... 2.3.2
s. 15(5).......... 2.3.2
s. 15(6).......... 2.3.2
s. 15(7).......... 2.3.2
s. 15(10).......... 2.3.2
s. 16 .... 2.2.3
s. 19 .... 2.2.3, 15
s. 19(2).......... 2.2.3
s. 20 .... 12.5.1, 12.5.4
s. 20(3).......... 12.5.1
s. 20(8).......... 12.5.1
s. 21 .... 2.2.1
s. 21(4).......... 12.5.1
s. 22 .... 12.5.3
s. 23 .... 12.5.4

Companies (Amendment) Act 1983— *contd.*
s. 23(1) 12.5.4
s. 23(8) 12.5.4
s. 23(10) 12.5.4
s. 23(13) 12.5.4
s. 24(2) 12.5.4
s. 26 .... 12.5.5
s. 26(2) 12.5.5
s. 27 .... 12.5.6
s. 28(1) 12.5.5
s. 29(1) 12.5.5
s. 30 .... 2.3.1, 12.5.5
s. 30(5) 12.5.5
s. 30(6) 12.5.5
s. 30(8) 12.5.5
s. 31 .... 12.5.5
s. 38 .... 12.4.6
s. 40 .... 1.5.9(2), 13.3.2, 15.5, 21.2
s. 40(2) 15.5
s. 41 .... 15.2
s. 41(1) 15.2
s. 41(2) 15.2.1
s. 41(3) 15.2
s. 41(4) 15.2.1
s. 42 .... 15.2
s. 43 .... 12.1.4
s. 43(3) 13.3.7
s. 44 .... 12.4.5
s. 45(1) 12.2.1, 12.2.4
s. 45(2) 12.2.1
s. 46(1) 12.2.1
s. 50 .... 12.2.4
s. 51 .... 12.2.1
s. 52 .... 2.3.4
s. 52(5) 2.3.4
s. 52(6) 2.3.4
s. 53 .... 2.3.3
s. 53(5) 2.3.3
s. 53(7) 2.3.3
s. 54 .... 2.3.3

Companies (Amendment) Act 1983— *contd.*
s. 56(1) .... 4.1.3(1)
s. 56(2) .... 4.1.3(1)
s. 57 .... 15.5
s. 58(1) .... 4.1.3(1)
First Sched. .... 4.1.4(5)
Second Sched. 4, 4.1.2
Second Sched., Pt I 2.3.1, 4.1.1
Second Sched., Pt II 4.1.1
Companies (Amendment) Act 1986 .... 1.2.1, 1.3.1
s. 3 .... 9.1.2
s. 4 .... 9.1.2
s. 13 .... 9.1.2
s. 14 .... 9.1.2
s. 15 .... 9.1.7
Companies (Amendment) Act 1990 ..... 10.1, 16.4.2, 18.1.4, 20, 20.1.1, ... 20.3.1, 20.5 20.6.6, 20.7.1, 20.7.5
s. 2(1) 20.3, 20.3.1
s. 2(2) 20.3, 20.3.1
s. 2(3) 20.3
s. 3 .... 20.1
s. 3(3) 20.1
s. 3(3A) 20.2
s. 3(3B) 20.2
s. 3A 20.5
s. 3A(1) 20.2.1
s. 3A(4) 20.2.1
s. 3B(1) 20.4
s. 3B(2) 20.4
s. 3C(1) 20.2
s. 3(6) 20.4
s. 3(7) 20.4
s. 3(8) 20.5.4
s. 3(9) 20.1
s. 4A 20.1.1
s. 4(2) 20.3.2
s. 4(5) 20.3.2
s. 5(1) 20.5
s. 5(2)(f) 20.5.3
s. 5(2)(h) 20.6.8

Companies (Amendment) Act 1990 — *contd.*
s. 5(4) 14.2.1
s. 5(A) 20.6.7
s. 6 .... 18.1.4, 20.5.2, 20.5.5
s. 6A 20.5.2
s. 7 .... 20.6.1
s. 7(5) 20.6.5
s. 7(5A) 20.6.5
s. 7(5B) 20.5.2, 20.6.5
s. 7(5C) 20.5.2, 20.6.5
s. 7(6) 20.6.3
s. 8(5) 20.6.2
s. 8(5A) 20.6.2
s. 9 .... 20.6.4
s. 10 .... 20.6.6, 20.6.7
s. 11 .... 20.6.9
s. 11(3) 20.6.9
s. 11(4) 20.6.9
s. 13(6) 20.6.5
s. 18 .... 20.7.2
s. 21 .... 20.7.2
s. 22 .... 20.7.3
s. 22(5) 20.7.3
s. 22(6) 20.7.3
s. 23 .... 20.7.4
s. 23(4A) 20.7.4
s. 24 .... 20.7.5
s. 24(4A) 20.7.5
s. 24(a) 20.7.5
s. 24(c) 20.7.5
s. 25 .... 20.7.5
s. 25A 20.4
s. 25(1) 20.7.5
s. 27 .... 20.7.5
s. 29 .... 20.6.6
s. 29(2) 20.6.6
s. 29(3) 20.6.6
s. 29(3A) 20.6.6
s. 29(3B) .... 20.6.6, 23.2.2(7)
s. 180 .... 1.2.2, 5.3.10

Companies (Amendment) Act 1999 .... 1.2.4
s. 2 .... 1.2.4
s. 4 .... 11.6
Companies Act 1963 .... 1.2.1, 1.2.2, 1.2.3, 2.2.3, 7.1.2, 17.5, 20.3.2, 21.6.3, 22.6
Pt XI 2.3.6
s. 2 7
s. 2(1) 12.5.3
s. 5 .... 2.2.1, 2.2.3, 4.1.4, 5.3.1
s. 5(2)(a) .... 2.1.1(1)
s. 5(2)(b) .... 2.1.1(2)
s. 6 .... 4.1.2
s. 6(1) 4.1.2, 4.1.4, 12.5.3
s. 6(1)(a) 4.1.3
s. 6(1)(b) 4.1.3
s. 6(2) 4.1.2, 4.1.5
s. 6(4) 4.1.2, 4.1.6, 12.1.1
s. 7 .... 4.1.1
s. 8(1) 6.1.1, 6.1.2
s. 8(2) 14.1.2
s. 10 .... 4.1.8, 15.4.2
s. 10(1) .... 4.1.4(5)
s. 10(4) .... 4.1.4(5)
s. 10(5) .... 4.1.4(5)
s. 10(6A) .... 4.1.4(5)
s. 10(8) .... 4.1.4(5)
s. 11 .... 4.2.1
s. 13 .... 4.2.1
s. 14 .... 4.2
s. 15(1) 4.2.2
s. 15(A) 15.3.2
s. 15(B) 15.3.3
s. 16 .... 4.1.1, 4.2.1
s. 18(1) 2.4.3
s. 18(2) 2.4.3
s. 19 .... 2.4.3
s. 20 .... 2.3.3
s. 21 .... 4.1.3(2)
s. 22(1) .... 4.1.3(2)
s. 23 .... 4.1.3(1), 4.1.3(3)

Companies Act 1963 — *contd.*
s. 23(2) .... 4.1.3(3)
s. 24 .... 4.1.3(1)
s. 24(1)(a) .... 4.1.3(1)
s. 24(1)(b) .... 4.1.3(1)
s. 24(4) .... 4.1.3(1)
s. 24(7)(a) .... 4.1.3(1)
s. 24(7)(b) .... 4.1.3(1)
s. 24(7)(c) .... 4.1.3(1)
s. 25 .... 4.3, 12.3.5
s. 25(1) 4.3
s. 27(1) 4.1.5
s. 27(2) 4.1.5
s. 28 .... 4.1.8
s. 29 .... 4.1.8
s. 30 .... 4.1.8
s. 31 .... 14.2.1
s. 31(1) 13.1.1
s. 31(2) 13.1.2
s. 32 .... 13.1.3
s. 33 .... 13.2.2
s. 33(1) 2.2.1, 2.2.3, 2.3.2
s. 34(1) 2.2.1
s. 34(2) 2.2.1
s. 36 .... 1.5.8(4), 2.2.1, 5.3.1
s. 37 .... 3.3.2
s. 37(1) 3.3.2, 3.3.3
s. 37(2) 3.3.2, 3.3.3
s. 38(2) 8.1.5
s. 47(1) 12.5.3
s. 49 .... 12.5.2
s. 49(1) 12.5.3
s. 49(3) 12.5.3
s. 53 .... 7.4.2, 12.5.3
s. 53(1) 7.4.2
s. 53(2) 7.4.2
s. 54 .... 7.4.2
s. 56 .... 12.5.3
s. 57 .... 12.5.3
s. 56(1) 7.4.2

Companies Act 1963 — *contd.*
s. 56(2) 7.4.2
s. 56(3) 12.5.2
s. 58(1)(a) 12.5.2
s. 58(1)(b) 12.5.5
s. 58(3) 7.4.2, 12.5.2
s. 58(4) 7.4.2, 12.5.2
s. 59 .... 12.5.6
s. 60 .... 1.5.9(1), 1.5.9(2), 14.2.4, 15.3.1, 15.3.2, 15.3.4
s. 60(1) 15.3, 15.3.1, 15.3.2, 15.3.3, 15.3.4
s. 60(2) 6, 15.3.1, 15.3.2, 15.3.4
s. 60(2)(a) 15.3.2
s. 60(2)(b) 15.3.2
s. 60(4) 15.3.2
s. 60(5) 15.3.2, 23.1.8
s. 60(6) 15.3.2
s. 60(8) 15.3.2
s. 60(9) 7.4.2
s. 60(10) 7.4.2
s. 60(11) 7.4.2
s. 60(12) 15.3.3
s. 60(13) 15.3.3
s. 60(14) 15.3.4
s. 60(15) 15.3.4
s. 60(15B) 15.3.3
s. 62 .... 12.5.7
s. 64 .... 15.1, 15.1.5
s. 65 .... 15.2.1
s. 66 .... 7.4.2
s. 68 .... 4.1.6
s. 70 .... 4.1.6, 12.6.2
ss. 72-77 .... 4.1.6
s. 72 .... 4.1.6, 15.4.1
s. 72(1) 15.2, 15.4.1
s. 72(2) 15.4.1
s. 72(2)(a) 15.4.1
s. 72(2)(b) 15.4.1
s. 72(2)(c) 15.4.1
s. 73 .... 4.1.6, 15.4.1
s. 73(3) 15.4.1

Companies Act 1963 — *contd.*

s. 74 .... 4.1.6
s. 75 .... 4.1.6, 15.4.1
s. 76 .... 4.1.6
s. 77 .... 4.1.6
s. 78 .... 12.4.6
s. 78(6) 12.4.6
s. 79 .... 12.1, 13.2.1
s. 81 .... 13.2.1, 16.2.4
s. 82 .... 13.2.6
s. 81(2) 13.2.6
s. 83 .... 13.2.3
s. 84 .... 13.2.4
s. 85 .... 13.2.1
s. 86 .... 12.1.2, 13.2.1
s. 86(3) 12.1.2
s. 87 .... 12.1.2, 13.2.6
s. 88 .... 12.1.3
s. 91 .... 17.1
s. 98 .... 16.4, 18.3.3, 20.5.2
s. 99 .... 17.5
s. 99(1) 16.6.1, 17, 17.1, 17.2.1, 17.2.5, 17.4, 17.5, 17.6
s. 99(2) 17.2.1, 17.2.12
s. 99(2)(a) 17.2.2
s. 99(2)(b) 17.2.3
s. 99(2)(c) 17.2.4
s. 99(2)(d) 17.2.5
s. 99(2)(e) 17.2.6
s. 99(2)(f) 17.2.7
s. 99(2)(g) 17.2.8
s. 99(2)(h) 17.2.9
s. 99(2)(i) 17.2.10
s. 99(2A) 17.2.11
s. 99(2B) 17.2.11
s. 99(10) 17.2.5
s. 100 .... 17.3
s. 100(3) 17.7
s. 100(4) 17.3
s. 101 .... 17.2.12
s. 103 .... 17.1

Companies Act 1963 — *contd.*

s. 104 .... 17.5
s. 106(1).......... 17.7
s. 106(2).......... 17.7
s. 109 .... 17.1
s. 107(1).......... 18.1.7
s. 107(2).......... 18.1.7
s. 110 .... 17.1
s. 113 .... 2.4.6
s. 113(4).......... 2.4.6
s. 114 .... 4.1.3(4), 5.3.5
s. 114(4).......... 4.1.3(4), 5.3.5
s. 116 .... 13.1.1, 13.1.4
s. 116(3).......... 13.1.4
s. 116(6).......... 13.1.4
s. 116(9).......... 13.1.4
s. 117 .... 13.1.4
s. 117(4).......... 13.1.4
s. 118 .... 12.1.3
s. 119 .... 12.1.4
s. 119(4).......... 12.1.4
s. 121 .... 12.1.4
s. 121(1).......... 12.1.4
s. 122(3).......... 12.1.4
s. 122(5).......... 12.1.4
s. 123 .... 12.1.5
s. 124 .... 12.1.4
s. 125 .... 22.9.1
s. 126 .... 22.9.1
s. 131 .... 2.2.2, 13.3.1
s. 131(1).......... 13.3.1
s. 131(2).......... 13.3.1
s. 131(3).......... 13.3.1
s. 131(6).......... 13.3.1
s. 132 .... 13.3.2
s. 133(1).......... 13.3.3
s. 134(b).......... 13.3.2, 13.3.3
s. 134(c).......... 13.3.4
s. 134(d).......... 13.3.6
s. 135 .... 13.3.2

Companies Act 1963 — *contd.*
s. 136(1) 13.3.5
s. 136(3) 13.3.5
s. 136(4) 13.3.5
s. 136(5) 13.3.5
s. 137 .... 13.3.8
s. 137(1) 13.3.8
s. 138 .... 13.3.8
s. 140 .... 13.3.1
s. 141 .... 13.3.3, 13.3.7
s. 141(5) 13.3.7
s. 141(8) .... 4.2.3, 7.6.2(1), 13.3.7, 15.3.2
s. 141(8)(c) 13.3.7
s. 142 .... 13.3.3, 23.1.7
s. 143 .... 13.3.7
s. 143(7) 13.3.7
s. 145 .... 13.3.9
s. 145(3A) 13.3.9
s. 146 .... 13.3.9
s. 146(4) 13.3.9
s. 147 .... 9.1.1
s. 148 .... 9.1.2, 13.3.1
s. 155(1) 13.1.3
s. 157 .... 9.1.2
s. 158 .... 9.1.2
s. 158(7) 9.1.2
s. 159 .... 13.3.1
s. 159(3) 13.3.1
s. 160 .... 9.2.9, 13.3.7
s. 160(1) 9.2
s. 160(2) 9.2.1, 9.2.3
s. 160(5) 9.2.3
s. 160(5A) 9.2.1
s. 160(6) 9.2.1, 9.2.3
s. 160(8) 9.2.2
s. 161(a) 9.2.3
s. 161(b) 9.2.3
s. 161(c) 9.2.1
s. 161(2A) 9.2.3
s. 161(3) 9.2.3

Companies Act 1963 — *contd.*
s. 161(4) 9.2.3
s. 162(5) 7.1.1
s. 163 .... 9.2.6
ss. 165-173 19
s. 174 .... 2.2.2, 7
s. 176 .... 7.1.1
s. 180 .... 7.1.5
s. 181 .... 7.1.1
s. 182 .... 7.1.4, 7.1.5, 13.3.7
s. 182(1) 7.1.4
s. 183 .... 7.1.1
s. 185 .... 7.4.4
s. 189 .... 7.4.4
s. 190 .... 7.4.2
s. 194 .... 1.5.13, 7.4.1
s. 194(2) 7.4.1
s. 194(3) 7.4.1
s. 194(5) 7.4.1
s. 194(7) 7.4.1
s. 195 .... 7.2, 7.4.3
s. 195(6) 7.2
s. 195(8) 7.2, 8.2.1
s. 195(10) 7.2
s. 195(10A) 7.2
s. 195(11A) 7.2
s. 195(11B) 7.2
s. 195(13) 7.2
s. 195(14) 7.2
s. 200 .... 9.2.8
s. 202 .... 23.1.8
s. 205 .... 7.1.4, 13.1.6, 13.2.6, 14, 14.2, 14.2.1, 14.2.2, 14.2.3,
.... 14.2.4, 14.2.5, 15.4.2, 20.5, 22.1.6, 22.2.5(1), 22.1.6
s. 205(1) 14.2.1
s. 205(3) 14.2.2, 14.2.3, 14.2.4
s. 205(6) 14.2.1
s. 205(7) 14.2.2
s. 207 .... 21.4, 22.1.3
s. 207(1)(g) 12.4.2
s. 208 .... 22.1.3

Companies Act 1963 — *contd.*
s. 213(f) .... 4.1.4(5), 14.2.3
s. 213 .... 21.4, 22.2, 22.2.4, 22.3.1
s. 213(a) 22.2.1
s. 213(c) 22.2.2
s. 213(d) 22.2.3
s. 213(e) 22.2.4
s. 213(f) .... 22.2.5, 22.2.5(1)
s. 213(g) .... 14.2.3, 22.2.5(1), 22.2.6
s. 213(h) 22.2.7
s. 213(i) 22.2.8
s. 214 .... 8.1, 22.2.4, 23.2.1
s. 214(a) 20.3, 22.2.4
s. 214(b) 20.3, 22.2.4
s. 214(c) 22.2.4
s. 215 .... 22.1.1, 22.1.2, 22.1.3, 22.1.5, 22.1.6
s. 215(c) 22.1.2
s. 216 .... 22.3.1
s. 218 .... 22.3.2, 23.1.2, 23.1.2(1), 23.1.2(2), 23.1.2(3)
s. 219 .... 22.3.2
s. 220(2) 22.3.1
s. 222 .... 22.3.2
s. 224 .... 22.3.3
s. 224(5) 22.3.3
s. 226 .... 22.3.1
s. 228 .... 22.4.4
s. 228(c) 22.4.5
s. 228(d) 22.4.4
s. 228(e) 22.4.5
s. 229 .... 22.3.2
s. 231 .... 21.6.2
s. 231(1) 22.5.1
s. 231(2) 22.5.2
s. 232 .... 22.4.2
s. 234(1) 22.6
s. 234(2) 22.6
s. 235 .... 22.6, 23.2.3(4)
s. 236 .... 22.6
s. 237 .... 22.6
s. 238 .... 22.6

Companies Act 1963 — *contd.*

s. 239 .... 22.6
s. 241 .... 22.6
s. 242 .... 22.6
s. 243 .... 1.4.4, 22.6
s. 244 .... 22.6, 23.2.2(7)
s. 244A 22.4.3, 22.6
s. 245 .... 1.4.4, 22.6
s. 245(5) 22.6
s. 245(7) 22.6
s. 245(8) 22.6
s. 245A 1.4.4
s. 245A(1) 22.6
s. 245A(2) 22.6
s. 246 .... 22.6
s. 247 .... 1.4.4, 22.6
s. 249(1) 22.8
s. 249(2) 22.8
s. 251 21
s. 251(1)(a) 21,21.1.1
s. 251(1)(b) 21, 21.1, 21.1.1
s. 251(1)(c) 21, 21.2, 21.2.1
s. 252 .... 21.1.1
s. 253 .... 21.1.1
s. 256 .... 1.5.9(1), 1.5.9(2), 21.1.2, 21.1.3, 21.3.3
s. 256(1)(c) 21.2
s. 256(2) 21.1.2
s. 256(5) 21.3.1
s. 256(8) 5.3.8, 21.1.2, 23.1.8
s. 256(9) 5.3.8, 21.1.2
s. 258(2) 21.1.4
s. 260 .... 21.6.5
s. 261 .... 21.3.2
s. 263(1) 21.8
s. 266(1) 21.2.2
s. 266(6) .... 21.2.2(2)
s. 267(2) .... 21.2.2(3)
s. 269 .... 21.2.2(4)
s. 273 .... 21.8
s. 275 .... 12.3.3, 23.2.3(4)

Companies Act 1963 — *contd.*
s. 276 .... 23.2.3(4)
s. 276A .... 21.1.4, 21.2.2(3)
s. 276(1)(a) 21.6.1
s. 276(1)(b) 21.6.2
s. 276(1)(c) 21.6.2
s. 276(1)(d) 21.6.2
s. 276(1)(e) 21.6.2
s. 280 .... 21.6.4
s. 281 .... 23.2.2(7)
s. 283 23
s. 283(1) 23.2.1
s. 283(2) 23.2.1
s. 284 23
s. 284(1) 23.2
s. 285 23
s. 285(2) .... 23.2.3(1)
s. 285(7)(b) .... 23.2.3(1)
s. 286 .... 23.1.3, 23.1.4, 23.1.5
s. 286(1) .... 23.1.3(1)
s. 286(2) 23.1.3
s. 286(3) .... 23.1.3(1)
s. 286(4) 23.1.3
s. 286(5) .... 23.1.3(1)
s. 288 .... 16.3, 16.4, 23.1.5
s. 290 .... 21.6.2, 22.5.3, 23.1.1
s. 290(3) 23.1.1
s. 290(6) 23.1.1
s. 290(9) 23.1.1
s. 297 .... 1.4.4, 10, 10.3.1, 23.1.8
s. 297(1) 10.3.2
s. 297(2) 10.3.2
s. 297(1)(a) 5.3.2, 10.2, 10.2.1, 10.2.3, 10.2.4
s. 297(1)(b) 5.3.3, 10.3
s. 297A 1.4.4, 8.2.3, 23.1.8
s. 297A(1) 10.1, 10.2.1
s. 297A(2) 10.2.2
s. 297A(2)(a) 10.2.2, 10.2.3, 10.2.4
s. 297A(2)(b) 10.2.2, 10.2.3, 10.2.4
s. 297A(3)(a) 10.1

Companies Act 1963 — *contd.*
s. 297A(4) 10.2.2
s. 297A(6) 10.2.3
s. 297A(8) 10.1
s. 298 .... 1.4.4, 7.8.6, 21.7, 23.1.7
s. 299 .... 1.4.4
s. 300 .... 21.1.4
s. 300A .... 21.1.4, 21.2.2(3)
s. 303 .... 22.3.2
s. 310 .... 21.8, 22.8
s. 311 .... 7.2, 22.9, 22.9.6, 22.9.7(1), 22.9.7(2)
s. 311A .... 22.9.7(2)
s. 311(1) 22.9.3
s. 311(3) 22.9.4
s. 311(5) 22.9.3, 22.9.4
s. 311(6) 22.9.6
s. 311(7) 22.9.6
s. 311(8) .... 22.9.7(1)
s. 311(8A) .... 22.9.7(1)
s. 314 .... 18.4.2
s. 315 .... 18.4.2
s. 316 .... 18.3.1
s. 316A(1) 18.3.2
s. 316A(2)(b) 18.3.2
s. 316(1)(1A) 18.3.1
s. 316(2) .... 18.2.3(2)
s. 319(2) 18.1.8
s. 322A(1) 18.4.1
s. 322B 18.1.5
s. 322C 18.4.2
s. 322C(3) 18.4.2
s. 352 .... 2.3.6
s. 353 .... 2.3.6
s. 354 .... 2.3.6
s. 357 .... 2.3.6
s. 358 .... 2.3.6
s. 370 .... 4.4
s. 371 .... 1.4.4
s. 378 .... 13.1.4
s. 379 .... 1.5.11

Companies Act 1963 — *contd.*
s. 382 .... 2.5.6(4)
s. 383 .... 2.5.6(4)
s. 383(2) .... 2.5.6(4)
s. 383(3) .... 2.5.6(4)
s. 391 .... 9.2.8
First Sched. 4, 4.1.1, 4.2.1
First Sched., Pt I 4.2.1
First Sched., Pt II 4.2.1
Third Sched. 12.5.3
Sixth Sched. 9.1.2
Seventh Sched. 9.2.7
Companies Act 1977
s. 4 .... 13.1.4
Companies Act 1985 20
Companies Act 1990 .... 1.2.3, 1.2.5, 1.3.1, 2.2.1, 4.1.6, 7.2, 7.3, 9.2.4, 10, 10.3.1, 11, 12.6.7, 15.1.5, 15.2.2, 15.2.3, 19.2.4(2), 19.6.4, 21.1.3, 21.6.3, 21.7, 22.6
Pt IV 1.2.4, 1.5.13, 12.6
Pt V 1.2.4, 11, 11.5, 11.7
Pt VII 8
Pt XI 15.2.1
s. 4 .... 5.3.10
s. 7 .... 19, 19.1, 19.2.1, 19.2.2, 19.2.3, 19.8
s. 7(3) 19.2.1
s. 8 .... 19, 19.1, 19.2.2, 19.2.3, 19.6.1, 19.8, 22.1.4
s. 9 .... 19, 19.2.4(1)
s. 10 .... 19, 19.2.4(5)
s. 10(1) .... 19.2.4(2)
s. 10(3) .... 19.2.4(3)
s. 10(4) .... 19.2.4(4)
s. 10(5) .... 19.2.4(5)
s. 10(6) .... 19.2.4(5)
s. 11 19
s. 11(1) 19.2.6
s. 11(2) 19.2.6
s. 11(3) 19.2.6
s. 11(4) 19.2.6
s. 12 19
s. 12(1) 19.2.6

Companies Act 1990 — *contd.*
s. 12(2) ... 21.1.4
s. 13 ... 19
s. 13(1) ... 19.2.4
s. 13(2) ... 19.2.4
s. 14 ... 19, 19.1, 19.3.1, 19.3.2, 19.4.1, 19.5, 19.7, 19.8
s. 14(3) ... 19.3.1
s. 14(5)(b) ... 19.3.2
s. 14(6) ... 19.3.3
s. 14(7) ... 19.3.3
s. 15 ... 19, 19.1, 19.4.1, 19.5, 19.7
s. 16 ... 12.6.6, 19, 19.5
s. 16(b) ... 19.5
s. 16(14) ... 19.5
s. 16(17) ... 19.5
s. 17 ... 19, 19.2.2
s. 18 ... 19, 19.2.4(5)
s. 19 ... 1.2.6, 19, 19.1, 19.1, 19.6.1, 19.6.4, 19.7, 19.8
s. 19A ... 19.6.2
s. 19(2) ... 19.6.4
s. 19(2)(f) ... 19.6.4
s. 19(3) ... 19.6.1
s. 19(4) ... 19.6.1
s. 19(6) ... 19.6.2
s. 19(9) ... 19.6.2
s. 19(10) ... 19.6.3
s. 20 ... 1.4.3, 19, 19.7, 19.8
s. 21 ... 1.2.6, 19, 19.6.4, 19.8
s. 22 ... 19, 19.8
s. 23 ... 19
s. 23A ... 19.8
s. 23(1) ... 19.8
s. 23(2) ... 19.2.4(2)
s. 23(3) ... 19.8
s. 24 ... 19
s. 25(2) ... 7.6.2
s. 25(3) ... 7.6.2
s. 26(1) ... 7.6.2
s. 26(3) ... 7.6.2
s. 27 ... 7

Companies Act 1990 — *contd.*
s. 28 .... 7.1.5
s. 29 .... 7.5, 21.6.6
s. 29(3) 7.5
s. 29(4) 7.5
s. 30 .... 7.6.1
s. 31 .... 1.5.9(1), 7.6.2(1), 7.6.2(2), 15.3.2, 16.1
s. 31(a) .... 7.6.2, 7.6.2(1)
s. 31(b) .... 7.6.2, 7.6.2(1)
s. 31(c) .... 7.6.2, 7.6.2(1)
s. 32 .... 7.6.2(1), 8.1.5
s. 33 .... 7.6.2(1), 8.1.5
s. 34 .... 7.6.2(1), 8.1.5
s. 34(2) .... 7.6.2(1)
s. 34(3) .... 7.6.2(1)
s. 34(4) .... 7.6.2(1)
s. 34(5) .... 7.6.2(1)
s. 34(6) .... 7.6.2(1)
s. 34(7) .... 7.6.2(1)
s. 34(8) .... 7.6.2(1)
s. 35 .... 7.6.2(1), 8.1.5
s. 36 .... 7.6.2(1), 8.1.5
s. 37 .... 7.6.2(1), 8.1.5
s. 38 .... 16.1
s. 38(2) .... 7.6.2(2)
s. 39 .... 7.6.2(2)
s. 40 .... 7.6.2(2)
s. 50 .... 7.1.5
s. 52 .... 7.8.4(3)
s. 53 .... 7.4.2
s. 53(1) 12.6.1
s. 54 .... 7.4.2
s. 55 .... 7.4.2
s. 56 .... 7.4.2
s. 57 .... 7.4.2
s. 59 .... 7.4.2
s. 64 .... 7.4.2
s. 67 .... 12.6.2
s. 70 .... 11.1.3
s. 72 .... 12.6.2

Companies Act 1990 — *contd.*
s. 73 .... 12.6.3, 12.6.5, 12.6.6
s. 74 .... 12.6.3
s. 75 .... 12.6.3, 12.6.4
s. 75(8) 12.6.3
s. 77(2) 12.6.2
s. 78 .... 12.6.2
s. 79 .... 12.6.4
s. 79(4) 12.6.4
s. 80 .... 12.6.5
s. 81 .... 12.6.6
s. 82 .... 12.6.6
s. 83 .... 12.6.6
s. 84 .... 12.6.6
s. 85(2) 12.6.6
s. 88 .... 12.6.5, 12.6.6
s. 88(5) 12.6.5
s. 98 .... 12.6.7
s. 98(2) 12.6.7
s. 98(3) 12.6.7
s. 98(5) 12.6.7
s. 98(6) 12.6.7
s. 99(1) 12.6.7
s. 101(1) 12.6.7
s. 101(4) 12.6.7
s. 102 .... 12.6.7
s. 104(2) 12.6.7
s. 107 .... 11.1.1, 11.1.2
s. 108 .... 1.2.4, 11.1.2, 11.4, 11.5, 11.6
s. 108(1) 11.1, 11.2, 11.3
s. 108(2) 11.1.4, 11.2, 11.3
s. 108(3) 11.2, 11.3
s. 108(4) 11.2
s. 108(6) 11.3
s. 108(7) 11.3
s. 108(11) 11.1.3
s. 108(10) 11.6
s. 109(1) 11.4
s. 109(2) 11.4
s. 109(4) 11.4

Companies Act 1990 — *contd.*
s. 110 ... 11.6
s. 110(2) ... 11.6
s. 110(3) ... 11.6
s. 111 ... 11.5
s. 112 ... 11.5
s. 113 ... 11.5
s. 115 ... 11.7
s. 115(1) ... 11.7
s. 115(5) ... 11.7
s. 115(7) ... 11.7
s. 116 ... 11.7
s. 122 ... 17, 17.2.11
s. 124 ... 21.6.6
s. 128 ... 21.1.3
s. 131(2) ... 21.6.3
s. 131(3) ... 21.3.2, 21.6.3
s. 131(5) ... 21.3.3
s. 135 ... 23.1.3, 23.1.3(1)
s. 137 ... 10.3.2
s. 138 ... 5.3.2, 5.3.3, 10.2, 10.3
s. 139 ... 1.4.4, 23.1.4
s. 139(3) ... 23.1.4
s. 140 ... 1.4.4, 5.3.9, 19.2.4(1), 23.1.6
s. 140(5) ... 23.1.3(1), 23.1.6
s. 141 ... 5.3.9, 23.1.6
s. 142 ... 7.8.6, 23.1.7
s. 147 ... 21.2.2(3)
s. 149 ... 8.1
s. 150 ... 1.4.4, 7.1.1, 8.1.1, 8.1.2, 8.1.3, 8.1.5, 8.1.6, 8.2.4, 9.1.1
s. 150(1) ... 3.2.4, 8.1, 8.1.1
s. 150(3) ... 2.2.3, 8.1.5
s. 150(4A) ... 8.1.1
s. 150(4B) ... 8.1.1
s. 151 ... 8.1.1
s. 152 ... 8.1.4
s. 155 ... 8.1.5
s. 155(5) ... 8.1.5
s. 157 ... 8.1.5
s. 159 ... 3.2.4, 8.2

Companies Act 1990 — *contd.*
s. 160 .... 1.4.4, 1.5.16, 3.2.4, 7.1.1, 7.1.5, 10.1, 10.2
s. 160(1)........................... 8.2.1
s. 160(1A)........................... 8.2.1, 8.2.3
s. 160(1B)........................... 8.2.1, 8.2.3
s. 160(2)........................... 8.2.2
s. 160(2)(a) 8.2.3, 8.2.4
s. 160(2)(b)........................... 8.2.3, 8.2.4
s. 160(2)(c) 8.2.3, 8.2.4
s. 160(2)(d)........................... 8.2.3, 8.2.4
s. 160(2)(e) 8.2.3, 8.2.4
s. 160(2)(f)........................... 8.2.3, 8.2.4
s. 160(2)(g) 8.2.3, 8.2.4
s. 160(2)(h) 8.2.3
s. 160(2)(i)........................... 8.2.3
s. 160(3A)........................... 8.2.3
s. 160(4)........................... 8.1.1, 8.2.4
s. 160(5)........................... 8.2.4
s. 160(6)........................... 8.2.4
s. 160(6A)........................... 8.2.4
s. 160(7)........................... 8.2.2
s. 160(8)........................... 8.2
s. 160(9A)........................... 8.2.2
s. 160(9B) 8.2.4
s. 161(1)........................... 8.2.5
s. 161(3)........................... 8.2.5
s. 161(5)........................... 8.1.5
s. 161 .... 8.1.6
s. 163 .... 8.2.5
s. 163(3)........................... 8.1.6, 8.2.5
s. 164 .... 8.2.5
s. 164(4)........................... 8.1.5
s. 168 .... 8.2
s. 163 .... 5.3.4
s. 163(3)........................... 5.3.4
s. 163(4)........................... 5.3.7
s. 165 .... 5.3.4
s. 165(2)........................... 5.3.4
s. 172 .... 18.3.2
s. 173 .... 18.1.8

Companies Act 1990 — *contd.*
s. 174 .... 18.1.8
s. 183 .... 9.2.1, 9.2.3
s. 184 .... 9.2.3
s. 185 .... 9.2.4
s. 186 .... 9.2.4
s. 186(5) 9.2.4
s. 187 .... 9.2.5
s. 187(1) 9.2.5
s. 187(2) 9.2.5
s. 192(6) 9.2.8
s. 194 .... 9.2.8
s. 196 .... 9.2.6
s. 196(3) 9.2.6
s. 197 .... 9.2.6
s. 197(4) 9.2.6
s. 202 .... 5.3.6, 9.1.1, 9.2.8
s. 202(5) 9.1.1
s. 202(9) 9.1.1
s. 202(10) 8.2.3, 9.1.1
s. 203 .... 1.4.4, 9.1.1
s. 203(1) 9.1.1
s. 203(2) 9.1.1
s. 204 .... 1.4.4
s. 204 .... 5.3.6, 9.1.1
s. 204(4) 5.3.6, 9.1.1
s. 206 .... 15.1
s. 207 .... 15.1
s. 207(2) 15.1.1, 15.2.2
s. 208 .... 15.1.2, 15.2.2
s. 208(e) 15.1.2
s. 209 .... 15.1.3, 15.2.2
s. 209(2)(a) 15.1.3
s. 209(3) 15.1.3
s. 209(4) 15.1.3
s. 209(5) 15.1.3
s. 209(6) 15.1.3
s. 210 .... 15.1.4
s. 211 .... 15.2.2
s. 211(2) 15.2.2

Companies Act 1990 — *contd.*
s. 211(3) 15.2.2
s. 212(a) 15.2.2
s. 212(b) 15.2.2
s. 213 .... 15.2.2
s. 214 .... 15.2.2
s. 217(1) 15.2.2
s. 218(1)(a) 15.2.2
s. 218(1)(b) 15.2.2
s. 218(1)(c) 15.2.2
s. 215 .... 15.2.2
s. 219 .... 15.1.6, 15.2.2
s. 219(6) 15.1.6
s. 220 .... 15.1.2
s. 222 .... 15.2.3
s. 222(4) 15.2.3
s. 226 .... 15.2.3
s. 228 .... 15.2.3
s. 229 .... 15.2.2
s. 224 .... 13.1.3
s. 230 .... 15.2.2
s. 232 .... 15.2
s. 251 .... 5.3.2, 10.1
s. 251(2A) 10.1
s. 239 .... 1.5.8(1)
s. 240 .... 8.1.6
s. 244 .... 9.3.1
s. 251 .... 1.4.4, 1.5.16
Companies Acts 1963-1990 .... 8.1.2
Companies Acts 1963-2001 ..... 1.1, 1.2.7, 1.4, 1.4.1, 1.4.3, 1.4.4, 1.5.1,
.... 1.5.5, 1.5.6 1.5.8(1), 1.5.8(2), 1.5.11, 1.5.13, 1.5.16, 2, 2.2,
.... 2.4.1, 2.4.2, 2.5.6(4), 3, 4.1.1 4.1.6, 4.2.2, 5, 5.1, 5.3, 7.4.1,
.... 7.7, 9.1.1, 12.3.4, 18, 23.2.1
Companies Amendment Acts 1990-1999 .... 20.1.1
Company Law Enforcement Act 2001 ..... 1.2.6, 2.2.1, 2.2.3, 4.1.6, 7.2,
.... 8.1.1, 8.1.5 19, 21.7, 22.6
s. 7 .... 1.4
s. 8(1) 1.4
s. 10(1) 1.4
s. 11 .... 1.4

Company Law Enforcement Act 2001 — *contd.*
s. 12 19
s. 12(1) 1.4.1
s. 12(2) 1.4.1
s. 12(5) 1.4.1
s. 13 .... 1.4.1
s. 14 .... 1.4.1, 7.4.2, 8.2.1, 11.7, 13.3.1, 19.2.2, ... 19.4.1, 19.5, 19.6.1, 22.1.4
s. 14(4) 1.4.1
s. 15 .... 1.4.1
s. 16 .... 1.4.2
s. 17 .... 1.4.3
s. 17(2) 1.4.3
s. 17(3) 1.4.3
s. 18 .... 1.4.3
s. 19 .... 13.3.9
s. 20 .... 19.2.1
s. 21 .... 19.2.2
s. 22 .... 19.2.5
s. 23 .... 19.2.5(2), 19.2.5(5)
s. 24 .... 19.2.6
s. 25 .... 19.2.4
s. 26 .... 19.3.1, 19.3.3
s. 27 .... 19.5
s. 28 .... 19.2.5(5)
s. 29 .... 19.6.1, 19.6.2
s. 30 .... 19.7
s. 31 .... 19.8
s. 32 .... 19.2.5(2)
s. 33 .... 19.8
s. 37 .... 11.7
s. 39 .... 15.2.2
s. 41 .... 8.1.1
s. 42 .... 8.2.1
s. 44 .... 22.6
s. 50 .... 7.8.6
s. 54 .... 10.1
s. 55 .... 1.4.4
s. 66 .... 1.4.4

Company Law Enforcement Act 2001 — *contd.*
s. 67 .... 1.5
s. 68 .... 1.5.1
s. 69 .... 1.5.2
s. 70 .... 1.5.2
s. 71 .... 1.5.3
s. 71(3) 1.5.3
s. 72 .... 9.2.5
s. 73 .... 9.2.8
s. 76 .... 7.6.2
s. 77 .... 7.6.2(1)
s. 78 .... 1.5.9(1), 7.6.2(1)
s. 79 .... 7.6.2(1)
s. 80 .... 4.1.1, 4.2
s. 80(3) 4.1.1, 4.2
s. 85 .... 4.1.4(5)
s. 86 .... 4.1.3(2)
s. 87 .... 4.1.3(3)
s. 88 .... 4.1.3(1)
s. 89 .... 15.3.2
s. 91 .... 7.2
s. 100 .... 2.5.6(4)
s. 101 .... 2.4.2
s. 102 .... 7.6.1
s. 103 .... 11.6
Corporation Tax Act 1976 .... 5.3.11
Electronic Commerce Act 2000 .... 1.5.8(1), 1.5.8(2)
English Companies Act 1985 7
s. 124A 22.1.4
English Insolvency Act 1986
s. 127 .... 23.1.2(2)
European Communities Act 1972 .... 1.3, 1.5.6
Finance Act 1986
s. 115 .... 23.2.2(5)
Finance Act 1995
s. 174 .... 23.2.2(5)
Insurance (No. 2) Act 1983 .... 23.1.2(3)
Registration of Business Names Act 1963 .... 4.1.3(2)
Registration of Title Act 1964 .... 17.2.5, 17.2.7

Statute of Limitations Act 1957 .... 12.1.4, 12.2.3, 23.2.1
s. 25 .... 12.2.3
Stock Transfer Act 1963 .... 13.2.1
Taxes Consolidation Act 1997
s. 882(3) 22.9.2
s. 1001 .... 23.2.2(5)
Tribunals of Inquiry (Evidence) Acts 1921-1998 .... 1.2.6

Table of Statutory Instruments

Companies Act 1963 (Section 24) Regulations 2001
(S.I. No. 571/2001)... 4.1.3(1)
Companies Act 1990 (Insider Dealing) Regulations 1992........... 11.1.2
European Communities (Branch Disclosures) Regulations 1993
(S.I. No. 395/1993) 1.3.1, 2.3.6
European Communities (Companies) Regulations 1973
(S.I. No. 163/1993)... 6.1.2
Reg. 4(1).. 2.4.4
Art. 6.. 6.1.2
Art. 6(2)... 6.1.2
Art. 6(3)... 6.1.2
European Communities (Companies Group Accounts)
Regulations 1992 (S.I. No. 201/1992)................................... 1.3.1
European Communities (European Economic Interest
Groupings) Regulations 1989 (S.I. No. 191/1989) 1.3.4
European Communities (Mergers and Divisions of
Companies) Regulations 1987 (S.I. No. 137/1987) 1.3.1
European Communities (Public Limited Companies
Subsidiaries) Regulations 1997 (S.I. No. 67/1997).................. 1.3.1
European Communities (Safeguarding of Employees Rights
on the Transfer of Undertakings) Regulations 1980 .... 18.2.3(3)
European Communities (Single-Member Private Limited
Companies) Regulations 1994 (S.I. No. 275/1994) 1.3.1
European Communities (Single-Member Private Ltd Companies)
Regulations 1994 (S.I. No. 275/1994)........................ 1.5.8(4), 2.2.2
Reg. 5(1).. 2.3.5
Reg. 5(2).. 2.3.5
Reg. 5(3).. 2.3.5
Reg. 6(1).. 2.3.5
Reg. 6(2).. 2.3.5
Reg. 6(3).. 2.3.5
Reg. 8(1)... 2.2.2, 13.3.1
Turnover Tax (Exempted Activities) (No. 1) Order 1963
(S.I. No. 163/1963)... 1.3.1

Rules

Rules of the Superior Courts 1986 .... 16.2.1, 22.3.1, 23.2
Ord. 46.. 13.1.5
Ord. 74..23.2.2(4)
Ord. 75A.. 20.1

European Union Legislation

Treaties

E.C. Treaty
Art. 48 .... 1.3
Art. 44(2)(g) 1.3
Art. 3(1) 1.3.5

Regulations

Regulation 2137/85 .... 1.3.4
Regulation 2157/2001 .... 1.3.3

Directives

Directive 2001/86 .... 1.3.3
Art. 7 .... 1.3.3
Directive 92/101 .... 1.3.1
Directive 60/1999 .... 1.3.1
First Directive 68/151 .... 1.3.1
Second Directive 77/91 .... 1.3.1, 2.2.3, 15
Third Directive 78/855 .... 1.3.1
Fourth Directive 78/660 .... 1.3.1
Fifth Directive 1.3.1
Sixth Directive 82/891 .... 1.3.1
Seventh Directive 83/349 .... 1.3.1
Eighth Directive 84/253 .... 1.3.1
Ninth Directive 1.3.1
Eleventh Directive 89/666 .... 1.3.1
Twelfth Directive 89/667 .... 1.3.1, 2.2.2
Thirteenth Directive 1.3.1
European Community Directive 89/592 11

1. DEVELOPMENTS IN COMPANY LAW

1.1 Companies in general

A company consists of a group of people who combine to achieve common objects; one such object may be the achievement of trading profits but this is not always the case. As will be seen later, a company can now even be formed with just one person. The majority of companies in Ireland are formed and registered with the Companies Offices under the Companies Acts 1963-2001 with the benefit of limited liability, *i.e.* the members of the company have no liability for the debts that the company owes to its creditors.

However, not all companies in Ireland are formed under the Companies Acts. There are chartered bodies, such as the Royal Irish Academy or the Royal College of Surgeons and Physicians, which were formed pursuant to a charter from the British Crown and preserved by the transitional provisions of the Irish Constitution and the relevant adapting legislation. There are companies, such as Aer Lingus Teoranta or An Post, which are established pursuant to statutes setting out the composition of the board of directors and the capital of the company. Certain types of corporate bodies with special objects, such as building societies and co-operatives, are registered and managed under their own relevant statutes.

The main advantages of a company is its shield of limited liability for members, its separate corporate personality, the free transferability of its shares, its management by a board of directors, and the options for raising of its capital. A partnership by comparison lacks many of these benefits. The disadvantages of a partnership are as follows:

1. A partnership is not a separate entity; it is merely the partners as a group working in a particular relationship with each other.

2. Each partner is liable for the debts of the partnership without limit (it is possible to register a limited partnership in which some partners have limited liability under the Limited Partners Act 1907, but the limited partners may not take part in the management of the business).

3. A partnership commonly dissolves on a change in the personnel of the partnership, whereas a company has perpetual succession, *i.e.* a change in members does not affect the life of the company.

4. A partnership, unlike a company, cannot create a floating charge over its assets.

5. A partner may not, without the consent of the other partners, transfer his shares in the firm, whereas shares in most companies are freely transferable.

6. A partnership's creditors have a right of action against the individual partners, whereas a company's creditors have no such right of action, as they are limited to pursuing the company itself for their debts.

1.2 The Companies Acts

1.2.1 Companies Act 1963

This Act is called the Principal Act as it is the main body and foundation of company legislation in the State. This Act was amended by the Companies (Amendment) Act 1977 (which *inter alia* modified the obligation to prepare a share certificate when dealing on the stock exchange and confirmed that a computer could be used for the keeping of certain company records), the Companies (Amendment) Act 1982 (which *inter alia* dealt with the appointment and qualification of auditors and the striking-off and restoration of a company to the Company Register), the Companies (Amendment) Act 1983 (which introduced the "plc" into Irish company law), and the Companies (Amendment) Act 1986 (which implemented and improved the provisions relating to the preparation of a company's accounts).

1.2.2 Companies (Amendment) Act 1990

The Companies Act 1963 was also amended by the Companies (Amendment) Act 1990. The latter Act introduced for the first time into Irish company law the notion of court protection for an ailing company. The process of examinership involves granting the company a breathing space from creditors while an insolvency professional, known as an examiner, drafts a survival plan for the company.

1.2.3 Companies Act 1990

This Act introduced the most far-reaching amendments to the Companies Act 1963. It was believed that the Principal Act did not go far enough to curb the potential abuses of the company entity and its limited liability by those in control. The Companies Act 1990 upgraded the procedure for the investigation of companies, introduced personal liability for reckless trading, introduced disqualification and restriction orders for errant company officers, prohibited loans by a company to its directors, and introduced stricter disclosure requirements for company accounts.

1.2.4 Companies (Amendment) Act 1999

This Act amends and extends Parts IV and V of the Companies Act 1990 to permit stabilising activity in relation to the issue for sale of securities and to provide for connected matters. Section 2 of the Companies (Amendment) Act 1999 declares that section 108 of the Companies Act 1990 (the insider dealing provisions) shall not be contravened by anything done in the State for the purpose of stabilising or maintaining the market price of securities, provided that the Stabilisation Rules contained in the Schedule to the Act are obeyed.

1.2.5 Companies (Amendment) (No. 2) Act 1999

The Company Law Review Group reviewed the examinership legislation (in the Companies (Amendment) Act 1990) in its report of December 1994. Part II of the Companies (Amendment) (No. 2) Act 1999 set about upgrading the examinership procedure in line with those recommendations. Part III of the Companies (Amendment) (No. 2) Act 1999 introduced exemptions for private companies from the requirements to have audited accounts.

1.2.6 Company Law Enforcement Act 2001

The provisions of the Company Law Enforcement Bill 2000 flowed directly from the recommendations in the Report of the Working Group on Company Law Compliance and Enforcement (the "McDowell Group"), which was published in March 1999. This group was established because of the Government's concerns at the emerging indications of serious abuses of company law. The report of the group confirmed the low level of compliance with company law and the extent to which company law is being enforced in Ireland. It found *inter alia* that

1. only 13 per cent of companies filed their annual returns on time in 1997;
2. most statutory offences were never prosecuted;
3. there were very few successful prosecutions for breaches of the Companies Acts;
4. those who were tempted to carry out serious breaches of company law had little to fear.

Wide-ranging recommendations were made by the group as to how companies should be made to pay more timely and due attention to their statutory obligations. In responding to the contents of the report, the Government has included virtually every recommendation contained in the report in the Company Law Enforcement Act 2001.

1.3 European developments

Under Article 48 of the E.C. Treaty, companies formed in accordance with the law of a Member State, having a registered office, central administration or principal place of business in the Community are entitled to the same freedom of movement as natural persons who are Member State nationals. Minority shareholders, creditors, employees, and third parties are to some extent protected by each Member State's company law. In order to prevent distortions, which might result when certain Member States offer more extensive protection than others, Article 44(2)(g) of the E.C. Treaty provides for the co-ordination, to the extent necessary, of safeguards for the protection of the interests of members and others, in place in the Member States, with a view to making such safeguards equivalent throughout the Community.

As a result of the possible conflict between these harmonising measures and domestic law, the European Communities Act 1972 provided that both the treaties and the existing and future Acts adopted by its institutions should be binding on the State and part of our domestic law. It also empowered Ministers to make regulations for the purpose of enabling this provision to have full effect. The E.U. law that affects the structure of the Irish companies code consists of the following:

1. the treaties of the E.U. which become part of the State's law by virtue of the European Communities Act 1972;
2. the regulations of the E.U. which have direct effect, *i.e.* no domestic legislation is necessary to implement the provisions of the regulations in Irish law;
3. the Directives of the community which do not generally have direct effect and which are implemented in the State by a statutory instrument; and
4. decisions of the Court of Justice of the E.U. on matters affecting company law.

1.3.1 European Directives

The First Directive 68/151 (implemented in Ireland by S.I. 163/1963) applies to both public and private limited companies. It requires the compulsory disclosure of legal documents (such as the memorandum and articles of the company) and the names and particulars of the company directors and agents of limited companies. These details must be kept with a Company Register (in Ireland this is the Registrar of Companies). The company name and other details must be printed on all company documents and correspondence. The Company Law SLIM (Simplification of Legislation for the Internal Market) Working Group on the Simplification of the First and Second Company Law Directives identified a need for simplifying the registration and disclosure requirements of the First Directive. Company disclosure documents stored on the national register should be stored in electronic form and a "European Business Register" should be established so that all data would be electronically available for consultation throughout the E.U.

The Second Directive 77/91 (implemented in Ireland by the Companies (Amendment) Act 1983) deals with the formation of public limited companies (plcs) and the maintenance of their capital. The Directive aims to protect the shareholders of the company and third parties dealing with the company. It sets out the information that such a company must include in its memorandum and articles of association and also sets out that this company must have a minimum capital base. This Directive was amended by Directive 92/101 (implemented in Ireland by the Companies Act 1990 and S.I. 67/1997) to deal with situations where a company purchasing shares in a plc, is actually controlled by that plc through shareholding or management influence.

The SLIM Working Group proposed a simplification of the Second Directive in relation to the capital requirements.

The Eleventh Directive 89/666 (implemented in Ireland by S.I. 395/1993) deals with public and private companies and deals with disclosure requirements for branches set up in one Member State. All foreign companies who have established a branch in a Member State must register information about the branch and the company. The branch must publish its parent company's main accounts in the relevant Member State. The SLIM Working Group recommended that when the "European Business Register" is established, disclosure could take place exclusively in the company's home state. A draft Tenth Directive provides for trans-national mergers, but it has faced difficulties on the topic of employee participation in the merger process.

The Third Directive 78/855 and the Sixth Directive 82/891 (both implemented in Ireland by S.I. 137/1987) deal with the merger and the division of plcs within the same Member State. The Directives oblige the directors of the companies to draw up draft terms for, and a reports on, the merger or division. The companies must appoint an independent person to examine the terms of the reports, which must be approved by the shareholders and confirmed by the court. The creditors of the company have a right to object to the court.

The Twelfth Directive 89/667 (implemented in Ireland by S.I. 275/1994) allows for the creation of a single-member private limited company (see Chapter 2).

The Fourth Directive 78/660 (implemented in Ireland by the Companies (Amendment) Act 1986) sets out various rules concerning the annual accounts of various limited companies. It offers a choice of formats for balance sheets and profit and loss accounts and sets out the information to be provided in the notes to the accounts. It obliges companies to have their annual accounts audited and their annual report verified as a true and fair view of the company's position. It provides for less severe accountancy rules in respect of small and medium-sized companies, which may produce abbreviated accounts. The thresholds for such companies are set out in the Directive and they are reviewed every five years. As of the most recent Directive 60/1999, a small company is defined as one with two of the following characteristics:

1. a total balance sheet of €3.125 million;
2. net turnover of €6.25 million;
3. less than 50 employees.

A medium firm is defined as one with two of the following characteristics:

1. a total balance sheet of €12.5 million;
2. net turnover of €25 million;
3. less than 250 employees.

The Seventh Directive 83/349 (implemented in Ireland by S.I. 201/1992) contains rules on the publication of consolidated accounts for groups of limited liability companies, showing the assets, liabilities, financial position, and profits and losses of the undertakings included in a consolidation as if the latter were a single undertaking.

The Eighth Directive 84/253 (implemented in Ireland by the Companies Act 1990) sets out the minimum standards of education and competency for company auditors.

The draft Fifth Directive concerns the structure and management of plcs and the powers and obligations of company bodies. The original text of the Directive was published in 1972 but the Directive encountered difficulties on the issues of employee participation and the choice of management structures. The draft Ninth Directive aimed to provide greater disclosure of the internal relationships within a corporate group. It was never formally proposed by the Commission. Both Directives now appear to be abandoned.

The draft Thirteenth Directive on takeovers was initially proposed in 1989 as the Commission wanted to develop a clear set of pan-E.U. rules in order to create a level playing field in takeover bids which would benefit European companies and minority shareholders by clarifying their rights and obligations. It was amended on a number of occasions in the face of strong opposition from some Member States. A company law group of experts was requested to examine the issues, and it produced a report in January 2002 making a series of recommendations, including the recommendation that the ultimate decision in a takeover bid must be with the shareholders. The future of the Thirteenth Directive remains unclear.

Details of the Directives are available at the Commission website, ***www.europa.eu.int***.

1.3.2 A European legal personality

On of the problems facing the E.U. company law harmonisation initiative is the *siége réel* approach of some Member States to the legal personality of a company. Under the *siége réel* approach, a company is only recognised by a Member State if it is incorporated in that Member State *and* it also has its headquarters or centre of operations in that Member States. Some Member States like Ireland adopt the incorporation theory, *i.e.* if the company is validly incorporated under the law of the State, it retains legal personality and remains governed by the law of the State of incorporation, even if it transfers its centre of operations to another country. Currently, the *siége réel* approach requires a company to be wound up in the host Member State and re-incorporated in the new Member State or to at least modify its memorandum and articles of association.

The E.U. Treaty provisions on the freedom of establishment imply that recognition be accorded to any company validly incorporated in a Member State and having its registered office there and thus also the right of a company to transfer its effective seat from one Member State to another without losing legal personality. It is argued by some that the transfer of the effective seat of a company has nothing to do with freedom of establishment and that it should be dealt with by a Directive harmonising the conditions for the recognition of companies in the Community. As the debate continues, it is important to note that a recent amendment in Ireland states that a company can no longer be incorporated in the State unless it proposes to carry out a business activity in the State (see section 42(1) of the Companies (Amendment) (No. 2) Act 1999 discussed at Chapter 2); and this may be interpreted as an obstacle to the exercise of the right of establishment.

1.3.3 A European company

E.C. Council Regulation No. 2157/2001 on a Statute for a European company (SE) was adopted by the Member States in October 2001 (with an accompanying Directive 2001/86 on employee participation). It facilitates the establishment of a European company – *Societas Europaea* or SE. This regulation, which has direct effect, comes into force on October 8, 2004, and facilitates the reorganisation of companies whose business is not limited to satisfying local needs. The SE will be a type of European public company, with a minimum capital of €120,000. Setting up an SE is not an alternative to establishing a new company but is an option available to companies that already exist. The Regulation allows an SE to be established in one of four ways: conversion; formation of a holding company; a joint venture, or through merger. The Regulation sets out a legal choice of management system and contains general rules on meetings, accounts and winding up. The basic principle is that the SE will be governed by the law that would apply to a plc in the Member States in which its registered office is situated. The registration of the SE will be published in the E.C. Official Journal.

Employee participation does not mean participation in the day-to-day management of the company, but participation in the supervision and strategic development of the SE. The standard principles on the participation of workers are set out in Article 7 of the Directive and they oblige the SE managers to provide regular reports, on the basis of which there is to be regular consultation of, and information to, a body representing employees. The Commission has determined that such consultation will eventually be the norm for large trans-national companies.

1.3.4 European Economic Interest Groupings ("EEIG")

Regulation 2137/85 (implemented in Ireland by S.I. 191/1989) provided for the establishment of the EEIG. The EEIG allows groups of companies, or any types of legal entity, to co-operate in economic activities across border within the E.U. while at the same time preserving their legal and economic independence. These businesses come together to pool their knowledge and resources where they have a common interest, such as firms of solicitors or auditors.

It is a corporate entity that operates like an international partnership and it can sue and be sued. There must be at least two members and one must be based in a different Member State. Its memorandum and articles of association must be registered in the Member State and the name of the entity must include the words European Economic Interest Grouping or the initials "EEIG". Employee participation in the EEIG is limited to 500 employees. When the SE comes into force in 2004 it is anticipated by many legal commentators that the use of the EEIG will decline across the E.U.

1.3.5 Cross-border insolvencies

European Council Regulation on Insolvency Proceedings came into effect across the E.U. (save for Denmark) on May 31, 2002. It provides a framework for common rules on cross-border insolvency proceedings. As a European Regulation it has direct effect and, therefore, as a matter of any Member State's domestic law, it does not have to be implemented into the domestic law concerned. Pursuant to the Regulation, the courts of the state where the company has its registered office will, generally have jurisdiction in insolvency proceedings. The provisions of the Regulation apply only where the debtor has its "centre of main interests". Article 3(1) (of the E.C. Treaty) states that a company's "centre of main interests" is, in the absence of proof to the contrary, situated in the country in which the company's registered office is located. See Chapter 22 for a further discussion on this Regulation and insolvency.

1.4 The Office of Director of Corporate Enforcement

Section 7 of the Company Law Enforcement Act 2001 established the Office of the Director of Corporate Enforcement. The Director of Corporate Enforcement took over the functions of the Minister for Trade, Enterprise and Employment in relation to the investigation and enforcement of the Companies Acts. The Director of Corporate Enforcement (the "Director") can now bring proceedings for non-compliance with the Companies Acts (along with the Registrar of Companies) and in a number of cases the Director may refer matters to the Director of Public Prosecutions.

Pursuant to section 8(1), the Director will hold office for a five-year renewable term and under such terms and conditions as shall be set out by the Minister. The Minister may, with the consent of the Minister for Finance, continue the appointment for a further period of five years. The Director is prohibited from holding any other office or employment in respect of which emoluments are payable.

Pursuant to section 10(1), the Minister may, for stated reasons, remove the Director from office. Where this occurs, the statements of reasons shall be presented to both Houses of the Oireachtas. Where the Director is nominated as a member of Seanad Eireann or as a candidate for election to either House of the Oireachtas or the European Parliament or where he becomes a member of a local authority, he shall cease to be a Director.

An Acting Director may be appointed under section 11 where the Director is out of the State, unable to perform the functions of the Director, suspended from the office of Director, or where there is a vacancy in the office of Director. The Acting Director can only act for a period of six months.

1.4.1 Functions of the Director of Corporate Enforcement

The functions of the Director are set out in section 12(1) of the Company Law Enforcement Act 2001 and they include the following:

1. to enforce the Companies Acts including the prosecution of offences by way of summary proceedings;
2. to encourage compliance with the Companies Acts;
3. to investigate incidences of suspected offences under the Companies Acts;
4. to refer cases to the Director of Public Prosecution for prosecution on indictment where the Director has reasonable grounds for believing that an indictable offence has been committed under the Companies Acts;
5. where it is necessary and appropriate, to supervise the activities of liquidators and receivers in the discharge of their duties under the Companies Acts;
6. to perform such other functions in respect of any matters to which the Companies Acts relate as the Minister considers appropriate;
7. to perform such other duties as may be assigned to him under the Companies Acts.

Section 12(2) makes it clear that the Director may do all such acts or things as are necessary or expedient for the purpose or the performance of his or her functions under the Companies Acts, and section 12(5) specifically provides for the independence of the Director in the performance of his functions. Under section 13 of the Company Law Enforcement Act 2001, the Director has the power to delegate in writing his powers to an officer of the Office of Director of Corporate Enforcement. Under section 15 both the Director and his staff are to be granted immunity from legal action against them personally in respect of anything done by them, in good faith, in the performance of their duties.

Pursuant to section 14 of the Company Law Enforcement Act 2001, several of the powers exercised by the Minister under the Companies Acts are transferred to the Director. It is set out in section 14(4) that the Director is to be named as the prosecutor in proceedings that were commenced by the Minister prior to this Act. However, the Director cannot be substituted for the Minister, where the Minister was a defendant in proceedings commenced prior to the Company Law Enforcement Act 2001.

1.4.2 Reporting obligations

The reporting obligations of the Director are set out in section 16 of the Company Law Enforcement Act 2001. The Director is required to report annually to the Minister, and this report will, in turn, be laid before each House of the Oireachtas within two months of its receipt. The Director will also report to the Minister on an ongoing informal basis. The Director must, when requested to do so, account to an appropriately established Committee of either House of the Oireachtas for the performance of his functions. When reporting to the Minister or to such a Committee, the Director shall not be required to furnish any information which would, in the opinion of the Director, be likely to prejudice the performance by him of any of his functions.

1.4.3 Information received by the Director of Corporate Enforcement

In cases where information is received by the Director in the performance of his functions, which has not otherwise come to the attention of the public, that information must not be disclosed, save in accordance with the law, by any person including the Director (section 17 of the Company Law Enforcement Act 2001). Any person who contravenes this provision is guilty of an offence. Section 17(2) permits the disclosure of information to a competent authority under section 20 of the Companies Act 1990. Where the information may relate to the commission of a possible offence under legislation other than the Companies Acts, section 17(3) permits the Director or an officer of the Director to disclose this information to a member of An Garda Siochana. Where the Competition Authority, An Garda Siochana or an officer of the Revenue Commissioners is of the opinion that an offence has been committed under the Companies Acts, that information may be disclosed to the Director or his officers under section 18.

1.4.4 Powers of the Director of Corporate Enforcement

The powers of the Director of Corporate Enforcement include *inter alia*

1. the power to apply for disqualification orders under section 160 of the Companies Act 1990 (see Chapter 8);

2. the power to apply for restriction orders under section 150 of the Companies Act 1990 (see Chapter 8);

3. the power to relieve the liquidators of insolvent companies from the obligation to make an application for a restriction order;

4. the power to prosecute all summary offences and to impose on-the-spot fines in respect of summary offences under the Companies Acts and under section 66 of the Company Law Enforcement Act 2001;

5. the power to apply to the High Court under section 371 of the Companies Act 1963 for an injunction to compel a company, any officer of the company, and any promoter, liquidator, or receiver of a company to comply with the provisions of the Companies Acts; and

The Director has the right to be informed by a voluntary or involuntary liquidator that any past or present officer, or any member or promoter, auditor, liquidator, or receiver of the company has been guilty of a criminal offence for which he is liable under section 299 of the Companies Act 1963.

The Director is given *locus standi* in respect of a number of provisions of the Companies Acts. The Director has the following rights:

1. the right to apply under section 243 of the Companies Act 1963 for a right to inspect the books and documents of a company in liquidation;

2. the right to apply under section 245 of the Companies Act 1963 for an officer of a company in liquidation to be examined by the court;

3. the right to apply under section 245A of the Companies Act 1963 for an order directing the officer under examination to pay money or deliver assets to the liquidator;

4. the right to apply under section 247 of the Companies Act 1963 for an order arresting an absconding contributory or officer of a company in liquidation;

5. the right to apply under sections 297 and 297A of the Companies Act 1963 in respect of the fraudulent and /or reckless trading of the company;

6. the right to apply under section 298 of the Companies Act 1963 in respect of a misfeasance committed against the company; and

7. the right to apply under section 139 of the Companies Act 1990 for an order for the return of assets improperly transferred, under section 140 of the Companies Act 1990 for an order that a company should contribute to the assets of a related company in liquidation, under section 203 of the Companies Act 1990 for an order imposing criminal liability for failure to keep proper books of account, and under section 204 of the Companies Act 1990 for an order imposing personal liability for failure to keep proper books of account (the *locus standi* for each section was introduced by an amendment to section 251 of the Companies Act 1990).

Section 55 of the Company Law Enforcement Act 2001 introduced a radical new power of freezing assets into the arena of company law. A company, director, member, liquidator, receiver, creditor, or the Director may apply to the court for an order that a director or other officer of the company may not remove his assets from the State or may not reduce his assets within or without the State, below a specified minimum amount. This power is only exercisable where:

1. the applicant has a substantive civil cause of action or right to seek a declaration of personal liability or damages against the respondent; and

2. where there are grounds for believing that there is a likelihood that the respondent will remove assets or dispose of his assets with a view to evading his or the company's obligations and frustrating an order of the court.

As this section is limited to civil actions, it may be used where the applicant is seeking to impose personal liability under the Companies Acts (see Chapter 5). There is no requirement for the applicant to give security for costs or an undertaking as to damages, and, in this regard, the section may become popular when pursuing errant company directors.

Details of the Office of the Director of Corporate Enforcement are available on-line at ***www.odce.ie***.

1.5 The Company Law Review Group (the "CLRG")

On foot of a Government decision, the Minister for Enterprise, Trade and Employment set up the CLRG in February 2000. The CLRG operated on an administrative basis until it was accorded statutory advisory status by section 67 of the Company Law Enforcement Act 2001. The establishment of the CLRG and the consolidation of the companies code were included among the recommendation of the Working Group on Company Law Compliance and Enforcement (the "McDowell Report").

1.5.1 Functions of the CLRG

According to section 68 of the Company Law Enforcement Act 2001, the function of the CLRG is to monitor, review, and advise the Minister for Enterprise, Trade and Employment on matters concerning the following:

1. the implementation, amendment and consolidation of the Companies Acts;
2. the introduction of new legislation relating to the operation of companies and commercial practices in Ireland;
3. the Rules of the Superior Court and case law judgments in so far as they relate to the Companies Acts;
4. the approach to issues arising from the State's membership of the E.U., insofar as they affect the operation of the Companies Acts;
5. the international developments in company law insofar as they provide lessons for improved State practice; and
6. other related matters, including issues submitted by the Minister to the Review Group for consideration.

1.5.2 Composition of the CLRG

The members of the CLRG shall be appointed by the Minister; the Minister shall also appoint its chairperson. The remuneration of the members shall be determined by the Minister and the Minister may, for stated reasons, terminate a person's membership of the CLRG (section 69 of the Company Law Enforcement Act 2001). The CLRG currently comprises social partners, the users of company law, and the administrators and regulators of company law.

Section 70 of the Company Law Enforcement Act 2001 sets out that the Minister must consult with the CLRG at least every two years and determine the programme of work to be undertaken by the Group, which programme may be amended by the Minister from time to time. This section also details how the CLRG should work in practice. The CLRG must hold such meetings as shall be necessary for the performance of its functions and it may make such arrangements for the conduct of its business and meetings as it considers appropriate. It is expressly set out that the CLRG may establish sub-committees and fix quorums for meetings. Where no chairperson is present at a meeting, the members may appoint one of their number to be a chairperson. A member of the CLRG who is unable to attend a meeting (other than a chairperson) may nominate a deputy to attend in his place.

1.5.3 Reporting obligations of the CLRG

According to section 71 of the Company Law Enforcement Act 2001, the CLRG must report to the Minister on its activities within three months of the end of every year, and the Minister must cause copies of the report to be laid before each House of the Oireachtas within a period of two months of the receipt of the report. This report must contain information in such form and on such matters as the Minister directs. According to section 71(3), the CLRG must, if so requested, provide a report to the Minister on any matter concerning the functions or activities of the CLRG or on any matter referred by the Minister to the CLRG for advice.

1.5.4 The First Report of the CLRG

The First Report of the Company Law Review Group (the "First Report") was launched by the Tanaiste on February 28, 2002. The statutory group's First Report, which concerns the CLRG's deliberations in the two-year period from February 2000 to December 2001, contains 195 recommendations, many of which, if implemented, will give rise to far-reaching reform. According to the First Report, these recommendations, "on approval by the Government, will be translated into legislation substantially reforming and amending the Companies Code and laying the basis for the consolidation of company law". According to the First Report, there is at least one area of our business environment which has not kept pace with the developments in the Irish economy and this is "the legal and regulatory framework in which Irish companies operate and which is intended to provide the legal context for investment, for risk-taking, for profit-making, for corporate governance and for compliance with public policy objectives and ethical standards; in short, our companies code". The main recommendations of the First Report are directed at creating what the CLRG calls a "world-class company law structure".

1.5.5 The CLS

Chapter 3 of the First Report recommends that the private company limited by shares ("CLS") should become the model company type in the Companies Acts (see Chapter 2 on the types of companies that can be established in the State). This would have the effect of greatly simplifying the regulatory regime for companies and of making the law clearer and more accessible. Currently, nine out of ten registered companies in Ireland are private companies limited by shares.

The CLS should be defined as a company which (a) has a share capital; (b) has the liability of its members limited by shares; and (c) by its constitution (i) restricts the rights to transfer its shares; (ii) limits the number of its members to 150, not including persons who are employed in the company; and (iii) prohibits any invitation to the public to subscribe for any shares or debentures of the company.

1.5.6 A Single Companies Act

Following the implementation of the extensive reform and restructuring proposed in the First Report, Chapter 3 states the intention to consolidate the 10 main Companies Acts and associated statutory instruments into a single Act. The consolidated Companies Act should be divided into two groups of law. The first group of law (Group A) will define the CLS and contain all company laws that apply to it. The second group of law (Group B) will reference and define the remaining types of companies and other bodies corporate and provide, by cross-reference to Group A, those provisions that apply to each type of company. The regulations concerning company law made under the European Communities Act 1972 should be included in the consolidated Companies Act without first being enacted as primary legislation.

1.5.7 Electronic transactions

The First Report recommends that company officers and company members should be facilitated to transact business electronically, *inter se*, and with the regulatory authorities so as to minimise the costs and to maximise the gain from efficiencies in time and convenience.

1.5.8 The simplification of corporate governance

The main recommendations to achieve simplification in the context of corporate governance are discussed below.

(1) Registers and inspections

All documents to be made available for inspection under the Companies Acts should be available at the company's registered office or such other place within the State as notified to the Registrar of Companies.

Where various company registers must be made available for inspection under the Companies Acts, the Minister should make an order to standardise register inspection and copying fees commensurate with the actual cost of the provision of copies. The Electronic Commerce Act 2000 should be taken as the principal legislation on the keeping of electronic records by a company under the Companies Acts and section 239 of the Companies Act 1990 should be repealed.

The requirements of directors to disclose directorships during the past 10 years should be reduced to five years (see Chapter 2).

See Chapters 2, 7, 12 and 13 on the current provisions relating to company registers and inspections.

(2) Meetings of members

All companies, other than plcs, should not have to hold an annual general meeting if the members of the company unanimously consent. However, the auditors of the company should have the power to demand an annual general meeting where it is proposed to pass a resolution changing the company auditors.

Any resolution of any company should be capable of being passed by a unanimous written resolution of the members, consisting of a number of pieces of paper and regardless of the rules set out in the articles of the company.

The Companies Acts should specify the notice required for meetings of the company rather than delegating the matter to the company's articles of association. Twenty-one days' notice should be required for an annual general meeting and meetings to pass a special resolution, and seven days' notice should be required for an extraordinary general meeting, save in the case of a plc where fourteen days' notice would be required. The company could increase these notice periods.

The giving of notice should be able to be achieved electronically and in accordance with the Electronic Commerce Act 2000.

See Chapter 13 on the provisions currently applying to members' meetings.

(3) Directors' meetings

Meetings of the directors of all companies ought, by statute, to be capable of being held by telephone or by other suitable electronic means unless the articles of the company specifically provide to the contrary. It is further recommended that written resolutions of the directors should be capable of consisting of separate pieces of paper signed separately.

See Chapter 7 for the current provisions applying to directors' meetings.

(4) Number of company members

It is recommended that the European Communities (Single-Member Private Limited Company) Regulations 1994 (discussed at Chapter 2) should be repealed and replaced with a statutory provision that private companies can be formed with one member or more and that any public company can be established with two members or more.

It is also recommended that section 36 of the Companies Act 1963, which provides for personal liability for members where the number of company members falls below the statutory minimum, be repealed.

See Chapters 2 and 5 for the current provisions applying to the number of company members.

1.5.9 Creditor protection

(1) The validation procedure for otherwise prohibited acts

The Report recommends a single validation procedure for transactions under section 60 of the Companies Act 1963 (where a company assists the purchase of its own shares, see Chapter 15), section 31 of the Companies Act 1990 (the prohibition on a company giving loans and other security to its directors or connected persons, see Chapter 7), and section 256 of the Companies Act 1963 (the directors' declaration of solvency in a voluntary winding up, see Chapter 21).

This single validation procedure would require the directors of the company to make a declaration stating that they are satisfied that the company is solvent at the time of the declaration, including a statement of the company's assets and liabilities at the time of the declaration and, further, setting out the benefit to the company of the transaction at issue. The directors should, where the court is satisfied that it is just and equitable, be personally liable for the company's debts where the declaration is made without reasonable grounds and the company is subsequently unable to pay its debts. Further, those directors and persons connected to them should be liable to indemnify the company where they have received a benefit from the transaction. In addition, a special resolution should be required to validate the proposed transaction. The requirement of the independent person's report should be dispensed with. The latter was only recently introduced in respect of section 31 of the Companies Act 1990 (by section 78 of the Company Law Enforcement Act 2001).

The Report also recommends that a breach of sections 60, 31 and 256 should be a criminal offence.

(2) The obligation to call a meeting where there is serious capital loss

The Report recommends that the obligation under section 40 of the Companies (Amendment) Act 1983 should be abolished in the case of private companies (see Chapter 15).

The obligation placed on auditors to state in their annual report whether, in their opinion, there existed at the balance sheet date a situation that would require the convening of an extraordinary general meeting of the company pursuant to section 40 of the Companies (Amendment) Act 1983 should be repealed for audit reports in respect of all companies.

1.5.10 Incorporation procedure

A simplified form of application for incorporation of private companies limited by shares should be approved for use, containing the following:

1. the company name, details of its first officers, address of the registered office, the company's activity within the State, and where it is carried on (Part I);
2. the company constitution containing the company name, the share capital clause, and the rules currently contained in the articles of association (Part II);
3. a signature section, in which the first officers of the company consent to acting as such, and which includes the current association or subscription clause, wherein the subscribers subscribe to the documents and verify their contents (Part III).

Part II only would be required to be re-filed in full where the constitution is altered after the date of incorporation. All existing requirements to make and file statutory declarations with the Companies Registration Office should be replaced with a requirement to make an unsworn declaration in the prescribed form, which the Registrar of Companies may accept in the relevant circumstances as sufficient evidence of compliance. It should be open to the board to authorise agents to sign documents electronically and to forward them directly to the Companies Registration Office, and the company should notify the Companies Registration Office of its designated electronic filing agents.

See Chapter 2 for the current provisions on incorporation and the Companies Registration Office.

1.5.11 Criminal acts and omissions

For the sake of clarity, the Director of Corporate Enforcement should be obliged to publish and maintain a complete list of offences under the Companies Acts, distinguishing between summary and indictable offences. Reliance on that list shall be a defence to any prosecution for failure to notify any person of the suspected commission of any offence on the list.

The minimum fine for summary offences should be €500, and the lowest maximum fine for indictable offences should be increased to €12,500. The recommendations are proportionate to the relative severity of the offences.

Section 379 of the Companies Act 1963 deals with the service of documents on a company. It is recommended that this provision be amended to include an obligation on all non-resident directors to nominate an address within the state for the service of criminal proceedings.

The nomination should be provided to the Registrar of Companies. Where false information is supplied, the matter should be referred to the Director of Corporate Enforcement or the Director of Public Prosecutions as appropriate.

1.5.12 The abolition of the ultra vires doctrine

In 1958 the *Cox Committee* stated that "the purpose of the doctrine of *ultra vires* had been largely defeated. It does not now give any protection to the shareholders or the creditors of the company and becomes a waste of time and paper". The CLRG recommends that private companies should have the same legal capacity as natural persons. A related recommendation is that all other companies should have an objects clause and be referred to as "limited capacity" companies.

So plcs will immediately be recognisable as being "limited capacity" companies and the other companies (companies limited by guarantee or unlimited companies) would have to use the letters "DAC" (designated activity company) as part of their name. The vast majority of companies in Ireland would be largely unaffected by such a change.

See Chapter 6 for the discussion of the current position of the doctrine of *ultra vires*.

1.5.13 Directors' duties

In the interests of clarity and completeness, the fiduciary duties of the directors of companies should be clearly set out in the Companies Acts. Currently, these duties are enumerated in the common law and they are not specifically expressed in the companies code (see Chapter 7).

The Report clarifies that no distinction should be made between the duties of executive and non-executive directors.

It recommends that certain laws that apply to companies generally could safely be disapplied to the private company limited by shares and, in this regard, the number of directors required for a CLS could be reduced from two to one. This is justified on the ground that many second directors in such companies are nominal only and fulfilling the statutory requirements. It will remain necessary to have a distinct company secretary.

As set out in Chapter 7, directors and secretaries of companies are obliged by Part IV of the Companies Act 1990 to notify the company of any interests they hold in the shares or debentures of the company or a related company. The Report recommends that this obligation should be disapplied where that interests falls short of one per cent of the issued share capital or debentures of the company and that the director or secretary ought to be required merely to disclose the fact of such an interest along the lines of the general disclosure under section 194 of the Companies Act 1963 (where he has an interest in company contracts).

1.5.14 Practice and procedure

It is recommend that a Commercial Division of the High Court be established to deal with business-to-business and business-to-State litigation. This Division should have a dedicated Companies List and an assigned judge.

1.5.15 Insolvency regulation

The Report recommends the introduction of professional regulation for insolvency regulators (liquidators, receivers, and examiners).

1.5.16 The effects of a strike-off

As the application to restore a company to the register can now be made in the Circuit Court, the Report recommends that the Circuit Court Rules Committee should draw up rules:

1. to simplify the procedures for applications to have the company restored; and
2. to facilitate a reduction in the costs of restoration by the establishments of a scale of measured costs.

The Companies Acts should be amended to award the applicant the costs of restoration against the company unless to do so would be in breach of the constitutional rights of any person. The Director of Corporate Enforcement should be given the power to require each person who was a director at the time of the strike-off to produce a statement of affairs for the company as at the date of strike-off and, on foot of this, he may decide if an investigation and consequent application to court for a disqualification order under section 160 of the Companies Act 1990 (see Chapter 8) or some other order under section 251 of the Companies Act 1990 (where a company is in liquidation) is appropriate.

See Chapter 22 on the restoration of the company to the register.

1.5.17 The Second Work Programme

The Second Work Programme 2002-2003 of the CLRG includes the review of shares and share capital, the winding up of companies, and a review of charges and securities. It will also examine the following:

1. the preparation of heads of a Bill in respect of the recommendations of the First Report;
2. the structure of a consolidated Companies Act;
3. the drafting of a one-document company constitution (*i.e.* the current memorandum and articles of association should be replaced by one document);
4. whether Ireland should have a State-funded public interest liquidation service.

The text of the First Report and details of this Second Work Programme are available on-line at ***www.clrg.org***.

2. COMPANY FORMATION

A company is an entity that is formed and registered in the Companies Registration Office under the Companies Acts 1963-2001. This corporate entity exists in law entirely separate from its owners, the shareholders, or members, and the directors who manage the company. The company is therefore an artificial legal person having a separate legal identity called a corporate personality, which is discussed at Chapter 5.

2.1 Limited and unlimited companies

All registered companies are either limited or unlimited. The promoters of the company, the persons who establish the company, must decide whether the members of the company are to be fully liable for the debts incurred by the company, in which case the company is unlimited, or whether their liability is restricted, in which case the company is limited.

2.1.1 Limited liability

If a company has limited liability, it means that members of the company are not liable for the debts due and owing to the company creditors. The members are simply liable to pay to the company whatever amount remains unpaid on their shares or on their guarantees. In certain circumstances this protection from general liability for the debts of the company may be removed by the court or by statute where the privilege of limited liability has been abused (see Chapter 5 on the imposition of personal liability on company officers or members for the debts of the company).

(1) A company limited by shares

Section 5(2)(a) of the Companies Act 1963 allows for the creation of a company where the liability of its members is limited to the amount, if any, unpaid on the shares held by them. This is company limited by shares. Such a company has an authorised share capital divided into shares of a fixed amount. This is the amount of shares that the company is authorised to issue and, once issued, it is called the issued share capital of the company. As discussed at Chapter 12, some investors or members of the company may not pay the full amount due to the company for the shares at the time of purchase. This is called unpaid share capital. In a company limited by shares, the responsibility of the members for debts of the company is limited to the payment of the remainder of the purchase price of their shares.

(2) A company limited by guarantee

Shares denote a trading company, and the shares frequently carry the right to a dividend, *i.e.* a share of the company's profits. Some companies may determine not to issue shares, particularly where the company is not incorporated with a view to making a profit. A company limited by guarantee does not issue shares and, therefore, will not have shareholders. Instead, the members have a form of personal membership and give a guarantee to the company to contribute a specified amount to the debts of the company. The guarantee is only triggered in the event that the company is wound up, and the member will be liable for the company debts to the extent of the figure in that guarantee (section 5(2)(b) of the Companies Act 1963). Companies limited by guarantee are common in the case of clubs, social societies, and property management companies which are not trading and do not require a capital base.

(3) A company limited by guarantee and having a share capital

This is a hybrid company where there are shareholders (who owe the company any unpaid amounts on their shares) who have also guaranteed to pay the company's liabilities up to a specified amount in the event that the company is wound up.

2.1.2 Unlimited liability

The members of an unlimited company have an unlimited liability for the debts of a company in the event of a company being unable to meet its debts when due. The member cannot be personally sued by the company creditors, and it is the company liquidator, the person who manages the liquidation of the company (discussed at Chapter 21), who must pursue the members for the company debts. These companies are commonly formed where there is no intention to trade. These companies are exempted from many financial disclosure requirements, they do not have to pay capital duty on the registration of the company, and the use of the company's capital base is left to the discretion of the company. An unlimited company may have a share capital but it is not an essential prerequisite.

2.2 Private and public companies

The limited or unlimited companies may be public companies or private companies depending on how the company proposes to raise its capital. A private company is prohibited from offering its shares or debentures to the public. A public company may raise its capital in this way but it must do so in accordance with the Companies Acts, The Stock Exchange rules and European regulations.

2.2.1 Private company

Private companies are very common in Ireland; they range from one-person or family owned entities and small enterprises that behave very much like partnerships (often called quasi-partnerships) to large-scale ventures. Section 33(1) of the Companies Act 1963 defines a private company as a company having a share capital. As a private company must always have a share capital, private companies consist of companies limited by shares, companies limited by guarantee having a share capital, and unlimited companies having a share capital.

Section 33(1) of the Companies Act 1963 also requires that a private company must adopt company rules (articles of association), which set out the following terms:

1. a limit of 50 company members;
2. a restriction on the transferability of the company's shares;
3. a prohibition on inviting members of the public to subscribe for shares or debentures in the company.

Where a private company contravenes any of these conditions, it does not lose its private status, but it loses certain legal privileges of its status. According to section 34(1) of the Companies Act 1963, it ceases to be entitled to the privileges and exemptions conferred on the private company such as the exemption from the obligation to annex an auditor's report to its annual return. It is open to the company or any other interested person to apply to court for relief on the ground that the breach was accidental or due to inadvertence or some other sufficient cause, or that it is just and equitable to grant relief (section 34(2) of the Companies Act 1963). Where a private company offers shares or debentures to the public, it is a criminal offence, according to section 21 of the Companies (Amendment) Act 1983, and the company and every officer in default is liable to a fine.

Under section 5 of the Companies Act 1963 a private company must have two or more members. Section 36 of the Companies Act 1963 provides for personal liability for the members of a private company where the membership of that company falls below two. If the company carries on business for more than six months with fewer than two members, every person who is a member of the company during the period after six months and who knows that it is carrying on business with fewer than two members, is liable for the whole of the debts of the company contracted during that time (see Chapter 5). As discussed in paragraph 2.2.2 below certain private limited companies can now carry on their business with just one member.

A private company is not required by statute to maintain a minimum capital. The value of the nominal share capital of the company may be fixed at the discretion of the promoters. However, where a restricted director becomes involved with a private company, that company must maintain a minimum paid-up share capital of €63,500, as prescribed by the Companies Act 1990 and as amended by the Company Law Enforcement Act 2001 (see Chapter 8).

2.2.2 Single-member private limited company

Further to the European Communities (Single-Member Private Limited Companies) Regulations 1994 (S.I. 275/1994), the formation of a one-member private limited company is possible. The regulations were introduced to give effect to the Twelfth E.U. Directive on single-member companies. This option is only available under the terms of the regulations to a private company limited by shares or a private company limited by guarantee and having a share capital.

However, these regulations do not remove the requirement that all companies must have two directors (section 174 of the Companies Act 1963). These companies are exempted from the requirement to hold annual general meetings under section 131 of the Companies Act 1963 as a result of Regulation 8(1). As there is no annual general meeting, the requirement to lay the profit and loss account, balance sheet, directors' report, and auditors' report before the annual general meeting is deemed satisfied where they are delivered to the sole member of the company. Rather than passing resolutions, the company decisions are commonly set out in writing.

The CLRG recommends the abolition of this category of company (see paragraph 1.5.8).

2.2.3 Public company

According to section 2 of the Companies (Amendment) Act 1983, a public company is defined as a company that is not a private company, and under section 5 of the Companies Act 1963 such a company must have at least seven members. The principal characteristic of a public company is that the company offers its share to the public. This is normally carried out by way of a document called a prospectus (see Chapter 12). Public companies can be limited or unlimited. The majority of public companies registered in the State have limited liability. The phrase "old public limited companies" refers to companies established under the Companies Act 1963, and they were simply limited companies that did not contain the provisions required by section 33(1) of the Companies Act 1963. The Companies (Amendment) Act 1983 implemented the Second E.U. Directive, which provided for the establishment of the public limited company, the "plc".

A plc is defined in section 2 of the Companies (Amendment) Act 1983 as a company which is limited by shares, which states in its memorandum that it is a public limited company, and which complies with the requirements of the Act as to registration. Section 5(2) of the Companies (Amendment) Act 1983 states that Registrar of Companies shall not register the memorandum of a plc unless the share capital set out in the memorandum, the company charter, is not less than the authorised minimum which is set at €38,100 under section 19 of the Companies (Amendment) Act 1983. Section 19(2) permits the Minister to increase the amount by order. There are a number of restrictions placed on a plc in respect of the allotment of this share capital to the public; these are discussed at Chapter 12. Where a restricted director acts for a plc, the plc must comply with the minimum capital requirements set out in section 150(3) of the Companies Act 1990 (as increased by the Company Law Enforcement Act 2001) and the plc must have a minimum paid-up share capital of € 317,500.

Where a private company converts to a plc or an old public limited company is re-registered as a plc, the same provisions must be observed. The old public limited companies were given three years from October 13, 1983, (the "transitional period") to re-register as a plc or another form of company. Section 12 of the Companies (Amendment) Act 1983 required that the directors of the company pass a resolution that the company be re-registered and lodge a statutory declaration that the capital requirements for a plc would be satisfied. Section 13 of the Companies (Amendment) Act 1983 provided for the imposition of penalties on the company and every officer in default where an old public limited company failed to re-register as a plc. Where the old public limited company failed to re-register as another form of company, section 16 of the Companies (Amendment) Act 1983 rendered the company and every officer in default guilty of an offence.

According to section 7 of the Companies (Amendment) Act 1983, it is no longer possible to establish a public limited company that is limited by guarantee and having a share capital.

2.2.4 The CLS

See Chapter 1.5.5 for the new model company recommended by the CLRG.

2.3 Conversion of companies

2.3.1 Conversion of a private company to a plc

Section 9 of the Companies (Amendment) Act 1983 provides for the re-registration of a private company as a plc. According to section 9(1)(a), the shareholders of the company must pass a special resolution (this resolution requires a 75 per cent majority) that the company should be re-registered. The resolution must alter the memorandum of the company to state that the company is a plc and that it has an authorised minimum share capital. The form of the memorandum should be in accordance with the model memorandum set out in Part 1 of the Second Schedule to the Companies (Amendment) Act 1983. The resolution may also make any necessary amendments to the articles of the company.

According to section 10(1) of the Companies (Amendment) Act 1983, a private company cannot re-register as a plc unless

1. the nominal value of the company's allotted share capital is not less than the authorised minimum (section 10(1)(a));
2. each of its allotted shares is paid up at least as to one-quarter of the nominal value of that share and the whole of any premium on it (section 10(1)(b));

3. where the company allotted shares in consideration for an undertaking to perform work or services, that undertaking has been performed (section 10(1)(c));

4. where the company allotted shares in consideration for an undertaking (other than to perform work or services), that undertaking has been performed or must be performed within five years from the time of allotment (section 10(1)(d)).

Pursuant to section 9(1)(b) of the Companies (Amendment) Act 1983, the director or secretary of the company must lodge an application to re-register with the Registrar of Companies together with a copy of the altered memorandum and articles. The following documents must also be submitted with the application:

1. a balance sheet of the company (prepared not more than seven months before the date of the application) together with an unqualified auditors' report in respect of that balance sheet (see Chapter 9 on auditor's reports);

2. a written statement from the company's auditors stating that in their opinion the amount of the company's net assets was not less than the aggregate of its called-up share capital plus undistributable reserves on the date of the balance sheet;

3. a copy of a report prepared in accordance with section 30 of the Companies (Amendment) Act 1983, where between the date of the balance sheet and the date of the application, the company accepted non-cash consideration for the payment of its shares (see Chapter 12);

4. a statutory declaration sworn by a director or secretary of the company swearing that the requisite special resolution has been passed, the conditions set out in section 10 have been satisfied, any report under section 30 has been prepared, and that between the date of the balance sheet and the date of the application there has been no change in the financial position of the company resulting in the amount of the company's net assets becoming less than the aggregate of its called-up share capital plus undistributable reserves.

Where the Registrar of Companies is satisfied that the company has complied with all its obligations under section 9 of the Companies (Amendment) Act 1983, the Registrar of Companies shall issue a certificate of incorporation stating that the company is a plc and the altered memorandum and articles take effect on this date. The certificate is conclusive evidence that the requirements of re-registration have been complied with and that the company is a plc.

2.3.2 Conversion of a plc to a private company

Under section 14 of the Companies (Amendment) Act 1983 a plc may convert to a private company on the passing of a special resolution resolving to re-register, amending the memorandum so that it no longer states that it is a plc, and amending the articles to include the conditions specified in section 33(1) of the Companies Act 1963. The application to re-register must be submitted to the Registrar of Companies by the director or secretary of the company together with a printed copy of the altered memorandum and articles of association.

Under section 15(2) of the Companies (Amendment) Act 1983 an application may be made to the court to cancel the resolution. The application may be made by a shareholder holding not less than five per cent of the nominal value of the issued share capital or any class thereof, by not less than five per cent of the company members (where the company is not limited by shares) or by not less than 50 members of the company. The court application must be made within twenty-eight days of the passing of the special resolution, and the applicant must not have consented to or voted in favour of the special resolution (sections 15(2)). The court may cancel the alteration, confirm the alteration, or confirm the alteration on certain terms and conditions. It is also open to the court to adjourn the application to facilitate the purchase of the dissentient members' shares (section 15(6) of the Companies (Amendment) Act 1983). Under section 15(7) of the Companies (Amendment) Act 1983) the court may make an order directing the company to purchase the shares of any member of the company and to reduce its share capital accordingly.

Notice of the application must be delivered to the Registrar of Companies under section 15(5) of the Companies (Amendment) Act 1983. Where the court hears an application under section 15 and makes an order canceling or confirming the special resolution, the company must deliver a copy of that court order to the Registrar of Companies within fifteen days or within such longer period that the court directs. Failure to comply with these obligations renders the company and every officer in default liable to a fine (section 15(10) of the Companies (Amendment) Act 1983).

Where no application has been made to the court to cancel the resolution and the period for making such an application has expired, the Registrar of Companies may issue a certificate of incorporation to the company. The company shall become a private company and the altered memorandum and articles of association take effect. The certificate of incorporation is conclusive evidence that the company is a private company and that the requirement of re-registration has been satisfied (section 14(5) of the Companies (Amendment) Act 1983).

2.3.3 Conversion of an unlimited company to a limited company

Section 20 of the Companies Act 1963 originally provided for the conversion of an unlimited company to a limited entity. According to section 54 of the Companies (Amendment) Act 1983, it is no longer possible to make this conversion pursuant to that section, and the relevant procedure is now set out in section 53 of the Companies (Amendment) Act 1983. This conversion is permitted on the condition that the members pass a special resolution and the requisite amendments are made to the memorandum and articles of association.

The resolution must state whether the company is to be limited by shares (in which case the amount of the nominal share capital of the company must be set out) or guarantee and make the attendant amendments to the memorandum and articles of association. The application for re-registration must be submitted by the director or secretary of the company together with a printed copy of the amended memorandum and articles of association. Where the Registrar of Companies issues a certificate of incorporation, the status of the company shall change from unlimited to limited, and the altered memorandum and articles take effect. According to section 53(5) of the Companies (Amendment) Act 1983, the certificate of incorporation is conclusive evidence that the requirement for re-registration has been complied with.

Section 53(7) of the Companies (Amendment) Act 1983 deals with the case of the re-registered company going into liquidation shortly after the conversion. A past member of the company who was a member at the time of re-registration shall be liable without limitation for the debts of the company contracted before the re-registration, in the event of the company winding up within three years of the date of the conversion.

2.3.4 Conversion of a limited company to an unlimited company

Section 52 of the Companies (Amendment) Act 1983 permits this conversion provided that the members of the company unanimously consent and strict procedural requirements are followed. The application must be submitted to the Registrar of Companies by the director or secretary of the company, and it must be accompanied by the following documents:

1. an assent to the re-registration signed by or on behalf of *all* the members of the company;
2. a statutory declaration made by the directors of the company that the assent was signed by all the members of the company or where someone signed on behalf of a member, the directors took reasonable steps to confirm that the person was lawfully entitled to sign on the member's behalf;
3. a printed copy of the memorandum and articles of the company incorporating any necessary alterations;
4. where no articles were previously registered by the company, a copy of articles to be registered.

Where the Registrar of Companies issues a certificate of incorporation, the status of the company shall change from limited to unlimited, and the altered memorandum and articles shall take effect. According to section 52(5) of the Companies (Amendment) Act 1983, the certificate of incorporation is conclusive evidence that the requirement for re-registration has been complied with. According to section 52(6) any past member of the company at the time of re-registration who does not become a member of the re-registered company shall have no greater liability in the case of a winding up than if the company had not been re-registered.

2.3.5 Conversion of a private company to a single-member private limited company or vice versa

According to Regulation 5(1) of the European Communities (Single-Member Private Limited Companies) Regulations 1994, where the membership of a private company, limited by shares or limited by guarantee and having a share capital, reduces to one member and all the shares of the company are registered in the name of the sole member, the company becomes a single-member private limited company. According to Regulation 5(2), the fact of the conversion, the date of the conversion, and the identity of the sole member must be notified to the Registrar of Companies within twenty-eight days. Regulation 5(3) states that a failure to deliver the notification will render the company and every officer in default liable to an offence.

A single-member private limited company will automatically convert to a private company limited by shares or limited by guarantee and having a share capital where the number of members increases above one according to Regulation 6(1) of the European Communities (Single-Member Private Limited Companies) Regulations 1994. According to Regulation 6(2) the fact of the conversion and the date of the conversion must be notified to the Registrar of Companies within twenty-eight days. Regulation 6(3) states that a failure to deliver the notification will render the company and every officer in default liable to an offence.

2.4 Foreign companies

Where a company incorporated outside the State establishes a place of business within the State, it is regulated by Part XI of the Companies Act 1963 and the European Communities (Branch Disclosures) Regulations 1993 (S.I. 395/1993). Any foreign company which has an established place of business in the State is required to deliver the following documents to the Registrar of Companies under section 352 of the Companies Act 1963:

1. a certified copy of the charter, statutes or memorandum and articles of the company or any other instrument constituting or defining the constitution of the company;
2. a list of the directors of the company and details of any other directorships held by the directors in Irish companies;
3. a list of the company secretaries and, where the secretary is a body corporate, its corporate name and the registered or principal office of the company;
4. the address of the company's principal place of business in the State;
5. the name and address of a person resident in the State who is authorised to accept the service of proceedings and any notices in respect of the company.

Section 353 of the Companies Act 1963 requires the company to deliver particulars of any alteration to those documents to the Registrar of Companies. Section 354 requires such a company to deliver its balance sheet and profit and loss accounts to the Registrar of Companies every calendar year. It is open to the company to seek a ministerial exemption from this requirement, and, further. this provision shall not apply to a company where its constitution would enable it to be registered as a private company in Ireland. If the company issues a prospectus in Ireland inviting investors to subscribe for shares or debentures in the company, the prospectus must state the country in which the company is incorporated and state whether the liability of the members is limited. All the company's bill-heads and letter-paper must state the name of the company, where it is incorporated, and the limited liability of the members. Section 357 of the Companies Act 1963 requires the company to give notice to the Registrar of Companies where it ceases to have a place of business within the State.

Pursuant to section 358 of the Companies Act 1963, where the company fails to comply with these provisions, the company and every officer or agent of the company who knowingly or wilfully authorises or permits the default shall be liable to a fine.

Similar provisions apply to a company that has not established a "place of business within the State" but it has established a "branch" within the State within the meaning of the European Communities (Branch Disclosures) Regulations 1993 (S.I. 395/1993).

In the English case of *Rakusens Ltd v. Baser Ambalaj Plastik Sanayi Ticaret Asi* (2002) it was not proven to the satisfaction of the court that the company had an established place of business in Great Britain under equivalent legislation. The Court of Appeal held that that it was insufficient to show that an agent of the company (as opposed to its employees) had established a place of business in the jurisdiction. The agent in this case was a commission agent who had no authority to conclude contracts on behalf of the foreign company.

2.5 Incorporation

2.5.1 Carrying on an activity in the State

As a result of section 42(1) of the Companies (Amendment) (No. 2) Act 1999, any company shall not be formed and registered under the Companies Acts unless it appears to the Registrar of Companies that the company proposes to carry on an activity mentioned in its memorandum in the State. The Registrar of Companies may accept a statutory declaration from the company's director or secretary or a solicitor involved in the formation of the company as sufficient evidence that this is the case.

Under section 42(2) the declaration must state that the purpose for which the company is being formed is to carry out an activity within the State, and the activity must be described together with the place or places it is proposed to carry on the activity. The declaration must also state the place, whether in the State or not, where the central administration of the company will normally be carried on. Where the company proposes to carry on two or more activities, the declarant must state the above details in respect of what he considers to be the proposed principal activity of the company. This provision was introduced to ensure that Irish registered companies have a real and genuine connection with the State and that they are not incorporated in this State to avoid regulatory obligations in other countries.

2.5.2 Documents required for registration

There are a number of documents that must be lodged with the Registrar of Companies at the Office of the Registrar by the promoters of the company when they are applying for the registration of a company. A memorandum of association of the company must be lodged irrespective of the category of company that the promoters are seeking to establish (see Chapter 4). The articles of association of the company must be lodged where it is proposed to establish a company limited by guarantee and having a share capital or an unlimited company. In the case of a company limited by shares or limited by guarantee and not having a share capital, the promoters have the option of submitting articles, and where no articles are submitted, the model articles in the Schedules to the Companies Acts are adopted (see Chapters 2 and 4).

The promoters must also submit a statement setting out the following:

1. the name of the company;
2. the registered office of the company;
3. the name, address, and signature of the company;
4. particulars of the directors, including their signatures;
5. a statutory declaration of a person named as a director or secretary of the proposed company or by a solicitor involved in the for-

mation of the company, that all the requirements of the Companies Acts as to registration have been complied with.

A simplified incorporation procedure is recommended by CLRG in its first Report as discussed at paragraph 1.5.10. Further details must be delivered to the Registrar of Companies under section 3A of the Companies (Amendment) Act 1982 (as inserted by section 101 of the Company Law Enforcement Act 2001) where any person named in the statement is disqualified under the law of another state from acting as a director or secretary of a body corporate or an undertaking. That disqualified person is under an obligation to ensure that a further statement is delivered to the Registrar of Companies setting out the following:

1. the jurisdiction in which he is so disqualified;
2. the date on which he became so disqualified;
3. the period for which he is so disqualified.

2.5.3 Certificate of Registration

Where the Registrar of Companies is satisfied with the documents submitted, he shall "certify under his hand that the company is incorporated" under section 18(1) of the Companies Act 1963. This is the date that corporate life begins according to section 18(2) of the Companies Act 1963. Section 5(4) of the Companies (Amendment) Act 1983 (replacing section 19 of Companies Act 1963) provides that the issue of the certificate of incorporation is "conclusive evidence" that all the requirements of the Companies Acts in respect of registration and matters precedent and incidental thereto have been complied with, that the association is a company authorised to be registered under the Companies Act, and that the company is duly registered. It is also conclusive evidence that a company is a plc if the certificate contains a statement to that effect (section 5(4) of the Companies (Amendment) Act 1983).

According to *Re Barned's Banking Company; Peels Case* (1867), the court is not permitted to look into matters prior to the certificate; Cairns L.J. stated that it would have "disastrous consequences" if a "person was allowed to go back and enter into an examination" of the original incorporation.

2.5.4 Obligations on registration

Within six weeks all companies incorporated with limited liability are required under Regulation 4(1) of the EC (Companies) Regulations 1973 (S.I. 163/1993) to publish in *Iris Oifigiuil* (an official Government publication) notice of the delivery to, or issue by, the Register of Companies of the following documents and particulars:

1. the certificate of incorporation of the company;
2. the memorandum and articles of association and any amendments thereto;
3. the text of every amended text of the memorandum and articles of association;
4. notice of the location of the company's registered office or any change thereto.

Where the company fails to comply with this regulation, the company will be unable to rely on the documents against any person unless the company can prove that the person actually had notice of the documents.

2.5.5 Commencement of business

Where a certificate of incorporation is issued to a private company, it may commence business immediately. In the case of a plc, section 6(1) of the Companies (Amendment) Act 1983 states that a plc "shall not do business or exercise any borrowing powers unless the registrar of companies has issued it with a certificate under this section". Such a certificate will only be issued where the nominal value of the company's allotted share capital is not less than the authorised minimum (€38,100) and a director or secretary delivers a statutory declaration to the Registrar of Companies stating the following:

1. that the nominal value of the company's allotted share capital is not less than the authorised minimum;
2. the amount paid up, at the time of the application, on the allotted share capital of the company;
3. the amount, or estimated amount, of the preliminary expenses of the company and the persons by whom any of those expenses have been paid or are payable; and

4. any amount of any benefit paid or given, or intended to be paid or given, to any promoter of the company, and the consideration for the payment or benefit.

Where such a certificate is issued, it is conclusive evidence that the company is entitled to do business and exercise any borrowing powers (section 6(6) of the Companies (Amendment) Act 1983). If the plc carries on business or exercises borrowing powers in contravention of this section, the company and every officer in default is liable to a fine. Bona fide outsiders who enter into transactions with the plc before the issue of the certificate are protected. The transaction remains valid, and, where the plc fails to comply with its obligations under the transaction within twenty-one days of being called upon to do so, the directors of the company are jointly and severally liable to indemnify the other party to the transaction in respect of any loss or damage caused by the failure of the company to comply with those obligations (section 6(8) of the Companies (Amendment) Act 1983).

2.5.6 Registered office of the company

Section 113 of the Companies Act 1963 (as substituted by section 4 of the Companies (Amendment) Act 1982) requires that a company must maintain its registered office within the State at all times and particulars of the location must be delivered to the Registrar of Companies with the application for registration. A notice of any change in the location of the registered office must be delivered to the Registrar of Companies within fourteen days after the date of the change (section 113(4)). Where the company does not comply with section 113, the company and every officer in default is liable to a fine. The company is required by the Companies Acts to retain, at the registered office, a number of its registers, such as the register of members (see Chapter 13), the register of debenture holders (see Chapter 17), the register of directors and secretaries (see Chapter 7), the register of directors' and secretaries' interests in shares (see Chapter 12), and the register of interests in shares in plcs (see Chapter 12).

2.6 Consequences of incorporation

2.6.1 Corporate personality

When a company is incorporated, it becomes a separate legal entity, distinct from its members and its directors. It has the power to do business in its own name, it has the capacity to hold its own assets, and it is regarded as a separate legal person by those who deal with it. It acquires rights, obligations, and duties that are different and distinct from those of its members.

2.6.2 Limited liability

One of the principal reasons why a company is incorporated is the allure of limited liability for the members in respect of the indebtedness of the company. As stated, limited liability is a statutory development and not a necessary consequence of the recognition of corporate personality (*Revenue Commissioners v. Bank of Ireland* (1925)).

2.6.3 Transfer of interests

Shares can easily be transferred between individuals, and the life of the company remains unaffected. In the case of a partnership, the transfer of partnership interests usually results in the dissolution of the partnership. Share transfer and transmission is discussed at Chapter 13.

2.6.4 Perpetual succession

A company continues to exist from the date of incorporation until it is struck off the company register by the Registrar of Companies. This is called the dissolution of the company. Therefore, the company continues regardless of any changes in membership or its directors.

2.6.5 Floating charges

The incorporation of a company enables a business to use charges over assets as security for borrowings. A floating charge is an equitable charge that hovers over assets which match a description and the company can continue to deal with those assets until the charge crystallises and becomes fixed on the assets remaining in that category. A fixed charge attaches to specific identifiable property and the company is restricted in its dealing with that asset. See Chapter 16 for a detailed discussion of fixed and floating charges.

2.6.6 The company can sue and be sued

One of the consequences of the separate corporate personality principle is that a company can be party to legal proceedings and may sue or be sued in its own name.

(1) Contract

A company has the capacity to enter its own contracts as discussed in Chapter 5. The shareholders of the company are not considered to be parties to such contracts entered into by the company, and, as a result, a shareholder cannot be personally sued under a company contract. It is not open to the shareholder to sue on foot of a contract entered into by the company unless the shareholder can bring the action in the form of a derivative action, *i.e.* in the name of the company. Such actions are limited in scope and are usually confined to cases where a fraud has been committed on the company. Further, where the action is successful, the order of the court must be made in the name of the company and not the shareholder (see Chapter 14 on derivative actions). Save where the shareholder can bring a derivative action, it is for the company to sue on foot of its contracts, and it is not open to the shareholder to plead that the company was acting as its agent when entering company contracts according to *Dunlop Pneumatic Tyre Co. Ltd v. Selfridge & Co. Ltd* (1915).

Equally a company has no claim or liability on foot of a contract entered into by a shareholder unless it can be established that the member was authorised, expressly or ostensibly, to enter into the contract as an agent for the company (see Chapter 6).

(2) Tort

There are certain torts which a company cannot suffer, such as assault, battery, or false imprisonment, because it is an artificial entity and not a natural person. It appears that a company may take an action for defamation on the ground that its business reputation has been damaged. In the Australian case of *Wiggins and anor v. Rigby et al* (2000) the Supreme Court of Victoria held that it was well established that a trading company could maintain an action for libel or slander for any words that are calculated to injure its reputation in the way of its trade or business. It was also held that an imputation concerning a director or officer of a company could reflect upon the company itself depending on the part that the director or officer is alleged to have played in the operations of the company and upon the extent to which one is identified with, or is considered to be, the alter ego of the other. However, it is for the company and not the company's shareholders to sue for compensation for any loss or damage. This is supported by the dicta of Carroll J. stated in *McSweeney v. Bourke* (1980), where she stated it was for the company to sue for a breach of duty and the consequent loss and damage if a financial consultant had been negligent in his advice to the company. This was because the company was the only client of the adviser and the adviser therefore assumed no duty of care to the shareholders. The company members may be able to sue for damages in tort where they can establish that the wrongdoer owed a duty of care directly to the shareholders of the company (see, for example, the duty of care owed by the company auditors in Chapter 9).

A company is commonly held to be vicariously liable for the tortious acts of its servants and agents, such as its directors or employees. Several cases have established that the company entity itself is capable of committing a tort through a person that is the directing mind and will of the company. In *Lennards Carrying Co. Ltd v Asiatic Petroleum Co.* (1915) the cargo on a ship was destroyed by fire as a result of the unseaworthy condition of the ship's boiler. The company that owned the ship could avoid liability for the accident if it happened without the "actual fault or privity" of the company. It was held by the House of Lords that a company itself could be liable for a tort, as the company could act through a person who was the active and directing will of the company. Viscount Haldane L.C. said that a "corporation is an abstraction" and that it has "no mind of its own any more than it has a body of its own; its active and directing will must consequently be sought in the person of somebody who for some purposes may be called an agent, but who is really the active and directing mind and will of the corporation, the very ego and centre of the personality of the corporation." A tort committed by such a person is a tort committed by the company.

This decision was applied in *The Lady Gwendolyn* (1965), a case where a ship crashed in fog. The relevant statute excluded vicarious liability, and the company could only be held liable for the accident if the damage occurred with the "actual fault or privity" of the company. The court considered the management structure of the company and determined that the assistant managing director was the embodiment of the company. The company, acting through that assistant managing director, had failed to ensure that the staff were properly instructed and, therefore, the company was held to be directly at fault for the accident.

(3) Crime

Like certain torts, there are crimes which a company, because of its artificial nature, is incapable of committing, for example the offence of bigamy. Where the punishment for a crime is limited to imprisonment, it is not possible to convict the company according to *R. (Cottingham) v. Justices of Cork* (1906). As the law develops it appears that it may be possible to prosecute the directors or controllers of the company for such an offence. It is considered that a company can be made personally amenable to criminal law on the basis of the actions and states of mind of persons who may be said to be its active and directing will.

In *Tesco Supermarkets Ltd v. Nattrass Ltd* (1972) a company was charged with breach of the Trade Descriptions Act by advertising products at prices other than those at which the products were actually sold. The statute provided that a person charged would not be liable if the act was that "of another person" and the person charged had taken "all reasonable precautions and exercised all due diligence" to avoid the commission of the offence. The manager of the particular store in which the breach occurred was considered to be to blame for the breach. The question was whether he was "another person" for the purposes of the Act or whether he could be identified with the company. Following *Lennard's Case*, it was stated that a company must act through a living person and if that person has a guilty mind, then "that guilt is the guilt of the company".

In *Tesco Supermarkets Ltd v. Nattrass Ltd* (1972) Lord Diplock stated that not everyone who acts for the company may be considered to be acting as the company. The only persons who could do so, according to Lord Diplock were "those natural persons who by the memorandum and articles of association or as a result of action taken by the directors or by the company in general meeting pursuant to the articles are entrusted with the exercise of the powers of the company." For the company to be liable, the delegate must have full authority to act independently of the instruction of the board of directors. The store manager could not be identified with the company since he was merely one person in a chain of control and was obliged to seek instruction. Similarly, in *R. v. P&O European Ferries (Dover) Ltd* (1991) two senior ship's officers were not considered to be high enough in the hierarchy of the company to be identified with it for the purposes of criminal liability. Turner J. did, however, acknowledge the possibility that a company could be convicted of manslaughter.

The net was cast somewhat wider in *Re Supply of Ready Mixed Concrete (No. 2)* (1995), where an undertaking by a company to the Restrictive Practices Court was breached by executives acting within the scope of their employment but without the knowledge of the board of directors. The board had, in fact, given instructions not to enter into arrangements that breached the undertaking. Nonetheless, the House of Lords attributed the acts and state of mind of the executives to the company for the purpose of determining whether the company was guilty of contempt.

The focus on the management structure of a company may in many cases be impractical and lead to considerable difficulty in securing a conviction against a company. This difficulty arose in *Meridian Global Funds Management Asia Ltd v. Securities Commission* (1995), a case which concerned a breach of securities regulations that required the purchaser of shares in a public issue to comply with certain notification requirements. The defendant was an investment management company, and its chief investment officer and senior portfolio manager, with the authority of the company, but unknown to the board or the managing director, acquired such shares. The required notification was not given. The High Court in New Zealand found that there had been a breach and that the knowledge of both officers was attributable to the company. The Court of Appeal found that the chief investment officer was the directing mind and will of the company, so his knowledge was attributable to the company. The Privy Council said that the proper course was to apply the primary rules of attribution contained in the company's constitution and implied by company law and the general rules of agency. But, in an exceptional case, where the application of those rules would defeat the intended application of a particular statutory provision to companies, a special rule of attribution had to be devised. This was such a case, as the ordinary rules of attribution could have little application in fast-moving securities markets. Accordingly, the knowledge of acquisition of a security was attributable to the company when the person who acquired it with the authority of the company had such knowledge. Therefore, the chief investment officer's knowledge was attributable to the company, regardless of whether he was the directing mind and will of the company.

(4) Developments in the area of Corporate Manslaughter

The evidential difficulty in successfully prosecuting a company for corporate manslaughter is that at common law, in addition to proving an *actus reus*, it is also necessary to identify an individual or individuals within the company who represent the company's directing mind and to show that he or they are personally guilty of gross negligence (the *mens rea*). This "identification" principle has caused considerable difficulties in prosecuting companies for corporate manslaughter, particularly in large companies where the chain of command is long and there are many people involved in the policy-making. In *R. v. P. & O. European Ferries (Dover) Ltd (1991)* the difficulties associated with the identification problem were highlighted. Here a ferry capsized and 192 people died. The identification doctrine was applied and it was held that a company could be charged with corporate manslaughter if one of its agents who represented a controlling mind of the company committed an act which fulfilled the requirements of manslaughter. Two directors and a senior officer were prosecuted for manslaughter but the case was withdrawn from the jury on the grounds that there was no evidence that they had formed the requisite criminal intent. The company therefore escaped conviction notwithstanding that a report of the disaster found that "[f]rom top to bottom the body corporate was infected with the disease of sloppiness".

At the moment the only manner of prosecuting these offences is via the Health and Safety Act 1989. The disquiet surrounding the use of the Health and Safety legislation for the redress of deaths in the workplace concerns the low fines and the invariable use of the lowers courts for the prosecution of offences. It is considered that these regulatory offences have a lower deterrent effect. The sanction for prosecution for corporate manslaughter is also a fine but the prosecution takes place in the higher courts. The attendant publicity and the element of moral culpability which attaches to a conviction for homicide and the consequent lowering of the reputation of the company and its senior officers is a powerful deterrent.

The Corporate Manslaughter Bill 2001 was a private member's bill introduced to address the difficulties in successfully prosecuting companies for manslaughter by lowering the bar for a successful prosecution. It came in the wake of increasing public concern at the rate of fatalities arising from industrial accidents and public frustration at the difficulties involved in holding bodies corporate liable in criminal law. The Bill proposed to provide for criminal liability for involuntary homicide on broader grounds than the foregoing "identification" principle alone would provide. The Bill was expressly based on the March 1996 report of the Law Reform Commission of England and Wales, *Legislating the Criminal Code: Involuntary Manslaughter*. This Bill has now lapsed but the provisions of the Bill are worthy of comment.

The Bill proposed that a company shall be guilty of manslaughter where it is managed or organised in a way that fails to ensure the health and safety of persons liable to be affected are not thereby threatened and (a) that failure amounts to conduct falling "far below the standard of care and attention it is reasonable in the circumstances to expect would be paid to ensuring that the health and safety of such person is not so threatened" and that (b) that failure is the cause of, or one of the causes of, the death of a person (not withstanding that the immediate cause of a person's death is that act or omission of another individual. Where this offence is committed by the company and the failure is proved "to have been attributable to recklessness or gross negligence on the part of a person who is a director, manager, secretary or other office, or an employee of the company" that person shall also be guilty of manslaughter.

One of the drawbacks of the Bill was that the "identification" principle still remained part of the law where the accident results, not in death, but in serious injury. Further, the Bill failed to target the company directors and the senior officers, making such persons and the company liable for the "sloppy" corporate policy and culture. The Bill should have focused on the remedies that can be ordered by the court to include orders compelling the management to make changes to how it devises and implements its entire safety system. If this Bill was introduced it would have seriously altered companies' responsibilities and duties and render all companies liable for criminal sanction in circumstances for which they are not currently liable.

(5) Breach of the Companies Acts

There are several provisions of the Companies Acts set out in later chapters that impose criminal liability for a breach of statutory obligations on the company and every officer of the company acting in default. Section 382 of the Companies Act 1963 sets out the procedure that applies, including the appointment of a representative of the company for the purposes of prosecution, where the company is prosecuted on indictment.

Section 383 of the Companies Act 1963 (as replaced by section 100 of the Company Law Enforcement Act 2001) defines what is meant by the phrase "officer in default" and this section came into operation on

October 1, 2001. An officer in default is defined as any officer who authorises or who, in breach of his duty as such officer, permits the default mentioned in the provision. There is a presumption under section 383(2) that the officer permitted the default unless he can establish that he took all reasonable steps to prevent it, or that, by reason of circumstances beyond his control, he was unable to do so. Section 383(3) places a positive duty on each secretary and director of a company to ensure that the requirements of the Companies Acts are complied with by the company. "Default" is defined to include a refusal or contravention.

Section 240 of the Companies Act 1990 (as amended by section 41 of the Companies (Amendment) (No 2) Act 1999 and sections 14 and 104 of the Company Law Enforcement Act 2001) states that where a person who is guilty of an offence under the Companies Acts and where no punishment is specified, that person shall be liable on summary conviction to a fine not exceeding €1,905 and/or imprisonment not exceeding twelve months. Where convicted on indictment, that person shall liable to a fine not exceeding €12,700 and/or imprisonment not exceeding five years.

3. COMPANY PROMOTERS

Promoters carry out the work that is necessary to bring a company into being. They prepare the incorporation documentation, identify the potential company subscribers, and in some cases secure contracts for the proposed venture. A promoter is regarded as a trustee owing fiduciary duties to the company that is being established, and it is, therefore, important to distinguish between the promoters and the professionals who are also involved in the establishment of the company.

The Companies Acts do not provide a definition of a promoter but in *Twycross v. Grant* (1877) Cockburn J. defined a promoter as "one who undertakes to form a company with reference to a given project and to set it going, and who takes the necessary steps to accomplish that purpose." In *Emma Silver Mining Co. Ltd v. Lewis & Son* (1879) Bowen J. stated that a promoter "is a term not of law but of business" and therefore the role of all persons involved in the formation of the company should be examined. A solicitor or an accountant who is retained for the formation of a company will not normally be a promoter unless that professional goes further and actively "promotes" the venture by, for example, seeking investors (*Re Great Wheel Poolgooth Ltd* (1883)).

3.1 Promoters' duties

As mentioned above, a promoter stands in a position of trust to the company and as a result owes the company certain fiduciary duties. The principal fiduciary duty is to act bona fide when forming the company. In *Whaley Bridge C.P. Ltd v. Green & Smith* (1878) Bowen J. stated that promoters' duties are based on the general principles of equity. The most controversial function carried out by the promoter is the purchase of assets on behalf of the new venture that are later sold by him to the company. When carrying out this function, he is prohibited from making any secret profit on the transaction when the property is later sold by him to the company.

3.1.1 Disclosure

The prohibition extends to a secret profit only. Therefore, if the potential gain is disclosed and the consent of the company is obtained, the promoter may retain any such profit or gain. It was originally held that the disclosure of the profit or gain could be made only to an independent board of directors, who must, according to Cairns L.J. in *Erlanger v. New Sombrero Phosphate Co.* (1878), "exercise an independent and intelligent judgement on the transaction." As the promoters commonly become the first directors of the company, an independent board of directors may not exist. In *Lagunas Nitrate Company v. Lagunas Nitrate Syndicate* (1899) Lindley M.R. stated that "it is impossible to hold that it is the duty of promoters of a company to provide it with an independent board of directors, if the real truth is disclosed to those who are induced by the promoters to join the company."

Therefore, it was accepted that the obligation of disclosure could be satisfied where such disclosure was made to the shareholders of the company in a general meeting. In some cases it may be appropriate to disclose the profit to potential future shareholders as in *Gluckstein v. Barnes* (1990). In this case it was sought to make the promoters account for an undisclosed profit. The promoters purchased discounted debentures in a company that was nearing liquidation. They proceeded to purchase the main asset of that company for £140,000 and sold the asset to a company that they had promoted for the sum of £180,000. The profit of £40,000 was disclosed to the public. The promoters failed to disclose that the liquidator of the ailing company paid the full value of the debentures from the proceeds of £140,000, resulting in a further profit of £20,000 for the promoters. This additional profit was disclosed to the initial members of the company who were also the promoters. The court held that this was not sufficient and the profit should have been disclosed to the future shareholders in the prospectus. They were held liable to repay the £20,000 secret profit that they had made from the undisclosed transaction.

In *Hopkins v. Shannon Transport Systems Limited* (1972) the promoters established a company to operate a River Shannon ferry service. Acting as a partnership, they acquired ferry vessels and options on terminal sites. Unknown to the subscribers, those acquisitions were partially funded by the issue of shares in the promoted company. The promoters later sold the land and vessels to the company at a profit. At the time of the transaction, these promoters were the only shareholders and directors of the company. The venture collapsed due to the lack of government grants and one of the promoters/partners sought his share of the profits arising from the sale of the assets to the company. The court held that the contract between the partnership and the company was voidable because full disclosure should have been made to the subscribers, as there was no independent board of directors.

In the case of a plc, it is common for a potential profit or gain to be disclosed in the prospectus that is issued to the public for the purpose of inviting investment in the new venture (see Chapter 12).

3.2 Breach of duties

3.2.1 Rescission

As noted in *Hopkins v. Shannon Transport Systems Ltd* (1972), the contract is voidable at the instance of the company where a promoter acts in breach of his fiduciary duties. It is, therefore, open to the company to rescind the contract. Rescission is, however, limited to cases where *restitutio in integrum* is possible, *i.e.* the parties involved can be restored to the original position and the courts will not allow rescission where injustice will be caused to a bona fide purchaser, someone who purchased the controversial assets in good faith, for value, and without notice of the secret profit. Even where *restitutio in integrum* is not possible, *Erlanger v. New Sombrero Phosphate Co.* (1878) held that the court may still order a rescission of the contract where the result is regarded as "practically just". However, in *Northern Bank Finance Corporation v. Charlton* (1979) the Supreme Court emphasised that the essence of rescission was *restitutio in integrum* and it could not be ordered where it resulted in one of the parties receiving property that it has never owned in the first place.

3.2.2 Damages

The promoter may be held liable to surrender the secret profit to the company as in *Gluckstein v. Barnes* (1990) (see above). It is also open to the company to confirm the contract and sue the promoter for damages for breach of contract and/or damages for misrepresentation in contract and/or damages for breach of his fiduciary duty. In *Re Leeds & Hanley Theatres of Varieties Ltd* (1902) it was held that the prospectus of the company should have disclosed the amount of the promoters' profit and the promoters were liable in damages to the company for the profit made.

3.2.3 *Where the company fails to take action*

One of the difficulties regarding actions for breach of fiduciary duties is that the promoters may have effective control of the company. If the company fails to take an action for a breach of fiduciary duty, it is open to the shareholders to take a derivative action in the name of the company on the ground that the breach of duty is a fraud on the minority (see Chapter 14). If the shareholder can establish that the promoter/director was in a fiduciary relationship not only with the company but also with the shareholder, then the shareholder may be able to take a personal action for a breach of duty against the promoter.

3.2.4 *Disqualification of promoters*

Section 150(1) of the Companies Act 1990 states that a restriction order made under that section will prohibit a director or shadow director of a company from acting in any way, either directly or indirectly, as a director or secretary of any company for a period of five years. It also prohibits that person from taking any part in the formation or promotion of any company during that time (see Chapter 8).

Under section 160 of the Companies Act 1990 a person may be subject to a disqualification order, and under section 159 of the Companies Act 1990 a disqualification order is defined so as to include a disqualification from taking part in the promotion, formation, or management, either directly or indirectly, of any company (see Chapter 8).

3.3 Pre-incorporation contracts

3.3.1 *Personal liability for promoters*

It may be the case that the promoter wishes to secure a contract for a new venture that is not yet incorporated. In many such cases the promoter seeks to enter the contract "on behalf of" the company. The difficulty is that the company does not yet exist and the promoter cannot be an agent of an unincorporated company. In *Kelner v. Baxter* (1966) three promoters purchased wine "on behalf" of an unincorporated company. The company was then formed and went into liquidation shortly afterwards. The creditor sought payment for the wine. It was held that the promoters were personally liable and it was stated that "where a contract is signed by one who professes to be signing 'as agent', but who has no principal existing at the time, and the contract would be altogether inoperative unless binding on the person who signed it, he is bound thereby, and a stranger cannot by a subsequent ratification relieve him from that responsibility."

In *Firth v. Stains* (1897) Wright J. set down conditions which must be satisfied in order to protect a purported "agent" from personal liability including that the agent must have had a competent principal at the time the act was done and that such principal must have been capable of doing the act himself before it can be subsequently ratified. This, of course, is impossible in the case of an unincorporated company.

3.3.2 Section 37 of the Companies Act 1963

Promoters, therefore, welcomed section 37(1) of the Companies Act 1963, which stated as follows:

> "[A]ny contract or other transaction purporting to be entered into by a company prior to its formation or by any person on behalf of the company prior to its formation may be ratified by the company after its formation and thereupon the company shall become bound by it and entitled to the benefit thereof as if it had been in existence at the date of such contract or other transaction and had been a party thereto."

This section captures contracts entered into by the unincorporated company itself and contracts entered into on its behalf. The latter contracts are only ratifiable under this section according to *Badgerhill Properties Ltd v. Cottrell* (1991) where the agent purported to make the contract in the name of the company.

The ratification may be carried out by the board of directors or by the members in a general meeting, depending on the terms of the articles of the company. In *HKN Invest OY v. Incotrade PVT Ltd & Ors* (1993) Costello J. noted that ratification does not have to be formal, citing the example of a one-person company. He also held that, in certain circumstances, a liquidator could ratify a pre-incorporation contract. In this case the pre-incorporation contracts were ratified by the liquidator. The promoters had received payments under these contracts, which were held in the personal bank account of one of the promoters. By ratifying the contracts, the liquidator was able to claim that the payments were being held by the promoters for the company on the basis of a constructive trust.

On ratification, the company is regarded as bound by the contract as if it had been in existence at the date the contract was entered into. Prior to the ratification of the contract, the agent who purported to act in the name of, or on behalf of, the company is personally liable on the contract according to section 37(2) of the Companies Act 1963. This personal liability applies even where the third party knew that the company was not yet incorporated (*Phonogram Ltd v. Lane* (1981)). However, section 37(2) allows for the agent to be indemnified in respect of that personal liability as it imposes this liability "in the absence of an express agreement to the contrary". Any disclaimer of liability by the promoter must be set out in clear and unambiguous terms.

3.3.3 Remuneration of the promoter

As a result of section 37(1) of the Companies Act 1963, any contract to pay remuneration to the promoter may be ratified by the company when it is incorporated. Where the contract is not ratified or the company is never established, it is open to the promoter to issue proceedings against any person who agreed to pay him for his services on the basis that personal liability for unratified contracts may be imposed under section 37(2).

4. COMPANY CONSTITUTION

The memorandum and articles of association are the fundamental constitution and regulations of any Irish registered company. As noted in Chapter 2, a memorandum and articles of association may, and in some cases must, be submitted to the Registrar of Companies in order to incorporate a company under the Companies Acts. It is open to a company to submit a model memorandum and/or articles of association which are set out in the First Schedule to the Companies Act 1963 and, in the case of a plc, in the Second Schedule of the Companies (Amendment) Act 1983.

The memorandum sets out a company's powers, and the articles set out the regulations that the company ought to follow when exercising those powers.

4.1 Memorandum of Association

The memorandum is often described as the company charter and the company must act at all times within the parameters of this document.

4.1.1 A model memorandum of association

A company should adopt a model memorandum of association when applying for incorporation or use a format "as near thereto as the circumstances permit" (section 16 of the Companies Act 1963). The following are the model memoranda provided by the Companies Acts:

1. model memorandum of association for a company limited by shares (First Schedule to the Companies Act 1963, Table B);

2. model memorandum of association for a company limited by guarantee and not having a share capital (First Schedule to the Companies Act 1963, Table C);

3. model memorandum of association for a company limited by guarantee and having a share capital (First Schedule to the Companies Act 1963, Table D, Part 1);

4. model memorandum of association for an unlimited company having a share capital (First Schedule to the Companies Act 1963, Table E, Part 1);

5. model memorandum of association for a plc limited by shares (Second Schedule to the Companies (Amendment) Act 1983, Part 1);

6. model memorandum of association for a plc limited by guarantee and having a share capital (Second Schedule to the Companies (Amendment) Act 1983, Part 11).

Section 7 of the Companies Act 1963 requires that the entire memorandum of the company must be printed or in a form acceptable under section 80 of the Company Law Enforcement Act 2001. Section 80 allows for the prior registration of a document setting out standard objects of the company, and the memorandum may contain a statement that it is to incorporate the text of that previously registered document. The memorandum and any such related document must then be read as an entire document according to section 80(3) of the Company Law Enforcement Act 2001. The memorandum must also be signed by each of the subscribers to the company (at least one in the case of a private company or seven in the case of a public company, see Chapter 2, in the presence of at least one witness.

4.1.2 Compulsory clauses

According to section 6 of the Companies Act 1963, the memorandum must include certain clauses depending on the category of company that is established.

Under section 6(1) the memorandum of every company must state the name of the company and the objects for which the company has been established. Under section 6(2) where a company is limited by shares or by guarantee, the memorandum must state that the liability of the members is limited. In the case of a company limited by a guarantee, the memorandum must specify the amount that the member must contribute to the company in the event that the company is wound up while he is a member or within one year after he ceases to be a member.

Section 6(4) requires that where a company has a share capital, the memorandum must state the authorised share capital and the division of that share capital into fixed amounts, *i.e.* the nominal value of each share (see Chapter 12). The memorandum must also state that no subscriber may take less than one share and that each subscriber must write his name opposite the share that he takes.

In the case of a plc, the memorandum must state that the company is a public company according to the Second Schedule to the Companies (Amendment) Act 1983. Although not required by section 6, the memorandum should also contain an association clause that sets out the details of the initial subscribers to the company.

4.1.3 Name clause

The name of a company limited by shares or by guarantee must include the word "limited" or "teoranta" as the last word of the name (section 6(1)(b) of the Companies Act 1963). The name of a plc must end with the word "plc" (public limited company) or "cpt" (cuideachta phoibli teoranta) (section 6(1)(a) of the Companies Act 1963).

(1) Exemption for a private limited company

The old section 24 of the Companies Act 1963 provided that a private limited company could apply for ministerial licence permitting the company to omit the word "limited" from its name where the company was established in order to promote *inter alia* commerce, art, science, religion, charity, or for the purpose of a similar object.

Section 24 was repealed and substituted by section 88 of the Company Law Enforcement Act 2001. The new section 24 of the Companies Act 1963 permits the Registrar of Companies to exempt a private limited company from this requirement where the following conditions are satisfied:

1. the objects of the company provide for the promotion of commerce, articles, science, education, religion, charity, or any other prescribed object (section 24(1)(a));
2. the memorandum of the company requires that the profits or any other income of the company be applied to the promotion of those objects and prohibits the payment of any dividend to its members (section 24(1)(b));
3. the memorandum of the company sets out that on the winding up of the company, its assets will be transferred to another company with similar objects (section 24(1)(b));
4. a director or secretary of the company must deliver a statutory declaration to the Registrar of Companies that the company com-

plies with section 24(1) (a) and (b). It is an offence to provide incorrect, false, or misleading information in the statutory declaration according to section 24(7)(a). The Registrar of Companies must refuse to register the private limited company without the words "limited" after its name where this statutory declaration is not delivered. The Companies Act 1963 (Section 24) Regulations 2001 (S.I. 571/2001) prescribes the form of the statutory declaration of compliance that is required to be made by the company under section 24(1)(a) and (b).

Section 24(4) of the Company Act 1963 states that the company must not alter its memorandum or articles of association in such a manner that it ceases to comply with those conditions. An alteration in contravention of this section is an offence under section 24(7)(b). Where it appears to the Registrar of Companies that an exempted company has carried on business other than the promotion of the objects stated in section 24(1)(a), has applied profits or income to other objects, or has paid a dividend to its members, the registrar may send a written direction to the company directing the company to amend its name to include the word "limited". The amendment must be carried out in accordance with the procedure set out in section 23 of the Companies Act 1963 (discussed below). The failure to comply with a direction under this section is an offence, according to section 24(7)(c) of the Company Act 1963, which may be summarily prosecuted by the Registrar of Companies.

Section 58(1) of the Companies (Amendment) Act 1983 states that this exemption procedure may not be used by a plc. Further, in the case of a plc, it is an offence under section 56(1) of the Companies (Amendment) Act 1983 of that Act for any person who is not a plc to carry on any trade, business, or profession using a name which includes "plc" or "cpt". It is also an offence under section 56(2) for a plc to use a name that may reasonably be expected to give the impression that it is a company other than a plc.

(2) Undesirable company names

A company name may not be registered where in the opinion of the Registrar of Companies it is "undesirable" according to section 21 of the Companies Act 1963 (as amended by section 86 of the Company Law Enforcement Act 2001). This decision was formally that of the Minister. The decision of the Registrar of Companies may be appealed to the court. A name may be "undesirable" for the following reasons:

1. it is offensive;

2. it suggests a connection with the State;

3. it is misleading;

4. it is identical to a name already on the register.

It is open to the court to direct that a company change its name where the company has been found guilty of the tort of passing-off, *i.e.* the name is similar to that of another company and the public are likely to be confused or misled as a result. In *Guinness Ireland Group et al v. Kilkenny Brewing Co. Ltd* (1999) Laffoy J. held that the tort of passing-off includes the incorporation of a company with a name likely to give an impression to the public that it is a subsidiary or branch of or associated with another company which has an established goodwill and that the intention of the company using the name is irrelevant.

Where the company proposes to trade under a name other than the name registered, the name must be registered under the Registration of Business Names Act 1963 (section 22(1) of the Companies Act 1963). The company must register the business name, the general nature of the business, the principal place of business, the name and registered office of the company, and the date of adoption of the business name. It is open to the Minister to refuse registration on the ground that the name is undesirable, and this refusal may be appealed to the court.

(3) Amendment of the company name

The amendment of the registered company name is carried out in accordance with the procedure set down in section 23 of the Companies Act 1963 (as amended by section 87 of the Company Law Enforcement Act 2001). The company must pass a special resolution of the members and obtain the approval of the Registrar of Companies. Prior to 2001 the amendment of the company name required the approval of the Minister. A new certificate of incorporation is issued incorporationg the change of name, and the change of name does not affect any legal proceedings issued against the company prior to the change. Where it later becomes apparent that the name of a company is "too like" the name of an existing registered company, the company may, and shall at the direction of the Registrar of Companies, change its name within six weeks of the direction or such longer period as may be permitted by the Registrar of Companies (section 23(2) of the Companies Act 1963). Failure to comply with a direction renders the company liable to a fine, and the Registrar of Companies may prosecute the offence.

(4) Liability for failing to display company name correctly or at all

Section 114 of the Companies Act 1963 sets out the regulations on the publication of the company name. The company name must be displayed outside the company office, engraved on the company seal, and set out on all business letters, official publications, cheques, promissory notes, bills of exchange, etc. Failure to comply with these regulations renders the company and every officer in default liable to a fine. Where the name of the company is not set out on a bill of exchange, promissory note, cheque, or order for money or goods, every officer of the company may be personally liable under section 114(4) of the Companies Act 1963 to the holder of those documents unless it is duly paid by the company. In *Penrose v. Martyr* (1858) the company secretary was held personally liable for the amount of a bill of exchange because of the incorrect description of the company's name. In *Rafsanjan Pistachio Producers Co-operative v. Reiss* (1990) an attempt by a director of the company to escape liability by seeking the rectification of a cheque failed.

(5) Liability for using the words "Ltd" or "Teo"

It is an offence for any person to trade or carry on business under the name or title of which "limited" or "teoranta" is the last word, unless it is duly incorporated with limited liability. The Director of Corporate Enforcement or the Registrar of Companies may apply to the court for an order that the person ceases to trade or carry on business with such a name if that person fails to comply with a notice directing him to cease within fourteen days (section 381 of the Companies Act 1963 as repealed and substituted by section 98 of the Company Law Enforcement Act 2001).

4.1.4 Objects clause

Under section 6(1) of the Companies Act 1963 the memorandum of every company must detail the objects for which the company is established. This clause sets the outer limits of the company's legitimate activities, and where the company enters a contract that is neither expressly nor impliedly in furtherance of its objects, it is *ultra vires* the company and void *ab initio*. Where the contract is *ultra vires*, it cannot be ratified by the shareholders of the company in general meeting. In *Ashbury Railway Carriage and Iron Co. Ltd v. Riche* (1875) the company was incorporated with *inter alia* the object of making and selling railway carriages. Without regard to the company's objects, its directors purported to contract to buy a concession for constructing a railway in Belgium. In this case, the contract was held to be void *ab initio* and unratifiable by the shareholders. This decision was followed in *Re German Date Coffee Co.* (1882) and *Re Jon Beauforte (London) Ltd* (1953).

It is, therefore, in the interests of all the outsiders who deal with the company to ensure that the company adheres to and observes the terms of the objects clause in the memorandum of association. The objects of the company may be virtually limitless as in the case of *Newstead v. Frost* (1980), but they cannot be illegal according to section 5 of the Companies Act 1963.

(1) Objects and express ancillary powers of a company

A company's memorandum will commonly set out a number of paragraphs entitled the "objects of the company", and the court will apply principles of construction to determine the actual capacity of the company. Where it appears that one paragraph embodies the main or dominant object of the company, all the remaining paragraphs will be treated as merely ancillary to this main object, and limited and controlled thereby (*Re Haven Gold Mining Co.* (1882)). Those ancillary paragraphs are called express ancillary powers, which are, by their nature, incapable of standing as independent objects of the company according to *Re Horsley & Weight Ltd* (1982).

In *Rolled Steel Products (Holdings) Ltd v. British Steel Corp. et al* (1985) Slade L.J. stated that the question is purely one of construction of that memorandum. He stated that each sub-clause "must be treated as containing a substantive object unless either (i) the subject of this sub-paragraph is by its nature incapable of constituting a substantive object or (ii) the wording of the memorandum shows expressly or by implication that the sub-clause was intended merely to constitute an ancillary power only". The case related to the giving of guarantees, and it was held that while this could constitute the objects of a company, in this case it was an ancillary power and not a substantive object. Slade L.J. also stated that these express ancillary powers may be exercised only "as may seem expedient for the furtherance of the objects of the company".

(2) Independent objects clause

If the memorandum incorporates an "independent objects" clause stating that "each sub-clause of this clause shall be construed independently of the other sub-clauses hereof, and that none of the objects mentioned in any sub-clause shall be deemed to be merely subsidiary to the objects mentioned in any other sub-clause", then the contents of each paragraph of the objects clause is a separate main object which can be individually pursued according to *Cotman v. Brougham* (1918). In this case the company underwrote and held shares in an oil company. Without the insertion of an independent objects clause, the company would have been limited in its activities to the development of rubber plantations and ancillary business. The investment was found to be *intra vires* as the independent objects clause permitted the purchase of shares and stocks in a company.

However, the independent objects clause will not transform what is in reality an express ancillary power into an object of the company according to *Re Introductions Ltd, Introductions Ltd v. National Provincial Bank Ltd* (1968).

(3) Implied ancillary powers of a company

The company may also have implied powers. The company can rely upon having implied powers to do "whatever may fairly be regarded as incidental to and consequential upon" its stated objects according to *A.-G. v. Great Eastern Railway* (1880). Necessary ancillary powers of this nature will be implied if they are not expressly stated in the memorandum and in so far as they are not expressly negatived or curtailed by the memorandum. Powers will also be implied by the court because of the particular nature of the company's business or undertaking. Before implying a power, two conditions must be satisfied. In the first instance there must be some reasonable connection between the company's objects and the power it seeks to exercise, it being insufficient for the company merely to show that it will benefit in some way by the exercise of the power (*Evans v. Brunner, Mond & Co.* (1921)). Second, it must be shown that the company will in fact benefit in some way, even though remote, from the exercise of the power (*Hutton v. West Cork Rly Co.* (1883)).

In *Parke v. Daily News Ltd* (1962) the court held that the company had no implied power to give £1.5m to its employees in redundancy and pension payments. The payments were not permitted by the objects, and the company had no express ancillary power to give them.

It was held that this power was not "reasonably incidental or consequential" upon the company's objects. In *Hutton v. West Cork Rly Co.* (1883) an implied power to give gratuities to servants or employees was denied. Such incidental powers that may be implied include the power to employ workers, borrow money or contract for the purchase of supplies.

An express ancillary power or an implied ancillary power must be exercised in furtherance of the objects of the company. Recent case law has softened in its approach to this restriction, and if the contract is one which, on true construction of the memorandum, "is *capable* of being performed as reasonably incidental to the attainment or pursuit of its objects, it will not be rendered *ultra vires* the company merely because in a particular instance its directors, in performing the act in its name, are in truth doing so for purposes other than those set out in the memorandum", according to *Rolled Steel Products (Holdings) Ltd v. British Steel Corp. et al* (1986).

(4) Bell Houses clause

It is also common for the objects clause to permit the company to carry on any trade or business in connection with the general business of the company that the directors believe to be advantageous to the company. This is called the "Bell Houses clause" and it is derived from the decision of *Bell Houses Ltd v. City Wall Properties Ltd* (1996). The effect of this clause was to make the bona fide opinion of the directors sufficient to determine whether an activity of the company is *intra vires.*

In general the powers of the company will be generously construed. This view is supported by Vaughan William L.J. in *A.-G. v. Mersey Railway Co.* (1907), where he stated the following:

> "You ought to give a wider construction to the ends of a memorandum of association creating and defining the powers of a purely commercial company having no compulsory powers and no monopoly than you would give to the words of a statute creating a monopoly ... having compulsory powers of land purchase."

According to *Palmer's Company Law* (25th ed., Vol. 1), "in modern law the courts are unlikely to hold a contract to be *ultra vires* the company unless, on a reasonable construction of the objects clause and the other clauses of the memorandum and articles, there are compelling grounds to arrive at that result".

Therefore, the ambit of the company's legitimate activities depends on the express objects in the memorandum, the express ancillary powers in the memorandum, and implied ancillary powers, and it appears the court will be generous in construing the ambit of these powers in the interests of protecting third parties contracting with the company.

(5) Alteration of the objects clause

The objects clause can be amended under section 10(1) of the Companies Act 1963 by a special resolution of the company members. Any such alteration must be bona fide and in the interests of the company as a whole according to *Re Cyclists' Touring Club* (1907). Where the company is a private company exempted from the use of the words "limited" or "teoranta" (see paragraph 4.1.3(1) above), the Registrar of Companies must receive at least ten days' notice of the proposed special resolution under section 10(8) of the Companies Act 1963 (this sub-section was amended by section 85 of the Company Law Enforcement Act 2001 as the company had to give such notice to the Minister prior to the amendment).

A shareholder of the company may apply to the court to overturn the alteration where the shareholder holds not less than fifteen per cent of the nominal value of the issued share capital or any class thereof. In the case of a company limited by guarantee, at least fifteen per cent of the members may make this application. It is also open to the holders of not less than fifteen per cent of the company's debentures to apply to the court to challenge the resolution where the debentures are secured by floating charges and they incorporate the right to object to an alteration of the company's objects. These debenture holders must receive at least ten days' notice of the meeting proposing to pass the special resolution.

The court application must be made within twenty-one days of the passing of the special resolution and the applicant must not have consented to or voted in favour of the special resolution (sections 10(4) and 10(5) of the Companies Act 1963). The court may cancel the alteration, confirm the alteration, or confirm the alteration on certain terms and conditions. It is also open to the court to adjourn the application to facilitate the purchase of the discontented shareholder's shares. Under section 10(6A) of the Companies Act 1963 (as inserted by Schedule 1 of the Companies (Amendment) Act 1983), the court may make an order directing the company to purchase the shares of any shareholder of the company and to reduce its share capital accordingly (see Chapter 15 for a discussion of capital reduction).

Notice of the alteration of the objects clause must be delivered to the Registrar of Companies within thirty-six days of the passing of the special resolution. If an application is made to the court challenging the alteration, the Registrar of Companies must be notified of the court application, and within fifteen days of the court order, a copy of the order and, where the alteration is confirmed, a copy of the amended memorandum must be delivered to the Registrar of Companies. Failure to comply with these notice requirements will render the company and every officer in default liable to a fine.

It is open to the court to wind up the company under section 213(f) on "just and equitable" grounds if there has been a failure of substratum, *i.e.* the company was formed with a particular purpose in mind and now discontinues that purpose (see Chapter 22).

4.1.5 Liability clause

Under section 6(2) of the Companies Act 1963 the memorandum must state that the liability of the members is limited where a company is to be limited by share or by guarantee. According to section 27(1) of the Companies Act 1963, no member is bound by an alteration that requires him to buy more shares in the company or that increases his liability to contribute to the share capital of, or pay money to, the company. Under section 27(2) of the Companies Act 1963 a member can waive this veto in writing.

4.1.6 Share capital clause

Section 6(4) of the Companies Act 1963 requires a company's memorandum to set out the total amount of the company's authorised share capital. This is the amount of share capital that the company is authorised to issue to shareholders and it is divided into shares of a fixed or nominal amount, called the "par" value of the shares. In the case of a private company, the value of the nominal share capital of the company may be fixed at the discretion of the promoters as there is no minimum set by the Companies Acts. However, where a restricted director becomes involved with another private company, that company must maintain a minimum capital as prescribed by the Companies Act 1990 and as increased by the Company Law Enforcement Act 2001 (see Chapter 8). Section 5(2) of the Companies (Amendment) Act 1983 provides that a plc must have a minimum authorised share capital of €38,100. The capital clause may divide the authorised share capital into share classes and designate the dividend and voting rights attached to those classes.

Section 68 of the Companies Act 1963 provides that the authorised share capital of a company may be increased by an ordinary resolution of the members where such an increase is in accordance with the regulations set out in the articles of the company. Under section 70 of the Companies Act 1963 the Registrar of Companies must be notified of the increase within fifteen days of the passing of the resolution. Failure to deliver this notice renders the company and every officer in default liable to a fine. Where the company proposes to reduce its capital, the procedure is strictly controlled by sections 72-77 of the Companies Act 1963 (see Chapter 15).

Any alteration that proposes to vary the rights attached to classes of shares must comply with the variation rules set out in Chapter 12.

4.1.7 Association clause

The subscribers, being the first shareholders and members of the company, agree to be bound by the terms of the memorandum. Each subscriber must sign his name at the bottom of the memorandum and indicate the number of shares held; each subscriber must take at least one share. That signature must be witnessed by at least one person.

4.1.8 Alternation of the memorandum in general

The non-compulsory clauses may be altered by a special resolution of the company under section 28 of the Companies Act 1963. Where the memorandum itself provides for a specific procedure for an alteration of these clauses, it must be followed by the company. The right to apply to the court to challenge the alteration under section 10 of the Companies Act 1963 also applies to these alterations. Section 29 of the Companies Act 1963 entitles the members of the company to request a copy of the memorandum of association of the company, and where the company fails to comply with the request, the company and every officer in default is liable to a fine. Section 30 of the Companies Act 1963 requires that all copies of the memorandum that are issued by the company must contain any alterations, and the failure to comply with this provision renders the company and every officer in default liable to a fine.

4.2 Articles of Association

The articles of the company are known as the rules of management of the company. The rules govern *inter alia* matters such as company meetings, the transfer of shares, voting rights, and the appointment and removal of company officers. According to section 14 of the Companies Act 1963, the entire articles must be printed or in a form acceptable under section 80 of the Company Law Enforcement Act 2001. Section 80 allows for the prior registration of a document setting out standard articles of the company, and the articles of association may contain a statement that it is to incorporate the text of that previously registered document. The articles and any such related document must then be read as an entire document, according to section 80(3) of the Company Law Enforcement Act 2001.

Section 14 of the Companies Act 1963 further requires that the articles are divided into paragraphs, numbered consecutively and signed by each subscriber to the memorandum in the presence of one witness. In the case of a conflict between the memorandum and the articles, the memorandum is the superior document, according to Carroll J. in *Roper v. Ward* (1981). However, the articles may be used to clarify ambiguities in the memorandum.

4.2.1 Model articles of association

It is optional for a company limited by shares or a company limited by guarantee and not having a share capital to lodge articles of association with the Registrar of Companies according to section 11 of the Companies Act 1963. Where no such articles are lodged, the model articles in the First Schedule of the Companies Act 1963 in Table A, Part I (in the case of a public company) or Part II (in the case of a private company) shall apply to the company limited by shares. If the company limited by shares does register articles of association the provisions of Table A will still apply to the company save where they are modified or excluded by the articles (section 13 of the Companies Act 1963).

Where no articles are lodged in the case of a company limited by guarantee and not having a share capital, the model articles in the First Schedule of the Companies Act 1963 in Table C shall apply to the company. If the company limited by guarantee and not having a share capital does register articles of association, the provisions of Table C will still apply to the company save where they are modified or excluded by the articles (section 13 of the Companies Act 1963).

In the case of a company limited by guarantee and having a share capital, the articles of the company must be lodged and they must be in accordance with the First Schedule of the Companies Act 1963 in Table D, Part III. In the case of an unlimited company, the articles must be lodged and they must be in accordance with the First Schedule of the Companies Act 1963 in Table E, Part II (in the case of a public company) or Part III (in the case of a private company). In both cases, the articles must be as near to the model forms as the circumstances admit (section 16 of the Companies Act 1963).

4.2.2 Alteration of the articles

According to section 15(1) of the Companies Act 1963, a company may alter its articles by a special resolution of its members. This statutory right to alter the articles of the company is protected by case law, as a number of decisions have stated that the company cannot deprive itself of this power to alter the articles (*Peter's American Delicacy Co. Ltd v. Heath* (1938-9) and *Allen v. Gold Reefs of West Africa Ltd* (1900)), and any provision that purports to so do is void. The alteration must not result in a conflict with the memorandum, the Companies Acts or the general law.

All alterations of the articles must be bona fide and in the interests of the *company as a whole* according to *Allen v. Gold Reefs West Africa Ltd* (1900), where Lindley M.R. in the Court of Appeal held that the power to alter articles is limited by the law, by the memorandum and by "those general principles of law and equity which are applicable to all powers conferred on majorities and enabling them to bind minorities. It must be exercised not only in the manner required by the law, but also bona fide for the benefit of the company as a whole and it must not be exceeded." In that case, the articles gave the company the power to take a lien (as security) on partly paid shares for all debts and liabilities of the member to the company. The company altered its articles to extend the right to take a lien to fully paid shares. A deceased member was the only member who had fully paid-up shares and his executors objected to the alteration. The company held that the alteration was valid as it was for the benefit of the company as a whole even if it happened to affect only one member.

Therefore, where the majority of the shareholders honestly decide that the alteration is for the benefit of the company as a whole, the court will uphold the decision unless no reasonable man could regard that decision as reasonable. This is the test to be applied according to

Shuttleworth v. Cox Brothers & Co. (Maidenhead) Ltd (1927). In this case, the articles provided that the directors of the company should be life directors unless one of six specified disqualifying events occurred. One of the directors failed to account for company money on 21 occasions within one year. This was not one of the six reasons for disqualification and the articles were altered to allow the other directors to resolve to remove him. This alteration was held to be valid. Aitkin L.J. stated that the test was whether the shareholders, in considering whether to alter the articles, "honestly intended to exercise their power for the benefit of the company" and it was not for the court to decide whether the alteration was actually for the benefit of the company. Aitkin L.J. placed a limit on the subjective test and stated that where the majority were acting in an oppressive manner, they could not be acting in good faith, and the alteration will be disallowed irrespective of the subjective considerations.

In *Allen v. Gold Reefs of West Africa Ltd* (1900) Lindley M.R. considered the phrase "the company as a whole" to mean the separate legal entity. However, in *Greenhalgh v. Arderne Cinemas Limited* (1950) the court came to a different conclusion and Evershed M.R. held that the phrase "company as a whole" did not mean the company as a commercial entity but the general body of the shareholders. Here, an alteration of the articles altered a pre-emption clause and allowed a direct sale of shares to non-members where an ordinary resolution was passed. A minority shareholder sought a declaration that this was invalid as it was not bona fide in the interests of the company as a whole. The alteration was held to be valid as the majority of the shareholders honestly believed that it was in the interests of the company as a whole. In a different context, Henchy J. in *G & S Doherty Ltd v Doherty* (1969) held that "for the benefit of the company as a whole" meant "the shareholders as a whole".

However, Evershed M.R. stated in *Greenhalgh v. Arderne Cinemas Ltd* (1950) that an alteration would be invalid were it to "discriminate between the majority shareholders and the minority shareholders so as to give the former an advantage of which the latter were deprived." This is similar to the statement of Henchy J. in *G & S Doherty Ltd v Doherty* (1969) where he held that the court would intervene where the majority were acting "for the ulterior purposes of benefiting themselves to the detriment of other shareholders". In *Clemens v. Clemens Bros. Ltd* (1976) Foster J. stated that the right of the majority shareholders is not boundless and that it is "subject to equitable considerations which may make it unjust to exercise [it] in a particular way."

4.2.3 Informal alteration of the articles

According to *Cane v. Jones* (1981), the articles may be altered informally if there is unanimous approval of all the members, as "it is a basic principle of company law that all the corporators, acting together, can do anything which is intra vires the company." This principle was endorsed by Costello J. in *Re Shannonside Holdings Ltd* (1993). However, section 141(8) of the Companies Act 1963 (see Chapter 13) allows for the passing of a special resolution without a meeting of the members where the special resolution is in writing and signed by the members. Therefore, an informal oral special resolution resolving to alter the articles of the company would not appear to be valid.

4.3 Section 25 contract

According to section 25(1) of the Companies Act 1963, the memorandum and articles of the company bind the company and every member of the company as if they had been signed and sealed by each member and contain covenants by each member to observe all the provisions of the memorandum and of the articles. This is called the section 25 contract, and when each member is registered on the register of members he becomes a party to this statutory contract. The section 25 contract is enforceable by members *inter se* (*i.e.* by one member against another), by members against the company, and by the company against the members. These parties are bound by the terms of the memorandum and articles and cannot act in disregard of any obligations imposed by those documents.

The contract is not a contract in the ordinary sense of the word according to Steyn J. in *Bratton Seymour Service Company Limited v. Oxborough* (1992), as it only affects members in their capacity as members of the company. *Hickman v Kent or Romney Marsh Sheepbreeders Association* (1915) held that the section 25 contract does not bind and cannot be enforced by outsiders, and it is only enforceable by members in their capacity as members. This is demonstrated in *Eley v. Positive Government Security Life Assurance Co. Ltd* (1876), where the articles of a company appointed a member as a solicitor to the company for life. He did not enter a contract of employment and eventually the company no longer used his services. He sued for breach of contract in his capacity as company solicitor and not his capacity as a member, and, as a result, it was held that he could not rely on section 25.

One member can sue another regarding a breach of a provision of the memorandum or articles, according to *Lee & Co. (Dublin) Ltd v. Egan (Wholesale) Ltd* (1978). In *Rayfield v. Hands* (1960) a pre-emption clause in the articles required a member who wished to transfer his shares to first offer them to the directors who were to purchase the shares at a fair price. The directors refused to buy the shares, and the court held that the clause was enforceable against the directors as fellow members on the basis that they were parties to the section 25 contract.

Section 25 entitles members of the company to enforce rights against the company and *vice versa*. A member can only enforce the personal rights that he has by virtue of membership. In Chapter 14 the cases of *Pender v. Lushington* (1877), *Edwards v. Haliwell* (1950) and *Byng v. London Life Association Ltd* (1990) illustrate instances where the members may enforce the terms of the articles against the company. The company may enforce the obligations placed on members under the section 25 contract. In *Hickman v. Kent or Romney Marsh Sheepbreeders Association* (1915) Ashbury J. found that the articles do create rights and obligations under a contract between the company and its members. The case related to a clause in the articles that required any dispute in a company to go to arbitration. A member took a court case and the company successfully sought a stay on the proceedings to force compliance with the arbitration clause because the clause bound the litigant as a member.

An outsider who is not be able to rely on the terms of the section 25 contract may be able to argue that the articles of the company are implied terms in his contract with the company. In *Re New British Iron Co.* (1989) a director of the company successfully argued that an article of the company setting out the remuneration of the directors was an implied term in his service contract with the company, and the director was able to claim arrears of remuneration when the company was liquidated.

4.4 Public documents

The memorandum and articles of a company are public documents which may be inspected by the public at the Office of Registrar of Companies on the payment of a small fee (section 370 of the Companies Act 1963). The public, and in particular those dealing with the company, are deemed to be on constructive notice of the terms of these documents. This principle has caused considerable hardship for third parties where a company contract was found to be *ultra vires* the company. Chapter 6 sets out the measures that have been developed to protect these third parties.

5. CORPORATE PERSONALITY

On the date that a company is incorporated by the Registrar of Companies (see Chapter 2) it is a separate legal entity with a corporate personality. The company can hold its own assets, enter its own contracts, file its own lawsuits, and open its own bank accounts. The notion of a company having a corporate personality was examined and endorsed by the court in 1897 in the case of *Salomon v. Salomon & Company Ltd* (1897). The directors of the company are the managers of this legal entity, and the members (the investors) are the owners of the company. There is said to be a corporate veil between the company and its managers and owners.

In the *Salomon* case, Lord Halsbury stated that the principle of corporate personality was to be applied provided that there was "no fraud and no agency" and only "if the company was real one and not a fiction or a myth". There have been a number of instances where the concept of the corporate personality has been abused by the directors or controlling members of the company. As a result, the Companies Acts have detailed situations where the corporate veil will be lifted or pierced and personal liability for an act of the company will be placed squarely on the directors, and in some cases the controlling members, of the company. The courts have also developed the circumstances where the corporate veil should be pierced.

The veil of incorporation may be lifted between the controllers (the directors or a controlling shareholder) and the company so that responsibility for the action is shared by the controllers. The veil may be lifted between company subsidiaries or between a parent company and its subsidiary. Alternatively, the court may determine to ignore the company entity and the corporate veil if it finds that the company is a "sham" or "device" and place responsibility fully on the controllers of the company.

5.1 The *Salomon* case

The infamous case which endorsed the concept of corporate personality is *Salomon v. Salomon & Company Ltd* (1897). Mr. Salomon ran a successful leather business as a sole trader. He then set up a company, with 20,007 shares of which he held 20,001 shares. The remaining six shares were held by his wife and five children as nominees for Mr. Salomon, meaning in effect that Mr. Salomon was in complete control of the venture. He sold the business to the company for £38,782. The company was to pay him 20,000 fully paid £1 shares and £8,782 in cash. The balance £10,000 remained payable to Mr. Salomon. He secured the payment of this debt when the company issued 100 debentures (loans) at £100, and each loan was secured by the creation of a floating charge over all the assets of the company. When the company later went into liquidation, Mr. Salomon was the controlling shareholder and a secured creditor. Mr. Salomon sought payment of his debt in preference to the ordinary unsecured creditors of the company.

The liquidator argued that the sole purpose of transferring the business to the company was to use it as an agent for himself and, accordingly, he should, as principle, indemnify the company against the debts of unsecured creditors. In the Court of First Instance the liquidator's view was accepted, and it was held that the creditors should be paid by Mr. Salomon. Vaughan Williams J. held that the subscribers of the memorandum, other than Salomon, held their shares as mere nominees for him, and Solomon's sole purpose in forming the company was to use it as an agent to run his business for him. On appeal, the Court of Appeal came to the same conclusion but for different reasons. It held that the creditors should be paid by Mr. Salomon on the basis that he had abused the privileges of incorporation and limited liability provided by the Companies Acts. According to Lopes L.J., these privileges should only be enjoyed by "independent bona fide members, who had a mind and will of their own, and were not mere puppets of an individual who, adopting the machinery of the Act, carried on his old business in the same way as before, when he was a sole trader". Consequently, Mr. Salomon had incorporated his business for an unlawful purpose. The court could not hold that the incorporation was void as the certificate of incorporation was conclusive evidence that it was incorporated (see Chapter 2), but it could give relief to the company's creditors by requiring Mr. Salomon to indemnify the company against the liabilities and to contribute to the company's assets a sum sufficient to meet its liabilities in full.

Mr. Salomon appealed to the House of Lords. Here the view of the Court of Appeal was unanimously rejected and the cornerstone of modern company law was put in place. It was held that the company was a separate legal entity and separate from its members. All that company law required was that there be seven subscribers to the memorandum, each holding at least one share and nothing was mentioned about independence. As the company was validly incorporated, the debts are debts of the company and not of the members. As Lord Halsbury L.C. stated, "the business belonged to [the company] and not to Mr. Salomon." Lord McNaughten L.J. stated as follows:

> "The company is at law a different person altogether from the subscribers to the memorandum; and, though it may be that after incorporation the business is precisely the same as it was before, and the same persons are managers, and the same hands receive the profits, the company is not in law the agent of the subscribers or a trustee for them. Nor are the subscribers as members liable, in any shape or form, except to the extent and manner provided in the Act."

It was, therefore, confirmed that a company could be created through the observance of the Companies Acts even where there was, in reality, only one person involved. The practical result of the case was that the company was a valid entity, the secured debentures were valid loans, and under the Companies Acts Mr. Salomon's debentures were paid in preference to the ordinary creditors of the company (see Chapter 23 for the rules on priority of distribution on a winding up).

5.2 The effect of the corporate veil

The principle of separate personality has been fully applied by the courts since the *Salomon* case, and, according to Lord Oliver in *Maclaine Watson & Company Ltd v. Department of Trade and Industry* (1989), "[t]he decision of *Salomon v Salomon & Company Ltd* is as much law today as it was in 1896".

At first glance the corporate veil appears to work to the benefit of the company controllers, as they are protected or veiled from the consequences of a company's actions and liabilities. However, there have been a number of cases where the corporate veil has worked to the detriment of the controllers. As already noted, a company is the beneficial owner of its own property and its members have no legal or equitable interest in that property (see *Short v. Treasury Comrs* (1948)). As a result, the shareholders cannot insure that property against a loss. In *Macaura v. Northern Assurance Company* (1925) the plaintiff sold all the timber on his estate to a company in exchange for company shares. The timber was insured in the plaintiff's own name. When it was destroyed by fire, the insurance company refused to pay on the basis that the plaintiff had no insurable interest in the timber given that it was owned entirely by the company. The court applied the *Salomon* principle finding that the timber belonged to the company who had failed to insure its interest in the timber.

It has been held in a number of cases that where compensation is payable in respect of a loss suffered by the company, the shareholders have no right to the payment as the loss is the loss of the company. In *O'Neill v. Ryan & ors* (1993) the plaintiff alleged that breaches in competition law by some of the defendants had caused a diminution in the value of his shares in the second-named defendant, Ryan Air Ltd. The Supreme Court held the actions of the defendants did not cause personal loss to the plaintiff as a shareholder and the action was struck out. It was held that "such a loss is merely a reflection of the loss suffered by the company. The shareholder does not suffer any personal loss". Blayney J. based his holding on a decision of the English Court of Appeal in *Prudential Assurance Company Ltd v. Newman Industries Ltd (No. 2)* (1982) wherein it was stated that "the plaintiff's shares are merely a right of participation in the company on the terms of the articles of association" and that the shares themselves are not directly affected by the wrongdoing. According to *Wilson v. Jones* (1866) a policy can be taken out by a shareholder to insure the success of a venture in which the company is engaged where the shareholder is insuring against the fall in value of his shares in consequence of the failure of the company's venture. The shareholder has an insurable interest in the maintenance of the value of his shares, which are his own property.

In *Roberts v. Coventry Corporation* (1947) the land held by the plaintiff was the subject of a compulsory purchase order. The plaintiff had granted a yearly tenancy in the land to a company in which the plaintiff was the majority shareholder. The plaintiff claimed compensation for loss suffered due to the cancellation of the company's tenancy. It was held that the loss was the loss of the company and the plaintiff was not entitled to compensation in respect of that loss.

In *Battle v. Irish Art Promotion Centre Ltd* (1968) it was held that the managing director of a company was separate and distinct from the company itself. The case involved a lawsuit issued against a company that was unable to afford legal representation. The managing director wished to be allowed to represent the company himself as a judgment against the company would reflect badly on his reputation. The court refused to allow him to represent the company because the judgment would be against the company and not against him. The court held that the correct procedure would be for the company to employ legal representation.

However, there are certainly examples of the doctrine working in favour of the shareholder, as in *Lee v. Lee's Air Farming Company Ltd* (1961). A deceased pilot owned all but one share in a company meaning that the company was a one-man company, as in the case of *Salomon*. He was also an employee of the company, and on his death his widow applied to receive employee benefits. It was held that entrepreneurs can participate in employee benefits by incorporating their business and then becoming employees. The *Salomon* principle was applied and it was held that the company was a separate legal entity, that he was an employee of that legal entity, and that the widow was entitled to recover the benefits.

The principal has also been successfully used by companies to avoid obligations. This was referred to as a "legal subterfuge" in the case of *Roundabout Limited v. Beirne* (1959). This case involved all the employees of a pub, which was owned by a limited company, joining a trade union. As the controllers of the company were unwilling to employ a unionised staff, they closed the pub and dismissed the staff. The union legally picketed the pub. The controllers of the company then set up a second company, which leased the pub. This second company had no employees, as its barmen were the company's directors. The new company could not be classed as an employer and, therefore, could not be subject to a trade dispute under the laws of the time. The second company successfully sought an injunction restraining the strikers. Dixon J. stated as follows:

> "[T]he new company is in law a distinct entity, as is the old company. Each company is what is known as a legal person. I have to regard the two companies as distinct in the same way as I would regard two distinct individuals. I must, therefore, proceed on the basis that a new and different person is now in occupation of the premises and carrying on business there."

As noted in Chapter 2, a shareholder cannot enforce a contract made by his company with another person. Likewise, a shareholder cannot be sued on contracts made by his company, according to *Daimler Co. Ltd v. Continental Tyre & Rubber Co. (Great Britain) Ltd* (1916), and the court cannot compel a shareholder to vote in a general meeting of the company in a way which will ensure that the company will fulfil its contractual obligations, according to *Northern Counties Securities Ltd v. Jackson & Steeple Ltd* (1974).

A member of a company cannot sue in respect of torts committed against it, nor can he be sued for torts committed by it unless he participates in committing them. In the case of *Shinkwin v. Quin-Contract*

Ltd and Quinlan (2000) the question before the Supreme Court was whether a controlling shareholder and manager of a company was liable for the personal injuries suffered by an employee. Fennelly J. stated as follows:

> "[O]n the one hand, a person might be the sole effective and controlling shareholder in a business run by a company but have no involvement in its day to day operations. He would have control of the company but not in the manner in which it conducted its operations. It is clear that such a person would not, without more, be responsible to employees injured by the negligent acts of the company…[t]hat would disregard the separate legal character of the company, the principle of limited liability and the rule in *Salomon v Salomon.* According to Fennelly J., the question to be answered was "did he involve himself so closely in the operation of the factory and, in particular, in the supervision of the plaintiff as to make him personally liable for any acts of negligence which injured the plaintiff?"

5.3 Lifting the veil by statute

The Companies Acts 1963-2001 provide a number of situations where the separate corporate personality of the company may be disregarded and personal liability for the company's actions may be imposed on the members or directors or officers of the company. According to Lord Diplock in *Dimbleby & Sons Ltd v. NUJ* (1984), the legislature must use clear and unequivocal language before the court will treat the principle of *Salomon* as having been dislodged.

5.3.1 Personal liability for the number of members

Under section 5 of the Companies Act 1963 a private company must have a minimum of two members and a plc must have a minimum of seven members. It is commonly the case that the membership of a company reduces where a member dies or where shares are transferred by one member to another. Section 36 of the Companies Act 1963 provides for the imposition of personal liability on the members' companies where the membership falls below the stated minimum. If the company carries on business for more than six months with fewer than the required members, every person who is a member of the company during the period after the six months and who knows that the company is carrying on business with fewer than the required members, is liable for the whole of the debts of the company contracted during that time.

As discussed in Chapter 2, certain private limited companies can now carry on their business with just one member, and the provision is, therefore, of relevance mainly in respect of plcs.

Statutory liability for reduced membership does not attach until the membership has remained below the statutory minimum for six months, and it attaches only in respect of debts contracted after that time. The sole shareholder may escape personal liability by transferring some of his shares during the six months to nominees or trustees for himself so that the number of members is restored to the statutory minimum before the six months expire.

The personal liability only applies in respect of debts contracted by the company during this time, and not in respect of claims for damages for breach of contract or tort, nor in respect of statutory claims against the company, such as taxation. Where the member of the company is liable under this section, he may be sued personally by the creditor, and it is not necessary for the creditor to seek a winding up of the company. The member is liable without limitation for the debts for which he is personally responsible under this section. Where the member is compelled to satisfy such a debt, he may seek an indemnity from the company, as the debt is still primarily the company's liability (see *Brook's Wharf and Bull Ltd v. Goodman Brothers* (1937)).

The First Report of the CLRG (see paragraph 1.5.8) recommends that section 36 of the Companies Act 1963 should be repealed as it has been described as an "ancient and obsolete rule" which "serve[s] no purpose in protecting the public or anyone else", according to *Nisbet v. Shepherd* (1994).

5.3.2 Personal liability for reckless trading

Section 297(1)(a) of the Companies Act 1963 (as inserted by section 138 of the Companies Act 1990) states that where "any person was, while an officer of the company, knowingly a party to the carrying on of any business of the company in a reckless manner", the court may impose personal liability for some or all of the company's debts on that person. It is important to note that the declaration of personal liability for reckless trading may only be made in respect of an officer of the company. The term "officer" includes directors, secretaries, shadow directors, auditors, liquidators, and receivers. See Chapter 10 for a discussion of reckless trading.

As noted in Chapter 10, an application in respect of reckless trading may be made only where the company is in insolvent liquidation (*i.e.* is unable to pay its debts when due) or where the company is under court protection (see Chapter 10 for a discussion of examinership). Section 251 of the Companies Act 1990 states that such an application may be made where the company is not in liquidation and where either a judgment, decree, or other order of the court in favour of a creditor remains unsatisfied, or it is proved to the court that the company is unable to pay its debts.

5.3.3 Personal liability for fraudulent trading

Section 297(1)(b) of the Companies Act 1963 (as inserted by section 138 of the Companies Act 1990) replaced the old provision providing for civil liability for fraudulent trading. It states that where "any person was knowingly a party to the carrying on of any business of the company with the intent to defraud creditors of the company, or creditors of any other person or for any fraudulent purpose", the court may impose personal liability for some or all of the company's debts on that person. The effect of this section is not limited to company officers. See Chapter 10 for a discussion of fraudulent trading.

An application for personal liability in respect of fraudulent trading may be made only where the company is in liquidation or where the company is under court protection. Liability under this section cannot be imposed simply because a company is insolvent or because the company was formed to escape liability for the debts incurred in the carrying on of a business. It is only where the persons responsible for the managing of the company's business have been guilty of dishonesty that personal liability may be imposed on them.

5.3.4 Personal liability for breaching a restriction or disqualification order

Restriction and disqualification orders are discussed at Chapter 8. Where the restricted director acts for a company in breach of a restriction order, or where a disqualified person acts for a company in breach of a disqualification order, section 163 of the Companies Act 1990 sets out the civil consequences of so acting.

According to section 163(3) of that Act, where the company goes into insolvent liquidation while that person is acting for the company or within twelve months of that person so acting, the liquidator or a creditor of the company may apply to the court for an order declaring that person to be personally liable without limitation for all or part of the debts of the company incurred during the period that the person was acting for the company.

Under section 165 of the Companies Act 1990 any person who acts on the directions or instructions of a disqualified person may be made personally liable for the debts of the company incurred during the period while he was so acting. Under section 165(2) relief from liability may be granted by the court where it is "just and equitable" to do so.

5.3.5 Personal liability for company name irregularities

Pursuant to section 114 of the Companies Act 1963 a company must comply with a number of regulations on the publication of the company name. The company name must be displayed *inter alia* on cheques, promissory notes, and bills of exchange. Where the name of the company is not set out on a bill of exchange, promissory note, cheque, or order for money or goods, every officer of the company may be personally liable under section 114(4) to the holder of those documents unless it is duly paid by the company. In *Penrose v. Martyr* (1858) the company secretary was held personally liable for the amount of a bill of exchange because of the incorrect description of the company's name.

5.3.6 Personal liability for failing to keep proper records

Pursuant to section 202 of the Companies Act 1990, a company has a statutory obligation to maintain proper books of account (see Chapter 9 for a discussion of proper books of account). Where a company goes into insolvent liquidation and where the court is of the opinion that a contravention of section 202 has occurred, the court may declare that one or more of the officers of the company (including the former officers of the company) shall be personally liable without limitation for all or part of the company's debts as shall be specified by the court (Section 204 of the Companies Act 1990). The court must be satisfied that the contravention of section 202 has either

1. contributed to the company's inability to pay its debts; or
2. resulted in substantial uncertainty as to the assets and liabilities of the company; or
3. substantially impeded the orderly winding up of the company.

It is open to the liquidator, creditor, or contributory of the company to make an application for the imposition of personal liability. The court will not impose personal liability (section 204(4)) where the officer can prove that he took all reasonable steps to ensure compliance by the company with section 202 or that he had reasonable grounds for believing, and did believe, that a competent and reliable person, acting under the supervision and control of a director of the company who was formally allocated such responsibility, was charged with the duty of ensuring that section 202 was complied with. When considering whether or not to impose personal liability on the officer, the court will consider the extent of the financial loss caused to the company by the contravention *(see Mehigan v. Duignan* (1997)).

In *Re Ashclad Ltd (In liquidation)* (2000), discussed at Chapter 9, the official liquidator made an application to the court for a declaration of personal liability under section 204 of the Companies Act 1990, and the court made a declaration of personal liability in the sum of £112,000 for the failure to keep proper books of account.

5.3.7 Capital requirements

Section 163(4) of the Companies Act 1990 deals with the situation where a restricted director proposes to act for a new company and that company receives notice of the restriction order. As discussed at Chapter 8, this company must put in place minimum capital requirements. If the company proceeds with the appointment without putting these capital requirements in place within a "reasonable period" *and* the new company goes into insolvent liquidation, the Act provides for the imposition of personal liability.

The liquidator, a contributory, or a creditor of the company may apply to the court for an order that every officer of the company who knew or ought to have known that the company had been so notified, shall be personally liable for such debts of the company as the court may direct. The court may grant relief to such an officer where it is just and equitable to do so.

5.3.8 Personal liability for an unreasonable declaration of solvency

As noted in Chapter 21, a company cannot be wound up voluntarily by the shareholders of the company unless the directors swear a declaration that the company is solvent, *i.e.* it is able to pay its debts when due.

The directors must exercise caution when swearing the declaration of solvency, as section 256(8) of the Companies Act 1963 imposes personal liability on the directors where the declaration of solvency is sworn and the company is found to be insolvent. An application to court under this section is commonly made by a liquidator or a creditor of the company.

The court will impose liability where it believes that the directors had no reasonable grounds for their opinion that the company was solvent. If the company's debts have not been paid within twelve months of the commencement of the winding up, there is a presumption under section 256(9) of the Companies Act 1963 that the director did not have reasonable grounds for making the declaration. This presumption can be rebutted by the directors by proving that they did have reasonable grounds.

5.3.9 Contribution and pooling orders on a winding up

Pursuant to section 140 of the Companies Act 1990, the liquidator or a creditor of the company under liquidation may apply to the court for an order directing that a related company contribute to the assets of the company that is under liquidation. The court must be of the opinion that it is just and equitable to make such an order and it will take into account the following:

1. the extent to which the related company took part in the management of the company in liquidation;
2. the conduct of the related company towards the creditors of the company that is in liquidation; and
3. the effect which the order is likely to have on the creditors of the related company.

The court will not make the order unless it is satisfied that the circumstances that gave rise to the winding up of the company are attributable to the actions or omissions of the related company. See Chapter 23 for a discussion of what constitutes a related company.

Where two or more related companies are in liquidation, the liquidator may apply to the court, pursuant to section 141 of the Companies Act 1990, for an order directing that the assets of the companies be pooled between the creditors of both companies. The court will only make this order where it is just and equitable to do so, and from the date of the order the companies shall be wound up as one company.

The court will have particular regard to the interests of the members of the companies and the rights of the secured creditors of either company shall not be affected. The unsecured debts of the companies rank equally among themselves. The court will take into account the following:

1. the extent to which any of the companies took part in the management of any of the other companies;
2. the conduct of any of the companies towards the creditors of any of the other companies;
3. the effect which the order is likely to have on the creditors of the related company;
4. the extent to which the circumstances that gave rise to the winding up of any of the companies are attributable to the actions or omissions of any of the other companies; and
5. the extent to which the businesses of the companies have been intermingled.

5.3.10 Related examinerships

Under section 4 of the Companies (Amendment) Act 1990 (as amended by section 12 of the Companies (Amendment) (No. 2) Act 1999), the court may, when appointing an examiner, appoint the examiner to a related company or grant the examiner the right to use his powers in respect of a related company (see Chapter 20).

5.3.11 Taxation

The legislature sought to ensure that individuals could not decrease their tax liability on business profits by retaining them in companies and receiving the same by way of loans or other distributions. The Corporation Tax Act 1976 introduced the concept of the "close company" which is defined to mean a company with five or fewer participants. Certain "distributions" of the company's profits made to the participators shall be caught in the taxation net.

5.4 Lifting the veil by the court

The court may use its discretion to set the separate legal personality of a company aside where the justice of the case requires it. In *State (McInerney) v. Dublin Co. Co.* (1984) Carroll J. stated that "[t]he arm which lifts the corporate veil must always be that of justice."

5.4.1 Avoidance of legal duty

There are a number of cases where the court has disregarded the separate legal personality of a company because it was formed or used to facilitate the evasion of legal obligations.

In *Cummings v. Stewart* (1911) a limited patent licensing agreement allowed the defendant to exploit the plaintiff's patent for consideration but not allowing him to sublet, transfer, or assign it without the plaintiff's consent. A proviso allowed the defendant to transfer the licence to a limited company he formed for the purpose of business connected with the licence. The defendant could not make a profit, and in an attempt to evade the royalties payable by him under the contract, he transferred the licence to a company formed by him, but not for the purpose of exploiting the licence. Meredith M.R. stated that "it would be strange indeed if [the Companies Acts] could be turned into an engine for the destruction of legal obligation and the overthrow of legitimate and enforceable obligations."

In *Gilford Motor Company Ltd v. Horne* (1933) the defendant had been employed by the plaintiff company and had entered into a valid agreement not to solicit the plaintiff's customers or to compete with it for a certain time after leaving its employment. After ceasing to be employed by the plaintiff, the defendant formed a company which carried on a competing business, and caused the whole of its shares to be allotted to his wife and an employee of the company who were to be appointed the directors. It was held that since the defendant in fact controlled the company, its formation was a mere "cloak or sham" to enable him to break his agreement with the plaintiff. The court set aside the separate legal personality of the company.

In *Re Bugle Press Ltd* (1961) the majority shareholders in a company wished to buy out the shares of the minority. They formed a company and transferred their shares and sought to acquire the minority shares under the statutory procedure for buying out a minority shareholding compulsorily when a company is being taken over. The court held that the new company was a "sham" and "bare faced attempt to evade a fundamental rule of company law".

In *Jones v. Lipman* (1962) the vendor sought to evade specific performance of the contract for sale by conveying the land to a moribund company which he "bought" for the purpose. The company had been formed by third parties and the vendor purchased the whole of their shares in his own name and in the name of a nominee. Both the vendor and the nominee had themselves appointed as the company directors. It was held that the acquisition of the company and the conveyance of the land was a mere "cloak or sham" for the evasion of the contract for sale, and the specific performance of the contract was ordered against the vendor and the company which he had acquired.

In *Crease v. Breachwood Motors Ltd* (1993) a company sought to avoid a judgment for damages for wrongful dismissal obtained against it by its manager by forming a new company to which it transferred all its assets and liabilities, except the judgment debt in favour of its dismissed manager. The company then procured its own dissolution by applying to the Registrar of Companies to strike it off the register of companies. It was held that the new company was bound by the judgment in view of the blatant attempt by the original company to evade its enforcement, but the new company was given time to plead any defence it might have before the judgment was entered against it.

However, this rule will not impose liability on a company if it takes steps to avoid entering into an obligation to the plaintiff at all. In *Adams v. Cape Industries plc* (1990) a company incorporated in England set up independently managed, but wholly owned, subsidiaries in foreign countries to manufacture the products of the group. It was held that breach by those subsidiaries of the obligations imposed on them by local law to ensure the safety of those employees did not result in the parent company being liable on judgments obtained in those foreign countries against the subsidiaries by their injured employees. The fact the that the parent company deliberately formed the subsidiaries in order to insulate itself from safety obligations imposed on them did not of itself impose liability on the parent company.

The court, therefore, requires some evidence of fraud or illegality in the avoidance of the law of legal obligations in order to justify the lifting of the corporate veil. In the case of *United States v. Milwaukee Refrigerator Transit Co.* (1905) Sanborn J. stated that

> "[a] corporation will be looked upon as a legal entity as a general rule....but when the notion of legal entity is used to defeat public convenience, justify wrong, protect fraud, or defend crime, the law will

regard the corporation as an association of persons." This is endorsed in a number of Irish cases.

In *Roundabout Ltd v. Beirne* (1959), discussed at paragraph 5.2 above, the court found no such fraud or illegality. In *Dublin County Council v. Elgin Homes Ltd* (1984) a company which had been granted planning permission went into liquidation before it could comply with the terms of that permission. The plaintiff sought to compel the company and its directors to complete the works. Barrington J. refused to lift the veil and compel the directors *qua* individuals to complete the works at their own expense, and drew a distinction between fraud and mismanagement. In *Dublin Co. Co. v. O'Riordan* (1986) Murphy J. found that the affairs of the company were being carried on with "scant disregard for the requirements of the Companies Acts" but that there was no evidence of "fraud or the misappropriation of monies." This was relied upon by Hamilton P. in *Dun Laoghaire Corporation v. Park Hill Developments Ltd & Ors* (1989) where Hamilton P. held that he had found "no evidence of any fraud or misrepresentation, no siphoning off or misapplication of funds, nor any negligence in the carrying out of the affairs of the company."

In *Mastertrade (Exports) Ltd et al v. Phelan et al* (2001) P sold 50 per cent of his interest in the Master Meet Group companies to T under a joint venture agreement. In breach of the terms of that agreement, T subsequently sold his shares to G, and P was unaware of this sale. When the group encountered financial difficulties P and T entered into negotiations (with T's agents acting on behalf of G). P offered to acquire the group for £2.5m. A counter offer of £2.75m was made which was binding under the terms of the joint venture agreement. Subsequently P commenced proceedings against T, G and the Master Meat Group. The Master Meat Group companies in turn commenced an action against P alleging several misappropriations. P applied to have that action struck out on the basis of G's alleged wrongdoing. P was asking the court to lift the corporate veil between the Master Meet Group companies and G. Murphy J. refused this application on the basis that the companies were not in breach of any agreement, had not induced a breach of agreement, and were not in any way tainted with illegality, deceit, or fraud. Murphy J. further held that the companies had not been used as an engine for the destruction of legal obligations or the overthrow of legitimate or enforceable claims. He held that while there may have been concealment which misled the public, there was no evidence before the court that "the sole object of the concealment was to cheat and mislead the public".

5.4.2 Implied agency

The court has made an inroad on the principle of a company's separate legal personality by implying in some cases that the company was acting as an agent for another company, or that the company held its property as a trustee for another company. If this is the case, the court may lift the corporate veil between those companies.

In the English case of *Smith, Stone and Knight Ltd v. Birmingham Corporation* (1939) Atkinson J. set out the six matters that the court will take into account in determining whether a subsidiary is carrying on its business as an agent of its holding company, as follows:

1. Were the profits of the subsidiary treated as the profits of the parent company?;
2. Were the persons conducting the business of the subsidiary appointed by the parent company?;
3. Was the parent company the "head and brains" of the trading venture?;
4. Did the parent company govern the adventure, decide what should be done and what capital should be embarked on the venture?;
5. Were the subsidiary company's profits made by the skill and direction of the parent company?;
6. Was the parent company in effective and constant control of the subsidiary?

In this case the subsidiary had been formed simply in order to separate formally the business carried on in its name from another business carried on by the holding company. The freehold of the premises and the assets of the business carried on in the subsidiary's name were never transferred by the holding company to the subsidiary. All the subsidiary's shares were held by, or in trust for, the holding company, and the subsidiary's directors were all directors of the holding company. Accounts in respect of the business carried on in the subsidiary's name were kept as part of the holding company's accounts, and the subsidiaries profits were dealt with as though they had been earned by the holding company. The defendant compulsorily purchased the land on which the subsidiary was based, and the plaintiff holding company successfully sought compensation. The defendant attempted to rely on the principle in *Salomon's* case and claimed the subsidiary was a distinct legal entity. However, Atkinson J. stated that *Salomon* does not apply to a situation where there is a specific arrangement between the shareholders (the holding company) and the company whereby the company *is* an agent of its shareholders (holding company) for the purpose of carrying on the business of the company.

It is considered that the "six points" could apply to a large number of subsidiary and holding company relationships. As a result, the courts have appeared to limit the agency concept to those cases where the application of the separate personality principle could cause an anomaly or injustice. In revenue cases the court shows the strongest inclination to treat subsidiaries as agents of their holding companies, so that the holding companies may be taxed in respect of the subsidiaries' profits. In *Apthorpe Surveyor of Taxes v. Peter Schoenhofen Brewing Co. Ltd* (1899) an English company was held liable for income tax on the profits of its wholly-owned American subsidiary. The English company had agreed to buy the assets and business of the American company as well as the whole of its share capital, and the assets were vested in the American company only as a matter of convenience. The American company was managed by directors appointed by the English company, but they acted as the board of the English company instructed them. The English company was carrying on the business of the American company as much as if the assets of the business were vested in itself.

In *Firestone Tyre and Public Company v. Llewellin* (1957) an American company formed a wholly-owned subsidiary in England to manufacture and sell its brand of motor vehicle tyres in Europe. The American company negotiated agreements with European distributors, and the subsidiary would fulfil the orders of the American customers. In practice the orders were sent directly to the subsidiary, and the orders were met without the American company being consulted. The subsidiary retained only affixed sums out of the proceeds of the sales, and the balance was forwarded to the American company. All except one of the directors of the subsidiary resided in England, and they managed the subsidiary's business free from the day-to-day control by the American company. The Court of Appeal and the House of Lords held that the American company was carrying on business in England through its English subsidiary acting as its agent, and it was, therefore, liable to pay United Kingdom income tax on the profits of the subsidiary. In the Court of Appeal Evershed M.R. based his decision on the "close direction" of the American company in all respects and on the fact that the articles were sold by the English company to the American customers on terms fixed by the American company. This decision is evidence of the broad approach taken by the court to the "agency" principle where tax liability is at issue.

5.4.3 Trusteeship

There are a number of cases where the court has used the concept of trusteeship to escape from the principle of separate legal personality. In order to avoid apparent injustice the court has held that the company was a trustee of its shareholders. In *Littlewood Mail Order Stores Ltd v. IRC* (1969) the court treated the property vested in the subsidiary as being held on behalf of the parent company where a contrary conclusion would have allowed the parent company to avoid a tax liability. In *Trebanog Working Men's Club and Institute Ltd v. Macdonald* (1940) a club was incorporated as an industrial and provident society in order to provide recreational facilities for its members. A committee, which managed the club, purchased liquor in the name of the club and sold it to the members. The club was prosecuted for selling the liquor without a licence. The case was dismissed by the court on the ground that there had been no sale, as the members were in reality the owners of the liquor when it was purchased on their behalf by the committee. The club held the liquor as trustees for the members, and the beneficial ownership of the liquor was vested in them collectively.

5.4.4 Single economic entity

Where the "justice of the case requires", the court will disregard the separate corporate personalities of companies within a group and treat the group as a single economic entity.

In *DHN Food Distributors Ltd v. Tower Hamlets LBC* (1976) a holding company carried on its business on land that was in the ownership of one of its wholly-owned subsidiaries. When the defendant issued a compulsory purchase order in respect of the land, the holding company sought compensation for the disturbance. The Court of Appeal upheld that claim for compensation. Denning M.R. endorsed the contention that courts had a general tendency to ignore the separate legal entities within a group and instead look at the economic identity of the whole group. Denning M.R. stated that this particularly applied when the holding company held all the shares in the subsidiary (a wholly-owned subsidiary), and could control it. He treated the business as being carried on by the group. The judgments of the court went on to state that there were other grounds upon which a successful compensation claim could be based, but it was the concept of the "single economic entity" that captured the imagination of the later courts.

The concept was adopted by Costello J. in *Power Supermarkets Limited v. Crumlin Investments Limited et al* (1981). The first-named defendant was the landlord of a large shopping centre, and the plaintiff leased a unit for a supermarket chain within the centre. The leasing contract included a clause that prohibited the defendant from leasing any other unit over 3,000 sq. feet for the sale of food or groceries. The centre encountered financial difficulties, and the first-named defendant sold all of its shares to another company, Cornelscourt Shopping Centre Limited, which was one of the Dunnes Stores group of companies. Many of the Dunnes Stores group companies were separate in name only as they were managed by the same group of people. The Dunnes Stores group wished to set up a retail unit at the shopping centre. They set up another company, Dunnes Stores (Crumlin) Limited, to set up a retail outlet. When that company was incorporated, Cornelscourt Shopping Centre Limited caused the first-named defendant to convey the freehold of a large unit to Dunnes Stores (Crumlin) Limited for a nominal consideration. When Dunnes Stores (Crumlin) Limited began to trade in the shopping centre, the plaintiff succeeded in getting an injunction preventing them from trading.

Costello J. held that Dunnes Stores (Crumlin) Limited were bound by the restrictive covenants in the original contract even though they were not party to it. The company was described as a "mere technical device and a company with a £2 issued capital which had no real independent life of its own". He stated that "if the justice of the case requires it", the court may treat two or more related companies as a single entity so that the business notionally carried on by one will be regarded as the business of the group "if this conforms to the economic and commercial realities of the situation".

The use of the words "the interests of justice" and the facts of the *Power Supermarkets* case appears to have developed into a principle that the court will only lift the corporate veil on the basis of the "single economic entity" principle where unjust consequences would otherwise be caused to outsiders.

In *Rex Pet Foods Ltd v. Lamb Bros (Dublin) Ltd et al* (1985) Costello J. refused to disregard the separate legal personalities of a group of companies under common ownership and control. It was argued that the plaintiff companies should be aggregated and be treated as one because:

1. the defendant acquired a 52 per cent shareholding in the plaintiff;
2. some of the directors of the plaintiff were directors of the defendant;
3. the defendant group became distributors for the plaintiff's goods;
4. the defendant discharged the creditors of the plaintiff from time to time;
5. invoices from the suppliers to the plaintiff company were sent directly to the defendant.

The court did not consider these factors as grounds for treating the companies as a single economic entity. Costello J. held that there was "no evidence to suggest that the funds of the plaintiff company were siphoned off into any of the defendant's companies in such circumstances as would raise an equitable claim to any assets of the defendant companies."

This approach was endorsed in *State (McInerney & Co. Ltd) v. Dublin Co. Co.* (1984), where a holding company claimed compensation where its subsidiary was refused planning permission. The parent company was held to have no proprietary interest in the land concerned; Carroll J. based this on the inchoate concept of what justice requires, and not on what suits the parent or group. Carroll J. stated as follows:

> "[T]he corporate veil is not a device to be raised or lowered at the option of the parent company or group. The arm which lifts the corporate veil must always be that of justice. If justice requires (as it did in the DHN case) the courts will not be slow to treat a group of subsidiary companies and their parent companies as one."

In *Lac Minerals Ltd v. Chevron Mineral Corp. of Ireland* (1995) Murphy J. held that there were two requirements for the lifting of the veil in these circumstances. Firstly, that the decisions of one company were so dominated by another that it refutes separate identity, and secondly, the requirements of justice.

In the recent English case of *Truster AB v. Smallbome et al (No. 2)* (2001) Sir Andrew Morritt V.-C. confirmed that the corporate veil would not be lifted in the interests of justice where no unconnected third party was involved.

Allied Irish Coal Supplies Ltd v. Powell Duffryn International Fuels (1998) sent out a note of caution to those seeking to treat companies as single economic entities. Allied Irish Coal Supplies alleged that the defendant was in breach of a commercial contract concerning the supply of industrial coal. Allied Irish Coal Supplies sued Powell Duffryn International Fuels, a wholly-owned subsidiary of Powell Duffryn plc., in early 1992. The plaintiff later became aware that the parent plc was selling the defendant, and the plaintiff feared that the plc was trying to distance itself from the defendant. The plaintiff applied to join the plc as a co-defendant. The plaintiff was also concerned that the defendant would have insufficient funds to pay the debt.

Laffoy J. refused to allow the plaintiff to join the plc as a co-defendant on the basis that to do so would be to breach the principle of separate corporate legal personality.

> "[I]n my view, it cannot be used to render the assets of a parent company available to meet the liabilities of a trading subsidiary, to a party with whom it has traded. The proposition advanced by the plaintiff seems to me to be so fundamentally at variance with the principle of separate corporate legal personality laid down in *Salomon v Salomon & Co.*, and the concept of limited liability, that it is wholly unstateable".

Murphy J. in the Supreme Court agreed with Laffoy J. stating as follows:

> "The corner stone of company law was put in place just one hundred years ago by the decision of *Salomon*. Not merely did that case decide that a company incorporated under the Companies Acts is a legal entity separate from its promoters and members, but it was recognised that this was so, even though the company was incorporated for that purpose and with the result that the distinction operated to the manifest detriment of those dealing with the company in the ordinary course of business."

Interestingly, Murphy J. also refused the application on a different point. He pointed to the interests of the creditors of the plc, the proposed co-defendant. He stated that making the assets of the proposed defendant available to the plaintiff could operate as an injustice to these creditors.

5.5 The character of a company

There are a number of legal obligations, such as tax liability, imposed on a company that is determined to be resident in the jurisdiction. In order to establish the residency of a company, the court must examine where the real control of the day-to-day operations of the company is carried out. This involves an examination of where the controllers of the company carry out their functions. This test for residency was laid down in *De Beers Consolidated Mines v. Howe* (1906), which examined whether a South African company was resident in England for tax purposes. Lord Lorebun looked to where the company "keeps house and does business and the real business is carried on where the central management and control actually abides." This is the "head and brains" test. In this case, the head office was in South Africa, and this is where the general meetings were held. Most of the directors lived in England, however, and most of the board meetings were held in England. It was at these meetings that the important business of the company, such as negotiation of contracts, policy decisions, application of profits, etc., was discussed and decided. Thus, as the company was controlled from England, it resided there for tax purposes. This test was endorsed in the Irish case of *John Hood & Co. Ltd v. Magee* (1918), where the court held that the company was controlled by its shareholders in the general meeting, and not by its managing director who resided in another jurisdiction.

It has been held that an examination of the character of a company does not involve the lifting of the corporate veil. In *Daimler Company Ltd v. Continental Tyre & Rubber Co. (Great Britain) Ltd* (1916) the issue was whether the plaintiff should be treated as an enemy alien during the First World War because it was owned by German shareholders and controlled from Germany, although its registered office was in England. Lord Parker did not agree that *Salomon's* case prevented the court from looking at the individual members in order to determine the character of the company.

Therefore, the rule in *Salomon's* case does not prevent the court from looking at the individual members of the company in order to determine its character and status and where it has its legal residence.

6. COMPANY CONTRACTS

As a separate corporate entity, it is beyond question that the company has the capacity to enter into contracts on its own behalf, and, according to section 38(2) of the Companies Act 1963, all such contracts entered into by a company "shall bind the company and its successors and all other parties thereto". There are, however, a number of instances where the company may claim, to the detriment of outsiders, that it is not in fact bound by the terms of the contract.

As stated in Chapter 4, the memorandum and articles of the company are public documents, as they are registered with the Registrar of Companies. Therefore, all outsiders dealing with the company are deemed to be aware of their contents. This is called the doctrine of constructive notice and it can have considerable harsh implications for outsiders dealing with the company. This chapter highlights those contracts that may be challenged by the company on the basis that the outsider had constructive notice of the contents of its memorandum and articles and, further, what remedies are available to the outsider to enforce those disputed contracts.

6.1 Contracts in breach of the objects of the company

Where the company enters a contract that is neither expressly nor impliedly in furtherance of its objects (see Chapter 4), it is *ultra vires* the company and void *ab initio.* Such a void contract cannot be ratified by the shareholders in a general meeting of the company.

The classical doctrine of *ultra vires* is based on the fact that companies and other corporate bodies are formed to fulfil the specific limited purposes or objects stated in the documents constituting them, and are intended by their founders and persons who become members of them, as well as by the statute which recognises their corporate status, to achieve those purposes or objects and nothing else. A company can therefore be restrained from acting outside its objects (see Chapter 14), and any attempt to do so is a nullity and produces no legally effective results.

The *ultra vires* rule is justified by the fact that the outsider is on constructive notice of the company's objects clause. In *Ashbury Railway Carriage and Iron Co. Ltd v. Riche* (1875) the company was incorporated with *inter alia* the object of making and selling railway carriages. Without regard to the company's objects, its directors purported to contract to buy a concession for constructing a railway in Belgium. In this case, the contract was held to be void *ab initio* and unratifiable by the shareholders. Lord Cairns held that the memorandum stated "affirmatively the ambit and the extent and vitality and power which by law are given to the corporation, and it states, if it is necessary to so state, negatively, that nothing shall be done beyond that ambit, and that no attempt shall be made to use corporate life for any other purpose than that which is so specified".

This decision was followed in *Re German Date Coffee Co.* (1882). This case concerned a company, using a Swedish patent, manufacturing coffee from dates. The memorandum specifically provided that the business of the company could only be carried out once the German patent had been obtained. It was held that the company must be wound up as it hadn't obtained the German patent and the main objects of the company could only be conducted when the German patent had been obtained.

In *Re Jon Beauforte (London) Ltd* (1953) the main object of the company was set out as costumiers and gown makers. The actual business carried on by the company was that of veneer panel makers. The company entered a fuel contract, which could be used in either business. As the objects clause is public knowledge, and the note paper of the company stated veneer panel maker, the fuel supplier was deemed to have constructive notice of the *ultra vires* nature of the contract, and it was unenforceable when the company went into liquidation.

The harsh consequences of the *ultra vires* rule and the doctrine are mitigated by two provisions that may be used by the company creditor to enforce the *ultra vires* contract against the company. It is important to note that these measures do not alter the fact that the contract is *ultra vires* the company.

6.1.1 Section 8(1) of the Companies Act 1963

Section 8(1) of the Companies Act 1963 states as follows:

> "Any act or thing done by the company, which, if the company had been empowered to do the same, would have been lawfully and effectively done, shall, notwithstanding that the company had no power to do such act or thing, be effective in favour of any person relying on such act or thing who is not shown to have been actually aware, at the time when he so relied thereon, that such act or thing was not within

> the powers of the company, but that any director or officer of the company who was responsible for the doing by the company of such act or thing shall be liable to the company for any loss or damage suffered by the company in consequence thereof."

In order to enforce a contract pursuant to this provision the contract must be a lawful contract, *i.e.* it could have been "lawfully and effectively" made by the company if the company had the relevant capacity in its memorandum of association. This means that the section cannot be used to enforce an illegal contract. In *Bank of Ireland v. Rockfield Ltd* (1979) a company attempted to buy its own shares in circumstances that were prohibited under the Companies Acts. The court held that section 8(1) could not assist the shareholder to enforce the *ultra vires* contract as the contract was not lawful in the first instance.

One important limitation on the section is that the person seeking to enforce the contract must not have been "actually aware" of the *ultra vires* nature of the contract. This has been interpreted to mean that the party to the contract must not have read the memorandum of the company. In *Northern Bank Finance Corp. v. Quinn and Achates Investment Co.* (1979) the defendant company entered into a guarantee contract that was *ultra vires* the memorandum of the company. The plaintiff sought to enforce the guarantee by relying on section 8(1) of the Companies Act 1963. The plaintiff unsuccessfully claimed that it was not aware of the corporate capacity of the defendant. Keane J. held that the "probabilities are" that the solicitor for the plaintiff did read the objects clause and came to the conclusion that the guarantee was within the capacity of the company. As a result, the solicitor was actually aware of the objects and that awareness was imputed to the plaintiff. Keane J. stated that the purpose of section 8(1) was to protect those who entered transactions without reading the memorandum, not those who had read it and did not understand it. This decision has been heavily criticised as some commentators believe that the protection of the section should be available to outsiders who read the memorandum of the company but who honestly and reasonably fail to appreciate the effect of the objects.

The section may be used by "any person" to enforce an *ultra vires* contract. Therefore, outsiders and any member or director of the company may rely on the section. It may, however, be difficult for the member or the director to prove to the court that they were not actually aware of the *ultra vires* nature of the contract.

6.1.2 E.C. (Companies) Regulations 1973

Article 6 of the E.C. (Companies) Regulations 1973 (S.I. 163/1973) states that a transaction entered into by an organ of the company (defined as the board of directors or a person registered as authorised to bind the company) shall be deemed to be within the capacity of the company "in favour of a person dealing with the company in good faith".

According to Article (6)(2), such a person shall be presumed to have acted in good faith unless the contrary is proven.

Article 6 is more limited in effect than section 8(1) of the Companies Act 1963. In the first instance Article 6 only covers contracts entered into by the board of directors and registered persons. Registered persons are those persons who are notified to the Registrar of Companies under Article 6(3) as authorised to enter transactions on behalf of the company. In the second instance, the Regulation only applies to transactions entered into by limited liability companies.

One of the important limitations on Article 6 is that the person seeking to enforce the contract must have acted in "good faith". This is interpreted as meaning that the person has acted with subjective honesty, and it is considered a higher standard than the test of actual awareness in section 8(1) of the Companies Act 1963. According to Lawson J. in *International Sales & Agencies Ltd v. Marcus* (1982) good faith exists where a person did not actually know of the *ultra vires* nature of the transaction or "where it can be shown that such a person could not in view of all the circumstances have been unaware that he was a party to an *ultra vires* contract". Therefore, the good faith requirement would not be satisfied if the party to the transaction was suspicious that the contract was *ultra vires* and failed to investigate the matter.

This Regulation does not, however, amend or repeal section 8(1) of the Companies Act 1963 and it is possible to argue that section 8(1) and Article 6 are separate causes of action for the enforcement of an *ultra vires* contract. Therefore, a party who read the memorandum of the company and failed to appreciate the capacity of the company may be able to rely on Article 6 provided that the party acted in good faith.

6.1.3 Abolition of ultra vires

The CLRG has recommended the abolition of the *ultra vires* rule in its first Report discussed at paragraph 1.5.12.

6.2 Contracts in breach of the express ancillary powers of the company

As set out at Chapter 4, an express ancillary power of the company must be exercised in furtherance of the objects of the company. There may be further express conditions on the exercise of those powers enumerated in the memorandum. It was originally held by the courts that the exercise of an express ancillary power, other than in furtherance of the objects of the company or in breach of the express conditions, was *ultra vires* the memorandum of association and void.

In *Re Introductions Ltd* (1968) the company was incorporated to provide tourist services. One of the sub-clauses of the objects clause gave the company power to borrow money. The company changed hands and it went into the business of breeding pigs and borrowed money to finance its activities. The lender was aware of the objects of the company and its new line of business. When the company went into liquidation, the liquidator claimed that the loan was an *ultra vires* contract. The pig breeding was prima facie *ultra vires* but the bank relied on the ancillary power of the company to borrow money. It was held that the power to borrow money was an express ancillary power, which was exercised in respect of *ultra vires* activities, and therefore the loan was void.

In *Thomas Williamson Ltd and anor v. Bailieborough Co-operative* (1986) the memorandum of the company stated that the defendant company could give a guarantee where the board was of the opinion that it was "directly or indirectly conducive or incidental to the business or trade" of the company. Costello J. held that a guarantee was *ultra vires* the company and void unless the board had expressed an opinion in the terms of the clause.

The courts developed a distinction between those contracts that were patently *ultra vires* when they were compared with the company's memorandum, and contracts that such a comparison did not show to be necessarily outside the company's powers. While the former contract was absolutely void, the latter contract was held to be enforceable by the other party against the company if, at the time when the contract was made, he did not know and had no reason to believe that the company entered into the contract in order to achieve a result that was *ultra vires.*

The case of *Rolled Steel Products (Holdings) Ltd v. British Steel Corp. et al* (1985) adopted this new approach to the exercise of express ancillary powers. The company had the express ancillary power to give guarantees "as may seem expedient", which was interpreted to mean "as may seem expedient for the furtherance of the objects of the company". Slade L.J. stated that whether or not this power was exercised in furtherance of the objects of the company did not affect the capacity to contract. He stated that the exercise of the power was always *intra vires* the company. According to Slade L.J., the exercise of an express ancillary power not in furtherance of the company's objects was an abuse of the directors' powers.

Slade L.J. referred to the case of *Re David Payne & Company Ltd* (1904), where the company had the power to borrow but it obtained a loan in order to use the money for an *ultra vires* purpose. According to Slade L.J., the use of the phrase *ultra vires* in that case referred to "*ultra vires* the directors' powers" and not *ultra vires* the company. The distinction has been accepted by *Parkes & Sons Ltd v. Hong Kong and Shanghai Banking Corp.* (1990), where the court stated that while a disposition may constitute a breach of duty on the part of the directors, it did not follow that it was *ultra vires* the company. In *Re Fredrick Inns Ltd* (1994) Blayney J. also distinguished between an abuse of directors' powers and a breach of the corporate capacity of the company.

However, Slade L.J. in *Rolled Steel Products (Holdings) Ltd v. British Steel Corp. et al* (1985) held that the outsider would not be permitted to enforce the contract where he entered into the transaction and was aware of the abuse of directors' powers. Therefore, an outsider who acts bona fide should not be punished for the actions of the company and the contract should be held as *intra vires*. This is supported by the dicta of Johnson J. in *Re Cummins Ltd: Barton v. Bank of Ireland (1939),* where the bank could not enforce a loan as it had knowledge of the wrongful purpose for which the loan was obtained by the company. In the aftermath of *Rolled Steel Products (Holdings) Ltd* it could be said that the bank knew of the abuse of the directors' powers.

It is therefore established that the exercise of an express ancillary power, other than in furtherance of the objects of the company or in breach of the express conditions, is considered a breach of the directors' powers. The transaction is enforceable against the company save where the outsider was aware of the irregularity.

6.3 Contracts without company authority

The company may be able to avoid the obligations under a contract on the ground that the person who negotiated the contract on behalf of the company did not have the appropriate authority to do so. The outsider may be able to enforce the contract on the basis that the person who entered the contract had the actual or ostensible authority to do so as an agent of the company.

6.3.1 Actual authority

The actual authority of an agent to bind a company may be set out expressly in the articles of the company, in the resolutions of the members of the company, or in the resolutions of the board of directors.

By the general law directors can act on behalf of the company only at general meetings at which their collective decisions are expressed by resolutions (*Re Athenaeum Life Insurance Society, ex p. Eagle Insurance Co.* (1858)). They have no power to act individually as agents of the company. This also applies to the chairman of the board of directors, who is distinguished from the others only by the fact that he presides at board meetings. The board may not delegate any of its powers to one or more of its members or any person, unless the articles empower it to do so, according to *Re County Palatine Loan and Discount Co, Re Cartmell's Case* (1874).

In practice the articles of the company contain the widest powers of delegation by the board, both to individual directors and to other agents chosen by the board. The articles of most companies empower the board of directors to appoint one or more of their number as a managing director and to delegate to him any of their powers either concurrently with or to the exclusion of the board. Model article 112 of Table A provides that the board of directors may delegate its authority to a managing director. Unless there is such an express power in the articles, a managing director cannot be appointed by the board according to *Boschoek Pty Co. Ltd v. Fuke* (1906). Even where there is such an express power, the appointment can be revoked by the board at any time. That managing director usually has actual authority to enter into commercial transactions on behalf of the company, as model article 112 is commonly adopted without qualification. If a company does not adopt model article 112 or its equivalent, then the outsider is deemed to know that no managing director can have actual authority.

The company secretary is the company's administrative officer. In 1887 the case of *Barnett, Hoares and Co. v. Slough London Tramways Co.* stated that the company secretary was "a mere servant; his position is that he is to do what he is told and no person can assume he has any authority to represent anything at all". It is his function to give effect to the decisions of the board of directors by drafting and signing contracts, drawing cheques on the company's bank account if the board authorises him to do so, conducting correspondence, keeping the company's records, and doing all other acts as are necessary. But the company's secretary has no power to make commercial decisions on the company's behalf, and the secretary is acting outside his authority if he borrows money in the company's name.

He also acts outside his authority if he negotiates contracts on the company's behalf unless the contract is authorised by the board or it is necessary for carrying on the administration of the company's organisation consistently with board decisions, such as the employment of staff or the acquisition of company equipment. In *Panorama Developments (Guilford) Ltd v. Fidelis Furnishing Fabrics Ltd* (1971) Lord Denning commented that the company secretary is a "much more important person nowadays", being a person who "regularly makes representations on behalf of the company and enters into contracts on its behalf…he is certainly entitled to sign contracts connected with the administrative side of a company's affairs". Therefore, apart from exceptional circumstances, the company is not bound by contracts entered into by its secretary.

If the articles of the company empower the directors to delegate their powers to any agent they choose, they may delegate to the secretary or even an employee. In a recent English case a company was held to be bound to a commission agreement entered into on behalf of the company by an employee. In *SMC Electronics Ltd v. Akhter Computers Ltd et al* (2001) an employee was employed with the title "Director of Power Supply Unit Sales" and his contract required him to perform such duties as may be reasonably associated with his job title. He was not formally appointed as a director of the company but he signed his name as "director" and this was done with the company's acquiescence. He entered into a commission agreement with a rival company, and when the rival company sought commission, this was denied by the defendant company on the grounds that the employee had no authority to agree the payment of the commission. It was held by the Court of Appeal that the employee had express actual authority to enter into the commission agreement, as it was reasonably associated with his job.

6.3.2 Implied authority

If a principal appoints an agent of a recognised class, he impliedly holds the agent out as having authority to do all acts on his behalf which an agent of that class is ordinarily empowered to do. If the principal restricts the authority of that agent, a transaction entered into by the agent in defiance of those restrictions, but within the limits of his apparent authority, is binding on the principal if the other party was unaware of the restrictions on that authority. Therefore, a person who deals with an agent who is unaware of restrictions imposed on the scope of his authority, can assume that he has the powers which an agent of that kind normally has and the company is estopped (*i.e.* prevented) from denying that this is so.

A managing director is invested with implied authority to carry on the company's business in the usual way, and to do all acts and enter all contracts necessary for that purpose. He can sign cheques and bills of exchange on the company's behalf (*Dey v. Pullinger Engineering Co.* (1921)), borrow money on the company's account, and give security over the company's assets (*Biggerstaff v. Rowatt's Wharf Ltd* (1896)), receive payment of debts owed to the company, guarantee loans made to the company's subsidiary, and indemnify persons who have given such guarantees themselves. In *Hely-Hutchinson v. Brayhead Ltd* (1968) the chairman of the company acted as a *de facto* managing director. Upon insolvency the company sought to refute his authority to sign letters of guarantee. The Court of Appeal held he had implied actual authority, as the board had over many months acquiesced in his acting as managing director.

The implied authority of a managing director is confined to commercial matters, according to *George Whitechurch Ltd v. Cavanagh* (1902), and in this case it was held that the managing director had no implied authority to approve transfers of shares in the company or to alter the register of members. An ordinary non-managing director or company secretary has no implied authority to act on the company's behalf save in the case of the implied authority of the secretary to negotiate contracts on the authority of the board and to do acts necessary for the administration of the company.

If a person negotiates a commercial contract with a director or secretary, the company will not be bound by the contract unless the board of directors has expressly delegated its power to enter the contract to that person or held that person out as having delegated powers by appointing that person as an executive director or a director with specific functions. A person dealing with a company is entitled to rely on the implied authority of a director or other agent only if he is unaware of the limits of the director's or agent's actual authority, or if nothing has come to his attention to make a reasonable man suspicious or cause him to make enquiries. In *Underwood (AL) Ltd v. Bank of Liverpool and Martins* (1924) a sole director endorsed cheques payable to the company specially to himself and paid them into his private bank account. It was held that the bank was put on enquiry by the unusual nature of the transaction, and since it had not enquired whether the endorsement was authorised, it was liable to the company for the conversion of the cheque.

6.3.3 Ostensible authority

A person who enters a contract on behalf of a company may not have the actual authority, express or apparent, to act as its agent at all. The contract may, however, be enforced against the company if the outsider can establish that the person acting on behalf of the company has the ostensible authority to bind the company. Henchy J. in the case of *Kett v. Shannon & English* (1987) distinguished between actual and ostensible authority. Actual authority exists when there is an actual agreement between agent and principal, whereas ostensible authority does not derive from a consensual arrangement and exists where the principal makes a representation "which is intended to convey, and does convey, to the third party that the arrangement entered into under the apparent authority of the agent will be binding on the principal."

The basis of this statement is Diplock L.J.'s dictum in *Freeman & Lockyer v. Buckhurst Park Properties (Mangal) Ltd* (1964). In that case the articles of the defendant company provided that the directors could appoint a managing director. No such director was ever appointed and one of the directors acted as a managing director with the knowledge of the other members of the board. While purporting to be the managing director of the company, he entered into a contract with the plaintiffs. The company later sought to repudiate the contract saying that the director had no actual authority to bind the company as he had not been formally appointed a managing director in accordance with the articles. The court held that the company was liable for the fees, as the director had the ostensible authority to bind the company. This was based on the representation of the board that he was the managing director with the actual authority to bind the company. The plaintiff could assume that he had been properly appointed and recover against the company.

Diplock L.J. provided a four-step test for establishing that an agent of the company has the ostensible authority to bind the company:

1. there must be a representation to the outsider by the company that the agent had the authority to enter the contract on behalf of the company;

2. the representation must be made by someone with the actual authority to manage the business of the company either generally or in respect of the specific matter to which the contract relates;
3. the outsider must have been induced by those representations to enter the contract, *i.e.* he relied on the representations;
4. the memorandum and articles of the company give the company the capacity to enter a contract of this kind, and to delegate authority to the agent to make such contracts.

The first prerequisite is that a representation must be made by the company to the outsider. It is not acceptable for the agent to represent himself as an agent capable of binding the company. According to *Armagas Ltd v. Mundagas SA* (1985), the representation which creates ostensible authority may take a "variety of forms, but the most common is a representation by conduct, by permitting the agent to act in some way in the conduct of the principal's business with other persons, and thereby representing that the agent has the authority which an agent so acting in the conduct of his principal's business usually has." The four-step test was applied by Laffoy J. in the case of *Ulster Factors Ltd v. Entonglen Ltd (in liquidation) and George Moloney* (1997), and Laffoy J. found that the representation in that case was a tacit representation. The transaction was to be authorised by the directors and the company secretary, but all the transactions were in practice authorised by one officer of the company. As the company did not communicate to the plaintiff that the transaction was to be authorised in a different manner, there was a tacit representation that the authorisation could be carried out by one officer.

In the second instance, the corporate agent who makes the representation must have the actual authority to make such a representation either generally or in respect of the particular issue in question. This will normally be the board of directors but it may be a managing director if it is within the scope of his actual or implied authority to make representations about the authority of the company's officers, employees, or agents to act on the company's behalf. Here the outsider is affected by the doctrine of constructive notice. If the company has not adopted model article 80 of Table A (or its equivalent), the company cannot have a board of directors and the outsider is deemed to be on notice of this fact. Therefore, the outsider cannot rely on a representation made by a board of directors. If the company has not adopted model article 112 of Table A (or its equivalent), the company cannot have a managing director and the outsider is deemed to be on notice of this fact. As a result, the outsider cannot rely on a representation made by a managing director. It is not sufficient to show that one or some of the company's directors have held out the pretended agent as having been regularly appointed and duly authorised; all members of the board must do so, or at least acquiesce in him being held out by other members of the board as being authorised to act on the company's behalf.

In the third instance, the outsider must have relied on the representation, and, according to *Dunn v. MBS Distribution Ltd* (1990), any evidence that the outsider did not rely on the representation is fatal to the case.

Finally, the company must have had the capacity to enter the contract in question. Further, the memorandum and articles of the company must permit an agent, such as the agent at issue, to bind the company. As mentioned previously, the memorandum and articles of association are public documents and the public are deemed to have constructive notice of their contents. A clear example is found in the *Mahony v. East Holyford Mining Company* (1875), where the articles provided for the board of directors to manage the company and that all moneys should be paid by cheque, signed as directed by the board. The subscribers to the articles acted as directors and secretary but were never formally appointed to these posts. A letter from the company to the bank stated that the board had resolved that the cheques be signed by two directors and countersigned by the secretary. A cheque was drawn and honoured by the bank. The company was estopped from avoiding liability for the cheque on the basis that the "directors" and "secretary" had no authority to sign the cheques. The court held that the board had acted within the ostensible authority that could have been conferred upon them.

6.3.4 Ratification of the contract

If the pretended agent lacks both actual and apparent authority to bind the company for which he claims to act, the other party to the contract cannot sue the company for breach of contract because there is no contract between them. If the contract is, however, ratified by the company, the contract is binding on the company. This ratification is normally carried out by the board of directors and it can be express or implied. In the latter case the ratification may be implied where the board carries out some of the obligations imposed on the company by the contract, or the board allows the company to benefit by the other party performing its obligations under the contract, or even where the board allows the other party to act on the assumption that the contract is binding on the company without warning him that it is not (see *Wilson v. West Hartlepool Rly Co.* (1865)). If the contract is one that could only be ratified by the members of the company in general meeting, the contract may still be binding on the company after ratification by the board if the outsider acted in good faith.

6.4 Contracts in breach of the company's internal rules

Under the doctrine of constructive notice the outsider is deemed to be aware of the contents of the memorandum and articles of the company. As a result the outsider is deemed to know the internal procedure that must be followed by the company when entering certain transactions. However, it is recognised that the outsider cannot be held responsible where those internal procedures have been breached without his knowledge. This is called the rule in *Royal British Bank v. Turquand* (1856) and it permits the outsider to assume that the requisite internal requirements have been followed when the company enters a transaction.

In *Turquand's* case the company issued a bond to borrow money under seal. The company memorandum and articles required that the company pass an ordinary resolution when issuing such a bond, and this was not complied with. The company subsequently argued that the bond was defective because the bearer had constructive notice of the internal rules of the company. This was rejected and the court stated that once the outsider read the memorandum and articles, "he would have the right to infer the fact of a resolution authorising that which on the face of the document appeared to be legitimately done."

6.4.1 The Rule in Turquand's case

The cases decided under the rule in *Turquand's* case usually involve three kinds of defect:

1. the defective appointment of a director, or a director continuing to act for a company after he has ceased to be a director;
2. failure to hold a properly convened board meeting to authorise the company to enter into the transaction;
3. a disregard of the limitations imposed on the directors' authority in the memorandum or articles of the company.

In *Allied Irish Bank Ltd v. Ardmore Studios International (1972) Ltd* (1973) the bank was aware of the internal requirements for the borrowing of money. The company had two directors and three directors were required for a quorum. The bank received a copy of a resolution signed by a director and the secretary *cum* managing director. This certified that a meeting had been held at which a resolution had been passed which allowed the company to borrow from the bank. The meeting was in fact irregular, as the third director had not received the statutorily required notice of the meeting. Therefore, the internal rules of the company were breached by the board of directors. The bank successfully relied in the rule in *Turquand's* case and enforced the loan against the company, as the court said that it was a "classic example" of an irregularity in the internal management of the company.

It is common for the articles to permit the company to fix its own quorum, and in that case the outsider may treat the transaction resolved upon at the board meeting as binding on the company even though no quorum is present, according to *Re Fireproof Doors Ltd* (1916). Even if the articles fix the quorum so that the outsider could discover the quorum by examining the articles, he is still not concerned to see that that number of directors in fact attended the board meeting, according to *Davies v R Bolton & Co.* (1894). The latter case also stated that the outsider is protected where an act is done by the directors, whether *de jure* or *de facto*, where the required board meeting was not held and the outsider assumes that the transaction has been authorised at a board meeting.

In *Ulster Investment Bank Ltd v. Euro Estates Ltd* (1982) a mortgage was challenged by the company on the ground that the quorum was not present at the meeting of the board of directors which authorised the affixing of the seal to the mortgage deed. The bank had read the memorandum and articles of the company and was aware of the required quorum. The bank successfully relied on the rule in *Turquand's* case, and the validity of the mortgage was upheld.

Many of the cases where there has been a defect in holding a board meeting have been concerned with the effectiveness of a document that purports to have been executed on the company's behalf at such a meeting. Documents executed at a board meeting at which a quorum was not present, but which appeared to have been properly executed, were held binding in favour of a mortgagee who was unaware of the irregularity (*see Glouster County Bank v. Rudry Merthyr Steam and House Coal Colliery Co.* (1895)). In *Davies v. R. Bolton & Co.* (1894) a debenture that appeared to be properly executed was held binding on the company even though no board meeting to authorise the issue was held at all.

The protection afforded by the rule in *Turquand's* case in respect of documents does not extend to forgeries. In *Ruben v. Great Fingall Consolidated Co.* (1906) a company was not bound by a forged document even where the person who took it believed that it was issued under a board resolution. In that case, a company's secretary fabricated a share certificate under the company's seal with his own signature and the signature of a director forged by him in attestation. It was held that the certificate could in no circumstances be binding on the company, even in favour of a person who relied on its apparent genuineness and advanced money on the security of it. This principle has been extended to an extent that endangers the protection afforded by the *Turquand's* rule. In *South London Greyhound Racecourses Ltd v. Wake* (1931) a share certificate bearing the company's seal and attested by a director and secretary of the company was held to be a forgery because the affixing of the company's seal had not been attested by a board resolution as required by the articles of the company. This decision had been criticised as incorrect on the basis that the rule in *Turquand's* case would allow the outsider to assume that the relevant board meeting was held.

6.4.2 The limitations of the rule

(1) The memorandum and articles

The outsider must have actually relied on the memorandum and articles of the company and, therefore, be aware of the internal rules that apply to the particular transaction. In *Rama Corporation Ltd v. Proved Tin and General Investments Ltd* (1952) the outsider had not even read the memorandum and articles and, therefore, it could not rely on the rule in *Turquand's* case.

(2) Matters of public record

The rule in *Turquand's* case cannot be relied upon by the outsider to save the transaction where the internal rule that is required for the transaction is a matter of public record. All special resolutions passed by the company must be notified to the Registrar of Companies (see Chapter 13). Once it is registered with the Registrar of Companies, it is a matter of public record, and all outsiders are deemed to be on constructive notice of it. In *Irvine v. Union Bank of Australia* (1877) internal regulations required a special resolution of members to allow directors to borrow above a certain amount. Such an amount was borrowed without a resolution, and it was held that the bank could not rely on *Turquand's* case. The bank had constructive resolution that the resolution had not been passed, as no copy of the resolution was filed in the Companies Office.

(3) Good faith

The outsider must act in good faith, and if he is actually aware of the irregularity, the rule in *Turquand's* case cannot be used to enforce the irregular contract. This excludes insiders in nearly all cases. In *Cox v. Dublin City Distillery Ltd* (1915) the internal rules stated that the directors were not allowed to vote on issues where they had a personal interest. Despite this, the directors issued debentures to themselves and outsiders as security for the advances to the company. The outsiders successfully relied on the rule in *Turquand's* case to enforce their debentures. The debentures issued to the directors were not upheld, as the directors could not rely on the rule in *Turquand's* case because they were deemed to have notice of the internal rules under which the resolutions were invalid.

If the transaction is of an exceptional nature, the outsider may be deemed to be on notice that there may be an irregularity and he is under a duty to investigate the matter. In *Underwood (AL) Ltd v. Bank of Liverpool & Martins* (1924) a director of the plaintiff endorsed cheques that were payable to the company to his own bank account with the defendant bank. The money was recovered from the bank on the basis that it failed to make ordinary enquiry into the director's actions, as Bankes L.J. stated that the "strangeness of his conduct" was material.

7. COMPANY DIRECTORS

Under section 174 of the Companies Act 1963 a company must have at least two directors. A director is defined as "any person who occupies the position of director by whatever named called" (section 2 of the Companies Act 1963). Therefore, the label will be ignored and the substance of the functions exercised by a person in relation to a company will be examined. Pursuant to the Companies Acts, the term "directors" includes a *de facto* director and a shadow director. A *de facto* director is a person who claims or purports to act as a director of a company in the absence of any formal appointment (see *Re Hydrodam (Corby) Ltd*(1994)). In *Re Kaytech International plc* (1999) the English Court of Appeal considered the meaning of a *de facto* director. The court held that there was no one test for determining whether a person was a *de facto* director, that there were a number of relevant factors, and that the issue was whether the individual in question had assumed the status and function of a director.

A "shadow director" is defined in section 27 Companies Act 1990 as someone who, while not formally appointed as a director, is deemed to be such because they are persons in accordance with whose directions or instructions the directors of a company are accustomed to act (unless the directions or instructions are given in a professional capacity). The definition of a shadow director was considered in *Secretary of State for Trade and Industry v. Derverell and anor* (2000) where Morritt J. in the English Court of Appeal held the following in relation to a similar provision in the English Companies Act 1985:

1. the definition was not to be strictly construed as it was intended to protect the public;

2. the purpose of the legislation was to identify those, other than professional advisers, with real influence in the corporate affairs of the company, but it was not necessary that their influence had to be over the whole field of its corporate activity;

3. what was a direction or an instruction had to be objectively considered by the court in the light of all the evidence;

4. non-professional advice could come within the meaning of "directions and instructions" and not all advice was excluded;

5. it was sufficient to show that the properly appointed directors or some of them cast themselves in a subservient role or surrendered their respective discretions.

7.1 Appointment, removal and remuneration of directors

7.1.1 Appointment

The first directors of a company are usually appointed by the subscribers to the memorandum of association and a statement of their details is delivered to the Registrar of Companies under section 3 of the Companies (Amendment) Act 1982. The procedure for subsequent appointments is commonly set out in the memorandum and articles of the company. The articles usually provide for the appointment of directors at a general meeting and where the members are proposing the appointment of a person as a director, other than a retiring director, they are required to give twenty-one days' notice to the company's registered office. In the event that a vacancy arises on the board, a replacement must be appointed by a special resolution of the members at a general meeting. The articles of association may permit the remaining directors to appoint a replacement who can hold the position until the next annual general meeting.

If permitted by the articles of association, a director may be appointed for life. Further, model article 110 permits the directors of the company to appoint a managing director and vest such powers in that person as they think fit (model article 112). Every director must consent to his appointment and that consent must be an informed consent (see *Re CEM Connections Ltd* (2000)).

There are no formal requirements for an individual to be a director; however, the following individuals are excluded:

1. a body corporate (section 176 of the Companies Act 1963);

2. an undischarged bankrupt (section 183 of the Companies Act 1963;

3. an auditor appointed to that company, its holding company or its subsidiary (section 162(5) of the Companies Act 1963);

4. a person subject to a restriction order under section 150 of the Companies Act 1990, unless the company meets the minimum capital requirements (see Chapter 8);

5. a person disqualified under section 160 of the Companies Act 1990.

Directors are not obliged by law to hold a certain amount of shares in a company which would "qualify" them to be directors, although companies can set such limits in the articles of association. Where a shareholding is required by the articles, section 180(1) of the Companies Act 1963 states that if they are not obtained within two months of his appointment, the office of director must be vacated.

7.1.2 Resident directors

According to amendments introduced by section 43 of the Companies (Amendment) (No.2) Act 1999, every company incorporated under the Companies Act 1963 must appoint an Irish resident director with effect from April 2000. Companies in existence prior to that date were obliged to appoint such a director by April 2001.

Under section 44(8) a person will be regarded as being resident if he is present in the Republic of Ireland in the previous twelve months for a period of at least 183 days, or in the previous twenty-four months for a period of at least 280 days. Under section 43(9) if a director who is resident in the State ceases, for whatever reason, to be a director and he is aware that as of the date of his resignation the company did not have a continuing resident director, he will be obliged to notify the Registrar of Companies of his resignation and of the fact that there is no resident director on the board. This must be done within fourteen days of his ceasing to be a director. Failing to so notify will place him in a position where he will continue to be personally responsible for the payment of any penalties or fines imposed on the company under Irish tax or company law (section 43 (11)).

Section 43(3) of the Companies (Amendment) (No.2) Act 1999 provides an alternative to the requirement to have a resident director. The company may opt to put in place a bond to the value of €25,400 against any fines or penalties that may be imposed on the company under Irish tax or company law.

Under section 44, if the company can demonstrate a real and continuous economic link with one or more economic activities in Ireland, the company can obtain a certificate from the Registrar of Companies showing that it is exempt from the requirement to have a resident director. The Registrar may withdraw this certificate in circumstances where he believes that the linkage has ceased.

7.1.3 Number of directorships

Under section 45 of the Companies (Amendment) (No.2) Act 1999, there is now a prohibition on a person holding more than twenty-five directorships. This includes shadow directorships. Certain directorships are exempted; these include directorships of a plc, an old public company or a company for which an exemption certificate under section 44 exists.

The legislation also excludes a wide variety of other directorships such as those in banks, recognised stock exchanges, stock exchange member firms, approved investment business firms, a company associated with a building society, etc. These directorships are only excluded where notice has been given to the Registrar of Companies that they fall within one of these categories and the Registrar of Companies certifies this in writing. Where the Registrar of Companies refuses to certify a directorship as exempted, the director may appeal to the Minister. It is open to the Minister to confirm the Registrar's decision yet direct that the directorship not be counted where to do otherwise would cause "serious injustice or hardship".

In cases where a person is a director of a holding company and any number of its subsidiaries, only one directorship will need to be counted towards the limit of twenty-five. If, after the commencement date, a person accepts a directorship that contravenes the new limit, he shall be guilty of an offence, and the directorship will be regarded as void under Irish company law.

7.1.4 Removal

The model article 92 of Table A provides that the first directors of the company must retire at the first annual general meeting (this article is commonly excluded by the articles of association). The model articles also state that one-third of the directors must retire on an annual basis. These directors are eligible for re-election. As mentioned, where a director fills a vacancy, that director must retire at the next annual general meeting, and he is also eligible for re-election.

The right of the members of a company to remove a director is conferred by section 182 of the Companies Act 1963. The members may, by ordinary resolution, remove a director before the expiration of his period of office, notwithstanding anything in the articles of the company or in any agreement between the company and the director. The members do not have this power in the case of a private company where the director is holding the office for life unless the memorandum and articles of association are amended to permit such a removal. In some cases the articles may require the passing of a special resolution. In *Coubrough v. James Panton & Co. Ltd* (1965) the removal of a director by an ordinary resolution was invalid, as the articles of association required a special resolution.

Section 182 requires certain statutory procedures to be followed where any such resolution is proposed:

1. twenty-eight' days notice must be given to all members;
2. the company must send a copy of that notice to the director concerned;
3. where the company receives written representations from the director, the members must receive notice of the same;
4. the directors may speak at the meeting proposing the resolution.

The right to hold this meeting is not absolute. In *Feighery v. Feighery & Co.* (1999) a director sought an injunction to restrain the company from holding the meeting to remove him. Laffoy J. held that the court had no jurisdiction to restrain a company holding a meeting proposing to remove a director because the effect of doing so would be to restrain the exercise of the company's statutory right under section 182(1) of the Companies Act 1963. However, in *McGilligan v. O'Grady* (1999) the Supreme Court held that the court did have jurisdiction to grant the injunction. Barron J. held that "no absolute reliance can be placed upon a statutory right given to the general meeting of a company when the exercise of that right is alleged to be wrongful." In the recent case of *Moore v. Xnet Information Systems Ltd et al* (2002) a director sought reinstatement and his salary pending the trial of the substantive action challenging his removal. The High Court considered that the balance of convenience favoured the continued payment of the director's salary and his right to receive all information he had previously received in his capacity as director. The balance of convenience did not, however, favour the reinstatement of the director.

In *Re Murphs Restaurants Ltd* (1979) two directors sought to remove a director of the company. The latter was also a member of the company and he applied to the court for relief under section 205 of the Companies Act 1963 (see Chapter 14) on the grounds of oppression and successfully sought the winding up of the company on just and equitable grounds. It is a stark reminder to companies that an attempt to remove a director for improper reasons may result in the liquidation of the company.

7.1.5 Disqualification

Model article 95 of Table A states that the director must vacate the office of director if any of the following apply:

1. the director does not hold any requisite share qualification and is disqualified under section 180 of the Companies Act 1963;
2. the director becomes bankrupt;
3. the director becomes of unsound mind;
4. the director resigns his office by notice in writing;
5. the director is convicted of an indictable offence;
6. the director is absent for six months without permission from directors' meetings.

As discussed in Chapter 8 a director may be disqualified pursuant to section 160 of the Companies Act 1990.

7.1.6 Remuneration

A director has no statutory right to receive remuneration for acting as a director. The articles of association commonly provide for the payment of the directors and it is open to the members in general meeting to determine the remuneration of the board. Where a director accepts remuneration that is in breach of the articles, he commits a misfeasance and he can be compelled by a liquidator to repay the money (see *Re Oxford Society* (1887)). The annual accounts of the company must disclose all payments of salaries and expenses to directors.

Many directors commonly negotiate a contract of employment with the company, but section 28 of the Companies Act 1990 requires that the members approve such a contract by special resolution where the contract is for a term in excess of five years with limited termination provisions. Section 50 of the Companies Act 1990 requires every company to keep a register of all contracts of employment entered into with directors. Section 182 of the Companies Act 1963 makes it clear that the statutory right to remove a director remains with the members irrespective of any terms negotiated in such a contract.

Where the contract is prematurely terminated by the company, the director has the usual rights to damages for wrongful dismissal. The company must follow fair procedures in any dismissal according to *Glover v. BLN Ltd* (1973) and the company cannot rely on a breach of contract or misconduct of a director where the same was unknown to the company at the time of the dismissal (see *Carvill v. Irish Industrial Bank Ltd* (1968)). The articles of association may, however, state that the company may terminate the contract at any time, as in *Read v. Astoria Garage Streatham Ltd* (1952), leaving the director with no right to bring a wrongful dismissal action.

7.2 Register of directors

Section 195 of the Companies Act 1963 requires that every company keep a register of its directors and secretaries at its registered office. The Companies Act 1990, the Companies (Amendment) (No 2) Act 1999, and the Company Law Enforcement Act 2001 have amended section 195 extending the contents of the register, the persons entitled to inspect the register, and the penalties for failing to comply with these provisions.

The contents of the register are set out in section 195 and it must contain the following information in respect of each director:

1. present and past name;
2. date of birth;
3. location of usual residence;
4. nationality;
5. business occupation; and
6. present and past directorships of bodies corporate incorporated in and/or outside the State (within the last 10 years).

There is a duty on every director to provide written information to the company for the purpose of the register and failure to do so is an offence (section 195(14)).

Section 195(6) of the Companies Act 1963 requires the company to notify the Registrar of Companies of any change of directors, secretary or particulars in the register within fourteen days of the date of the change. Any notification of appointment of a director sent to the Registrar of Companies must be accompanied by a consent to act by that director and, further, the notification must state whether or not that person is disqualified by the law of another state from acting as a director/ secretary of a body corporate (section 195(8) as inserted by section 91 of the Company Law Enforcement Act 2001).

The register must be open to any member for inspection free of charge and any other person may inspect the register on the payment of a fee (section 195(10)). Where an inspection is refused, the company and every officer in default shall be liable to a fine and it is open to the court under section 195(13) to make an order compelling an inspection. A member can also request a copy of the register from the company (section 195(10A)).

Where a company fails to notify the Registrar of Companies that a person has ceased to be a director or secretary of the company, that person may send a notice to the company requesting that the company notify the Registrar of Companies immediately of the resignation/ removal/retirement of that person (section 195(11A) of the Companies Act 1963 as inserted by the Companies (Amendment) (No 2) Act 1999). The notice must state that if the company fails to do so, that person will send documentary proof of having ceased to be a director/secretary to the Registrar of Companies and every officer of the company. Where there is no response by the company, such documentary proof should be forwarded to the Registrar of Companies and every company officer under section 195(11B) of the Companies Act 1963.

Where the Registrar of Companies receives such a notice and as a result there are no recorded directors of the company, the Registrar of Companies may exercise his power to strike the company off the register for failing to carry on business under section 311 of the Companies Act 1963 (see Chapter 22).

7.3 Meetings of directors

It is the board of directors that carry out the management of the company. As noted above, it is open to the directors to appoint a managing director. The model article 101 of Table A is commonly adopted and it states as follows:

1. the directors can meet for the dispatch of business, adjourn and otherwise regulate their meetings as they think fit;

2. questions arising at meetings shall be decided by a majority of votes;

3. where there is an equality of votes, the chairman has the casting vote;
4. a director may summon a meeting at any time;
5. if the directors so resolve, it shall not be necessary to give notice of a meeting to a director resident outside the State.

There is no need for written notice of meetings unless the articles demand it. Save where the articles set out a specific period of notice that must be given to directors, "due notice" will be required, *i.e.* reasonable notice according to *Holland et al v. McGill et al* (1990). Model article 102 of Table A states that, unless otherwise set out in the articles of association, the quorum for a directors meeting is two directors. Model article 103 of Table A states that where the number of directors falls below the designated quorum, they may meet only to increase the number to the quorum or to call a general meeting.

Under model article 105 of Table A the directors may appoint a committee of directors from their number, and any act of the committee, or of a meeting of directors, shall be valid where it is later discovered that one of the directors was invalidly appointed or disqualified (model article 108 of Table A). Under model article 109 of Table A the directors may hold informal meetings and a written resolution signed by all the directors entitled to notice of a meeting shall be valid as if it had been passed at a directors' meeting. In *Buchanan (Peter) Ltd v. McVey* (1954) it was held that if all of a corporation agree to a certain course, however informal the manner of their agreement, it is an act of the company and binds the company subject to its not being *ultra vires* or illegal.

Model article 89 of Table A states that the minutes of a board meeting must be kept, as they are prima facie evidence of what took place.

7.4 Disclosure of interests

7.4.1 Disclosure of Interests in Contracts

Section 194 of the Companies Act 1963 requires a director to disclose any direct or indirect interest in contracts or proposed contracts with the company at a meeting of the directors of the company. Section 194(2) requires the declaration to be made as follows:

1. at the first board meeting at which the proposal to enter the proposed contract is raised;

2. if the director was not interested at the time of this meeting, at the first meeting after he acquires his interest, when it is discussed; or

3. where the director becomes interested after the contract has been entered, at the first meeting after this occurs.

According to *Guinness plc v. Saunders* (1988) the declaration must be made to a duly convened full board meeting.

Section 194(3) of the Companies Act 1963 states that a general notice may be given to the directors to the effect that the director is a shareholder in a specified firm that is interested in a contract that the company may enter into. He may also give a general notice that he is to be regarded as interested in a contract that the company may enter into with a specified person who is "connected" to the directors within the meaning of the Companies Acts. This general notice should either be given at a meeting of the directors of the company or the director concerned must ensure that it is read at the next meeting after it has been given. It is an offence not to make this declaration in accordance with section 194, with the possible sanction of the director being fined. Section 194(5) of the Companies Act 1963 requires that every declaration and notice shall be entered in a book kept by the company which shall be open for inspection by a director, secretary, auditor, or member of the company. The book must also be available at every general meeting of the company. The company and every officer of the company in default of these provisions is liable to a fine. It is open to the court to make an order compelling inspection.

There is no actual requirement that this interest be approved, as the provision merely requires disclosure. However, it is set out at section 194(7) that the rules of law restricting directors of a company from having an interest in company contracts still apply (see paragraph 7.8.3).

7.4.2 Disclosure of Interests in Shares & Debentures

Section 190 of the Companies Act 1963 required a company to maintain a register disclosing, in relation to each director and secretary, any interest in the shares or debentures of the company or any related company. That section was replaced by sections 53, 54, 56, 57 and 59 of the Companies Act 1990.

Section 53(1) of the Companies Act 1990 requires a director/secretary of a company to notify the company in writing of any interests in shares in, and debentures of, the company, its subsidiaries, its holding company or fellow subsidiaries. The director/secretary must notify the company of that interest within five days of the section coming into force and if they are unaware of their interests on that day, they must notify the company within five days of becoming aware (section 56(1)).

Section 53(2) of the Companies Act 1990 requires the directors/secretary to notify the company of the following events:

1. any event as a result of which he ceases to be interested or becomes interested in any such shares or debentures (the notification must include the price paid for the shares or debentures);

2. the entering into any contract to sell such shares or debentures (the notification must include the price received for the shares or debentures);

3. the assignment by him of any rights to subscribe in shares or debentures of the company (the notification must include the consideration received for assignment);

4. the grant to him of any right to subscribe for shares or debentures in the company's subsidiaries, holding company or fellow subsidiaries, the exercise of that right or the assignment of that right (the notification must include the date on which the right was granted, the period within which the right is exercisable, consideration for the grant, the price to be paid for the shares and the consideration received for any assignment of the right).

The above events must be notified to the company within five days of the event or of becoming aware of the event (section 56(2)).

The obligations set out in section 53 of the Companies Act 1990 do not apply in respect of shares held in a body corporate that is a fully owned subsidiary of another body corporate (section 53(10)). A person who fails to comply with these obligations under section 53 is guilty of an offence (section 53(7)). Further, no right or interest of any kind whatsoever, in respect of those shares or debentures, shall be enforceable by that director/secretary either directly or indirectly (section 58(3)). It is open to the director/secretary to apply to the court for relief under section 58(4) of the Companies Act 1990, and the company may grant relief where it is satisfied that the default was accidental, due to inadvertence or some other sufficient cause, or where it is just and equitable to grant relief. No relief will be granted where it appears that the default has arisen as a result of a deliberate act or omission on the part of the director/secretary.

Section 54 of the Companies Act 1990 defines what is meant by an "interest" in shares and debentures. An "interest" refers to "any interest of any kind whatsoever" and includes the following:

1. where the director/secretary enters into a contract for the purchase of shares or debentures;
2. where the director/secretary is entitled to exercise rights in relation to those shares or debentures;
3. where the director/secretary is entitled to control the exercise of rights in relation to those shares or debentures;
4. where the director/secretary has a right to call for the delivery of those shares or debentures;
5. where the director/secretary has an option in respect of shares or debentures;
6. where the director/secretary is entitled to exercise control over one-third or more of the voting power of a body corporate that is interested in the shares or debentures;
7. where the director/secretary is a shadow director of a body corporate that is interested in the shares or debentures;

Any of the above "interests" held by a spouse or a minor child of a director or secretary are also captured (section 64 of the Companies Act 1990).

The following "interests" are not captured according to section 55 of the Companies Act 1990:

1. the interest of a bare trustee;
2. an interest in remainder or reversion;
3. any discretionary interest;
4. a life interest under an irrevocable settlement where the settlor has no interest in the income or property;
5. interests subsisting under unit trusts;
6. interests under schemes under the Charities Acts 1961;
7. interests held by stockbrokers;
8. any other interests prescribed by the Minister.

Pursuant to section 59 of the Companies Act 1990 every company must keep a register of these interests and the register must be maintained at the company's registered office (or where the register of members is kept), and it must be open for inspection by any member of the company without payment of a fee or any other person on the payment of a fee. Any member or any other person may also request a copy of the register on the payment of a fee. Any failure to allow an inspection or to allow a copy to be obtained shall expose the company and every officer of the company who is in default to a fine (section 60(10)). It is open to the court to compel an inspection of the register (section 60(11)). The register must be presented at the company's annual general meeting, and it may be inspected by any person attending that meeting (section 60(9)). Where the company does not comply with section 60(9) of the Companies Act 1990, the company and every officer of the company who is in default is liable to a fine.

Under section 66 of the Companies Act 1990 (as amended by section 14 of the Company Law Enforcement Act 2001), where it appears to the Director of Corporate Enforcement that a contravention of section 53 may have occurred, he may appoint one or more inspectors to carry out an investigation and report to him on any contraventions.

7.4.3 Disclosure of directorships

As set out at paragraph 7.2, section 195 of the Companies Act 1963 requires a director to disclose and make available in the company's registered office, details of any other companies in which he holds the position of director.

7.4.4 Disclosure of payments

Sections 185 and 189 of the Companies Act 1963 provide that directors must disclose payments to be made to directors in connection with share transfer. Failure to comply with this requirement may result in the directors holding the proceeds on trust for the company.

7.5 Substantial property transactions

Section 29 of the Companies Act 1990 aims to prevent directors from abusing their position of trust. Shareholder approval is required in respect of the sale to, or purchase from, a director of the company or of its holding company (or a person connected to that director) of a substantial non-cash asset of the company. Approval must take the form of an ordinary resolution of the shareholders.

The section only applies where the non-cash asset is of "requisite value", *i.e.* not worth less than €1,270 and exceeding €63,500 or ten per cent of the amount of the company's relevant assets. "Relevant assets" means net assets (the aggregate of the company's assets minus the aggregate of the company's liabilities) if accounts have been prepared or the amount of called-up share capital if no accounts are prepared (see Chapter 12 for a definition of called-up share capital). Any violation of this requirement will render the agreement and the transaction voidable at the instance of the company under section 29(3) unless restitution of the money or the asset is no longer possible, or the company has been indemnified for any loss or damage suffered, or the rights of a bona fide purchaser for value without notice would be affected, or the arrangement is, within a reasonable period, affirmed by the company in general meeting.

Where the transaction is voidable the director (or the person connected with the director) and any other director of the company who authorised the arrangement shall be liable to account to the company for any gain which he made directly or indirectly from the transaction and shall be liable to indemnify the company for any loss or damage resulting from the transaction (section 29(4)). That person shall not be liable if he can prove that at the time of the transaction he was unaware of the circumstances constituting the contravention.

All such transactions must be accompanied by certificates of compliance with section 29, and the transfer deeds have to include such certification. This certificate will say either that the parties are not connected or that they are connected but the resolution was passed.

7.6 Prohibited transactions

7.6.1 Share options

Section 30 of the Companies Act 1990 (as amended by section 102 of the Company Law Enforcement Act 2001) prohibits a director from acquiring options to buy or sell certain shares and debentures in the company; in particular, the directors may not reserve the right to acquire or to sell shares at a fixed future date and price. The reason for this prohibition was the fear that, otherwise, directors may be tempted to buy shares and attempt to influence their price. This prohibition extends across the divisions between a holding company and its subsidiary.

7.6.2 Loans, quasi-loans and credit transactions

Section 31(1)(a) of the Companies Act 1990 precludes a company from giving a loan or a quasi-loan to its director, shadow director, director of its holding company, or persons connected with such a director ("prohibited persons"). Section 25(2) of the Companies Act 1990 defines a "quasi-loan" as any arrangement whereby a third party pays money or reimburses expenditure incurred by a prohibited person on the understanding that he will be reimbursed by the company.

Section 31(1)(b) of the Companies Act 1990 prohibits a company from entering a credit transaction as a creditor for a prohibited person. Section 25(3) of the Companies Act 1990 deals with a "credit transaction" and sees it as hire purchase and similar arrangements such as conditional sales, leases, licences in return for periodical payments, and any other transfer of assets or services done on the basis of deferred payment.

Section 31(1)(c) of the Companies Act 1990 prohibits a company from giving a guarantee or other security in connection with a loan, quasi-loan, or credit transaction made by any other person to a prohibited person.

The prohibitions cover "those who are connected with such a director". Under section 26(1) of the 1990 Act (as amended by section 76 of the 2001 Act) this includes a spouse, parent, brother, sister, child, a partner as defined under the Partnership Act 1890, and a trustee where the director or his family are beneficiaries. Under section 26(3) of the Companies Act 1990, as amended, it includes a body corporate controlled by the director, *i.e.* he, alone or with another director or person connected with the director, is interested in one half or more of the equity share capital or is entitled to exercise one half or more of the voting power at any general meeting of the body corporate.

(1) The exemptions under sections 32 to 37

Section 32 of the Companies Act 1990 permits such arrangements with prohibited persons where the entire value of the arrangements is less than ten per cent of the relevant assets of the company. The definition of relevant assets is set out at paragraph 7.5. This section only applies in respect of arrangements under sections 31(1)(a) and 31(1)(b) above. If the value of the company's relevant assets significantly changes, there is provision for the arrangement to be reduced to less than ten per cent of the relevant assets within two months (section 33 of the Companies Act 1990, as amended by section 77 of the Company Law Enforcement Act 2001).

Section 34 of the Companies Act 1990 (as amended by section 78 of the Company Law Enforcement Act 2001) allows a transaction under section 31(1)(c) above if:

1. the entering into the guarantee is, or the provision of the security is given, under the authority of a special resolution of the company passed within the previous twelve months; **and**

2. the company has forwarded with each notice of the meeting at which the special resolution is to be considered, a copy of the statutory declaration which complies with section 34(2) and 34 (3); **and**

3. the company delivers to the Registrar of Companies a copy of the statutory declaration within twenty-one days of the giving of the guarantee or the granting of the security.

Pursuant to section 34(2) of the Companies Act 1990, the statutory declaration shall be made by the majority of directors at a directors' meeting not earlier than twenty-four days before the meeting to pass the special resolution. Section 34(3) requires that the declaration shall include *inter alia* the following information:

1. the circumstance in which the guarantee/security is to be provided;

2. the nature of the guarantee/security, the persons for whom the loan, etc., is to be made;

3. the purpose for which the company is providing the guarantee/security;

4. the benefit which will accrue to the company directly or indirectly because of the guarantee/security; and

5. the opinion of the declarants that the company will be able to pay its debts when due.

Section 34(4) requires that this declaration must be accompanied by a report drawn up by an independent person who is qualified to be an auditor of the company, which must state whether in the opinion of the independent person the statutory declaration is reasonable.

According to section 34(5) if the director did not have reasonable grounds for the opinion that the company would be able to pay its debts when due, the court may (on the application of the liquidator, member, creditor, or contributory of the company) declare that the director is personally liable without limitation for the company's debts. If the company is wound up within twelve months of making the statutory declaration and its debts are paid within twelve months of the commencement of the winding up, it will be presumed, until the contrary is shown, that the director did not have reasonable grounds for his opinion.

According to section 34(6) of the Companies Act 1990, the special resolution may be passed in accordance with the procedure set out in section 141(8) of the Companies Act 1963, *i.e.* a resolution signed by all the members entitled to attend and vote at a general meeting. The date that the last member signs shall be the date that the resolution is effective. Where this procedure is used by the company, the statutory declaration must be sworn not earlier than twenty-four days before the signing of the special resolution.

According to sections 34(7) and 34(8) of the Companies Act 1990, if all the members entitled to vote fail to vote in favour of the special resolution, then the resolution is not valid until 30 days have expired. An application may be made to the court to cancel the special resolution within twenty-eight days of the resolution being passed. A person who has voted in favour of the special resolution is barred from applying for such a cancellation.

Section 35 of the Companies Act 1990 (as amended by section 79 of the Company Law Enforcement Act 2001) allows for intercompany transaction within the same group. A company may make a loan or quasi-loan to any company which is its holding company, subsidiary, or a subsidiary of its holding company, or may enter into a guarantee or provide any security in connection with a loan or quasi-loan made by any person, to any company which is its holding company, subsidiary, or a subsidiary of its holding company. It also allows a company to enter into a credit transaction as creditor for any company which is its holding company, subsidiary, or a subsidiary of its holding company, or to enter into a guarantee or provide any security in connection with any credit transaction made by any other person, for any company which is its holding company, subsidiary, or a subsidiary of its holding company.

Section 36 of the Companies Act 1990 states that section 31 does not prohibit a company from providing any of its directors or shadow directors with funds to meet vouched expenditure properly incurred or to be incurred by him for the purposes of the company or for the purpose of enabling him properly to perform his duties as an officer of the company and section 36 does not prohibit a company from doing anything to enable any of its directors to avoid incurring such expenditure.

Section 37 of the Companies Act 1990 allows a company to make any loan or quasi-loan or enter into any credit transaction as creditor for any person if the company enters into the transaction concerned in the ordinary course of its business, and the value of the transaction is not greater, and the terms on which it is entered into are no more favourable, in respect of the person for whom the transaction is made, than that or those which the company ordinarily offers, or it is reasonable to expect the company to have offered, to or in respect of a person of the same financial standing as that person but unconnected with the company.

(2) Breach of section 31

A transaction which breaches section 31 of the Companies Act 1990 is voidable at the instance of the company unless:

1. restitution of the money or asset which is the subject-matter of the transaction is no longer possible; or
2. where the rights of a bona fide with value without notice person would be affected if the transaction was rendered void; or
3. where the company has been indemnified for the loss or damages suffered by it.

Every prohibited person and any director of the company who authorised the transaction shall be liable to account to the company for the gain that he has made directly or indirectly as a result of the prohibited transaction and is liable to indemnify the company for any loss or damage suffered as a result (section 38(2) of the Companies Act 1990) unless that person can prove that he was unaware that the transaction contravened section 31. According to *Currencies Direct Ltd v. Ellis* (2001) public policy does not prevent a company from recovering a loan that had been made to directors in breach of section 330 of the English Companies Act 1985 as the loan is voidable and not void. This section is similar to section 31 of the Companies Act 1990.

Where the company goes into insolvent liquidation and the court considered that any prohibited transaction contributed materially to the company's inability to pay its debts or has impeded the orderly winding up, then the court may on the application of the liquidator, contributory or creditor of the company declare that any person who benefited from the transaction shall be personally liable for some or all of the debts of the company (section 39 of the Companies Act 1990).

Section 40 of the Companies Act 1990 states that a company officer who authorises or permits the company to enter into a transaction prohibited by section 31 is guilty of a criminal offence if he knew, or had reason to believe, that the company was contravening the section.

7.7 Powers of directors

Model article 80 of Table A is commonly adopted by companies and it states that the business of the company shall be managed by the board of directors. The directors must act subject to the Companies Acts and any regulations made thereunder. The directors must act subject to the directions from the members where that power in question was not given exclusively to the directors, *e.g.* in *Royal British Bank v. Turquand* (1856) the power to borrow was reserved by the members.

There are certain powers that remain with the members and which cannot be delegated to the directors, such as the power to sanction matters by a special resolution, *e.g.* section 60 restricts a company from purchasing its own shares and a special resolution cast by the members is required if the company proposes to carry out such a purchase. Further, the power to alter the articles and memorandum of association remains with the members.

Power will revert to the members where the director dies or becomes incapacitated or for some other reason is unable to act. Power will also revert to the members if the director exceeds his authority.

7.8 Directors' duties

A director will always owe a fiduciary duty to the company because, *inter alia*, they are agents of the company, and the relationship between principal and agent will always give rise to fiduciary duties. In the English case of *JJ Harrison (Properties) Ltd v. Harrison* (2002) the English Court of Appeal commented on the source of directors' fiduciary duties stating that, on the appointment of a director, a director assumes the duty of a trustee in relation to the company property. Where a director takes possession of his company's property, it was held that such possession "is coloured from the first by the trust and confidence by means of which he obtained it". Importantly, the court held that where a director has abused his trust and had possession of the company property, he could not plead the statute of limitations or laches in defence to the company's claims against him.

The standard duties of fiduciaries in a company (and *mutatis mutandis* of a trustee in a trust situation) include the following:

1. duty to exercise their powers bona fide and for the benefit of the company as a whole;
2. duty to exercise due skill, care and diligence;
3. uty to avoid conflicts between the interests of the company, and their own personal or business interests.

The CLRG recommends that these fiduciary duties should be set out in the Companies Acts (see paragraph 1.5.13).

7.8.1 Duty to exercise their powers bona fide and for the benefit of the company as a whole

Whether or not the directors acted bona fide is judged subjectively, as it was held by Greene M.R. in the case of *Re Smith & Fawcett Ltd* (1942) that directors "must exercise their discretion bona fide in what they consider - not what the court may consider - to be in the interests of the company." Lord Finlay in *Hindle v. Cotton (John) Ltd* (1919) stated:

> "[W]here the question is one of abuse of powers, the state of mind of those who acted, and the motive in which they acted, are all important, and you may go into the question of what their intention was, collecting from the surrounding circumstances all the materials which genuinely throw light upon that question of the state of mind of the directors so as to show whether they were honestly acting in discharge of their powers in the interests of the company, or for some other reason."

The case of *Regentcrest plc (in liquidation) v. Cohen & anor* (2001) Jonathan Parker J. expressed continued support for the subjective approach.

The subjective test was used in the Irish case of *Clarke v. Workman* (1920) where a decision of the board of directors was challenged on the basis that they had acted in breach of the fiduciary duty which they owed to the company by fettering their discretion in the exercise of their power. The court looked at the intentions and the perceived intentions of the directors concerned. Ross J. stated that the directors:

> "were bound to consider the interests of all the shareholders, unfettered by any undertaking or promise to any intending purchaser … if they failed in any of these matters, they disabled themselves from performing their duty to the shareholders and nothing that they did would in the eye of the law be held to have been done in good faith."

A fetter upon the exercise of discretion is not always fatal as in *Fulham Football Club Ltd v. Cabra Estates plc* (1994) where O'Neill L.J. stated that "it is trite law that directors are under a duty to act bona fide in the interests of their company. However, it does not follow ... that directors can never make a contract by which they bind themselves in the future exercise of their powers in a particular manner." The question should be asked as to whether the fetter conferred a substantial benefit on the company.

Other cases have a adopted a slightly different approach stating that the court should examine the substantial purpose behind the exercise of a particular power, with regard being had to the bona fide beliefs of the directors and their judgment in relation to matters of management, and the issue then being whether this exercise of the power in question was, on balance, a proper one. This was the approach of Wilberforce L.J. in *Smith (Howard) Ltd v. Ampol Petroleum Ltd* (1974). Here two companies were already shareholders in a third company and proposed to make a take-over bid for that company. The third company however allotted shares to an outside company who was willing to make a higher bid in order to enable it to complete the take-over. At first instance, Street J. held that the primary purpose of the allotment had been to reduce the shareholding of the two companies in question, in order that the appellant may complete the take-over. This was an improper purpose and the allotment was accordingly declared to be invalid. This decision was appealed to the Privy Council, where it was upheld.

However, an allotment to fight off a take-over bid may be acceptable and in the case of *Teck Corporation Ltd v. Millar* (1972) it was held that the directors may reasonably:

> "consider who is seeking control and why ... If they say that they believe there will be substantial damage to the company's interests then there must be reasonable grounds for that belief. If there are not, that will justify a finding that the directors were actuated by an improper purpose."

In *Nash v. Lancegaye Safety Glass (Ireland) Ltd* (1958) where an allotment left one shareholder with fifty-one per cent of the shares, it was held that this was an abuse of fiduciary powers by the director, and invalid. Dixon J. observed that the exercise of this power may have dual purposes. However, he refused to accept that the mere fact that the directors may have the object of benefiting the company, in addition to other improper purposes, could justify the course of action taken. However, in *Re Jermyn Street Turkish Baths Ltd* (1971) an allotment leaving one individual in a controlling position was held legal because it was vital to the survival of the company and was, therefore, in its interests.

7.8.2 The duty to exercise proper skill, care and diligence in the discharge of their duties

In *Charitable Corporation v. Sutton* (1742) it was stated by Hardwicke L.J. that:

> "[directors] may be guilty of acts of commission or omission, of malfeasance or nonfeasance … By accepting a trust of this sort, a person is obliged to execute it with fidelity and reasonable diligence; and it is no excuse to say that they had no benefit from it, but that it was merely honorary; and therefore, they are within the case of common trustees."

In *Re City Equitable Fire Insurance company Ltd* (1925) Romer J. stated that the standard of care owed by a director was as follows:

1. a director need not exhibit in the performance of his duties a greater degree of skill than may reasonably be expected from a person of his knowledge and experience;
2. a director is not bound to give continuous attention to the affairs of his company. His duties are of an intermittent nature to be performed at periodical board meetings and at meetings of any committee of the board upon which he happens to be placed. He is not, however, bound to attend all such meetings, though he ought to attend whenever, in the circumstances, he is reasonably able to do so;
3. in respect of all duties that, having regard to the exigencies of business and to the articles of association, may properly be left to some other official, a director is, in the absence of grounds of suspicion, justified in trusting that official to perform such duties honestly.

In *Dorchester Finance Co. Ltd v. Stebbing* (1989) Foster J. found that the signing of blank cheques by a non-executive director was negligent and a failing to exhibit the necessary skill and care in the performance of a director's duties.

7.8.3 The duty to avoid conflicts of interest between the director and the company

The breach of this duty is judged objectively and therefore the motives of the directors are immaterial. In *Regal (Hastings) Ltd v. Gulliver* (1942) Lord Russell stated as follows:

> "The rule of equity which insists on those, who by use of a fiduciary position make a profit, being liable to account for that profit, in no way depends on fraud or absence of *bona fides* or upon such questions or considerations as whether the profiteer was under a duty to obtain the source of the profit for the plaintiff or whether he took a risk or acted as he did for the benefit of the plaintiff, or whether the plaintiff has in fact been damaged or benefited by his action. The liability arises from the mere fact of a profit having in the stated circumstances being made. The profiteer however honest and well-intentioned cannot escape the risk of being called upon to account."

In *Industrial Development Consultants v. Cooley* (1972) the managing director of the plaintiff company unsuccessfully tried to secure a contract on behalf of the company. He later resigned and took up the contract. The plaintiff company sought to make him account for the profit he had made. The court held that he had breached his fiduciary duties by using information he received as a director, for his own ends. He was, therefore, forced to account to the company for the profit that he had made. Here the company had not even a chance to consider the business opportunity and there was no disclosure. The court based its decision on the facts that "he embarked on a deliberate policy and course of conduct which put his personal interest as a potential contracting party ... in direct conflict with his pre-existing and continuing [obligations] as a managing director of the plaintiffs." If the company was given the opportunity to consider and reject the contract, the result may be different, as in *Peso Silver Mines Ltd v. Cropper* (1966) where the company had rejected the business chance, and the directors were not, therefore, liable to account for the profits that they had made. The English case of *Gencor ACP et al v. Dalby et al* (2000) held that it was no defence to claim that the company would not have taken up the particular business opportunity. A director could only escape accountability for profits made where he had obtained the prior approval of the company's shareholders after full disclosure.

CMS Dolphin Ltd v. Simonet and anor (2001) confirmed that the director was liable for the profits made where he expropriated a business opportunity and he was so liable whether he exploited the diverted opportunity personally or through a company.

A contract between the director or a company or firm in which he has an interest, and the company of which he is a director, is voidable at the instance of that company. In *Aberdeen Railway Company v. Blaikie Bros* (1854) such a contract was held voidable at the instance of the company and Cranworth L.C. emphasised the fiduciary nature of the duties of a director and his obligation to act in the best interests of the company. He stated as follows:

> "[I]t is a rule of universal application that no-one, having such duties to discharge, shall be allowed to enter into engagements in which he has or can have a personal interest conflicting or which, possibly, may conflict with the interests of those whom he is bound to protect. So strictly is this principle adhered to that no question is allowed to be raised as to the fairness or unfairness of a contract so entered into."

In *Craven Textiles Engineers Ltd v. Batley Football Club Ltd* (2001) the court held that it would not avoid the contract if it could not do what was practically just to restore the parties to the position they had been in before the contract was made.

As discussed at paragraph 7.4.1 the director is statutorily obliged to disclose such interests to the company. Furthermore, unless the articles of association provide otherwise, a director is not permitted to vote at board meetings concerning contracts in respect of which he is interested, nor can he be among the quorum (the minimum number of persons who constitute a valid formal meeting) for such a vote.

7.8.4 The beneficiaries of those duties

It was a long accepted principal of company law that the directors owed their duties to the company itself, and not to the shareholders, creditors, employees, or any other category.

The principal was faithfully followed in *Percival v. Wright* (1902), where directors purchased shares from shareholders at a favourable price. The shareholders later discovered that the board of directors was in negotiations to sell the company for a higher price per share. The shareholders sought to have the transfer set aside as the transaction was in breach of fiduciary duty to the shareholders. Swinfen-Eady J. held that there was no obligation to disclose the negotiations to the shareholders and that such a duty "would place directors in a most invidious position, as they could not buy or sell shares without disclosing negotiations, a premature disclosure of which might well be against the best interests of the company."

The principal was reiterated in the recent English case of *Dawson International plc v. Coets Paton plc.* (1989), where Cullen L.J. restated the law as follows:

> "It is well recognised that directors owe fiduciary duties to the company ... These fiduciary duties spring from the relationship of the directors to the company, of which they are its agents... I see no good reason why it should be supposed that directors are, in general, under a fiduciary duty to the shareholders, and in particular current shareholders with respect to the disposal of their shares in the most advantageous way. The directors are not normally the agents of the current shareholders... What is in the interests of the current shareholders who are sellers of their shares may not necessarily coincide with what is in the interests of the company. The creation of parallel duties could lead to conflict. Directors have but one master, the company."

(1) Shareholders

The old Canadian case of *Allen v. Hyatt* (1914) provides the departure point for this area. Directors will stand in a fiduciary relationship to shareholders where they expressly undertake obligations to those shareholders. The company directors induced shareholders to give them options to buy their shares, on the basis that it would help them negotiate an amalgamation with a third company. The directors then exercised their option and made personal profits. The Privy Council held that the directors must account to the shareholders for the profit they had made. Viscount Haldome stated that "the facts in the present case were widely different from those in *Percival v. Wright*, and their lordships thought that the directors must here be taken to have held themselves out to the individual shareholders as acting for them on the same footing as they were acting for the company itself, that was, as agents."

This was the basis of the more recent New Zealand decision of *Coleman v. Myers* (1977), where such a duty was also found on the facts. The *factors* that were held to assist in finding fiduciary duties to the shareholders were as follows:

1. dependence upon information and advice;
2. existence of a relationship of confidence;
3. the significance of some particular transaction for the parties; and

4. the extent of any positive action taken by the director to promote it.

In Ireland the matter was considered in *Crindle Investments v. Wymes* (1998) and it was held that company directors do not merely by virtue of their offices, owe a fiduciary duty to the individual members. However, in particular circumstances a company director may owe a fiduciary duty to individual shareholders.

(2) Creditors

Despite the general rule, directors also owe certain duties to creditors. The Australian case of *Walker v. Wimbourne* (1976) established that "the directors of a company in discharging their duty to the company must take account of the interests of its shareholders and creditors. Any failure by the directors to take into account the interests of creditors will have adverse consequences for the company as well as for them."

The New Zealand case of *Nicholson v. Permakraft (NZ) Ltd* (1985) limited this duty to cases where the company was insolvent. Cooke J. stated:

> "[T]he duties of directors are owed to the company. On the facts of particular cases this may require the directors to consider *inter alia* the interests of creditors. For instance creditors are entitled to consideration, in my opinion, if the company is insolvent or nearly-insolvent or of doubtful solvency or if a contemplated payment or other course of action would jeopardise its solvency… In a situation of marginal commercial solvency such creditors may fairly be seen as beneficially interested in the company or contingentlyso."

Street C.J. in the Australian case of *Kinsella v. Russell Kinsella Property Ltd* (1986) accepted this limitation on the duty owed to the creditors. He held that "where a company is insolvent the interests of the creditors intrude." The first Irish case to consider the matter was *Parkes & Sons Ltd v. Hong Kong & Shanghai Banking Corp.* (1990) where Blayney J. referred to Street C.J. in *Kinsella* and accepted that directors of insolvent companies do owe duties to the creditors. In *Re Frederick Inns* (1994) Blayney J. held that the directors of a company do owe duties to the creditors when the company is insolvent, stating:

> "[A]s soon as a winding up order has been made the company ceases to be the beneficial owner of its assets, with the result that the directors no longer have power to dispose of them... Once the company clearly had to be wound up and its assets applied *pro tanto* in discharge of its liabilities, the directors had a duty to the creditors to pre-

serve the assets to enable this to be done, or at least not to dissipate them."

(3) Employees

In *Parke v. Daily News Ltd* (1962) an attempt to make *ex gratia* payments to employees was held to be *ultra vires,* despite the fact that the majority of the shareholders of the company supported it. The Court of Appeal held that there was no authority to support the proposition that directors are entitled to consider the interests of the employees, irrespective of any resulting benefit to the company. Section 52 of the Companies Act 1990 now states as follows:

1. the matters to which the directors of a company are to have regard in the performance of their functions shall include the interests of the company's employees in general, as well as the interests of its members;

2. accordingly the duty imposed by this section on the directors shall be owed by them to the company (and the company alone) and shall be enforceable in the same way as any other fiduciary duty owed to a company by its directors.

The section has attracted much criticism as, while the directors are obliged to have regard to the interests of the employees, that duty is owed to the company and not the employees. This appears to leave the employees with an effective remedy where there is failure to consider their interests.

7.8.5 Silent directors

It has long been accepted that a silent or non-executive director cannot escape liability where there is a breach of directors' duties on the ground of non-involvement in the day-to-day running of the company (see *Re Hunting Lodges Ltd* (1985)). The Australian case of *Southern Cross Interiors Pty Ltd and anor v. Deputy Commissioner of Taxation* (2001) considered the novel concept of "sexually transmitted debt". In this case the directors of a company in insolvent liquidation (a husband and wife) were sued for "insolvent trading"' (like reckless trading) and one statutory defence available to the directors was to prove that due to illness or some other "good reason" he or she did not take part at that time in the management of the company. The wife claimed such "good reason" on the basis that she had accepted the appointment at her husband's request, was told that it was a formality, was unaware of directors' duties, and did not participate in the management of the company because of the trust and confidence she had placed in her husband. Palmer J. recognised that certain people had disabilities and that wills can be overborne. He referred to the Australian Law Reform Commission's concept of "sexually transmitted debt" where the relationship of dependence and emotional ties between a husband and wife may dominate a transaction and it is that relationship and not the appreciation of the reality of the responsibility for the debt that is the predominant factor in the partner accepting liability. He held that the law should recognise that a wife's failure to appreciate her responsibility as a director due to a deferral to her husband may be a "good reason" for the purpose of the statutory defence. Palmer J. did state that it would only be in rare cases that a wife would be able to establish such a defence.

7.8.6 Misfeasance

Section 298 of the Companies Act 1963 (as amended by section 142 of the Companies Act 1990 and section 50 of the Company Law Enforcement Act 2001) may be used against the directors of a company where the company is in liquidation and it appears that the director has "misapplied or retained or become liable or accountable for any money or property of the company or has been guilty of any misfeasance or other breach of duty or breach of trust in relation to the company". A liquidator, a creditor, a contributory or the Director of Corporate Enforcement may apply to the court for an order requiring the director to restore the cash/property or pay compensation to the company. In *Re Simmon Box (Diamonds) Ltd* (2000) it was held that a director who was responsible for the loss of the company's assets (diamonds) while on a foreign trip and who did not put adequate insurance cover in place, was grossly negligent and was liable for misfeasance and ordered to make substantial contributions towards the assets of the company.

8. RESTRICTION AND DISQUALIFICATION

Part VII of the Companies Act 1990 introduced for the first time a mechanism for applying to the court to restrict or disqualify directors and other officers of companies.

8.1 Restriction orders

Section 150(1) of the Companies Act 1990 states that a restriction order will prohibit a person from acting in any way, either directly or indirectly, as a director or secretary of any company for a period of five years. It also prohibits that person from taking any part in the formation or promotion of any company during that time. According to section 149 such an application may be made where, either at the commencement of the winding up or during the course of the winding up, it is proved to the court that the company is insolvent, *i.e.* unable to pay its debts within the meaning of section 214 of the Companies Act 1963 (see Chapter 22).

The application may be made in respect of any person who is a director or shadow director of the company at the date of the winding up or who held that position within the twelve months prior to the commencement of the winding up. The rationale behind the new procedure was to control errant directors who simply move on to another company leaving large numbers of unpaid creditors in their wake. In *Business Communications Ltd v. Baxter & Parsons* (1995) Murphy J. stated that the objective of the section was to "prevent the abuse by directors of their special position to the detriment of outsiders."

When the court makes a restriction order, a court officer must notify the Registrar of Companies, who must maintain a register of all restricted directors (section 153 of the Companies Act 1990).

8.1.1 Locus standi

Pursuant to section 150(4A) of the Companies Act 1990 (as inserted by section 41 of the Company Law Enforcement Act 2001) an application for a restriction order may be made by the following:

1. the Director of Corporate Enforcement;

2. a liquidator;

3. a receiver.

Prior to 2001 there was concern that the "friendly liquidator" in a voluntary liquidation may be slow to apply to the court in appropriate situations (see *Business Communications Ltd v. Baxter & Parsons* (1995)). In the case of an involuntary liquidation, it is open to the court to compel the liquidator to make an application. Shanley J. in *La Moselle Clothing Ltd (in liquidation) and Rosegem Ltd (in liquidation) v. Djarnel Soualhi* (1998) felt that directors in voluntary liquidations "are permitted to avoid the sanction of section 150 of the Companies Act, 1990, by the fortuitous circumstance of a voluntary winding up or indeed a receivership." This concern was addressed in the Company Law Enforcement Act 2001 by the express granting of *locus standi* to the Director of Corporate Enforcement.

In *Re Steamline Ltd (in voluntary liquidation)* (1998) Shanley J., in the interests of "promoting rather than restricting" the remedy available under section 150(1) of the Companies Act 1990, held that any one of the class of persons entitled to bring an application for a disqualification order under section 160(4) of the Companies Act 1990 (a member, contributory, officer, employee, receiver, liquidator, examiner of any company - see paragraph 8.2.4) could bring an application under section 150, as the legislature would have intended these applicants to have a "like interest in relation to applications to restrict directors." Section 150(4A) now clarifies the class of persons with the *locus standi* to make the application for a restriction order.

It is open to the court to direct that the costs of the application (including any costs incurred in investigating the matter) be discharged by the director against whom a restriction order is made (section 150(4B) of the Companies Act 1990 as inserted by section 41 of the Company Law Enforcement Act 2001). This provision addresses creditors' concerns about the dilution of the remaining company funds during court applications.

The liquidator is obliged to notify the court if the restricted director is acting as a director, secretary, or promoter of any other company and he is of the opinion that the interests of that other company or its creditors are in jeopardy as a result. The court may make whatever order it deems fit under section 151 of the Companies Act 1990. Failure to so notify the court is an offence.

8.1.2 Director defences

Once the court is satisfied that the company is in insolvent liquidation and that the person sought to be restricted is a director/shadow director of that company, the applicant is entitled to a restriction order unless the court is satisfied of one of the following:

1. the director/shadow director has acted honestly and responsibly in relation to the affairs of the company and there is no other reason why it is just and equitable to make a restriction order; or

2. the director/shadow director held that position solely as a nominee of a financial institution who has provided credit facilities to the company *and* the financial institution was not given any personal guarantee by a director for those credit facilities; or

3. the director/shadow director held that position solely as a nominee of a venture capital company who has purchased shares in the company.

According to Shanley J. in *Re Steamline Ltd (in voluntary liquidation)* (1998) the burden is on the directors to prove that they acted honestly and responsibly. The meaning of "honestly and responsibly" has been examined by the courts. In *La Moselle Clothing Ltd (in liquidation) and Rosegem Ltd (in liquidation) v. Djarnel Soualhi* (1998) Shanley J. stated that "the simple fact that a company fails is not evidence of a lack of responsibility nor indeed is it evidence of dishonesty". He stated that "a director, broadly complying with his obligations under the provisions of the Companies Acts and acting with a degree of commercial probity during his tenure as a director of the company, will not be restricted on the grounds that he has acted irresponsibly." However, in the case before him Shanley J. felt that the director of two companies had not acted honestly and responsibly. The factors which influenced him to make the order included *inter alia:*

1. the director made no attempt to wind up the companies or to stop trading, even though it was clear the companies were insolvent;

2. there were a number of withdrawals and unaccounted for expenses made at a time when the company was clearly insolvent;

3. the director forgave debts owed by related companies;

4. the director was also very unforthcoming with the books and records of the companies after it was placed in liquidation.

Shanley J. set out five factors that should be considered in deciding whether the directors have acted responsibly:

1. the extent to which the director has or has not complied with any obligation imposed on him by the Companies Acts ;
2. the extent to which his conduct could be regarded as so incompetent as to amount to irresponsibility;
3. the extent of his responsibility for the company's insolvency;
4. the extent of his responsibility for the net deficiency in the company's assets at the time of its winding up or thereafter;
5. the extent to which his conduct of the affairs of the company has displayed a lack of commercial probity or want of proper standards.

In *Re Dunleckney Ltd* (1999) Carroll J. was satisfied that a failure by a director to fulfil the statutory obligation to file a statement of affairs, and the director's subsequent failure to explain why this had not been done, constituted sufficient reason to impose a restriction order.

In *Re Squash (Ireland) Ltd* (2001) McGuinness J. stated that whether or not a director had acted responsibly was to be judged by an objective standard. She stated that in relation to insolvent companies "commercial errors may have occurred, misjudgments may well have been made; but to categorise conduct as irresponsible I feel that one must go further than this". She endorsed the five factors set out by Shanley J. in *La Moselle*. While she felt that the directors' conduct was open to criticism in this case, she did not feel that it merited a restriction order. In *Re Steamline Ltd (in voluntary liquidation)* (1998) the court refused the application for a restriction order as the directors had proved to the satisfaction of the court that they held an honest belief in the ability of the company to survive and prosper, displayed no want of commercial probity, and they did nothing to contribute to the insolvency of the company.

In *Re Gasco Ltd* (2001) McCracken J. considered an application for a restriction order in respect of two directors and one shadow director where the liquidator had found virtually no books and records of the company. McCracken J. found a clear implication that there had been no records or that they had been destroyed. The lack of records meant that the liquidator could not find evidence of substantial payments made to the company and that this was evidence of serious irresponsibility. He made a restriction order in respect of the shadow director. In refusing to restrict the second director, McCracken J. accepted the evidence of that director that he had recognised serious problems in the company, that he had assisted in drawing up a business plan and, when he realised it was inadequate, he refused to go along with it, and that he had then been effectively excluded from the management of the company and had later resigned. While finding that the third director was naïve, he found that he had relied on the other directors and, on the balance, he had acted honestly and responsibly.

In *Re Costello Doors Ltd* (1995) Murphy J. stated that the maintenance of proper books and accounts and the employment of appropriate experts would go a long way to discharge the onus that the directors behaved responsibly.

Non-executive directors are clearly covered by the ambit of section 150 of the Companies Act 1990. Murphy J. in *Re Costello Doors Ltd* (1995) commented *obiter* that it is not good enough for a director to plead non-involvement with the company, stating:

> "I do not accept that anybody who agrees to act as director of a company can be excused from acting responsibly merely because he or she is a friend, relative or spouse of the proprietor of the company and accepts the office to facilitate the proprietor without being prepared to involve himself or herself in any aspect of the management of the company."

This view was endorsed in *Re Vehicle Imports Ltd* (2000) where Murphy J. stated that there was no doubt that the duties of directors extended to non-executive directors and that the conduct of the latter should be examined to ascertain whether or not it was responsible.

8.1.3 Duration of the restriction

As noted above, the period of the restriction order is set out as five years. In the light of *Business Communications Ltd v. Baxter & Parsons* (1995), it appears that the court does not have the discretion to make a restriction order for a shorter period.

The question of when the five years should commence was considered in *Duignan v. Carway* (2000). The liquidator issued a motion seeking a restriction order but he failed to proceed with the motion for a further five years. When the liquidator sought to reactivate the motion, the directors made an unsuccessful application to the court to have the motion dismissed on the grounds of delay. O'Donovan J. dismissed the argument that the restriction order must date from the commencement of the proceedings and held that the five-year period commences whenever the court says it is to commence. On the question of delay, O'Donovan J. found that the delay was inordinate and inexcusable. However, he referred to the case of *Primor plc v. Stokes Kennedy Crowley* (1996) where the Supreme Court held that "even where the delay was both inordinate and inexcusable, the court must exercise a judgment on whether in its discretion, on the facts the balance of justice was in favour of or against the case proceeding". O'Donovan exercised his discretion and allowed the section 150 motion to proceed. He found that the directors' plea of general prejudice arising from the delay, *i.e.* the imputation that they were not honest and responsible, was not sufficient. Evidence of specific prejudice suffered as a result of the delay should have been put before the court. Further, he was influenced by the fact that the public interest requires that unsuitable persons should not be directors, and that public interest would overcome the delay in any case.

8.1.4 Section 152 and lifting the order

Section 152(1) of the Companies Act 1990 permits the restricted person to apply to the court for a lifting of the order and the court may accede to the application if it is just and equitable to do so and on whatever conditions it deems appropriate. The application must, however, be made within one year of the court making the restriction order.

In *Robinson v. Forrest* (1999) a restriction order was sought in respect of two directors. One of the directors contested the application. Shanley J. held that he had acted honestly, but not responsibly and he was restricted. Shanley J. placed a stay (a period of postponement) on the restriction order affecting this director. Notwithstanding the fact that the restriction order was not yet effective, the director applied to the court under section 152. Laffoy J. allowed the application and lifted the order on just and equitable grounds. She was influenced by the fact that Shanley J. had placed a stay on the order in the first place and, further, she believed that the deterrent effect of the order had been achieved. The director had argued *inter alia* that he had established another company and was a director on the board, it was his sole means of livelihood, and it was fully tax compliant.

The applicant is obliged by section 152(2) of the Companies Act 1990 to notify the liquidator of the company the insolvency of which caused him to be restricted. The liquidator must in turn notify the creditors and the contributories of the company who are entitled to appear at a section 152 hearing and give evidence.

8.1.5 Acting when restricted

The restricted company may, under certain conditions, go on to work for another company. Where a company (the "new" company) complies with the minimum capital requirements set out in section 150(3) of the Companies Act 1990 (as increased by the Company Law Enforcement Act 2001), a restricted director may act as its director, secretary, or promoter. Pursuant to section 150(3), a plc must have a minimum paid-up share capital of €317,500, and any other company must have a minimum paid up share capital of €63,500.

Section 155(5) obliges the restricted director, at least fourteen days prior to his appointment, to give notice to the new company that he is a restricted person under section 150 of the Companies Act 1990.

Section 163 (4) deals with the situation where the new company receives this notice and proceeds with the appointment without putting these capital requirements in place within a "reasonable period" *and* the new company goes into insolvent liquidation. The liquidator, a contributory, or a creditor of the company may a apply to the court for an order that every officer of the company, who knew or ought to have known that the company had been so notified, shall be personally liable for such debts of the company as the court may direct. The court may grant relief to such an officer where it is just and equitable to do so.

On the appointment of the restricted person, section 155 states that the new company cannot exercise the following statutory rights:

1. the exceptions available under section 60(2) of the Companies Act 1963 permitting a company to provide financial assistance in the purchase of its own shares (see Chapter 15);
2. the power to allot shares for non-cash consideration; and
3. the exceptions available under sections 32-37 of the Companies Act 1990 permitting a company to give a loan, quasi-loan or credit transaction to a director or a person connected with a director (see Chapter 7).

It is open to the new company to apply for relief to the court under section 157 of the Companies Act 1990 in respect of an act or omission in breach of section 155. The court will grant relief where it is just and equitable to do so. However, where the new company received notice from the restricted director that he was so restricted, the company is not entitled to relief under this section. Section 157 also grants *locus standi* to any person adversely affected by the breach to apply to the court for relief.

Section 161(5) deals with the situation where this new company goes into insolvent liquidation after the restricted person has been appointed. Where the new company goes into insolvent liquidation within five years of the winding up of the company that caused the director to be restricted in the first place, the liquidator of the new company must report this matter to the court. The court has the discretion to disqualify the restricted director for such period as it thinks fit.

8.1.6 Breach of the order

Section 161 states that a breach of a restriction order is an offence and the restricted person shall be disqualified for a period of five years or for whatever period decided by the court where he is convicted on indictment. Where the restricted director acts for a company in breach of the section 150 restriction, the company may recover any payments made to the restricted person. Where the company goes into insolvent liquidation while that person is acting for the company or within twelve months of that person so acting, the liquidator or a creditor of the company may apply to the court for an order that the restricted person be made personally liable for the debts of the company incurred during the involvement of the restricted person (section 163(3) of the Companies Act 1990).

8.2 Disqualification orders

Section 159 of the Companies Act 1990 defines a disqualification order as the disqualification from acting as an auditor, director, officer, receiver, liquidator, examiner (or any other capacity) in relation to any company, and the disqualification from taking part in the promotion, formation or management, either directly or indirectly, of any company. A person affected by a disqualification order may apply to the court for relief pursuant to section 160(8) of the Companies Act 1990, and the court may grant such relief where it is just and equitable to so. Disqualification orders have a wider remit than restriction orders as the latter are limited to company directors.

The disqualification order must be notified to the Registrar of Companies who must keep a register of the persons subject to a disqualification order under section 168 of the Companies Act 1990.

8.2.1 Automatic disqualification

Sections 160(1) and 160(1A) of the Companies Act 1990 (as amended by sections 14 and 42 of the Company Law Enforcement Act 2001) provide for the automatic disqualification of a person.

Section 160(1) states that a person who is convicted of an indictable offence in relation to a company or an offence involving fraud or dishonesty (whether in connection with a company or not) shall be subject to a disqualification order for five years from the date of the conviction or for such period as the court directs.

Section 160(1A) states that a person who fails to deliver details of any disqualification in another jurisdiction to the Registrar of Companies when delivering a statement of directors (section 3A(1) of the Companies (Amendment) Act 1982) or a notification of appointment of directors (section 195(8) of the Companies Act 1963), or who delivers false or misleading details, shall be deemed to be disqualified. The period of disqualification shall be the unexpired period of disqualification set out in the foreign disqualification order (section 160(1B)).

8.2.2 Court-ordered disqualification

Pursuant to section 160(2) of the Companies Act 1990, a disqualification order may be made by the court on its own initiative, or further to an application by specified persons. In the latter case the applicant is obliged by section 160(7) to give ten days' notice to the person in respect of whom the application is intended. In the English case of *Secretary of State for Trade and Industry v. Langridge* (1991) the equivalent provision requiring ten days' notice was held directory and not mandatory in character, *i.e.* the failure to give notice is a procedural irregularity and not something that renders the order void or voidable.

Unlike restriction orders, the court may exercise its discretion concerning the length o*f the disqualification. In Re Sevenoaks Stationers (Retail) Ltd* (1990) it was held that a serious disqualification should warrant ten years, with lesser offences getting six to ten years, and two to five years. It is open to the court to impose a restriction order in lieu of a disqualification order (section 160(9A) of the Companies Act 1990).

8.2.3 Court grounds

The grounds that may be pleaded for a court ordered disqualification are as follows:

1. fraud - section 160(2)(a): where a person is guilty of fraud in relation to the company, its members or creditors, while acting as a promoter, officer, auditor, receiver, liquidator, or examiner of the company;

2. breach of duty - section 160(2)(b): where a person is guilty of any breach of duty while acting as a promoter, officer, auditor, receiver, liquidator, or examiner of any company;

3. fraudulent/reckless trading - section 160(2)(c): where a person has been declared personally liable for the debts of a company as a result of fraudulent or reckless trading under section 297A of the Companies Act 1963;

4. unfitness to manage - section 160(2)(d): where the conduct of any person while acting as a promoter, officer, auditor, receiver, liquidator, or examiner makes him unfit to be concerned in the management of a company;

5. inspector's report - section 160(2)(e): where, in the light of an inspector's report, the conduct of the person makes him unfit to be concerned in the management of the company;

6. default under the Companies Acts - section 160(2)(f): where a person has persistently been in default in relation to the "relevant requirements" defined as failing to file/deliver to the Registrar of Companies any return, account, or other document as required under the Companies Acts. This will be "conclusively proved" by showing that within the five years preceding the application for disqualification, the person has been found guilty of three or more defaults in relation to those requirements (section 160(3)(a) and (b));

7. books of account - section 160(2)(g): where a person has been guilty of two or more offences under section 202(10) of the Companies Act 1990 for failing to keep proper books of account;

8. striking off of a company - section 160(2)(h): where a person was a director of a company when the company received a letter warning that it would be struck off the register of companies (see

Chapter 22) and that company was later struck off the register under section 12 of the Companies (Amendment) Act 1982. According to section 160(3A) a person will not be disqualified under this ground where he can show to the court that the company had no liabilities when it was struck off or that any liabilities existing at that time were discharged prior to the application for the disqualification order.

9. disqualified in another jurisdiction - section 160(2)(i): where a person is disqualified under the law of another state from acting as a director or secretary of a body corporate and the court is satisfied that if the conduct that gave rise to the said order had occurred or arisen in the State, it would have been proper to disqualify that person. A person may be disqualified under this ground notwithstanding that he is already subject to a disqualification order under section 160(1A). Where a person is also disqualified under section 160(2)(i), the period of disqualification will begin on the expiry of the period of disqualification set out in section 160(1B) (see paragraph 8.2.1).

8.2.4 Court applicants

The persons that have *locus standi* to make the applications under the above grounds are set out in sections 160(4), 160(5), 160(6) and 160(6A) of the Companies Act 1990 and are as follows:

1. the Director of Corporate Enforcement may make an application for a disqualification order under any of the grounds as set out in section 160(6A);

2. the Director of Public Prosecutions may make a disqualification application pursuant to grounds as set out in paragraphs (a), (b), (c), (d), (e), (f) and (g);

3. the Registrar of Companies may make an application under ground (f);

4. in respect of grounds (a), (b), (c) and (d) an application may be made by the members, the contributories, the creditors, officers, employees, receivers, liquidators, examiners, or creditors of any company in respect of which the person, whom it is sought to have disqualified, has, or is proposing to, act as officer, auditor, receiver, liquidator or examiner, or has been or is concerned or taking part, or is proposing to be concerned or take part, in the

promotion, formation or management. Where the application is made by a member, contributory, employee, or creditor, the court may require security for the costs of the application.

Pursuant to section 160(9B) of the Companies Act 1990, the court may order that any person disqualified, or alternatively restricted under section 150, may be ordered to discharge the costs of the application, and in some cases this may include the costs of investigating the matter prior to the application.

8.2.5 Liability for breach of the order

Section 161(1) of the Companies Act 1990 states that the breach of a disqualification order is an offence and under section 161(3) that person will have his period of disqualification extended for a further ten years. According to section 163 of the Companies Act 1990, where a person acts for a company in breach of a disqualification order, the company may recover any payments made to the disqualified person. Where the company goes into insolvent liquidation while that person is acting for the company or within twelve months of that person so acting, the liquidator or a creditor of the company may apply to the court for an order that the disqualified person be made personally liable for the debts of the company incurred during the involvement of the disqualified person (section 163(3) of the Companies Act 1990).

Section 164 of the Companies Act 1990 criminalises the behaviour of any person who acts on the directions or instructions of a disqualified person, and under section 165 that person may be made personally liable for the debts of the company incurred during the period while he was so acting.

8.2.6 Disqualifying conduct

In *Re Newcastle Timber Ltd and Atwood Ltd* (2001) McCracken J. stated that the purpose of the provision was not to punish the individual but to protect the public against the future conduct of companies by persons whose past record as directors has shown them to be a danger to creditors and others.

Murphy J. in *Business Communications Ltd v. Baxter & Parson* (1995) stated that the directors had a much stronger burden of proof to satisfy the court that they should not be disqualified.

In *Re Cladrose Ltd* (1990) Harman J. stated:

> "[The power to disqualify] is a power to be exercised to protect the public against those who display lack of commercial probity, rip-off the public in colloquial terms or otherwise shelter a totally rash and unjustified venture behind the shield of limited liability so that they themselves do not suffer when their rash venture fails, as was predictable, but leave the creditors at large to suffer."

In *Re Bath Glass Ltd* (1988) Peter Gibson J. considered that, on an application for a disqualification order, the court could look at the conduct of the director as a director of other companies, in addition to the insolvent company, in order to determine whether there was conduct that would justify the making of a disqualification order. The court stated that the conduct of the directors must be sufficiently serious to conclude that the director is unfit to be concerned in the management of a company:

> "[T]he court must be satisfied that the director was guilty of a serious failure or failures whether deliberately or through incompetence, to perform those duties of directors which are attendant on the privilege of trading through companies with limited liability."

This will depend upon all the circumstances of the case. The incurring of debts will not of itself be indicative of unfitness unless the directors knew or ought to have known the company was trading while insolvent at the risk of creditors. In this case the fact that there was no dishonesty, that the directors made financial commitments to the company themselves, that they produced regular forecasts and budgets regarding the company, and that they believed the company could continue to trade not without rational foundations, influenced the court. The court concluded that the conduct was not sufficiently serious to make them unfit to be concerned in the management of a company.

In *Re Keypak Homecare Ltd* (1990) the court emphasised that mere commercial misjudgment was not sufficient to render the persons unfit. They must display "a lack of commercial probity, but that may include gross negligence or total incompetence". While the directors in this case were unfit to be involved in the management of a company, and should therefore be disqualified, Harmon J. considered that they did make substantial efforts to mitigate the wrong, resulting in the creditors recovering quite a large proportion of the debts owed to them.

In *Re Landhurst Leasing* plc (1999) it was held that gross negligence, which did not import any dishonesty or contravention of commercial morality, was sufficient grounds for disqualification. It appears that the Irish courts are in agreement as Shanley J. did comment *obiter* in *La Moselle Clothing Ltd (in liquidation) and Rosegem Ltd (in liqui-*

dation) v. Djarnel Soualhi (1998) that "in an extreme case of gross negligence or total incompetence, disqualification could be appropriate." This is supported by McCracken J. in *Re Newcastle Timber Ltd and Atwood Ltd* (2001).

In *Re Bradcrown Ltd; Official Receiver v. Ireland* (2001) the court held that the leaving of all relevant judgments to professional advisers could amount to an abdication of responsibility for which a director should be punished by disqualification. In this case the director had relied on professional advice but had not asked any questions and had thereby abdicated responsibility. He was disqualified for two years.

In *Re CB Readymix Ltd; Cahill (official liquidation) v. Grimes* (2002) the Supreme Court confirmed that a *de facto* liquidator could be disqualified and, further, held that it was permissible for the High Court in making disqualification orders to distinguish between different offices and to impose conditions on the exercise of any particular office.

A nominee director may also be disqualified. In the English case of *Official Receiver v. Vass and anor* (1999) Blackburne J. disqualified a nominee director of a company that went into liquidation from acting as a director for twelve years. The nominee director was a nominee director of 1,313 English companies and a secretary of 513 English companies. The court held that the fact that he had held himself out as a director of so many companies and had abrogated his responsibilities for those companies by reason of merely acting as a nominee, was an extremely serious matter and was deserving of a substantial period of disqualification.

As stated above, the court has the discretion to impose a restriction order where the conduct of the directors does not justify a disqualification order (see *Re Newcastle Timber Ltd and Atwood Ltd* (2001)).

9. COMPANY ACCOUNTS, AUDITORS AND ANNUAL RETURNS

9.1 Company accounts

9.1.1 Books of account

Sections 202 to 204 of the Companies Act 1990 (replacing section 147 of the Companies Act 1963) set out the requirements for keeping proper books of account. According to section 202 of the Companies Act 1990, every company must keep proper books of account on a continuous and consistent basis that

1. correctly record and explain the transactions of the company;
2. will at any time enable the financial position of the company to be determined with reasonable accuracy;
3. will enable the directors to ensure that any balance sheet, profit and loss account, or income and expenditure account of the company complies with the requirements of the Companies Acts; and
4. will enable the accounts of the company to be properly audited.

The books of account must give "a true and fair view of the state of the affairs of the company and explain its transactions". In particular there must be

1. an entry of all sums received and expended daily by the company;
2. a record of the assets and liabilities of the company;
3. a record of all goods purchased and sold together with all invoices relating to the same;
4. a statement of all stock held by the company at the end of each financial year and a record of all stocktakings; and
5. a record of all services provided by the company, if services are provided, and a record of the attendant invoices.

The books of account must be kept at the registered office of the company or such other place as the directors think fit (section 202(5)). If the books of account are kept outside the State, accounts and returns that disclose the financial position of the company with reasonable accuracy must be kept at a place within the State (section 202(61)). The books of account or these accounts and returns must be open to inspection by an officer of the company at "reasonable times". According to section 202(9), the books of account must be preserved by the company for six years.

Where a company fails to comply with the above requirements and a director of the company fails to ensure such compliance (or is responsible for the default), that director will be guilty of an offence under section 202(10) of the Companies Act 1990 unless he can prove to the court that he had reasonable grounds for believing, and did believe, that a competent and reliable person was charged with the duty of ensuring that those requirements were observed. The director will not be sentenced to imprisonment for the offence unless the court is of the opinion that the offence was wilfully committed.

Where a company goes into insolvent liquidation, every officer of the company shall be guilty of an offence (section 203(1) of the Companies Act 1990) where the court is of the opinion that a contravention of section 202 has either:

1. contributed to the company's inability to pay its debts; or
2. has resulted in substantial uncertainty as to the assets and liabilities of the company; or
3. has substantially impeded the orderly winding up of the company.

Section 204 of the Companies Act 1990 deals with imposing personal liability for the debts of the company on the officers of the company in this situation. It is open to the liquidator, creditor or contributory of the company to make an application for the imposition of civil liability.

The court will not impose criminal liability (section 203(2)) and/or personal liability (section 204(4)) where the officer can prove that he took all reasonable steps to ensure compliance by the company with section 202 or that that he had reasonable grounds for believing, and did believe, that a competent and reliable person, acting under the supervision and control of a director of the company who was formally allocated such responsibility, was charged with the duty of ensuring that section 202 was complied with. When considering whether or not to impose personal liability on the officer, the court will consider the extent of the financial loss caused to the company by the contravention (see *Mehigan v. Duignan* (1997)).

In *Re Ashclad Ltd (In liquidation)* (2000) the official liquidator made an application to the court for a declaration of personal liability under section 204 of the Companies Act 1990 and a restriction order under section 150 of the same Act in respect of the company's directors. In relation to the books of account the liquidator established *inter alia* that bank statements, purchase ledgers, lodgments to the company's bank accounts, and the cheques payment book were not made available in relation to certain periods, the sales ledger was kept by the company but it was incomplete, cash payments to the company and certain direct debits were unaccounted for, audited accounts were missing and no records were kept in relation to PAYE or PRSI or VAT. The liquidator claimed that, as a result, he was unable to determine the financial position of the company with reasonable accuracy, together with the identity of suppliers to the company, the use to which monies of the company had been put, identity of the recipients of cash payments, and the identity and whereabouts of the assets and liabilities of the company. Geoghegan J. held that, as a consequence of those deficiencies, there was quite obviously substantial uncertainty as to the company's assets and liabilities and that its orderly winding up was being impeded. He found that at least £100,000 was wrongly withdrawn from the company, and he added £12,000 for the liquidator's expenses in trying to ascertain the assets and liabilities of the company. The court made a declaration of personal liability in the sum of £112,000 for the failure to keep proper books of account in contravention of section 202 of the Companies Act 1990. The directors were also restricted under section 150 of the Companies Act 1990 (See Chapter 8).

9.1.2 Annual accounts

Section 148 of the Companies Act 1963 requires every company to present a profit and loss account (and, where the company is not trading, an income and expenditure account) and balance sheet to every annual general meeting of the company. Failing to comply with this provision will render every director of the company guilty of an offence and he will not be sentenced to imprisonment for such an offence unless the court is of the opinion that the offence was committed wilfully. It is a defence to prove that he had reasonable grounds for believing, and did believe, that a competent and reliable person was charged with the duty of ensuring that this section was complied with.

According to section 3 of the Companies (Amendment) Act 1986, every balance sheet must give a "true and fair view" of the state of affairs of the company, and the profit and loss account must give a "true and fair" view of the profit and loss of the company for the financial year. Additional necessary information must be provided where the balance sheet/profit and loss account would not provide sufficient information to comply with this requirement. Section 4 of the Companies (Amendment) Act 1986 provides that every company's balance sheet and profit and loss account must contain the information set out in the Sixth Schedule to that Act.

The balance sheet must be set out in one of two formats detailed in the Sixth Schedule. The balance sheet will detail the share capital and debentures of the company, the fixed assets, the capital reserves and details of the company's indebtedness. The profit and loss account will detail the profits and losses of the company since the last statement, and it must be prepared in one of four formats set out in the Sixth Schedule. Less stringent requirements are put in place for medium- and small-sized firms (See Chapter 1 for a description of small and medium firms).

The annual accounts must be accompanied by an auditors' report under section 157 of the Companies Act 1963 (see paragraph 9.2.6 below). The annual accounts must also be accompanied by a directors' report under section 158 of the Companies Act 1963. The directors' report is a report on the state of affairs of the company and, where the company is a holding company, a report on the state of affairs of the company and its subsidiaries as a group. It must also set out the amount, if any, that the company should pay in dividends and the amount which the directors propose that the company should carry by way of capital reserves. It must also detail the companies in which the company holds shares where the shareholding consists of more than 20 per cent of the voting rights of the former. Pursuant to section 158(6A) of the Companies Act 1963 (as inserted by section 90 of the Company Law Enforcement Act 2001) the report must contain a statement of the measures taken by the directors to secure compliance with section 202 of the Companies Act 1990. The report must be signed by two directors. Failing to take reasonable steps to comply with this provision will render the director of the company guilty of an offence and he will not be sentenced to imprisonment for such an offence unless the court is of the opinion that the offence was committed wilfully. It is a defence to prove that he had reasonable grounds for believing, and did believe, that a competent and reliable person was charged with the duty of ensuring that this section was complied with (section 158(7) of the Companies Act 1963).

Section 13 of the Companies (Amendment) Act 1986 further requires that the report of the directors contain the following information:

1. a fair view of the development of the business of the company and its subsidiaries during the financial year;
2. particulars of any important events affecting the company and any of its subsidiaries since the end of the financial year;
3. an indication of likely future developments in the business of the company and its subsidiaries;
4. an indication of the activities of the company and its subsidiaries in the field of research and development;
5. an indication of branches of the company outside the State, indicating the country where they are situate.

Section 14 of the Companies (Amendment) Act 1986 requires that the directors' report set out the details of any purchase by the company of its own shares, whether by forfeiture or otherwise.

9.2 Company auditors

According to section 160(1) of the Companies Act 1963 every company is statutorily obliged to appoint an auditor at each annual general meeting of the company.

9.2.1 Appointment of auditors

Section 160(6) of the Companies Act 1963 provides that the directors of the company may make the first appointment of the company's auditor who holds office until the conclusion of the first annual general meeting. The first annual general meeting will then appoint the auditor who will hold the office until the conclusion of the next annual general meeting. The auditors of a company retire at every annual general meeting. However, section 160(2) provides that the retiring auditor, however appointed, shall be re-appointed without any resolution being passed unless

1. he is not qualified for re-appointment;

2. a resolution has been passed at that meeting appointing somebody instead of him or providing expressly that he shall not be re-appointed;

3. he has given the company notice in writing of his unwillingness to be re-appointed.

Where no auditors are appointed or re-appointed at an annual general meeting, the Minister may appoint a person to fill the vacancy and the burden is placed on the company under section 160(5A) of the Companies Act 1963 (as inserted by section 183 of the Companies Act 1990) to inform the Minister within one week that auditors must be appointed. The directors or the shareholders in a general meeting have the power to fill a casual vacancy arising in the office of auditor. Where a general meeting proposes to fill a vacancy, extended notice, *i.e.* twenty-eight days, must be given to the company (section 161(1)(c) of the Companies Act 1963) and a copy of the notice must be sent to the auditor whose ceasing to hold the office caused the vacancy.

9.2.2 Remuneration of auditors

Section 160(8) of the Companies Act 1963 provides that the remuneration of the auditor of a company shall be as follows:

1. in the case of an auditor appointed by the directors or by the Minister, the remuneration may be agreed by the directors or by the Minister respectively;

2. subject to the above, remuneration shall be fixed by the members at a general meeting or in such manner as the members at the annual general meeting may determine. It is common for the annual general meeting to determine that the directors fix the remuneration.

9.2.3 Removal of auditors

Pursuant to section 160(6) of the Companies Act 1963 the first appointed auditor may be removed and replaced by the members at a general meeting. The members must give fourteen days' notice to the company of the person they have nominated to replace the first-appointed auditor. The latter must be given notice of the proposed removal, and he has the right to make the representations discussed below.

Further, under section 160(2) it is open to the members not to re-appoint an auditor at an annual general meeting. Extended notice of twenty-eight days is required where it is proposed to appoint an auditor other than a retiring auditor, or where it is expressly provided that a retiring auditor should not be re-appointed (section 161(1)(a)). Section 160(5) of the Companies Act 1963 (as inserted by section 183 of the Companies Act 1990) now provides that the auditors of a company may be removed at any time by the company by means of an ordinary resolution at a general meeting. Extended notice must also be given of such a resolution (section 161(1)(b)). A copy of the notice must be given to the retiring auditor or the auditor being removed.

Where notice of the proposed resolution is received, the auditor has the right pursuant to section 161(3) of the Companies Act 1963 to make written representations of "reasonable length" to the company which must be notified to the members. The company must send a copy of the representations to the members unless otherwise ordered by the court under section 161(4). The company or an aggrieved person may apply to the court to restrain the publication of the representations, and the court may do so where it is satisfied that the auditor is abusing the right to make representations in order "to secure needless publicity for a defamatory matter".

Under section 161 (2A) of the Companies Act 1963 (as inserted by section 184 of the Companies Act 1990) an auditor who has been removed has a right to attend, and be heard at, the general meeting at which it is proposed to fill the vacancy, he has a right to attend the next annual general meeting at which his office would have naturally expired, and he has the right to attend any meeting which concerns his business as a former auditor. The company is obliged to give notice of the resolution removing the auditor to the Registrar of Companies within fourteen days of the resolution being passed and failure to give such notice is an offence.

9.2.4 Retirement/resignation of auditors

Before the passing of the Companies Act 1990 an auditor could not retire during the year. He was obliged to wait until the next annual general meeting, at which stage he could indicate that he did not want to be re-appointed. Section 185 of the Companies Act 1990 now enables an auditor to resign by serving a notice to that effect on the company. This notice takes effect on the day specified on the notice. The statement must indicate that there are no circumstances connected with the resignation which the auditor considers should be brought to the notice of the members or creditors, or, alternatively, such circumstances should be stated.

The company must send a copy of the notice to the Registrar of Companies within fourteen days. Where the notice states that there are circumstances which should be brought to the attention of the members or creditors, the company must send a copy within fourteen days from service to every person who is entitled to be sent copies of the accounts. Failure to circulate a notice is a criminal offence and the company and every officer in default may be liable to penalties. The notice need not be circulated, however, where the court, on the application of the company or any person claiming to be aggrieved, is satisfied that it contains material which has been included to secure "needless publicity for a defamatory matter". In *Jarvis plc et al v PriceWaterhouseCoopers* (2001) the court considered section 394 of the English Companies Act 1985 which is similar to the Irish section 185. The auditors of a company sought to send a statement to the members of a company regarding their resignation. The company applied to the court claiming that the auditors were seeking needless publicity. Lightman J. considered that section 394 was designed to forewarn the public and not to protect auditors' goodwill. It was also held that it would be presumed that auditors who make a statutory statement were acting in faithful discharge of their duty and not for any ulterior purpose unless the contrary was shown.

An auditor resigning under these provisions may also, under section 186 of the Companies Act 1990, require the holding of a general meeting of the company for the purpose of considering any account or explanation he may wish to give the meeting of the circumstances connected with his resignation. He also has the same right to attend and be heard at company meetings as an auditor who has been removed (see paragraph 9.2.3) under section 186(5) of the Companies Act 1990.

9.2.4 Qualifications of auditors

Secion 187 of the Companies Act 1990 (as amended by section 72 of the Company Law Enforcement Act 2001) outlines the qualifications required before a person can act as the auditor of a company. Section 187 (1) provides that a person shall not be appointed as an auditor of a company unless at least one of the following conditions are met:

1. he is a member of a body of accountants recognised by the Minister for the purposes of the section who holds a valid practising

certificate from such a body (bodies recognised by the Minister include the Institutes of Chartered Accountants in Ireland, Scotland, England and Wales, the Institute of Certified Public Accountants in Ireland, and the Chartered Association of Certified Accountants);

2. he holds an accountancy qualification which in the opinion of the Minister is not less than that required for membership of such bodies and would entitle him to be granted a practising certificate by such bodies of accountants;
3. he was authorised by the Minister before February 3, 1993, and is for the time being authorised by the Minister to act;
4. he is a person undergoing training and will later obtain a practising certificate;
5. he is a person declared by the Minister to be so qualified to act as an auditor as he holds either a qualification entitling him to audit accounts under the law of a specified foreign country or a specified accountancy qualification recognised under the law of another country.

Section 187(2) of the Companies Act 1990 outlines the categories of persons who are disqualified from appointment as auditors. These include the following:

1. an officer or servant of the company, *e.g.* a director or secretary;
2. a person who has been either an officer or a servant during a period in respect of which accounts would have to be audited by him if he were an auditor;
3. a parent, spouse, brother, sister or child of an officer of the company;
4. a person who is a partner of, or is in the employment of, an officer of the company;
5. a person who is disqualified from acting as an auditor of the company's holding company or one or more of its subsidiaries;
6. a body corporate.

If a person becomes so disqualified during the term of his office, he must vacate the office and give notice in writing of the reason for his disqualification. Failure to give such a notice is an offence. The Director of Corporate Enforcement may request the auditor to produce evidence of his qualification, and if the same is not produced within thirty days or such longer period as the Director may allow, the auditor may be guilty of an offence according to section 187(12)(a) of the Companies Act 1990 as inserted by section 72 of the Company Law Enforcement Act 2001.

9.2.5 Rights of auditors

Section 163 of the Companies Act 1963 outlines that the auditor has the right of access at all reasonable times to the books and accounts of the company and he is entitled to require from the officers of the company such information and explanations as he thinks necessary for the performance of his duties as auditor. Every auditor is also entitled:

1. to attend any general meeting of the company;
2. to receive all notices of and other communications relating to any general meeting which any member of the company is entitled to receive;
3. to be heard at any general meeting that he attends on any part of the business of the meeting which concerns him as an auditor.

Under section 196 of the Companies Act 1990 subsidiaries (and their auditors) are now statutorily obliged to give information and explanations to the auditors of their holding companies where that information or explanation is reasonably required. This obligation only applies to subsidiaries incorporated within the State and in any other case the duty is on the holding company to obtain the requisite information or explanation. It is an offence if the company or the auditor fails to comply with the request within a period of five days. It is a defence under section 196(3) to plead that it was not reasonably possible for the officer to comply with the requirement within the five-day period, but that it was complied with as soon as it was reasonably possible to do so after the expiration of the five days.

Section 197 of the Companies Act 1990 makes it a criminal offence where false statements are made to the auditors of a company. An officer (a company employee is expressly included for this purpose) who knowingly or recklessly makes a statement that is "misleading, false or deceptive" is guilty of an offence. An offence is also committed where an officer fails to provide any information or explanation sought by the auditors within two days of the request where that information or knowledge is within his knowledge or procurement. It is a defence under section 197(4) to plead that it was not reasonably possible for the officer to comply with the requirement within the two-day period, but that it was complied with as soon as it was reasonably possible to do so after the expiration of the two-day period.

9.2.6 The Auditors' report

The auditors must report to the members on the accounts examined by them, and on every balance sheet, every profit and loss account, and all group accounts laid before the company in general meeting during their tenure of office. The report must contain statements as to the matters set out in the Seventh Schedule to the Companies Act 1963:

1. whether they have obtained all the information and explanations which, to the best of their knowledge and belief, were required for the purpose of their audit;

2. whether, in their opinion, proper books of account have been kept by the company so far as appears from their examination of those books;

3. whether the company's balance sheet and profit and loss account are in agreement with the books;

4. whether, in their opinion, and to the best of their information and according to the explanations given to them, the accounts give the information required by the Acts in the manner so required, and give a true and fair view, in the case of the balance sheet, of affairs at the year end and, in the case of the profit and loss account, of the profit or loss for the year; and

5. in the case of a holding company submitting group accounts, whether, in their opinion, the group accounts were properly prepared in accordance with the Acts and give a true and fair view of the state of affairs and profit or loss of the company and subsidiaries dealt with thereby, so far as concerns the members of the company.

Under section 15 of the Companies (Amendment) Act 1986 the auditors must state whether, in their opinion, the information given in the directors' report is consistent with the accounts for that financial year.

9.2.7 Liability of auditors

In *Re Kingston Cotton Mill Co. (No. 2)* (1896) Lopes L.J. stated that "an auditor is not bound to be a detective - he is a watchdog but he is not a bloodhound". In *Thomas Gerrard & Sons Ltd (1968)* the auditors gave an unqualified report based on stock figures which had been falsified by a director. This falsification was done by including non-existent stock and by altering invoices. It was held that the auditors were under a duty to make an exhaustive inquiry once they had come across the altered invoices. Having failed to do so, they were liable to the company for the cost of recovering excess tax paid and for dividends and tax not recovered, since this loss was the natural and probable result of the breach of duty. Therefore, an auditor must act as a reasonably careful and competent auditor would act and he is liable to the company for a loss caused by negligent performance of his duty.

An auditor cannot be exempted by the company from such liability according to section 200 of the Companies Act 1963. However, the court may relieve him of such liability if he is found to have acted honestly and reasonably (section 391 of the Companies Act 1963).

This duty was extended to the prospective purchasers of the company's shares in *Sisk (John) & Son Ltd v. Flinn* (1984). Here the plaintiff claimed, and it was accepted by the court, that the auditors owed a duty to take reasonable care in auditing the accounts of the company and that this duty was owed not only to the company itself but also to prospective purchasers of shares in the company. It was held that auditors know, or ought to know, that the accounts that they audit will be relied on by prospective purchasers in deciding whether to buy shares in the company. In *Kelly v. Haughey Boland & Co.* (1989) the defendant auditors had failed to attend and observe a client company's stocktaking for over twenty years. Purchasers of the company suffered loss as a consequence of inaccurate stock figures in the accounts. The court held that the test is whether the auditors knew, or reasonably should have foreseen, at the time that the accounts were audited, that a person might rely on the accounts. However, the House of Lords in *Caparo Industries plc v. Dickman* (1990) sought to impose a limit on the potential liability of auditors by declining to accept that auditors owed a duty of care to all prospective investors.

In *Killick and anor v. Pricewaterhouse Coopers (a firm)* (2001) the court held that an auditor owed a duty to shareholders in the circumstances of the case. Here the articles of association of the company provided that if a shareholder wished to transfer his shares, they have to be offered in the first instance to the company's employee trust, the company itself or shareholders selected by the directors at a market price determined by the company's auditor. A shareholder died triggering a compulsory sale of the shares. The auditors valued the shares at £2.10 each and they were sold to the company's employee trust for that price. The shareholder's executors had valued the shares at £4.00 and they successfully sued the auditors for damages. Neuberger J. stated that the auditor in these circumstances did owe a duty of care to the shareholders in the conduct of the valuation.

Section 194(1) of the Companies Act 1990 (as amended by section 74 of the Company Law Enforcement Act 2001) places a duty on the company auditors where the company is not keeping proper books of account under section 202 of the Companies Act 1990. Where the auditors form the opinion that the company is not acting in accordance with section 202 they must serve a notice to that effect on the company "as soon as may be", and must also notify the Registrar of Companies within seven days of the notice. If the auditors fail to take such steps, a criminal offence is committed, and certain penalties are stipulated. They do not have to take these steps if the contraventions are minor or immaterial.

There is also a new obligation (inserted by section 74 of the Company Law Enforcement Act 2001) which came into force in November 2001. Section 194(5) of the Companies Act 1990 now requires auditors to report to the Director of Corporate Enforcement where they have reasonable grounds for believing that the company, or an officer or agent of the company has committed an indictable offence under the Companies Acts. The reporting obligation is underpinned by a corresponding protection to auditors where they are required to make a report to the Director. This portection is set out in section 194(6) of the Companies Act 1990 which states that no professional or legal duty to which an auditor is subject by virtue of his appointment as an auditor of a company shall be regarded as contravened by, and no liability to the company, its shareholders, creditors or other interested parties shall attach to, an auditor, by reason of his compliance with an obligation imposed on him by or under this section. The Director of Corporate Enforcement has issued a Decision Notice (Decision Notice D/2002/2) on the operation of section 194(5) which is a comprehensive document examining the section and setting out the auditors' obligation. Appendix 2 of the Notice sets out a complete schedule of all indictable offences under the Companies Acts 1963-2001 and it includes an

Indictable Offences Report Form which auditors are invited to use in reporting the commission of indictable offences to the Director.

Under section 192(6) of the Companies Act 1990 (as amended by section 73 of the Company Law Enforcement Act 2001), where a disciplinary committee or a tribunal of a body of accountants has reasonable grounds for believing that an auditor has committed an offence under the Companies Acts, that committee or tribunal must provide a report to the Director of Corporate Enforcement.

9.2.8 Exemption to obligation to appoint an auditor

In certain cases a small company may be exempt from the statutory obligation to have its annual accounts audited. Under section 32 of the Companies (Amendment) (No.2) Act 1999, where directors of a private company are of the opinion that the conditions in section 32(3) are satisfied by the company in respect of a financial year (and the preceding financial year), then the company is exempted from the requirement to appoint an auditor under section 160 of the Companies Act 1963. The conditions set out at section 32(3) include *inter alia* that the amount of the company turnover does not exceed €317,500, the balance sheet of the company does not exceed €1,905,000, the number of employees does not exceed fifty, and the company is not a subsidiary of another.

Under section 33 of the Companies (Amendment) (No.2) Act 1999, any member or members of the company holding one-tenth or more of the total voting rights may prevent the company from availing of the exemption in a given year. It is open to these members to request that the accounts of the company are audited and that the exemption is not availed of by the company.

Section 34 provides that a company may discontinue the appointment of a person as an auditor where it avails of the exemption and that auditor is required to serve a notice on the company to the effect that there are no circumstances which would affect the decision to be exempted from the obligation to audit. If there are any such circumstances, they must be stated in the notice. Under section 35 the company must appoint an auditor as soon as possible after it becomes clear that any of the conditions necessary for availing of an exemption no longer apply during a year in which it is being availed of. Failure to comply with these provisions is an offence.

9.3 Annual returns

Section 125 of the Companies Act 1963 was amended and replaced by section 59 of the Company Law Enforcement Act 2001. Under the new section 125(1) of the Companies Act 1963 every company must make an annual return to the Registrar of Companies "once at least in every year". The annual return is in effect the publication of the affairs of the company. If a company fails to comply with this obligation, section 125(2) of the Companies Act 1963 provides that it is an offence and that the Registrar of Companies can prosecute some or all of the following:

- the company;
- every officer of the company who is in default;
- any person in accordance with whose directions or instructions the directors of the company are accustomed to act (shadow directors) and to whose directions or omissions the default is attributable.

9.3.1 Contents of the annual return

The annual return must include the following:

- the address of the registered office of the company;
- where the register of members is maintained;
- where the register of debentures is maintained;
- a statement of the total indebtedness of the company in respect of all mortgages and charges required to be registered under section 99 of the Companies Act 1963 (see Chapter 17);
- the particulars of the directors and secretaries;
- if the company has a share capital, all the details of the share capital.

The documents to be annexed to the annual return are set out in section 128 of the Companies Act 1963 (as amended by section 244 of the Companies Act 1990) and they are as follows:

- a written copy of every balance sheet laid before the annual general meeting of the company held during the period to which the return relates as certified by both a director and a secretary of the company;

- certified copy of the auditors' report and the directors' report as it relates to each balance sheet;
- whenever these documents are in a language other than Irish or English, a translation in Irish or English certified in the prescribed manner to be the correct translation.

The requirements of section 128 do apply to a private company that is exempted from the requirement to have its accounts audited by virtue of section 32 of the Companies (Amendment) (No.2) Act 1999 discussed above. According to section 129 of the Companies Act 1963 a private company must annex a certificate signed by both a director and by a secretary of the company that the company has not, since the date of its last return or, in the case of its first return, since the date of incorporation, issued any invitation to the public to subscribe for any shares or debentures in the company.

9.3.2 Annual return date

The date when the annual return was to be filed with the Registrar of Companies was set out in section 127 of the Companies Act 1963. This section was also repealed and replaced by section 60 of the Company Law Enforcement Act 2001. Prior to the Company Law Enforcement Act 2001 the obligation of a company to file its annual return was linked to the holding of its annual general meeting and this was considered unsatisfactory by the Registrar of Companies. A company was required to hold an annual general meeting each year and to file a statutory return with annexed accounts made up to a date being fourteen days after the annual general meeting. The difficulty for the Registrar of Companies was that he was unaware of when a company held its annual general meeting and therefore he was unaware whether the company had missed the filing deadline.

The new section 127 of the Companies Act 1963 introduces the Annual Return Date, the ARD. This is a readily ascertainable date on which the company's annual return must be submitted to the Registrar of Companies each year. This will improve compliance as the Registrar of Companies will now be in a position to issue reminder notices. A company is given twenty-eight days from its ARD to file and register its statutory annual return. After the expiration of the twenty-eight days, the company will incur a late filing fee.

According to section 127(2) of the Companies Act 1963 an existing company will be allocated an ARD on the anniversary of the date of its most recent annual return prior to the commencement of section 60 of the Company Law Enforcement Act 2001. A new company which is incorporated after that commencement date will be allocated a first ARD six months after the date of incorporation of the company and no accounts must be attached to this annual return (section 127(5) and (7) of the Companies Act 1963). The subsequent ARD falls on the anniversary of that first annual return date (section 127(6) of the Companies Act 1963). The accounts which must accompany the second annual return shall cover a period commencing with the date of incorporation and ending not earlier than nine months prior to the date to which the annual return is made up.

An existing company may modify its ARD within twelve months of the commencement of section 60 of the Company Law Enforcement Act 2001 and it has the option of extending its ARD once in a five year period. The new ARD must be within six months of the current ARD.

If a company fails to comply with this obligation, section 127(12) of the Companies Act 1963 provides that it is an offence and that the Registrar of Companies (section 127(13) of the Companies Act 1963) can prosecute some or all of the following:

- the company;
- every officer of the company who is in default;
- any person in accordance with whose directions or instructions the directors of the company are accustomed to act (shadow directors) and to whose directions or omissions the default is attributable.

9.3.3 Late filing fee

The Companies (Fees) Order 2001 (S.I. 477/2001) provides for a progressively increasing late filing fee where an annual return is not received by the Registrar of Companies on time.

10. RECKLESS AND FRAUDULENT TRADING

The offence of "fraudulent trading" was prohibited by the old section 297 of the Companies Act 1963, but the provision was infrequently used against the officers of the company as the burden of proving "fraud" was considered unduly onerous. It was considered that the applicant had to discharge an almost criminal burden of proof in order to succeed. As a result of the changes introduced by the Companies Act 1990 the remit of the actions that may be taken against persons or officers of the company have been greatly extended. It is possible to pursue those involved in the company for personal liability for reckless or fraudulent trading and, in the appropriate case, criminal liability for fraudulent trading.

10.1 Reckless and fraudulent trading

According to section 297A(1) of the Companies Act 1963 (as inserted by section 138 of the Companies Act 1999) an application in respect of reckless and fraudulent trading may only be made where the company is in liquidation or where the company is in examinership under the Companies (Amendment) Act 1990. Section 251 of the Companies Act 1990 states that an application may be made where the company is not in liquidation and where either of the following applies:

1. A judgment, decree, or other order of the court in favour of a creditor remains unsatisfied.

2. It is proved to the court that the company is unable to pay its debts, taking into account contingent and prospective liabilities.

Under this section it must be clear to the court that the principal reason for the company not being wound up is the insufficiency of its assets.

The application under section 797A(1) of the Companies Act 1963 may be made by a receiver, examiner, liquidator, creditor or contributory of the company. In the case of an application under section 251 of the Companies Act 1990, the application to the court may also be made by the Director of Corporate Enforcement (section 251(2A) of the Companies Act 1990 as inserted by section 54 of the Company Law Enforcement Act 2001).

There are three important limitations on reckless trading applications:

1. in the case of a reckless trading application, the liquidation must be an insolvent liquidation according to section 297A(3)(a) of the Companies Act 1963;
2. where the application is made by a creditor or contributory of the company, the creditor or contributory of the company must be able to prove to the court that it suffered loss or damage as a result of the reckless behaviour complained of;
3. according to section 297A(8) of the Companies Act 1963, a reckless trading application cannot relate to the carrying on of the business of the company while it was under court protection, *i.e.* examinership.

As set out in Chapter 8, a person who is made liable for fraudulent or reckless trading may also be made subject to a disqualification order under section 160 of the Companies Act 1990.

10.2 Reckless trading

The Companies Act 1990 introduced for the first time the concept of civil liability for the reckless trading of a company. This means that it is open to the court to impose personal liability for all or part of the debts of the company on a person that the court believes is responsible for a company trading recklessly. Section 297A(1)(a) of the Companies Act 1963 (as inserted by section 138 of the Companies Act 1990) states that where "any person was, while an officer of the company, knowingly a party to the carrying on of any business of the company in a reckless manner", the court may impose personal liability for some or all of the company's debts on that person.

It is important to note that the declaration of personal liability for reckless trading may only be made in respect of an officer of the company. The term "officer" includes directors, secretaries, shadow directors, auditors, liquidators, and receivers. An application for fraudulent trading is not so limited.

10.2.1 Section 297A(1)(a) and the subjective test

Lynch J. in *Re Hefferon Kearns Ltd (No 2)* (1993) considered the meaning of the word "reckless". He referred to *Shawinigan v. Vodkins*

(1961), where it was stated that "recklessness is gross carelessness - the doing of something which in fact involves a risk whether the doer realises it or not: and the risk being such, having regard to all the circumstances, that the taking of that risk would be described in ordinary parlance as reckless." Lynch J. noted that this meaning of recklessness was approved in *Donovan v. Landys Ltd* (1963). These cases clearly considered recklessness objectively. The objective test means that a person is liable even where he does not contemplate risks of a course of action but a "reasonable man" would have contemplated those risks (this is called the "Caldwell" test of recklessness).

However, Lynch J. considered that the use of the word "knowingly" in section 297A(1)(a) of the Companies Act 1963 clearly suggested that a subjective test is to be applied when considering whether or not to make a declaration of personal liability under section 297A(1)(a). The subjective test means that a person is reckless only if he actually contemplates the risks involved in a course of action and goes on to consciously run those risks (this is called the "Cunningham" test of recklessness). Lynch J. stated that the inclusion of the word "knowingly" "requires that the director is party to carrying on the business in a manner which the director knows very well involves an obvious and serious risk of damage to others and yet ignores that risk because he does not really care whether such others suffer loss or damage or because his selfish desire to keep his own company alive overrides any concern which he ought to have for others."

10.2.2 Section 297A(2)(a) and (b) and the objective test

Section 297A(2) goes on to expand the reckless trading provision by stating that an officer will be "deemed" to have traded recklessly. *i.e.* to have been knowingly a party to the carrying on of the business of the company in a reckless manner if either of the following apply:

1. he was a party to the carrying on of such business and, having regard to the general knowledge, skill and experience that may be reasonably expected of a person in his position, he ought to have known that his actions and those of the company would cause loss to the creditors of the company, or any of them (section 297A(2)(a)); or

2. he was party to the contracting of a debt by the company and did not honestly believe on reasonable grounds that the company would be able to pay the debt when it fell due for payment as well

as all the other debts (taking into account contingent and prospective liabilities) (section 297A(2)(b)).

Lynch J. in *Re Hefferon Kearns Ltd (No. 2)* (1993) clearly felt that both of these provisions were to be treated objectively. Lynch J. believed that the use of the words "'general knowledge, skill and experience that may be reasonably expected of a person in his position" in section 297A(2)(a) and the words "reasonable grounds" in section 297A(2)(b) supported the conclusion that officers are to be judged by what "they ought to have known and not merely on what they in fact knew".

Before the court may make a declaration under section 297A(2)(b) above, the court will consider whether the creditor in question was, at the time the debt was incurred, aware of the company's financial state of affairs and, notwithstanding such awareness, nevertheless assented to the incurring of the debt (section 297A(4)). This section has the effect of limiting the effectiveness of section 297A(2)(b).

10.2.3 Section 297A(6) and relief

Pursuant to section 297A(6) of the Companies Act 1963, an officer of a company who is the subject of a declaration under section 297A(1)(a) may apply to the court for relief from personal liability on the grounds that he acted "honestly and responsibly" in relation to the conduct of the affairs of the company. The court has interpreted this section as meaning that the officer has to act both honestly, which is subjective, and responsibly which is judged objectively by the standards of the reasonable officer.

It should be emphasised that this section only refers to relief where a declaration is made under section 297A(1)(a). There is no mention of such relief where a declaration is made pursuant to sections 297A(2)(a) or (b). However, in *Re Hefferon Kearns* Lynch J. considered that the court retained its old common law discretion to grant relief where a person has acted honestly and responsibly and could grant relief in respect of a declaration made under sections 297A(2)(a) and (b).

10.2.4 Reckless trading

The combined effect of the above provisions is that it is open to the applicant to prove that a company officer knew or ought to have known that the company was trading in a reckless manner. It is then for the officer to prove that he acted not only honestly but also in accordance with the standards of the average reasonable officer.

In *Re Hefferon Kearns Ltd* the company went into examinership. It had three main contracts for construction work, but in the first six months the records showed a net loss. However, the directors were optimistic of its chances of success. Later in that year, two of the directors borrowed money to fund the company incurring personal liability. Later, the books of account displayed serious financial problems, and the directors decided that a review of the trading position was required. After that, they chose to prioritise one of the three contracts and, within some months, debts had been discharged. However, the company was still unable to make payments as they fell due, and it was decided that two of the contracts would be abandoned and the third pursued as the best means of ensuring repayment of the creditors. The minutes of that meeting indicate that the paramount objective was achieving fairness among the creditors. However, the attempts failed and the creditors appointed an examiner to the company. An application was made to the court seeking a declaration of personal liability for reckless trading.

Lynch J. considered the subjective nature of section 297A(1)(a) and that the director "had good reason to believe that the company would be able to pay all creditors falling due" and he was not satisfied that the director was knowingly party to the carrying on of the business of the company in a reckless manner within the meaning of section 297A(1)(a). In this regard he emphasised that the director was concerned about the effects on creditors of the state of affairs, had attempted to achieve profitable trading, had guaranteed the debts of the company, and was willing to surrender his shareholding for the benefit of the company.

In considering section 297A(2)(a), he stated that under this section there must be found a knowledge or imputed knowledge that the director's actions or those of the company would cause loss to creditors. In the circumstances of that case, Lynch J. concluded that the director had good reason to believe the company would be able to pay its creditors and that he reasonably expected no further losses to be incurred. There was, therefore, no evidence to satisfy this test of deemed recklessness in section 297A(2)(a).

In considering section 297A(2)(b), Lynch J. held that after a certain stage, it was apparent that the company would not be able to pay its debts as they fell due, and from then on the director was deemed to be trading recklessly within the meaning of this section. This finding was made despite the fact that the director was acting bona fide and in the interests of creditors. He went on to absolve the director form liability calling on the general discretion of the court mentioned above stating that it "would not be in the interests of the community that whenever there might appear to be any significant danger that a company was going to become insolvent, the directors should immediately cease trading and close down the business."

10.3 Fraudulent trading

Section 297A(1)(b) of the Companies Act 1963 (as inserted by section 138 of the Companies Act 1990) replaced the old provision providing for civil liability for fraudulent trading. It states that where "any person was knowingly a party to the carrying on of any business of the company with the intent to defraud creditors of the company, or creditors of any other person or for any fraudulent purpose", the court may impose personal liability for some or all of the company's debts on that person. As mentioned above the section is not limited to company officers.

This section has been interpreted as incorporating the subjective test by the use of the words "knowingly" and "intent". Therefore, the applicant for a declaration of personal liability for fraudulent trading must prove that the person actually believed that the company was trading fraudulently. This creates the danger that a person who sees nothing wrong with his conduct of the business may escape liability notwithstanding that the rest of the business community finds that conduct objectionable. However, in *Aktieselskabet Dansk Skibsfinansiering v. Brothers et al* (2001) the Court of Appeal in Hong Kong stated that that the person could not rely on a private standard of honesty not shared by the community. Yet the court cautioned that care had to be taken when invoking the reasonable man concept.

10.3.1 Intent to defraud

The question of what constitutes an intention to defraud was tackled by the English courts when considering the equivalent provision in English legislation. In *Re (WC) Bros Ltd* (1932) Maugham J. stated that "if a company continues to carry on business and to incur debts at a time when there is to the knowledge of the directors no reasonable prospect of the creditors ever receiving payment of their debts, it is in general a proper inference that the company is carrying on business with intent to defraud.' In *Re Patrick and Lyon Ltd* (1933) the requisite intent was considered as "actual dishonesty involving, according to current notions of fair trading among commercial men, real moral blame." This is in line with Dixon J. in the Australian case of *Hardie v. Hanson* (1960) where he stated that "the intent to defraud creditors must be express or actual or real, nothing constructive, imputed or implied will do."

The following Irish cases predate the changes introduced by the Companies Act 1990, but they continue to provide useful guidance to the meaning of "intent to defraud". In *Re Alimumin Fabricators Ltd* (1984) the company kept two separate sets of accounts, one for official use and the other for the private use of the company controllers. The directors also concealed payments to the company that were made in cash. O'Hanlon J. found that the directors in question should be personally liable without limitation of liability for the debts of the company. He stated that the privilege of limited liability should not be open to those who would use it as a cloak or a shield to conceal a fraudulent system of carrying on business for their own personal enrichment and benefit.

In *Re Kelly's Carpetdrome Ltd* (1983) there were no proper books of account and it appeared that financial documentation was being deliberately destroyed. The assets of the company transferred to a connected company to avoid the payment of revenue debts. Costello J. imposed personal liability for all the debts of the company.

In *Re Hunting Lodges Ltd* (1985) the main asset of the company, a pub called "Durty Nellies" was sold for the sum of £480,000. It was arranged that £200,000 of the purchase price would be paid directly to one of the directors and not to the company's account. Carroll J. held that the term "any business of the company" (as it appeared in the old section 297) did not require the existence of a course of dealing which was found to be fraudulent. The court held that a single transaction could be sufficient to come within the section. Carroll J. moreover stated that "it is not necessary that there should be a common agreed fraudulent intent. If each of the participants acts for a fraudulent purpose then each may be liable." Carroll J. found different levels of liability on the basis of different levels of involvement in the fraudulent behaviour. One director was found liable without limitation, and another's liability (a director's wife) was as little as £12,000.

Inaction by a person may not be sufficient to impose liability for fraudulent trading as in *Re Maidstone Building Provisions Ltd* (1971) the failure of the company's secretary or the company's financial adviser to warn the directors of the company's insolvency and its possible consequences was not held to justify a declaration of liability on the grounds of fraudulent trading. In *Morris v. Banque Arabe et Internationale d'Investissment SA (No. 2)* (2000) Neuberger J. stated that where it was sought to make a person, who was not an officer of the company, liable for fraudulent trading, it was necessary to show that the person had participated in the fraudulent acts of the company. It was not necessary to show that such a person carried on or assisted in the carrying on of the company's business. In *Morphites v. Bernasconi et al* (2001) the English Companies Court held that in order to establish "intent to defraud creditors" or "fraudulent purpose", a liquidator must establish (a) that the respondent took an active part in carrying on the relevant business of the company and in doing so he intended to defraud creditors, or (b) that he had some other fraudulent purpose and that he acted dishonestly. It was not necessary to prove that credit had in fact been incurred since it was not necessary to prove a victim's reliance on the fraud as in the case of the tort of deceit.

10.3.2 Criminal liability for fraudulent trading

Section 297(1) of the Companies Act 1963 (as amended by section 137 of the Companies Act 1990) states that if any person is knowingly a party to the carrying on of the business of a company with intent to defraud creditors of the company or creditors of any other person or for any fraudulent purpose, that person shall be guilty of an offence.

Section 297(2) sets out the penalties that can be imposed by the court. A prosecution under this section is not limited to where a company is in liquidation or examinership.

11. INSIDER DEALING

The statutory offence of insider dealing did not exist prior to the Companies Act 1990 and complaining shareholders had to make do with attempting to mould their case into a breach of fiduciary duty by the officers of the company. As noted in Chapter 7, this is not always an easy task as a special relationship between the officer/director and the shareholders must be established. The English legislation providing for criminal penalties for insider dealing was in place since 1980. In the light of the European Community Directive 89/592 requiring the co-ordination of regulations on insider dealings, Part V of the Companies Act 1990 introduced much needed legislation in this jurisdiction. The provisions of Part V outlaw insider dealing and put in place civil and criminal penalties for the offence.

11.1 Unlawful dealings by connected persons

Section 108(1) of the Companies Act 1990 states that it is unlawful for any person who is, or at any time in the last six months has been, connected with a company to deal in any securities of that company if, by reason of his so being, or having been, connected with that company, he is in possession of information that is not generally available, but, if it were, would be likely to materially affect the price of those securities ("material information").

11.1.1 Securities

Securities are defined in section 107 of the Companies Act 1990 to mean any shares, debentures, or other debt securities issued or proposed to be issued, whether in the State or otherwise and for which dealing facilities are, or are to be, provided on a recognised stock exchange, including any right, option or obligation in respect of those shares, debentures or debt securities.

11.1.2 Dealing

Dealing is defined in section 107 of the Companies Act 1990 to mean acquiring, disposing of, subscribing for or underwriting the securities, or making or offering to make, or inducing or attempting to induce a person to make or to offer to make an agreement of the following kind:

1. for or relating to acquiring, disposing of, subscribing for, or underwriting the securities; or

2. for the purpose, or the purported purpose, of securing a profit or gain to a person who acquires, disposes of, subscribes for, or underwrites the securities or to any of the parties of the agreement in relation to the securities.

11.1.3 Being "connected"

Section 108(11) of the Companies Act 1990 states that a person is "connected" with the company if any of the following apply:

1. he is an officer of the company or a related company. An officer includes a director (including a shadow director), secretary, employee, liquidator, examiner, auditor, receiver and any person administrating a compromise with creditors on behalf of the company;

2. he is a shareholder of the company or of a related company;

3. he occupies a position that may reasonably be expected to give him access to the material information because of a professional or business relationship with the company or a related company or because he is an officer of "substantial shareholders" in the company or a related company.

A related company is defined as a subsidiary or holding company or fellow subsidiaries. A substantial shareholder is one who holds more than the "notifiable percentage" set out in section 70 of the Companies Act 1990. The notifiable percentage is five per cent and where a shareholder obtains a shareholding in excess of five per cent he is under an obligation to notify the company.

11.1.4 Extension to other companies

Section 108(2) of the Companies Act 1990 states that it is unlawful for any person who is, or at any time in the last six months has been, connected with a company to deal in any securities of any other company if, by reason of his so being, or having been, connected with the first-mentioned company, he is in possession of material information that relates to any transaction (actual or contemplated) involving both those companies or involving one of them and the securities of the other, or to the fact that any such transaction is no longer contemplated.

11.2 Unlawful dealings by unconnected persons

Section 108(3) of the Companies Act 1990 prohibits a person who is in possession of material information in relation to securities from dealing in those securities if he has received the information either directly or indirectly from another person and he knows, or ought to have known, that the other person is a "connected" person and therefore precluded from dealing with those securities under sections 108(1) and (2).

A person precluded from dealing with securities by sections 108(1), (2) and/or (3) cannot procure another person to deal in those securities according to section 108(4) of the Companies Act 1990. Further, such a precluded person cannot communicate material information to any other person if he knows, or ought reasonably to know, that the other person will make use of the material information for the purpose of dealing, or causing or procuring another person to deal in those securities.

11.3 The company's right to deal

Section 108(6) of the Companies Act 1990 prohibits a company from dealing in securities where any officer of the company is precluded from dealing in the same securities under sections 108(1), (2) or (3) due to the possession of material information.

Section 108(7) of the Companies Act 1990 states that a company may proceed with such dealing only where

1. the decision to enter the transaction was taken by a person other than the precluded officer; and

2. there was a written agreement in place that the material information was not communicated or that advice was not given to that person by the precluded officer; and

3. the information was not communicated and the advice was not given.

A company is not prohibited from dealing in the securities of another company solely because its officer is in possession of information, which he obtained during the performance of his duties, consisting simply of the fact that his company proposes to deal in the securities of that other company (section 108(8) of the Companies Act 1990).

11.4 Civil liability for insider dealing

Section 109(1) of the Companies Act 1990 states that where a person deals, or causes or procures another person to deal, in securities in a manner outlawed by section 108 of the Companies Act 1990 or communicates information in any such manner, that person shall be subject to personal liability. That person shall be liable to compensate any other party to the transaction who was not in possession of the material information. The compensation consists of the loss caused to that party due to the difference between the price at which the securities were dealt in and the price they would have been likely to have been dealt in if the material information had been generally available. That person is also liable to account to the company that issued the securities for any profit made from the transaction.

Section 109(2) of the Companies Act 1990 states that where the precluded person can prove to the court that he has already paid compensation or repatriated profits as a result of the transaction, the amount payable under section 109(1) will be reduced.

Section 109(4) of the Companies Act 1990 places a limitation on the time within which an action for civil liability can be taken. The aggrieved party must commence this action within two years of the completion of the transaction.

11.5 Criminal liability for insider dealing

Section 111 of the Companies Act 1990 states that a person who deals in securities in contravention of section 108 is guilty of a criminal offence. That person is liable on summary conviction to a term of imprisonment not exceeding twelve months and/or a fine of €1,270 and, where he is convicted on indictment, to a term of imprisonment not exceeding ten years and/or a fine of €254,000.

Liability is also extended to a person who deals on behalf of another, if he has reasonable cause to believe or ought to conclude that the dealing is in contravention of section 108 (section 113 of the Companies Act 1990).

Section 112 of the Companies Act 1990 states that a person convicted of an offence is restricted from dealing for a period of twelve months from the date of the conviction. If a transaction was initiated but not completed prior to a conviction under section 111, the transaction may be completed where the board of directors, committee of management or a manager of a recognised stock exchange is satisfied in writing that

1. the transaction was initiated but not completed before the date of the conviction; and
2. the rights of an innocent third party will be prejudiced if the transaction is not completed; and
3. the transaction is not unlawful under Part V of the Companies Act 1990.

11.6 Exempt transactions

Section 110 of the Companies Act 1990 (as amended by section 4 of the Companies (Amendment) Act 1999 and section 103 of the Company Law Enforcement Act 2001) lists the transactions which are not affected by section 108 as follows:

1. the acquisition of shares under a will or on intestacy;
2. the acquisition of shares under an employee profit sharing scheme where the scheme is approved by the Revenue Commissioners and the members of the company, and where all permanent employees have the right to participate on equal terms;
3. the acquisition of a right to shares in a company pursuant to a tax scheme approved by the Revenue Commissioners.

Section 110(2) of the Companies Act 1990 also exempts the following transactions where they are entered into in good faith:

1. the purchase of a share qualification by a director in compliance with the articles of association of the company;
2. a transaction entered into by a person in compliance with obligations under an underwriting agreement;

3. a transaction entered into by a personal representative of a deceased person;

4. a transaction entered into by a trustee, liquidator, receiver or examiner in the performance of his duties;

5. a transaction by way of, or arising out of, a mortgage or charge on securities or a mortgage, charge, pledge or lien on documents of title to securities.

Transactions entered into by a Minister of the Government or the Central Bank in pursuance of monetary, exchange rate, national debt management or foreign exchange reserve policies are also exempt (section 110(3)).

Section 108(10) of the Companies Act 1990 provides an additional exemption where a person who intends to deal in securities gives twenty-one days' notice to the recognised stock exchange of his intention to deal in those securities. The notice must state that he intends to deal in those securities seven days after the publication of the company's interim accounts and before the expiry of fourteen days after the publication. The stock exchange must publish this notice. The person must not otherwise be taking advantage of material information.

11.7 Role of the stock exchange

The "relevant authority" (the board of directors, committee of management or a manager) of a recognised stock exchange is under a statutory duty to notify the Director of Corporate Enforcement where it appears that a person has committed an offence under Part V of the Companies Act 1990 (section 115 of the Companies Act 1990 as amended by section 37 of the Company Law Enforcement Act 2001). The relevant authority must furnish such information or provide such inspection facilities as the Director of Corporate Enforcement may require (section 115(1)). There is also a duty on every member of a recognised stock exchange to report any suspected offence to its relevant authority.

Where the court is of the opinion that an offence has been committed and no such report has been furnished by the relevant authority, it may, by its own motion or on the application of an interested person, direct that a report be furnished in accordance with section 115(1) of the Companies Act 1990. Section 115(5) also gives the Director of Corporate Enforcement the power to direct a relevant authority to make such a report.

Where the Director of Corporate Enforcement or the Director of Public Prosecutions institutes proceedings as a result of an offence under Part V, the relevant authority, the officers of the company at issue and every other person in possession of relevant information must give all assistance in connection with the proceedings where he or they are reasonably able to give.

Section 115(7) of the Companies Act 1990 states that the relevant authority of a recognised stock exchange shall only be liable in damages for anything done or omitted to be done under Part V where the relevant authority acted in bad faith.

Where a relevant authority receives a request for information from a similar authority of another Member State of the European Union which is exercising functions relating to unlawful dealing whether within or outside the State, the relevant authority must notify the Director of Corporate Enforcement, and it is under an obligation to assist with the request unless directed not to do so by the Director (section 116 of the Companies Act 1990 as amended by section 14 of the Company Law Enforcement Act 2001).

11.8 Stabilisation of share price

It was unclear whether or not Irish law formerly permitted those responsible for a flotation to attempt to control the vagaries of the post-floatation market, by strategic dealing in those shares, to minimise price volatility. An analogy may be drawn with the way in which central banks buy and sell currency with the aim of correcting volatility within currency markets In the context of shares, this exercise is known as price stabilisation, and has been permitted by legislation and stock exchange rules elsewhere.

Technically speaking, before the introduction of Companies (Amendment) Act 1999 price stabilising interventions might have contravened the insider dealing provisions of the Companies Act 1990. This was true not only of price stabilising acquisitions and disposals of shares on the Irish stock exchange but also of deals done pursuant to underwriting agreements, or agreements to buy securities in future, and agreements consequent on these it was therefore decided to enact legislation permitting price stabilisation.

The Companies (Amendment) Act 1999 amends and extends Parts IV and V of the Companies Act 1990 to permit stabilising activity in relation to the issue for sale of securities and to provide for connected matters. Section 2 of the Companies (Amendment) Act 1999 declares that section 108 of the Companies Act 1990 shall not be contravened by anything done in the State for the purpose of stabilising or maintaining the market price of securities, provided that the Stabilisation Rules contained in the schedule to the Act are obeyed.

A person acquiring or disposing of any interest in five per cent or more voting shares in a publicly quoted company must notify the company of this fact (see Chapter 12). Section 3 states that notification will be unnecessary for such acquisitions and disposals in three circumstances:

- the purpose must be to stabilise or maintain the market price of securities; and
- where the acquisition or disposal takes place in Ireland, it must conform to the Stabilisation Rules, or if outside Ireland, to the law of the jurisdiction where it takes place; and
- the acquisition or disposal must only occur during the stabilisation period.

The Companies Act 1990 provided an exemption from certain underwriting and other transactions entered into in good faith. In section 4 of the Companies (Amendment) Act 1999, special provision is made for exempting good faith agreements to underwrite securities, agreements, in advance of dealing facilities being provided by a recognised stock exchange for securities, to acquire or subscribe for a specified number of such securities, so that transactions thereby effected do not infringe the insider dealing rules.

The Companies (Amendment) Act 1999 also revoked the Companies Act 1990 (Insider Dealing) Regulations, 1991 (S.I. 151/1991) and the Companies Act 1990 (Insider Dealing) Regulations, 1992 (S.I. 131/1992).

12. COMPANY SHARES

12.1 Shares

Section 79 of the Companies Act 1963 states that "the shares or other interests of any member in a company shall be personal estate, transferable in a manner provided in the articles of the company, and shall not be of the nature of real estate." A share is an item of intangible personal property, as you cannot see it or touch it. It is considered a chose in action as the shareholder has the right to protect his share in legal proceedings.

Each share grants the shareholder the status of a company member. Membership involves a series of personal rights arising from the terms of the memorandum and articles of association (see paragraph 12.3.5 below). A member also has a proprietary interest in the company itself, as he is in effect the owner of the company. However, the company is a separate entity owning its own assets and undertakings, and a shareholder cannot claim to be the owner of these assets.

12.1.1 Share capital and par value

A share must have a nominal or par value under section 6(4) of the Companies Act 1963. The memorandum of association will set out the authorised share capital of the company, which is the limit of the capital that the company is authorised to issue. The authorised share capital is divided into shares of a fixed amount, *i.e.* €100,000 divided into 100,000 shares at par value of €1 each. This nominal value is the measure of the shareholder's liability to the company, and a measure of the shareholder's interest in and against the company. Commonly, the nominal value will not reflect the actual market price of the shares. The issued share capital represents the nominal capital raised by the company on the issue of shares. Any premium raised on the issue of shares by selling at a price above the nominal value is called a share premium and this is lodged in a share premium account. Chapter 15 sets out the rules that have been established in order to maintain and protect this pool of capital.

12.1.2 Share certificates

A share certificate is issued by the company as tangible evidence of a person's title to the company's shares. The share certificate is not a negotiable instrument, according to *Mills v. Shields* (1950), as it is not possible to transfer a shareholding without amending the register of members.

Under section 86 of the Companies Act 1963, each shareholder must be issued with a share certificate within two months of an allotment of shares or within two months of the lodgment of a share transfer. Where the company fails to issue the certificate under section 86, the company and every officer in default is liable to a fine. It is open to the person entitled to the certificate to notify the company of its default and to request the company to issue the certificate. If the company fails to comply within ten days, it is open to that person to apply to the court for an order directing the delivery of the share certificate within the time specified in the order. The costs of such an application must be borne by the company and any officer responsible for the default (section 86(3) of the Companies Act 1963).

It should be remembered that section 86 of the Companies Act 1963 allows for the conditions of the share issue to provide that a share certificate will not be issued.

According to section 87 of the Companies Act 1963, the share certificate is prima facie evidence of the title of the member to the shares. A share certificate is, therefore, not conclusive evidence that the person indicated thereon actually owns the shares covered by the certificate. It may be the case that the incorrect name or the incorrect number of shares appears on the certificate. However, the certificate is commonly relied on by third parties, and the company will be estopped form denying the facts set out in the certificate. In *Re Bahaia and San Francisco Railway Co.* (1868) Cockburn L.J. stated that a share certificate "is a declaration by the company to all the world that that the person in whose name the certificate is made out, and to whom it is given, is a shareholder in the company, and it is given by the company with the intention that it shall be so used by the person to whom it is given, and acted upon in the sale and transfer of shares." In this case the company was liable to compensate a third party who relied on an inaccurate share certificate.

In *Bloomenthal v. Ford* (1897) the share certificate stated that the share was fully paid-up. This was inaccurate and the company was estopped from any further calls in respect of that share. However, the company will not be liable to pay compensation to a third party where the certificate was forged, according to *Ruben v. Great Fingall Consolidated Co.* (1906). This decision was based on the fact that the certificate was not issued by a person authorised to do so by the company and, therefore, it was not issued, or the representation was not made, by the company. However, each case of forgery must be considered on its own facts as the reasoning in *Ruben* was rejected in *Lloyd v. Grace, Smith & Co.* (1912).

12.1.3 Share warrants

A public company, where its article of association so provide, may issue share warrants in respect of shares that are fully paid under section 88 of the Companies Act 1963. The warrant is issued under the seal of the company stating that the bearer of the warrant is entitled to the shares specified therein. It is open to the company to include a right to the payment of future dividends on those shares. The shares included in the warrant can then be simply transferred by the delivery of the warrant.

When a share warrant is issued, the name of the shareholder entered on the register as holding those shares is stricken from the register of members as if he had ceased to be a member (section 118 of the Companies Act 1963). The following particulars are then entered on the register under section 118:

1. the fact of the issue of the warrant;
2. a statement of the shares included by the warrant together with the reference numbers of the shares;
3. the date of the issue of the warrant.

Where the articles of the company provide, the bearer of the warrant is entitled to be registered as a member when the warrant is surrendered. The date of the surrender must be entered on the register. The company is responsible for any loss incurred by any person where it enters the name of the bearer of a share warrant on the register of members without the share warrant being surrendered or cancelled.

12.1.4 Calls

A company may agree to allot shares where the shareholder only pays part of the full consideration due for the shares. This is because the company has the right to make a call in respect of those shares, *i.e.* demand the unpaid amounts. It will be set out in the articles of association that it is the duty of every shareholder to meet those calls and pay what remains unpaid on a share. Where the shareholder transfers those shares, he is no longer liable for such calls save where he transfers the shares to a minor. A shareholder remains liable for calls in respect of his shares even where the company goes into liquidation, as the liquidator will make calls for the balance of the share payment in order to swell the creditors' fund.

The articles of the company commonly set out the rules that must be followed when making a call for unpaid capital. Model article 15 of Table A sets out that the directors have the power to make a call and do so by passing a resolution of the board of directors. The calls should be made *pari passu* unless the articles provide otherwise. This effectively means that the shareholders, or a class of shareholders, should be treated equally and asked to pay the same amount at the same time. Under *Alexander v. Automatic Telephone Co.* (1900) the power of directors to make calls must be exercised bona fide and for the benefit of the company as a whole. An injunction can be obtained to prevent a mala fide call.

Further, model article 15 sets out that no call can be more than twenty-five per cent of the nominal value of the share in respect of which the call is being made and that the relevant member must have at least fourteen days' notice of the time and place of payment. Model article 21 states that the directors may agree to receive all or part of the moneys uncalled and unpaid in respect of shares where the member is willing to pay the money in advance of a call. It is provided that the directors may agree to pay interest on the advance to such a member at a rate of five per cent per annum. The rate of interest may be varied by the shareholders in general meeting. In *Sykes Case* (1872) this power was exercised by the directors concerning their own shares in a situation where a company was insolvent. The money advanced was then used to pay the directors fees. This was held to be mala fide and illegal.

Where the call is unpaid, the company is barred from enforcing the payment after a period of twelve years has elapsed under the Statute of Limitations Act 1957. Model article 18 of Table A provides that an unpaid call carries an interest rate of five per cent per annum from the date that the call was due. It is open to the directors to waive the whole or any part of that interest.

The articles may give the directors the right to forfeit the shares in respect of which calls remain unpaid. Under the model articles of Table

A the directors may serve a notice on the shareholder requiring the payment of the call together with any applicable interest within fourteen days of the date of the notice. The notice must state that the shares will be forfeited where the notice is not complied with. Such a forfeiture of shares is not a capital reduction requiring the sanction of the court (see Chapter 15). Model article 37 states that the shareholder ceases to be a member of the company on the date of forfeiture but remains liable for the payments due to the company.

Where the directors comply with the requisite procedure set out in the articles and duly forfeit the shares for non-payment of the call, it is not open to the shareholder to seek relief from the court according to the case of *Ward v. Dublin North City Milling Co.* (1919). It is open to the company to cancel or re-issue the shares. In the case of a plc, the plc must cancel the forfeited shares within three years of the forfeiture if they have not been re-issued (section 43 of the Companies (Amendment) Act 1983). If this cancellation has the effect of reducing the capital of the company below the authorised minimum (see Chapter 2), the plc must re-register as another form of company and failure to do so will render the company and every officer in default guilty of an offence. However, a plc will rarely make calls as most of its shares will be fully paid-up on allotment.

A member may surrender his shares in anticipation of such a forfeiture provided that the surrender is permitted by the articles of the company (see Chapter 2).

12.2 Dividends

12.2.1 Distributions

The extent of a shareholder's rights depends both on the provisions of the memorandum and articles of the company and the terms attached to the issue of the shares. One of the most fundamental shareholder right is the right to be paid a dividend by the company. All company distributions must be paid out of the profits of the company that are available for distribution. Under section 51 of the Companies (Amendment) Act 1983, a distribution captures all distributions of the company's assets to members excluding the issue of bonus shares, the authorised redemption of the company's shares, the authorised reduction of the company's capital, and the distribution of assets on a winding up. Therefore, a distribution includes the payment of a dividend to shareholders and, according to section 45(1) of the Companies (Amendment) Act 1983, a dividend may be paid by the company only out of its profits that are available for distribution. Section 45(2) defines such profits as the company's accumulated realised profits (in so far as they have not been previously distributed or capitalised) less its accumulated, realised losses, (in so far as they have not been written off in a reduction or reorganisation of capital).

The statutory obligation to pay dividends out of profits is a product of the capital maintenance rules (see Chapter 15). The court may have to examine a "payment", and if it constitutes a dividend, it must be paid out of distributable profits. In *Igote Ltd v. Badsey Ltd* (2001) the Supreme Court held that where a share subscription agreement stated that it would "distribute" money to subscribers, this suggested the payment of a dividend and not the discharge of a commercial debt. As a result, the sum could only be paid out of profits.

Pursuant to section 46(1) of the Companies (Amendment) Act 1983, a plc may only make a distribution where its net assets are not less than the aggregate of its called-up share capital and its undistributable reserves, and the distribution does not result in its net assets falling below that aggregate. The undistributable reserves are made up of the company's share premium account, the capital redemption reserve fund, and any reserve that the company is prohibited from distributing either by law or under its memorandum and articles of association. It also includes the amount by which the company's accumulated unrealised profits (in so far as they have not been previously capitalised) exceed its accumulated unrealised losses (in so far as they have not been previously written off in a reduction or reorganisation of capital).

12.2.2 Declaration of a dividend

Where the memorandum and articles of the company permit, the company has a discretion to apply its profits to the payment of a dividend amongst its members. It is only on a declaration that a dividend be paid that the members can sue in the case of non-payment. While there is no obligation on the company to declare a dividend according to *Bond v. Barrow Haematite Steel Co.* (1902), the memorandum and articles of association may impose such an obligation in certain circumstances.

The articles of the company should set out the procedure for the declaration of a dividend. Model article 116 of Table A states that "the company in a general meeting may declare dividends, but no dividend shall exceed the amount recommended by the directors." This gives the directors the effective power on this issue, and the members cannot force the directors to declare a dividend according to *Scott v. Scott* (1943). Model article 117 of Table A gives the power to the directors to declare interim dividends, without any input from the members. These dividends are prima facie payable in cash, and, according to *Wood v. Odessa Waterworks Company* (1889) they are payable in cash where the articles are silent on the matter. It is open to the articles to provide for the payment of dividends by way of non-cash assets of the company.

12.2.3 Declared but unpaid dividends

Once the dividend is declared by the company it becomes payable to the members who have the right to sue for payment of arrears, subject to the terms of the memorandum and articles and the terms of the resolution declaring the dividend. According to Kenny J. in *Re Belfast Empire Theatre of Varieties* (1963), an action for an unpaid dividend may be brought within twelve years of the declaration or declared date of payment, whichever is later, under the Statute of Limitations Act 1957. This was because he considered that the section 25 contract was similar to an instrument under seal. However, the English authority of *Re Compania de Electricidad de la Provencia de Buenos Aires Ltd* (1980) held that an unpaid dividend was a simple contract debt and, as a result, the period of limitation of six years applies to any such action. The latter position appears to be the accepted authority on the matter. The articles may provide for forfeiture of unclaimed dividend within a lesser period and in *Ward v. Dublin North City Milling Company Ltd* (1919) a period of three years was upheld. This right to sue for arrears is personal to the shareholder, and the transferee of the shares cannot sue.

Declared dividends cease to be debts of the company once a winding up commences and the right to sue for the dividend is deferred. Once a liquidation begins, all assets including profits form part of the creditors fund according to Kenny J. in *Wilson (Inspector of Taxes) v. Dunnes Stores (Cork) Ltd* (1976). The shareholder does not lose his entitlement to the dividend, and it is taken into account in calculating his portion of the surplus.

12.2.4 Unlawful dividends

Section 50 of the Companies (Amendment) Act 1983 states that a member is obliged to repay to the company any amount paid by way of dividend in breach of section 45(1) above. In *Re Exchange Banking Co. Re Flitcrofts case* (1882) the directors were held liable to repay an amount paid out in dividends where they had inaccurately stated the position with regard to certain assets. In *Re Thomas Gerrard & Sons Ltd* (1968) the auditors were held liable to the company for dividends paid where the auditors failed to follow-up suspicions that the assets of the company had been overstated.

In *Bairstow et al v. Queens Moat Houses plc* (2001) the English Court of Appeal considered whether the directors of the company were accountable for unlawfully paid dividends. It was held that that dividends could only be paid in accordance with a company's financial statements that had been drawn up in the proper format and laid before the company in general meeting and that the directors could not go behind the figures for the company's "distributable profits" as disclosed by the accounts prepared, signed and laid before the company by them. The court held that the directors were accountable for the payment of unlawful dividends paid contrary to statute, whether or not the dividends were demonstrably paid out of capital and regardless of whether the company was solvent or insolvent.

12.3 Shareholders' rights

12.3.1 Dividends

As set out in paragraph 12.2, a shareholder's right to the payment of a dividend depends on the terms of the memorandum and articles of association and the conditions attached to his shares. However, once a dividend is duly declared by the company in respect of his shares, the shareholder has the right to receive the dividend and may issue proceedings in respect of the same.

12.3.2 Right to attend meetings and vote

All shareholders are equally entitled to attend general meetings and exercise a vote unless the terms of their shareholding provide otherwise. It is open to the company, where the terms of the memorandum and association permit, to issue voting and non-voting shares.

Unless otherwise provided in the articles, all members must receive notice of meetings even when they are not entitled to attend or vote. Where a member has not been informed, the meeting is invalid at common law according to *Smyth v. Darley* (1849). However, the articles of the company normally provide that any accidental failure to give notice, or non-receipt of notice will not invalidate a meeting. See Chapter 13 for a discussion of the voting procedure at general meetings.

12.3.3 Right to participate in a winding up

The members of the company are entitled to receive any surplus assets after the company's debts and the expenses of the liquidation have been discharged by the liquidator according to section 275 of the Companies Act 1963. It is open to the company to state in its memorandum of association that no surplus is to be distributed to the members, but such a prohibition was not upheld by the court in *Re Merchant Navy Supply Association Ltd* (1947). It appears that the court will uphold the prohibition where the company sets out an express alternative destination for any surplus, as in *Liverpool & District Hospital v. AG* (1981). See Chapter 23 on the distributions to members in a winding up.

12.3.4 Statutory rights

It will be evident throughout this text that shareholders are granted a large number of statutory rights under the Companies Acts. They are granted the right to inspect and receive copies of the various registers maintained by the company (registers of members, directors and secretaries share holdings). The annual accounts must be presented to the annual general meeting, and the shareholders have the right to demand and receive copies of balance sheets of subsidiary companies. The members are also given express access to the court in order to vindicate those rights.

Further, the members may petition the court for a winding up of the company or may seek remedies where they are being oppressed or disregarded by those running the company.

12.3.5 Personal rights

When a person becomes a shareholder of a company, he is automatically deemed to be a party to a statutory contract by virtue of section 25 of the Companies Act 1963. Section 25 states that the provisions of the memorandum and articles of the company will bind the company and members to the same extent as if they had been signed and sealed by each member. Farwell J. stated in *Borlands Trustee Company v. Steele* (1901) that "the contract contained in the articles of association is one of the original incidents of the share." The members and the company are bound by the terms of these documents and they may enforce these terms against each other.

The shareholders are said to have a personal right to vindicate these terms. In *Edwards v. Haliwell* (1950) the shareholders challenged a breach of the company's articles where the directors purchased the shares of an outgoing member, and in *Rayfield v. Hands* (1960) the shareholders challenged a breach of the articles which provided that no director decisions could be valid where two or more dissent. These are considered to be breaches of personal rights of the shareholders, and the shareholder in these cases is trying to protect his personal interests and not the interests of the company. See Chapter 14 on the vindication of personal rights.

12.4 Classes of shares

Prima facie, all shareholders are entitled to the same rights and interests in the company. This is because all shares are said to rank equally. *i.e. pari passu*. McNaughten L.J. stated in *Birch v. Cropper; Re Bridgewater Navigation Co. Ltd* (1889) that "every person who becomes a member of a company limited by shares of equal amount becomes entitled to a proportionate part in the capital of the company, and, unless it be otherwise provided by the regulations of the company, entitled as a necessary consequence, to the same proportionate part in all the property of the company".

Therefore, the regulations of the company may provide for different classes of shares with different rights and obligations attached. The memorandum or articles of the company must allow the creation of classes of share. The articles cannot, however, make such a provision where the memorandum provides expressly that all shareholders are to be treated equally. In *Campbell v. Rofe* (1933) it was stated that if the memorandum expressly provides for equality of the shareholders, that provision cannot be modified by the articles. Where model article 2 of Table A is adopted by the company, it allows the creation of any shares with any rights or restrictions.

12.4.1 Ordinary shares

The most common category of shares issued by a company is that of ordinary shares. These shares carry the rights and duties expressed in the memorandum and articles of the company. They are considered to be speculative shares due to the fact that where the company trades profitably in a particular year, the ordinary shareholder may receive a large dividend. However, if the company trades very badly, they run the risk of getting no dividend at all. Where the company goes into liquidation, these shareholders are normally last in line to receive any surplus distribution by the liquidator.

12.4.2 Preference shares

These shares are expressed to carry certain preferential rights over other categories of shares. A share may have preferential dividend, capital and/or voting rights.

A share is preferred as to dividend where the shareholder is to be paid his dividend prior to the ordinary shareholders. Normally this dividend follows the normal rules of dividend payment and it is only payable when it is declared by the directors or general meeting. It is open to the terms of the issue of the share to state that the fixed dividend is payable every year even without a declaration. In *Re Lafayette Ltd* (1950) the court considered the terms of the articles and held that the right to dividend did not require a declaration.

Where a dividend is not declared in any trading year due to insufficient profits, it is presumed that the shareholder is entitled to have the arrears paid the next time profits are available for distribution, *i.e.* the arrears are carried forward by the company. This is because preferential dividends are presumed to be cumulative according to *Webb v. Earle* (1875). In *Re Lafayette Ltd* (1950) the articles of the company declared that

> "the holders of the preference shares shall be entitled to receive out of the profits of the company a cumulative preferential dividend for each year of six per cent per annum on the amount for the time being paid on the preference shares held by them respectively, such dividend shall be cumulative, and arrears thereof shall be the first charge on the subsequent profits of the company."

The court held that the arrears were an automatic charge on any future profits. While it depends on the terms of the articles, the arrears are usually paid in priority to ordinary shareholder dividends when profits are made by the company.

This presumption is rebutted where it is expressly stated in the terms of issue that the dividend is non-cumulative, or that the dividend is to be paid only out of "profits available for dividends" for a particular year as in *Webb v. Earle* (1875). Where the shares are non-cumulative shares, the arrears of dividend are not carried forward to the next year.

If the profits for the distribution are large, the ordinary dividends may well exceed the preferential dividends. In *Will v. United Lankat Plantations Co.* (1914) the preference shareholders, who had already received their fixed dividend, attempted to participate in the remaining profits. The House of Lords held that once a shareholding is preferential concerning a particular right, it is deemed that this is an exhaustive definition of the rights of that shareholding. It is of course open to the articles of the company or the terms of the issue of the shares to provide that preferential shareholders can participate in the general profits of the company.

Whether arrears of cumulative preference shares are payable on winding up depends on the wording of the articles of the company and the terms of the issue of the shares. These may provide that the preference extends to a winding up, and if so, the arrears will be paid. If the articles and the terms of issue are silent as to a preference to arrears on a winding up, but the shares are preferred as to capital, then arrears will also be paid. Under section 207(1)(g) of the Companies Act 1963, claims for cumulative preference dividends which have been declared but not paid will be met after all non-member creditors have been discharged, but will be paid as a preferential debt. In *Re Imperial Hotel (Cork) Ltd* (1950) the articles gave preference shareholders the right to an annual six per cent dividend including all arrears "independent of any recommendation by the board of directors, and independent of any declaration of dividend by the company in a general meeting..." This was held to be an annually occurring debt of the company, and, on liquidation, it was owed in preference to the claims of ordinary shareholders. Courtney states that shares which are preferential as to dividend are assumed to be non-participatory concerning profit once the preferential dividend is paid, unless the terms of the shareholding contradict this.

A share may be preferential as the shareholder is entitled to have his capital investment returned before the ordinary shareholders where the company goes into liquidation.

12.4.3 Redeemable shares

These are shares which can be bought back by the company after a fixed period of time; they are discussed at Chapter 15.

12.4.4 Other categories

Deferred or founders' shares were commonly issued to the founders of the company and they carried special rights such as the right to a fixed dividend. These shares are now rarely issued.

Treasury shares are discussed at Chapter 15 and they are shares that are redeemed by the company and retained on the company books. The company is prohibited from exercising voting or dividend rights in respect of these shares.

Bonus shares are issued when a company capitalises profits, revenue reserves, or some other fund. These bonus shares are issued to existing members in proportion to their entitlement to dividend and they are fully paid-up.

12.4.5 Lien on shares

Model article 11 of Table A allows the company to place liens on the company's shares. A lien is a right to retain possession of an item of personal property pending the payment of a sum due in respect of that property. According to article 11, a company has a "first and paramount" lien on a share that is not fully paid-up in respect of money called or payable in respect of that share. The articles may also state that the company has a lien on a share that is not fully paid-up in respect of any debts owed to the company by the shareholder. Model article 12 of Table A permits a company to sell such a share on giving fourteen days' notice to the registered holder of the share demanding the payment of an amount due. Model article 13 of Table A permits the directors to authorise a person to transfer the share to the purchaser where the registered holder fails to execute the transfer.

A company lien will act in priority to all other charges on the share save where the company has notice of any prior equitable claims or interests in the share (see *Bradford Banking Co. v. Briggs Son & Co.* (1886)). A plc is prohibited by section 44 of the Companies (Amendment) Act 1983 from creating a lien over its shares save where a lien is created in respect of amounts unpaid on the shares.

12.4.6 Variation of class rights

The articles of the company commonly detail the rights and duties attached to each class of share issued by the company. The articles may, as we have seen, be altered by a special resolution of the members.

Where the articles set out a specific procedure for the variation of the rights attached to share classes, that procedure must be followed. Section 78 of the Companies Act 1963 deals with the situation where the memorandum or the articles set out that the rights of a class could be varied subject to the consent of a specified number of the holders of that class of shares or subject to a resolution passed by the class. Section 78 states that the rights of a class of shares can be lawfully varied where this procedure was followed. Section 78 also provides that the holders of not less than ten per cent of the affected class who did not consent or vote in favour of the resolution can apply to the court to have the variation cancelled. Such an application must be made within twenty-eight days of when the consent was given or the resolution passed, and the variation cannot take effect until it is confirmed by the court.

If the court is of the opinion that the variation would "unfairly prejudice" the shareholders of the class represented by the applicant, it can disallow the variation. The company has twenty-one days to forward a copy of the order to the Registrar of Companies, and failure to comply with this requirement renders the company and every officer in default liable to a fine. The decision of the court is final and the applicant may only appeal to the Supreme Court on a point of law.

Where the rights attached to the class of shares are set out in a document other than the memorandum, and the articles fail to set out any procedure for a variation of those rights, section 38 of the Companies (Amendment) Act 1983 provides that these rights may be varied only where three-quarters of the shareholders in the affected class consent in writing and the variation is sanctioned by a special resolution at a general meeting of that class. The right set out in section 78 of the Companies Act 1963 to apply to the court to have the variation cancelled, also applies in respect of a variation pursuant to section 38 of the Companies (Amendment) Act 1983. Where the rights are attached to the class of shares by the provisions of the memorandum and the articles fail to set out any procedure for a variation of those rights, section 38 of the Companies (Amendment) Act 1983 states that the class rights may be varied only by the consent of all the shareholders of the company.

A variation of rights is defined to include an abrogation in section 78(6) of the Companies Act 1963. The courts have examined what is meant by a variation. In *Greenhalgh Cinemas v. Arderne Cinemas* (1946) the subdivision of a class of ordinary shares was held not to affect the rights of another class of ordinary shares even where the subdivision diluted the latter's control of the company. In *White v. Bristol*

Aeroplane Co. Ltd (1953) Lord Evershed M.R. drew a distinction between rights affected as a matter of business and rights affected as a matter of law. Here the issue of bonus shares to ordinary shareholders had the effect of reducing the existing preference shareholders' holdings. These decisions have been criticised.

12.5 Share allotment

12.5.1 Power to allot shares

Where a company issues its shares, it is called an allotment. Model article 5 of Table A gives the power to allot shares to the company directors but this article must be read in conjunction with section 20 of the Companies (Amendment) Act 1983. Section 20 states that this power of allotment can only be exercised by the directors where they are authorised to do so by an ordinary resolution of the company or by the articles of association. Notice of the passing of the resolution must be delivered to the Registrar of Companies within fifteen days. This authority may be given for a particular allotment or on a general basis, and conditions may be attached to the authority. Under section 20(3) the authority must state the maximum number of shares to be allotted and the date on which the authority will expire. The expiration date must be not more than five years from the date of the resolution or, in the case of the first allotment of the company, not more than five years from the date of incorporation. The authority may be revoked or varied by the company in general meeting.

Section 21(4) of the Companies (Amendment) Act 1983 states that the authority may be renewed by the shareholders in a general meeting for a further period not exceeding five years. The resolution must state the amount of shares that may be allotted and the date of expiration of the authority. The directors may allot shares under an authority after the expiration of the five years where the contract to allot was entered into by the company before five years expired. An allotment in violation of section 20 shall be valid according to section 20(8), but any director who was knowingly and willfully involved in a contravention of this section is guilty of an offence and may be fined.

Section 20 of the Companies (Amendment) Act 1983 does not apply in the following cases:

1. where shares are allotted to the subscribers to the memorandum of association;

2. where shares are allotted pursuant to an employees' share scheme;

3. where there is a right to subscribe for, or convert any security into, shares other than the allotted shares.

12.5.2 Allotment

Where an application is made for shares in a company, it is deemed to be an offer to enter into a contract for the shares. The offer is deemed to be accepted and the contract is complete when the company issues a notice to the applicant that the requested shares have been allotted. This notice must be issued by the company within a reasonable time. As discussed in Chapter 13, no person is a member of the company until his name is entered on the register of members. In the case of public companies they may issue a letter of allotment, which can be accepted by the applicant, or he can renounce his right to become a member in favour of another person. The applicant or the other person then returns the letter of allotment with a request to be registered as a company member.

The company is required, within one month of the allotment, to notify the Registrar of Companies of the number and amount of shares allotted, the names and addresses of the shareholders, and the amounts paid or due on the shares (section 58(1)(a) of the Companies Act 1963). This is called the "return of the allotment" and failure to deliver the return to the Registrar of Companies will render every officer of the company in default liable to a fine under section 58(3). That officer may apply to the company for relief, and the court has the discretion to grant relief and extend the time for the delivery of the return under section 58(4) where it is satisfied that the failure was accidental or due to inadvertence or that it is otherwise just and equitable to do so.

The applicant is entitled to revoke his application at any time before the issue of the notice of allotment. Such a revocation must be made within a reasonable time according to *Crawley's Case* (1869). However, in the case of a plc, an application is irrevocable until after the expiration of nine days after the day on which the prospectus is issued (section 56(5) of the Companies Act 1963). This restriction does not apply where a director, promoter, or any other person who authorised the issue of the prospectus, has issued a notice under section 49 of the Companies Act 1963 which relieves him from responsibility for misstatements in the prospectus.

The directors' powers of allotment must be exercised bona fide and in the best interests of the company. In *Nash v. Lancegaye Safety Glass (Ireland) Ltd* (1958) an allotment increased a shareholder's shares so that he became a majority shareholder. It was held that this was an abuse of fiduciary powers by the director; the resolution which authorised it was, therefore, invalid. Dixon J. recognised that such allotments may have the object of benefiting the company, in addition to other improper purposes. However, the object of benefiting the company "would not suffice to validate the resolutions if the motives were partly improper." In *Re Jermyn Street Turkish Baths Ltd* (1971) an allotment leaving one individual in a controlling position was held bona fide because it was vital to the survival of the company and, therefore, in its interests.

In the case of a takeover bid, it is not acceptable for the directors to allot shares in order to protect their own positions according to *Hogg v. Cramphorn Ltd* (1966). However, in *Teck Corporation Ltd v. Millar* (1972) it was held that the directors may reasonably consider who is seeking control and why. If they believe there will be substantial damage to the company's interests, then the allotment may be for a proper purpose. In the absence of reasonable grounds for that belief, the directors will have acted with an improper purpose.

12.5.3 Allotments to the public

One of the most common ways a plc offers shares to the public is by means of a prospectus. Section 2(1) of the Companies Act 1963 defines a prospectus as "any prospectus, notice, circular, advertisement or other invitation, offering to the public for subscription or purchase any shares or debenture of a company". An offer to the public includes an offer of shares to any section of the public according to section 6(1) of the Companies Act 1963. The Third Schedule of the Companies Act 1963 sets out the required contents of the prospectus as including *inter alia*

1. details of the share and loan capital of the company;
2. details of the company directors, including information as to their remuneration and any interests they hold in the company's shares;
3. details of promoters and auditors of the company;
4. details of the property acquired, or to be acquired, from the proceeds of the issue;

5. a report by the auditors of the profits and losses of the company and its subsidiaries in the preceding five years, together with a statement of their assets and liabilities in the latest company accounts.

Section 47(1) of the Companies Act 1963 requires that the company deliver a copy of the prospectus to the Registrar of Companies on or before the date of its publication.

Public companies may be exempt from the requirement to issue a prospectus in a number of circumstances; these include where the share issue is a bona fide invitation to enter into an underwriting agreement, where the shares are not offered to the public, where the issue is limited to the company's existing shareholders or debenture holders, where the issued shares are identical to a prior issue two years before which are dealt with on a recognised stock exchange, or where the stock exchange grants an exemption from the requirements of the Third Schedule.

Where a plc is allotting shares, the following considerations must be taken into account:

1. pursuant to section 53 of the Companies Act 1963, a plc cannot allot shares unless the allotment will raise a minimum subscription, which is defined as an amount that, in the opinion of the directors, must be raised by the issue in order to provide for certain specified matters such as working capital and/or the payment of preliminary expenses. An allotment in contravention of this provision is voidable at the instance of the allottee within one month of the allotment;

2. pursuant to section 22 of the Companies (Amendment) Act 1983, a plc cannot allot any share capital offered for subscription unless the capital is subscribed in full or the terms of the offer specifically allow for the allotment of capital where the offer is not fully subscribed;

3. pursuant to section 56 of the Companies Act 1963, a plc cannot allot shares until four days have expired since the date of the issue of the prospectus, in the case of a prospectus issued generally to the public. It is open to the prospectus to set out a longer period. Any breach of this provision renders the company officers liable to a fine;

4. pursuant to section 57 of the Companies Act 1963, any allotment of shares is void where permission for the shares to be dealt on a

specified stock exchange has not been applied for within three days of the issue of the prospectus and the prospectus stated that such an application would be made. The allotment is also void where the permission has not been granted within six months of the closing of the subscriptions.

Where the prospectus of a company contains a mis-statement, each director, promoter, or any person who authorised the issue of the prospectus is liable to compensate any person who subscribed for shares on the basis of the document and has suffered a loss as a result of the untrue statement (section 49(1) of the Companies Act 1963). Section 49(3) states that the following defences may be raised in such an action:

1. the person withdrew his consent to acting as a director of the company prior to the issue of the prospectus, and it was issued without his consent;

2. the prospectus was issued without his knowledge or consent and, on becoming aware of it, he gave public notice that it was issued without his knowledge or consent;

3. after the issue of the prospectus and before any allotment, he withdrew his consent to the untrue statements and gave reasonable public notice on their withdrawal and the reason therefore;

4. he has reasonable grounds for believing that the statement was true, or he relied on a statement in a report by an expert whom he reasonably believed to be competent, or he relied on a statement in an official public document.

Section 50 of the Companies Act 1963 imposes criminal liability for such a mis-statement on any person who authorised the issue of the prospectus, but it is a defence if that person can prove that the statement was immaterial or that he believed on reasonable grounds up to the time of the issue of the prospectus that the statement was true.

12.5.4 Pre-emption rights

Section 23 of the Companies (Amendment) Act 1983 grants the existing shareholders of a company a statutory right of first refusal in respect of an allotment of shares. This is called the statutory right of pre-emption, and it extends to that amount of the new issue that is equal in proportion to the shareholders' existing shareholding. Under section 23(8) of the Companies (Amendment) Act 1983 the shareholder must be given twenty-one days to consider the offer. Under section 23(1) the directors of the company cannot allot those shares until this period has expired or the offer of pre-emption has been rejected by the relevant shareholders. The pre-emption rights are not available to preference shareholders and they are not available where the new issue relates to an employees' share scheme (section 23(13)). Pre-emption rights do not apply where the new issue will be allotted for non-cash consideration.

In the case of a private company, these pre-emption rights may be over-ridden by the memorandum and articles of the company, or by special resolution (section 23(10)). In the case of any company, where there is a general authority to allot shares in accordance with section 20 of the Companies (Amendment) (Act) 1983, the directors may be given the power to modify or exclude the pre-emption rights by the articles or a special resolution of the company (section 24(2) of the Companies (Amendment) (Act) 1983). Where the directors are authorised to allot shares under section 20, a special resolution of the company may permit the directors to modify or exclude the pre-emption rights in respect of a particular allotment where the directors have recommended such a course of action. In the latter case the directors must provide a written explanation of the reasons for the recommendation with the notice for the general meeting.

Pursuant to section 23(11) of the Companies (Amendment) Act 1983, any contravention of section 23 will not invalidate the allotment, but it will render the company and every officer who knowingly authorised or permitted the contravention, jointly and severally liable to compensate the person to whom the offer should have been made. The action for loss or damages cannot be commenced after the expiration of two years from the date the notice of the allotment was delivered to the Registrar of Companies.

12.5.5 Consideration for an allotment

Section 26 of the Companies (Amendment) Act 1983 allows shares to be paid for "in money or money's worth (including goodwill or expertise)". Therefore, shares may be allotted for cash or for non-cash consideration. Further, the entire amount of consideration does not have to be paid on allotment. Where the shares are not fully paid-up at the allotment stage, the balance is called uncalled share capital and, as discussed at paragraph 12.1.4, that balance may be called by the directors in accordance with the procedure set out in the Companies Acts and the memorandum and articles of association. In the case of a plc, at least twenty-five per cent of the nominal value of the shares allotted to a shareholder must be paid up on allotment (section 28(1) of the Companies (Amendment) Act 1983).

When shares are allotted for non-cash consideration, the written contract of allotment or a memorandum of an oral contract must be delivered under section 58(1)(b)of the Companies Act 1963 to the Companies Registration Office within one month of the allotment. The adequacy of the consideration is of no concern to the court; in *Re Leinster Contract Corporation* (1902) shares allotted for worthless patents were upheld, as the consideration must be sufficient but it does not have to be adequate.

A plc is subject to several restrictions when allotting shares for non-cash consideration. Section 26(2) of the Companies (Amendment) Act 1983 states that a plc cannot accept an undertaking to perform future services as consideration for an allotment. Where the company breaches this prohibition, the shareholder is liable to pay the value of the shares together with any premium on those shares to the company. Any person who later purchases these shares is liable to pay this amount unless he can prove that he did not have actual notice of the contravention of the prohibition.

A plc is also prohibited under section 29(1) of the Companies (Amendment) Act 1983 from allotting shares in consideration for an undertaking that can be performed more than five years from the allotment date. Where the contract of allotment does not breach this provision, any variation of the contract that would result in a contravention is void. If the company breaches this prohibition, the shareholder is liable to pay the value of the shares together with any premium on those shares to the company.

All non-cash consideration accepted by a plc for a contract of allotment must be independently valued by a independent person appointed by the company during the six months immediately preceding the allotment (section 30 of the Companies (Amendment) Act 1983). That independent person must be qualified to be appointed as the company auditor under section 30(5). The independent person may obtain a valuation of the consideration from a relevant expert who is not a servant or officer of the company, its holding company, or its subsidiary. The independent person must prepare a report that shall be provided to the proposed allottee. Pursuant to section 30(6) of the Companies (Amendment) Act 1983, the report should contain the following:

1. the nominal value of the shares to be wholly or partly paid for by the consideration proposed;
2. the amount of any premium payable on those shares;
3. a description of the consideration;
4. where the independent person has valued the consideration, details of the method used to carry out the valuation and the date of the valuation;
5. where another person has valued the consideration, details of that person, including his knowledge and experience in such a valuation, details of the method used to carry out the valuation, and the date of the valuation;
6. the extent to which the nominal value of the share and any premium are to be treated as fully paid up by the consideration and/or by cash.

The report must be accompanied by a note according to section 30(8) of the Companies (Amendment) Act 1983 setting out the following facts:

1. where the valuation was carried out by another person, that it appeared reasonable to the independent person to have a valuation carried out by another person;
2. that the valuation carried out was reasonable;
3. that there has been no material change in the value of the consideration since the date of the valuation;
4. that the consideration as valued together with any cash paid up on the shares is not less than the nominal value of the capital to be treated as paid up and premium.

The allottee is personally liable to the company for so much of the nominal value of the shares as was to be treated as paid up by the consideration where the allottee has not received the report or the allottee is aware that there has been some other contravention of section 30. The independent person is entitled to obtain from the officers of the company the information that he believes is necessary to enable him to carry out the valuation. It is an offence under section 31 of the Companies (Amendment) Act 1983 for any person to knowingly or recklessly make a statement to the independent person that is false, misleading, or deceptive in a material particular.

12.5.6 Issue of shares at a discount

Section 27 of the Companies (Amendment) Act 1983 states that it is illegal for a company to issue shares at a discount. Where the company contravenes this provision, the shareholder is liable to pay that discount, together with any interest, to the company. Some companies try to avoid this restriction by offering a commission to a shareholder for subscribing for shares. Section 59 of the Companies Act 1963 permits a company to pay commission, not exceeding ten per cent of the price at which the shares are issued, in order to induce shareholders to invest in the company.

12.5.7 Issue of shares at a premium

There is no prohibition on issuing shares at a premium. Where the company allots shares at a price greater than the nominal value of the shares set out in the memorandum of the company, the excess is regarded as a premium which must be lodged in a share premium account. It is treated like capital which is subject to the capital maintenance rules set out in Chapter 15. Section 62 of the Companies Act 1963 applies the normal rules of capital maintenance to this account, and it may only be used by the company in a limited manner. Section 62 permits the company to use the share premium account for the following purposes:

1. the payment of unissued shares which are then issued to members as bonus shares;
2. writing off preliminary expenses of the company;
3. writing off expenses or commission on the issue of shares or debentures;
4. providing for the premium payable on the redemption of redeemable preference shares or debentures of the company.

12.6 Disclosure of interests in shares

Part IV of the Companies Act 1990 imposes disclosure obligations on certain persons where they acquire shares in a company.

12.6.1 Shares held by the company directors and the company secretary

As set out in Chapter 7, the directors and secretary of the company must notify the company of any interest they have in the shares or debentures of the company. Section 53(1) of the Companies Act 1990 requires a director and/or secretary of a company to notify the company in writing of any interests in shares in, and debentures of, the company, its subsidiaries, its holding company, or fellow subsidiaries. The company must keep a register for this purpose.

12.6.2 Disclosure obligations where shares are held by individuals in a plc

In the case of plc, a person must notify the plc of any "notifiable interest" acquired in the plc (section 67 of the Companies Act 1990). The "notifiable interest" is set out in section 70 of the Companies Act 1990 as five per cent or more in nominal value of the relevant share capital of the company, *i.e.* the issued share capital of the company that carries voting rights (the temporary suspension of voting rights in respect of certain shares shall be ignored when determining the relevant share capital). This percentage may be raised or lowered by the Minister. The obligation to notify the plc is triggered where the shareholder's interest reaches the notifiable level, or in the case of a shareholder already holding such a percentage, where the interest falls below the level. The plc must receive this notification within five days of these events occurring.

Section 77(2) of the Companies Act 1990 defines what is meant by an "interest" in the shares of a plc. An "interest" refers to "any interest of any kind whatsoever" and a person has an interest in shares where

1. a person enters into a contract for the purchase of those shares;
2. a person is entitled to exercise rights in relation to those shares;
3. a person is entitled to control the exercise of rights in relation to those shares;
4. a person has a right to call for the delivery of those shares;
5. a person has an option in respect of those shares.

Any of the above interests held by a person's spouse or a minor child must be taken into account in determining whether that person has reached a notifiable percentage (section 72 of the Companies Act 1990).

The following interests are not captured according to section 78 of the Companies Act 1990:

1. an interest held as a bare trustee;
2. an interest held in remainder or reversion;
3. any discretionary interest;
4. a life interest under an irrevocable settlement where the settlor has no interest in the income or property;
5. interests subsisting under unit trusts;
6. interests under schemes under the Charities Acts 1961;
7. interests held by the President of the High Court in an estate before representation is raised;
8. interests held by lending institutions as security for a loan to a company;
9. any other interests prescribed by the Minister.

12.6.3 Disclosure obligations where shares are held by groups in a plc

It is open to a number of individuals to attempt to evade the individual disclosure obligations by entering into an agreement with others to purchase shares in a plc whereby each individual agrees to purchase shares below the notifiable percentage. In this case the plc is called the "target company". However, sections 73 of the Companies Act 1990 provides for this possibility and treats a person who is a party to the agreement as interested in the shares held by the other when calculating whether or not he has a notifiable interest. The agreement must satisfy the following conditions:

1. the agreement must be between two or more persons and must include a provision for the acquisition by one or more of them of shares carrying voting rights in a plc;
2. the agreement must impose obligations or restrictions on one or more of the parties as to the use, retention, or disposal of the shares;

3. the agreement must not be an agreement for the underwriting of shares in a company.

An "agreement" includes an informal "arrangement" and any "undertakings, expectations or understandings" under such arrangement where there is "mutuality" in the undertakings, expectations or understandings of the parties to it.

Where an agreement to acquire shares in a target company satisfies these criteria, a person is treated as being interested in the shares in which the other parties to the agreement are interested, whether the shares were acquired pursuant to the agreement or not (section 74). All parties to the agreement should be aware of the shares held in the target company by each party to the agreement, and section 75 of the Companies Act 1990 obliges each party to the agreement to notify the other parties of any acquisition of shares in the plc. Under section 75(8) of the Companies Act 1990 the person has five days within which to notify the other parties of such an acquisition.

12.6.4 Penalties for a breach of the disclosure obligations

Section 79 of the Companies Act 1990 deals with a failure by an individual to comply with these disclosure obligations. Where an individual fails to make the requisite notification to the plc, gives a statement to the plc which he knows to be false, or recklessly makes a false statement, or fails to comply with his obligations under section 75, no right or interest in respect of the shares in the plc shall be enforceable by him, whether directly or indirectly, by action or legal proceeding. It is open to the affected person to apply to the court for relief under section 79(4) of the Companies Act 1990 on the grounds that the default was accidental or due to inadvertence or some other sufficient cause or that it is just and equitable that the court grant relief. The court will not exercise its discretion to grant such relief if it appears that the default has arisen as a result of a deliberate act or omission of the shareholder. In *Re Telecom Eireann plc* (1999) Kelly J granted relief under section 79(4) of the Companies Act 1990 where the failure to comply with the statutory requirement was due only to inadvertence and where no person had been prejudiced by the failure.

Failure to comply with the notification obligations, including the notification obligation under section 75, is a criminal offence (section 79(7)). In relation to section 75, it is a defence for the individual to prove that it was not possible for him to give the notice to the other person or persons to the agreement within the proper period and that it remains impossible to give that notice or that he gave the notice as soon as it became possible for him to do so.

12.6.5 Register of interests maintained by the plc

Section 80 of the Companies Act 1990 requires every plc to maintain a register of interests in its shares. The company is obliged to note all notifications made pursuant to the disclosure obligations. Where the company receives notification that a shareholder has ceased to be a party to an agreement captured by section 73, the company is obliged to note that fact on the register. The register must be kept for a period of six years where the company ceases to be a plc. The register must be kept with the register of directors' and secretaries' interests. The company and every officer in default is liable to a fine where the register is not maintained in accordance with this provision.

The register must be available in accordance with section 88 of the Companies Act 1990. Under section 88 the register must be open for inspection every day for at least two hours per day. Inspection is open to the members of the company free of charge and to any other person on the payment of a fee. The register must also be open to the inspection of any person attending the annual general meeting of the company both before and during the meeting. Copies of the register must be provided within ten days of the company receiving a request. Where the company fails to comply with this provision, the company and every officer in default is guilty of an offence and is liable to a fine. It is open to the court under section 88(5) to make an order compelling an inspection or the provision of copies.

12.6.6 Investigation of membership by a plc

Section 81 of the Companies Act 1990 empowers a plc to investigate its share membership. The plc may issue a notice in writing to any person whom the company knows or has reasonable cause to believe to be, or at any time in the last three years to have been, interested in the shares comprised in the company's relevant share capital (*i.e.* voting shares). The company can seek confirmation as to whether the person is or was so interested. Where the person holds or has held such an interest, the company may request further particulars of that interest, including information on any agreements captured by section 73. The response must be given in writing and within a reasonable time specified in the notice. The company is obliged under section 82 of the

Companies Act 1990 to note on the register of interests that a notice was issued, the date on which it was issued, and the information obtained as a result.

Under section 83 the members of the company, holding not less than one-tenth of the paid-up capital carrying voting rights, may require the company to carry out an investigation under section 81. The members must give reasonable grounds for requiring the company to exercise those powers, and the company must comply with the request. Where the company fails to comply, the members or one of them may apply to the court for an order requiring the company to exercise its powers under section 81. The court must be satisfied that it is reasonable to make such an order. Where an investigation is carried out pursuant to section 83, the company must prepare a report that is made available for inspection at the company's registered office for a reasonable period of time (section 84 of the Companies Act 1990). If the investigation is not concluded within three months of the requisition, the company should prepare and make available interim reports every three months. The report must be kept by the plc for six years. Where the company fails to comply with these provisions regarding the report and/or the interim reports, the company and every officer in default is liable to a fine. The report should be available for inspection along with the register of interests in accordance with section 88 of the Companies Act 1990 (discussed above).

Where a person who is or was interested in the shares of a company, fails to comply with a notice served in accordance with section 81, that person is guilty of a criminal offence. It is open to the company to apply to the court for an order imposing restrictions on the transfer of his shares under section 16 of the Companies Act 1990 (see Chapter 19). Section 85(2) of the Companies Act 1990 permits the company or any aggrieved person to apply to the court for relief from the restrictions.

12.6.7 Disclosure orders in respect of a private company

The Companies Act 1990 introduced a procedure allowing a wide variety of persons to obtain information regarding the interests held by other persons in the shares or debentures of a private company (section 98). The order can require disclosure of interests of any kind in the shares or debentures of the company that are presently held or were held during the period specified in the court order.

Any person who has a financial interest in the company may apply to the court for a disclosure order in respect of all or any of the shares or debentures of the company (section 98(2) of the Companies Act 1990). Section 98(6) defines persons having a "financial interest" as including members, contributories, creditors, employees, co-adventurers, examiners, lessors, lessees, licensors, licencees, liquidators, or receivers of the company. The application must be supported by such evidence as the court requires (section 98(3)). Under section 99(1) of the Companies Act 1990 a person intending to apply to the court for a disclosure order must give at least ten days' notice of his intention to the company and to the person to whom the order is intended to be directed. The applicant must also notify any person specified by the court and if the person so notified is open to appear and adduce evidence at the hearing of the application.

The court will make a disclosure order if it is just and equitable to do so and the financial interest of the applicant would be prejudiced by non-disclosure (section 98(5)). Under section 101(1) of the Companies Act 1990 the court may vary or rescind the disclosure order. It is also open to the court to specify a person, group or class of persons to which the order applies. Where it is just and equitable to do so and the financial interests of the applicant would not be prejudiced, the court may exempt the following from the requirements of a disclosure order:

1. any person or class of persons;
2. any interest or class of interest in shares or debentures;
3. any share, group or class of shares;
4. any debenture, group or class of debentures.

The court can also impose conditions or restrictions on the rights attached to the shares or debentures under section 101(4) of the Companies Act 1990. It is open to any person whose interests are affected by the restrictions to apply for relief from all or any of those conditions. The court has the discretion to grant relief where it considers that it is just and equitable to so.

Where the applicant for the disclosure order is successful, he is under an obligation to deliver a notice of the making of the order, together with a copy of the order, by registered post to the following:

1. the company's registered office;
2. the Registrar of Companies;

3. the registered holder of any shares in respect of whom the order is made;
4. such other person as the court thinks fit.

Pursuant to section 102 of the Companies Act 1990 the applicant must deliver the order within seven days of the making of the order. The applicant must also, within the same time period, cause the publication of a notice of the making of the disclosure order in two daily newspapers circulating in the district of the registered office of the company.

Where the person who is subject to the disclosure order fails to comply with the order within the period specified in the order or makes a statement to the court which he knows to be false or recklessly makes a statement to the court which is false, he cannot enforce any right or interest in any of the shares or debentures in any action or legal proceedings. It is open to the affected person to apply to the court for relief under section 104(2) of the Companies Act 1990 on the grounds that the default was accidental or due to inadvertence or some other sufficient cause or that it is just and equitable that the court grant relief. The court will not exercise its discretion to grant such relief if it appears that the default has arisen as a result of a deliberate act or omission of the shareholder.

13. COMPANY MEMBERSHIP

13.1 Membership

13.1.1 Original subscribers

Once a company is registered by the Registrar of Companies, the original subscribers to the memorandum of association become the members of the company. This is because section 31(1) of the Companies Act 1963 states that "the subscribers of the memorandum of a company shall be deemed to have agreed to become members of the company, and, on its registration, shall be entered as members on its register of members." According to *Nicol's Case* (1885) a subscriber is a member even if the subscriber's name is not entered on the register of members. However, a subscriber cannot be treated as a member where all of the authorised shares of the company have been allotted to others without shares being allotted to the subscriber (see *Mackley's Case* (1875)).

Under section 116 of the Companies Act 1963 the name of the subscriber should be entered on the register of members within twenty-eight days of the registration of the company, and where the company fails to comply with this requirement, the company and every officer in default is liable to a fine.

13.1.2 Subsequent members

All subsequent persons who agree to become members of the company, and have their name entered in the register of members are members of the company under section 31(2) of the Companies Act 1963. A person becomes a member of a company where the company allots shares directly to that person, where an existing shareholder transfers shares to that person, or where shares are transmitted to the person on the death or bankruptcy of an existing member.

A person may also be treated as a member of a company where he allows his name to appear and/or remain on the register when in fact he holds no shares. He will be estopped from denying that he is a member. If a person is entered in the register of members without consent and then does some act consistent with membership, estoppel will again prevent a denial of membership (see *Linz v. Electric Wire Company of Palestine*). This is because persons who examine the register of members are entitled to rely on it as an accurate record of the company members according to *Oakes v. Turquand* (1867).

13.1.3 Eligible members

Where it is permitted by the articles and memorandum of association, it is open to other companies, foreigners, bankrupts, minors, and persons of unsound mind to become members of companies. A minor can purchase or inherit shares in a company and is liable to pay any calls on those shares. However, a minor can repudiate his membership while he is a minor or on reaching eighteen years of age. In the latter case, the minor should act promptly to repudiate his membership and any act consistent with membership during this time may result in an affirmation of membership. Where a minor repudiates his membership, he may be able to recover any money paid up on the shares where no consideration for the shares was given by the company.

As discussed in Chapter 15, a company is restricted from owning its own shares.

A company is also prohibited from becoming a member in its holding company under section 32 of the Companies Act 1963. Section 32 is a complete prohibition on a subsidiary (or its nominees) becoming a shareholder in its holding company, and any allotment or transfer of such shares is void. Section 155(1) of the Companies Act 1963 defines the subsidiary-holding company relationship. One company is deemed to be a subsidiary of another where the latter is a member of it and controls the composition of its board of directors, or holds more than half in nominal value of its equity share capital, or holds more than half in nominal value of its shares carrying voting rights (other than voting rights which arise only in specified circumstances). One company is deemed to be a subsidiary of another where the first-mentioned company is a subsidiary of any company which is that other's subsidiary.

Control of the board means an absolute right to appoint or remove all, or a majority of, the directors. Equity share capital means the issued share capital of the company excluding any part of the issued share capital that limits participation in a distribution of dividend or capital to a fixed amount. When deciding whether a company holds more than half in nominal value of the equity share capital or shares carrying voting rights of another company,

1. shares held or powers exercisable by the first-mentioned company as a fiduciary/trustee shall not be taken into account;

2. shares held or powers exercisable by the first-mentioned company as a result of a debenture or a trust deed securing the debenture shall not be taken into account;

3. shares held or powers exercisable by the first-mentioned company because it is a lending institution and the shares are held as security for a lending transaction shall not be taken into account;

4. shares held or powers exercisable by its nominees or by nominees of the subsidiaries of the first-mentioned company are to be taken into account.

The exceptions to the prohibition are set out in section 32 as follows:

1. where the subsidiary is a personal representative of the holding company's shares left by a member of the holding company under a will or on intestacy;

2. where the subsidiary is a trustee and holds the shares in the holding company as trust property (the holding company cannot be beneficially interested in the trust);

3. where a company is a member of another company and later becomes a subsidiary of that other.

However, section 224 of the Companies Act 1990 has broadened the capacity of a company to hold shares in its holding company once certain capital safeguards are met. Under section 224 there are two formalities that must be complied with, and failure to comply with them may leave the directors of the subsidiary personally liable for the total amount paid for the shares in the holding company:

1. The contract for the acquisition of the shares must be approved by the members of both companies. If the shares are to be purchased on a recognised stock exchange, an ordinary resolution is sufficient. If the shares are to pass by any other method, then a special resolution is required.

2. The consideration for the purchase contract must come out of the distributable profits of the subsidiary. The profits of the subsidiary available for distribution must be treated as being reduced by the total cost of the shares acquired, and the subsidiary may not exercise any voting or dividend rights in relation to those shares.

13.1.4 The register of members

Every company must maintain a register of members under section 116 of the Companies Act 1963 and it should state the following:

1. the names and addresses of each member;
2. the shares/stock held by each member;
3. the share numbers and the amount paid up in respect of those shares;
4. the date of becoming a member.

These details must be entered within twenty-eight days of a person becoming a member of the company. The register must record the date that a person ceases to be a member within twenty-eight days of the person so ceasing. Where the person ceases to be a member of the company as a result of a transfer or transmission of the shares, the entry must be made within twenty-eight days of the company receiving satisfactory evidence that the membership has ceased (section 116(3) of the Companies Act 1963). The register must be kept at the registered office of the company, or such other office within the State and so notified to the Registrar of Companies. The register cannot be kept outside the State (section 116(6) of the Companies Act 1963). Where the company defaults in complying with these requirements, the company and every officer in default is liable to a fine (section 116(9) of the Companies Act 1963).

Where a company has more 50 members, as in the case of a plc, an index of the names of the members must be kept by the company pursuant to section 117 of the Companies Act 1963. The index must be kept with the register of members, and failure to comply with section 117 renders the company and every officer in default liable to a fine (section 117(4) of the Companies Act 1963).

According to section 378 of the Companies Act 1963, the register must be in "legible form", and, according to section 4 of the Companies Act 1977, section 378 allows the company to maintain a computerised register.

Pursuant to section 119 of the Companies Act 1963, the register of members and the index of names must be open for inspection every day for at least two hours per day. In accordance with section 121 of the Act, the register and index may be closed for 30 days per year where notice of the closure is given by the company. Inspection is open to the members of the company free of charge and to any other person on the payment of a fee. Copies of the register and index must be provided within ten days of a request. Where the company fails to comply with this provision, the company and every officer in default is liable to a fine. It is open to the court under section 119(4) of the Companies Act 1963 to make an order compelling an inspection or the provision of copies. Section 356(6) of the English Companies Act 1985 is materially identical to section 119(4) of the Companies Act 1963. In *Pelling v Families Need Fathers Ltd* (2002) the Court of Appeal considered the scope of section 356(6). The court held that the court was not compelled under this section to make an order of inspection. It stated, however, that the scope of judicial discretion to refuse the order was narrow. The circumstances in which the court might refuse to make the order were said to include: where the request has been complied with or where the request is physically impossible to comply with because the register had been destroyed or lost; or where an undertaking has been offered to the court in lieu of the making of a formal order. It was further held that the court should balance the applicant's right to access to the register for the purpose of legitimately communicating with members, on the one hand, and the company's understandable concerns about the detrimental effect of an unqualified order for the disclosure of the names and addresses of the members.

The register is not conclusive evidence of membership of a company, and, according to section 124 of the Companies Act 1963, it is prima facie evidence of membership. Therefore, an entry on the register may be voidable for fraud, misrepresentation, or incapacity. However, once a winding up of a company commences, a voidable registration cannot be pursued according to *Oakes v. Turquand* (1867). An entry on the register may also be void for mistake. Under section 122(5) of the Companies Act 1963 the register may be rectified by the company to correct any error or omission, provided that the rectification does not adversely affect the rights of any person or where such an affected person has consented to the alteration. Such a rectification must be notified to the Registrar of Companies within twenty-one days.

It is open to an aggrieved person, a company member, or the company to apply to the court for the rectification of the register under section 122(1) where:

1. the name of any person is entered on or omitted from the register without sufficient cause; or

2. there is a failure to register a cessation of membership.

A note of caution was sounded by the Supreme Court of New South Wales, where an application for the rectification of the company register was refused on the ground that the applicant failed to join the company as a defendant in the proceedings (*Autodata v. Gibbons* (2000)). The court has wide powers in the matter to grant or refuse an order for rectification and may award compensation for any loss sustained by any aggrieved person. Under section 122(3) of the Companies Act 1963 the court may decide a dispute as to the title to shares and any question necessary or expedient to be decided for rectification of the register. Such an application could be brought in circumstances where the registration has been effected on the basis of a misrepresentation and it should be rectified to put the name of the real owner back on (see *Stewart's Case* (1886)). However, the applicant seeking the rectification must act promptly according to *Sewell's case* (1868).

13.1.5 Registration of beneficial interests

The registration of beneficial interests in the company is not permitted by section 123 of the Companies Act 1963, which states that no notice of any trust, express, implied, or constructive, shall be entered on the register.

In the case of *Rearden v. Provincial Bank (*1896), Porter M.R. explained that this rule existed in order to save the company from "the responsibility of attending any trusts or equities whatever attached to their shares, so that they might safely and securely deal with the person who is registered owner, and with him alone, recognising no other person and no different right." The rule excludes the company from disputes, breaches of trust liability, and prevents it from becoming an unwilling trustee. In *Societe Generale de Paris v. Walker* (1885) it was held that the company was within its rights to act this way and the registered party was the legal holder of the shares as far as the company was concerned. However, the court stated that while the trust agreement could be ignored by the company, it remained valid between the legal holder of the shares and the beneficiary of the shares. This is supported by *Hardoon v. Belilios* (1901), where it was held that the trustee was entitled to be indemnified by the sole beneficial holder of the shares for the amount of the calls on those shares.

Model article 7 of Table A incorporates this principle and extends it. According to article 7, except as required by law, no person shall be recognised by the company as holding any share upon trust, and the company is not bound by, or compelled in any way to recognise, any equitable, contingent, future or partial interest. Therefore, the company is not "bound" to recognise its shares as held on trust, but it may decide to do so and it may make a reasonable request to a member to furnish the company with information as to the beneficial ownership of shares. Even where the company opts to recognise the beneficial interests in the shares, it cannot enter those beneficial interests on the register of members because of the prohibition in section 123 of the Companies Act 1963.

While a company is not bound to recognise beneficial interest, it cannot ignore the interest where the company is on notice of it. In *Rearden v. Provincial Bank* (1896) it was held that the company, which had notice of the fact that the legal owner of the shares was merely a trustee, could not ignore that and create a lien over the shares in order to discharge a debt of the trustee to the company. This was contrary to good faith, and the rule exists for the benefit of the company and not to permit them to commit frauds or knowingly take the benefit of them.

Order 46 of the Rules of the Superior Courts 1986 allows the beneficial owner of shares to file a "stop notice" and an affidavit setting out the beneficial interest in the company with the High Court Central Office, and then to serve it on the company. This obliges the company to inform the beneficial owner of any attempt by the trustee to transfer the shares, or have the dividend paid to another, and then delay such transfer or payment by eight days to allow the beneficial owner to act.

13.1.6 Termination of membership

The membership of a company may be terminated in a number of ways. The most common termination occurs on the transfer of shares and the entry of the name of the transferee on the register. Shares may also be transmitted (involuntarily transferred) where a member dies or is declared bankrupt. An action by the company may terminate membership such as a forfeiture of the shares, the redemption of shares, or a sale by a company under its lien over the shares. An order of the court may result in a termination of membership, *e.g.* an order for the sale of shares under section 205 of the Companies Act 1963.

13.2 Share transfer and transmission

A member of a company may assign his share or shares in a number of ways. Where the shareholder voluntarily assigns his shares, it is called a transfer. Where the assignment is involuntary, it is called a transmission, and this commonly occurs where the shareholder dies or is declared bankrupt. On the death of a member, his shares are transmitted to his personal representatives. On the bankruptcy of a member, the shares vest in the official assignee appointed to his property under the Bankruptcy Act 1988.

13.2.1 Share transfer

Under section 79 of the Companies Act 1963 a share is "personal estate, transferable in the manner provided by the articles of the company". It is, therefore, open to a company to place conditions or restrictions on the transfer of its shares. Where the shares are fully paid, they may be effectively transferred by using a "stock transfer form" executed by the transferor in accordance with the Stock Transfer Act 1963. The transfer of unpaid shares must comply with the procedure for share transfer set out in the articles of a company, and in most cases a document similar to the stock transfer form is used.

Section 81 of the Companies Act 1963 provides that a company cannot register or transfer shares unless a proper instrument of transfer has been delivered to the company which sets out the shares being transferred and the names of the transferor and transferee.

Where the member is transferring all of his shares, he should deliver the share certificate to the transferee. The transferee must complete the stock transfer form, pay the stamp duty of one per cent and deliver the form together with the share certificate to the company for registration. Once the transferee is registered, the old share certificate is cancelled and a new one is issued to the transferee under section 86 of the Companies Act 1963 within two months of the registration

Where the member is transferring part of his shares, then the share certificate together with the transfer must be lodged by the transferor with the company under section 85 of the Companies Act 1963. The company will then certify the transfer of the shares, which constitutes a representation by the company that it has received documents that show a prima facie title to the shares in the transferor. Where that certification is made negligently and a person acts on the faith of it, the company is liable to that person as if the certification had been made fraudulently provided that he can prove that he relied on the certification (see *Longman v. Bath Electric Tramways* (1905)). The instrument of transfer will be marked with the words "certificate lodged" and returned to the transferor. The transfer is then delivered to the transferee, who pays the stamp duty and lodges the instrument with the company. When the transfer is registered, the company issues two new share certificates, one for the transferor and another for the transferee.

The transferee becomes the holder and legal owner of the shares only when his name is entered in the register of members.

13.2.2 Pre-emption rights

Pre-emption rules are commonly contained in the articles of association of a private company, as such a company must place a restriction on the transfer of its shares under section 33 of the Companies Act 1963. A pre-emption clause in the articles of association requires the transferor to first offer his shares to the existing members of a company before transferring those shares to third parties. In *Re Hafner* (1949) Black J. stated that a "statutory right of transfer is given independently of the articles, but it is a right which may or may not be restricted by the articles." These pre-emption rights should not be confused with the statutory pre-emption rights exercisable on an allotment by the company (discussed at Chapter 12).

In *Phelan v. Goodman et al* (2001) Murphy J. stated that the pre-emption rights guaranteed by the articles of the company were breached by an agreement that involved the transfer of the beneficial ownership of shares. He relied on *Lyle and Scott Ltd v. Scotts Trustees* (1959), which stated that "a shareholder who has transferred, or pretended to transfer, the beneficial interest in a share to a purchaser for value is merely endeavouring by the subterfuge to escape from the pre-emptory provisions of the articles".

Where the shareholder must offer the shares to his fellow members, the price is agreed between the parties, and, in the absence of such agreement, the price is commonly settled by the company's auditors. In *Dean v. Price* (1954) it was held that the auditors may be liable to a party who suffers a loss as a result of a negligent valuation of such shares. Where the articles of the company clearly indicate that the shareholders are to be bound by a pre-emption obligation, the court will enforce such provisions (see *Lyle & Scott Ltd v. Scotts' Trustees* (1959)). In *Re Benfield Greig Group plc, Nugent and anor v. Benfield Greig Group plc et al* (2000) the articles of the company provided that the shares were to be offered to the company's employee trusts at a market value to be determined by the company's auditor or an external and independent valuer appointed by the directors. The executors of a shareholder challenged the valuation and the court held that the valuation was final and binding since the parties had agreed to be bound by the articles which provided for this and there was no evidence of manifest error.

13.2.3 Registration of the transfer

A transfer of shares "is not legally complete until the transferee has been registered in the books of the company" according to *Tangney v. The Clarence Hotels Company Ltd et al* (1933). The transferor is not obliged to procure the registration of the transferee as a member of the company. However, it is now common for the parties to use a share purchase agreement on the transfer of shares whereby the transferor undertakes to assist with the registration of the transferee. Section 83 of the Companies Act 1963 states that the company shall register the transferee where such an application is made by the transferor.

Therefore, in the absence of an agreement to the contrary, it is the duty of the transferee to procure registration according to *Skinner's Case* (1885). Prior to such registration, the unregistered transferee has equitable rights in relation to the shareholding. Any dividend received by the transferor should be paid over to the transferee (unless the shares are sold ex-dividend), and the transferor indemnifies the transferee against any calls or liability on the shares before registration of the transfer. In *Phelan v. Goodman and Taher* (2001) Murphy J. held that this indemnity was in respect of the shares themselves and did not encompass a continuing obligation on the part of the transferor or representations made by the transferor in respect of the balance sheet or profit and loss account.

The transferor is still recognised as the legal holder of the shares, and the transferee has no legal rights to vote at the company meetings. In the English case of *Musselwhite and anor v. CH Musselwhite & Son* (1962), it was confirmed that the unpaid transferor was entitled to exercise his voting rights in respect of its share. In *Kinsella v. Alliance and Dublin Consumers Gas Co.* (1982) Barron J. held that "persons entitled to stock must be registered in the register of shareholders. Until they are, they are not entitled to vote. This is a well established principle and I would be wrong not to follow it." However, these voting rights cannot be exercised in a manner adverse to the interests of the transferee. In *O'Gorman et al v. Kelleher et al* (1999) Carroll J. stated that "if an unpaid vendor of share were to vote deliberately so as to damage the purchaser, or contrary to the interests of the purchaser, who is the beneficial owner, it seems to me that he could be restrained by the court of equity".

13.2.4 Refusal to register a transfer

Where the power to do so is granted by the articles of the company, directors may have a power to refuse to register the transfer. Further, directors will have a duty to refuse to register if the transfer is completed in contravention of conditions or restrictions for share transfers set out in the articles of association.

Model article 3 of Table A may be adopted by the company; it gives the sweeping power to the directors of a company to refuse to register a transfer without even giving a reason. The only real basis for the transferee to challenge this is that of mala fides - the exercise of powers not in the interest of the company. In *Re Hafner* the applicant, whose transfer was refused, was able to show that the directors had refused to register the transfer in order to prevent the applicant challenging "bloated emoluments" paid to the directors. The directors challenged the action on the basis that article 3 of Table A allowed the directors to refuse a registration without stating the reasons for the refusal. The court interpreted the directors' continuing silence as evidence of bad faith in the particular circumstances and invalidated their refusal to register. Black J. stated that "in order to interfere, the court must not only find that the directors had an invalid motive, but it must also find that they had no valid motive that might be itself sufficient."

The burden of proving mala fides is heavily placed on the transferee. In *Re Smith and Fawcett Ltd* (1933) the executors of a member's estate submitted a stock transfer form transferring the shares to the executors. The directors refused to register the transfer stating that one director of the company would purchase half of the shares to maintain the current control structure of the company and the rest of the shares could be transferred to the executors. The court held there was not sufficient evidence that the directors had not acted bona fide in refusing to register the transfer to the executors. Greene M.R. stated:

> "[I]n the present case the article is drafted in the widest possible terms, and I decline to write into that clear language any limitation other than a limitation which is implicit by law, that a fiduciary power of this kind must be exercised bona fide in the interests of the company. Subject to that qualification, an article in this form appears to me to give the directors what it says, namely, absolute and uncontrolled discretion."

In the light of this case, it appears that there is a presumption that the directors have acted in good faith, and the transferee has a heavy onus to rebut the presumption. Further, the test of whether or not the directors have acted bona fide is subjective. In *Lee & Company (Dublin) Ltd* (1978) it was held that a director who sells shares must vote in favour of their registration.

It may be that the articles allow the directors a more limited discretion to refuse registration. Some articles of association may permit the directors to refuse registration where it is not in the best interests of the company that the transferee becomes a company member. In *Tangey v. The Clarence Hotels Company Ltd* (1933) registration was declined on the basis that the transferee is "not a desirable person to admit to membership". The directors refused to register a transfer on this ground despite the fact that the transferee had been a director and member of the company for many years. This refusal was overturned by the court as a result. The power to refuse registration on this ground is limited, as the directors may only have regard to the transferee's personal qualities (see *Re Bede Steam Company* (1917)).

Also, the power to refuse registration must be exercised within a reasonable time, or it will lapse. Unless the registration is refused within a reasonable time, the transferee will be entitled to have his shares automatically registered. This is a consequence of the fundamental transferability of shares and the fact that the directors did not exercise their power to interfere with this. In *Re Hackney Pavilion Ltd* (1924) an executrix sought to be registered the deceased's shares. The two directors reached a deadlock on the decision and there was no resolution either way. Ashbury J. said that the power to decline must be actively exercised and it was not. Therefore, the shares were registered. A reasonable period is accepted to be two months, as section 84 of the Companies Act 1963 requires that the transferee be informed of a refusal to register within two months.

13.2.5 Unregistered transfers

If the company refuses to register a transfer, the transferor, as the registered shareholder, holds the shares in trust for the transferee as his nominee. In *Casey v. Bentley* (1902) it was held in the case of an unlimited company that there is no implied term in a contract for the sale of shares that the transferee will be registered. In this case, the transferor remained in danger of liability as a member of an unlimited company and had to pay the dividend she received over to the transferee as beneficial owner. The legal owner is, therefore, considered a trustee for the equitable owner, and must pay any dividend that accumulates on the shares, vote, or exercise any right as instructed by the transferee; and, finally, the transferor should assist with the registration of the equitable owner by handing over the executed transfer and the share certificate.

Forged transfers are null and void. The transferor can compel the company to restore the name of the true owner of the shares to the register if a company registers a forged transfer and removes the true owner from the register. The company can claim against persons submitting a forged transfer if the company thereby suffers any loss even where the person was unaware of the forgery. The company may have to compensate an innocent third party who takes a transfer of the forged shares and pays value for them.

13.2.6 Transmission on death or bankruptcy

On the death of a member of a company, the shares automatically vest in the personal representative of the deceased shareholder. Under section 87 of the Companies Act 1963 the company must accept the Grant of Probate (in the case of a will) or the Letters of Administration (in the case of intestacy, *i.e.* no will) as sufficient evidence of the title of the personal representatives. It is open to the personal representatives to apply for the registration of the transmission under section 81(2) of the Act. However, section 82 provides that the personal representatives may transfer the shares without becoming members of the company. The model articles of Table A provide that the personal representatives must elect to register as members of the company or transfer those shares within 90 days. Where the personal representatives opt to transfer the shares, the directors retain the right to refuse registration of the transmitee (equivalent to the transferee). The transmittee has the right to take an action against the company for oppression under section 205 of the Companies Act 1963.

Where shares were held jointly by shareholders, the surviving owner of the joint shares becomes the sole owner upon the death of the other.

Under section 44(1) of the Bankruptcy Act 1988, the shares of a member automatically vest in the official assignee appointed to carry out the bankruptcy. The official assignee may be registered as a member of the company or may transfer shares. If the shares are too onerous, it is open to the official assignee to disclaim them.

13.3 Shareholders' meetings

13.3.1 Annual general meeting

An annual general meeting is an opportunity for the company members and directors to examine the health of a company. It is primarily focused on the presentation and examination of the annual accounts (see Chapter 9). According to section 131(1) of the Companies Act 1963, there is a statutory obligation on every category of company incorporated in the State to hold an annual general meeting. Section 140 of the Companies Act 1963 states that every annual general meeting must be held within the State and any business transacted outside the State is void. However, such a meeting will be valid where the articles allow for annual general meetings outside the State and the members of the company unanimously consent to such a meeting or resolve to hold the meeting elsewhere at the preceding annual general meeting.

Section 131(1) of the Companies Act 1963 also requires that an annual general meeting is held every calendar year, not more that 15 months after the previous one. Newly incorporated companies get an 18-month period from incorporation within which to have their first meeting under section 131(2). Where there is a default in holding a meeting in accordance with section 131(1), the Director of Corporate Enforcement, further to the application of any member of the company, may call or direct the calling of a meeting, and it is open to the Director to direct that one member of the company present in person or by proxy shall constitute a meeting (section 131(3) of the Companies Act 1963 as amended by section 14 of the Company Law Enforcement Act 2001). Where the Director so directs an annual general meeting and it is not held in the year in which the default occurred, it shall not be treated as the annual general meeting for that year unless the company resolves that it be treated as the annual general meeting of the company. The obligation to hold an annual general meeting is placed on the company officers who will be held liable to a fine under section 131(6) of the Companies Act 1963 if the obligation is breached. In *Re Muckross Park Hotel Ltd* (2001) the company and its directors were successfully prosecuted for the failure to hold an annual general meeting in 1999 despite having been notified by the Department of Enterprise, Trade and Employment on a number of times.

Single-member private limited companies can resolve to dispense with the holding of an annual general meeting under section 131 of the Companies Act 1963 as a result of Regulation 8(1) of the European

Community (Single-Member Private Limited Companies) Regulations 1884.

As mentioned above, the annual general meeting primarily considers the annual accounts of the company. As discussed in Chapter 9, section 148 of the Companies Act 1963 requires the directors of the company to present the annual accounts of the company to the members at an annual general meeting. These accounts include the company's balance sheet, profit and loss account (or income and expenditure account in the case of a not for profit company), the auditors' report and the directors' report. Where model article 53 of Table A is adopted by the company, the ordinary business of an annual general meeting also involves the declaration of a dividend, the election of directors in place of those retiring, the re-appointment of auditors, and the fixing of the remuneration of auditors. Anything else that is considered at an annual general meeting is termed "special business". This may change from company to company, depending on the particular articles adopted. It is open to the company members to give notice of any resolution they wish to propose at an annual general meeting.

Under section 159 of the Companies Act 1963, a copy of the balance sheet, the profit and loss, and the reports must be sent to the members, any debenture holders, and any other entitled persons, at least twenty-one days before the annual general meeting. It is open to all the members who are entitled to be present and vote at the annual general meeting to agree to accept accounts sent less than twenty-one days before the annual general meeting (section 159(3)).

13.3.2 Extraordinary general meetings

Where a general meeting is not an annual general meeting, it is called an extraordinary general meeting. Pursuant to section 132 of the Companies Act 1963, such a meeting must be convened by the directors of the company on the requisition of the company members holding at least one-tenth of the paid-up share capital of the company that carries voting rights. The requisition must state the objects of the meeting and be signed by the requisitioners and deposited at the registered office of the company. The directors have twenty-one days from the date of the deposit to convene a meeting to be held within two months. If the directors fail to act, the requisitioning members may hold the meeting themselves within three months of that deposit date. Any expenses incurred by the members due to the directors' failure to call the meeting, shall be paid by the company out of any fees or remuneration due to the directors. Section 134(b) further provides that members themselves may call a meeting of the company unless the articles of the company state otherwise. This provision allows two or more members holding not less than one-tenth of the share capital of the company, or five per cent of the members where there is no share capital, to call a meeting.

Under section 135 the court may direct that a meeting of the company be called, held, and conducted, either by way of its own motion or on the application of a director or any member of the company who has the right to vote at general meetings. It is open to the court to direct that one member present in person or by proxy shall be deemed to constitute a meeting. Where model article 50 of Table A is adopted by the company, it is open to a director of the company to call a meeting.

There is no statutory obligation on a director to convene a general meeting save in the case of section 40 of the Companies (Amendment) Act 1983 where the company incurs serious capital loss (see Chapter 15).

13.3.3 Notice for meetings

In order to convene a general meeting of a company, all persons entitled to attend and vote at a general meeting of a company must receive a notice of the meeting. This includes the members and the auditors of the company unless the articles of the company provide otherwise. The notice must be in writing specifying the place, the day, and the hour of the meeting. In the case of special business, it must also state the nature of the special business to be transacted (model article 51 of Table A). In the case of *Re Moorgate Mercantile Holdings* (1980), it was held that a notice of a general meeting must be clear and precise in its substance, and each shareholder must be fully appraised so that he may decide whether he should attend the meeting or not. It is open to a member of the company to seek to restrain a meeting of the company where insufficient particulars of the meeting have been provided (see *Jackson v. Munster Bank* (1884-85)).

Section 133(1) of the Companies Act 1963 requires a minimum notice period of twenty-one days for an annual general meeting of every company. In the case of a private company, a general meeting to consider an ordinary resolution requires seven days' notice. In the case of a public company, fourteen days' notice of a general meeting to consider an ordinary resolution is required. The articles of the company may provide for a longer (but not a shorter) period of notice. The notice periods set out in the Act or in the company's articles may be avoided if the auditors of the company and all members entitled to vote at the general meeting agree.

Where a special resolution is being proposed at a general meeting of a private or public company, section 141 requires twenty-one days' notice to be provided to the members of the company. The notice required under section 141 can be avoided where not less that 90 per cent of the holders of the nominal value of shares entitled to vote and attend the meeting so agree. Section 142 requires extended notice of twenty-eight days to be given by the company of the intention to pass a resolution on specific matters, being to remove or appoint an auditor (see Chapter 9) or to remove a director from office or appoint a substitute in his place after removal (see Chapter 7).

Section 134(b) states that the notice of a general meeting shall be served in accordance with the model articles unless the articles of the company provide otherwise. *Re Union Hill Silver Co.* (1870) stated that it was not necessary to serve notice on a person who was abroad and *Allen v. Gold Reefs of West Africa Ltd* (1900) stated that the personal representatives of a deceased member are not entitled to be notified unless they are on the register of members. Under model article 52 of Table A, the accidental omission to give, or accidental non-receipt of, notice is not sufficient to invalidate the meeting. However, in the English case of *Bradman v. Trinity Estates plc* (1989), the fact the postal notices were not received during a postal strike was held sufficient to allow an injunction preventing the holding of the meeting.

13.3.4 Quorums

Section 134(c) of the Companies Act 1963 states that two members of a private company and three members of any other company shall constitute a quorum unless the articles of the company state otherwise. A quorum is the minimum number of persons required to attend before the general meeting can commence business. Where model article 54 of Table A is adopted by the company, the general meeting of a public company must have at least three members present in person in order to have a valid quorum. Under model article 5 of Part II of Table A, the general meeting of a private company must have two persons present or present by proxy. It is, however, open to the Director of Corporate Enforcement or the court to direct that one member present in person or by proxy shall constitute a valid meeting.

The quorum must be present when the meeting proceeds to business. In the case of *Re Hartley Baird Limited* (1954), it was held that if the quorum is present when the meeting commences, then even if they leave during the meeting, it is validly constituted and decisions are valid. Model article 55 states that if the quorum is not present within 30 minutes of the appointed time, the meeting will be dissolved where it was requisitioned by the members, and, in all other cases, it will be adjourned to the same day in the following week at such place and time as the directors determine. If the quorum is not present at the adjourned meeting within 30 minutes of the appointed time, then whatever members are present shall constitute a quorum.

If a meeting is not properly constituted, the outcome of the meeting is voidable and the court has a discretion as to whether to set aside the particular resolutions or not.

13.3.5 Proxies

A proxy is the name given to a person who is appointed by a member of the company for the purpose of attending and voting at a general meeting. Section 136(1) of the Companies Act 1963 gives every member of a company who is entitled to attend and vote at a general meeting, the right to appoint a proxy. The proxy has the same right as the member to speak at the meeting and to vote on a show of hands and on a poll.

In the case of a company having a share capital, every notice calling a general meeting must state with reasonable prominence that the member has the right to appoint a proxy. Where the company defaults in complying with this requirement, every officer of the company in default is liable to a fine under section 136(3).

Under section 136(4) members cannot be compelled to submit proxy forms to the company more than forty-eight hours before the meeting. Any article requiring this is void. Where invitations to appoint a person or one of a number of persons as proxies are sent to only some of the members at the company's expense, every officer of the company who knowingly and wilfully authorises the issue of those invitations is liable to a fine under section 136(5) of the Companies Act 1963. Such an officer shall not be liable where a company member requested a proxy form naming a proxy or a list of persons willing to act as a proxy and such a list is generally available to the other members of the company.

The structure that a proxy form should take is set out in model article 71 of Table A. It must indicate who is appointed as proxy and it may be the chairman, another member of the company or any other individual. If the member appointing the proxy is a company, the proxy must be signed by two directors and sealed. A general proxy gives the right to represent the member at more than one general meeting whereas a special proxy may relate to one general meeting. Where the proxy is a "two way" proxy, the member instructs the proxy how to vote on a particular proposal. Where there is no such instruction, the proxy may exercise his own discretion on how to vote. A proxy may be revoked by the member at any time before the general meeting unless, according to *Spiller v. Mayo (Rhodesia)* (1926), it is made for valuable consideration and is expressed to be irrevocable. Under model article 73 of Table A, a vote given in accordance with a proxy where the member has died, become insane, revoked the proxy or transferred his shares, shall be valid unless the company received notice of these matters before the commencement of the meeting at which the proxy was exercised.

13.3.6 The chairman

Section 134(d) of the Companies Act 1963 states that the company members may elect a chairman of a general meeting save where the articles of the company provide otherwise. Model article 104 of Table A permits the directors of the company to appoint a director as a chairman of the board meetings, and under model article 56 of Table A that chairman also presides as the chairman of every general meeting. The model articles also provide that where the chairman fails to attend the meeting or is unwilling to act, it is open to the directors to appoint a director to preside as chairman. Failing this, the chairman is appointed by the members. Pursuant to model article 58 of Table A, the chairman may adjourn the meeting with the consent of the members. The chairman must adjourn the meeting if directed to do so by the members. The next meeting may only deal with the unfinished business of the adjourned meeting, and fresh notice must be served on the company members where the meeting is adjourned for 30 days or more. In *Kinsella v. Alliance and Dublin Gas Consumer's Company* (1982) Barron J. held that the chairman had no power to adjourn a meeting contrary to the wishes of the majority.

13.3.7 Resolutions

Ordinary resolutions are resolutions that require a simple majority of the votes cast.

Under section 141 of the Companies Act 1963 special resolutions need to be passed by not less than three-fourths of the votes of members. Special resolutions are required for matters such as the alteration of the company's authorised capital, a reduction in the company's share capital, a change of company name, a resolution to wind up the company, or the variation of share class rights.

According to section 141(5) of the Companies Act 1963, the terms of any resolution (special or ordinary) before a general meeting may be amended by an ordinary resolution provided that the terms of the amended resolution will be such that adequate notice of that resolution was given to the members. Therefore, no amendment is permissible to the substance of a special resolution, according to *Re Moorgate Mercantile Holdings* (1980), and any amendment to an ordinary resolution should only be permitted where the amendment is within the scope of the original resolution (*Re Betts & Co. Ltd v. Macnaughton* (1910)).

Informal resolutions are permitted by section 141(8), which provides that a resolution in writing signed by all the members of the company entitled to attend or vote at a general meeting will be deemed to be valid. Such a resolution will take effect on the date that the last member signs the resolution. Section 141(8)(c) states that this informal procedure cannot be used in relation to a resolution under section 160 (the removal of an auditor) or a resolution under section 182 (the removal of a company director).

Section 143 requires that a copy of the following company resolutions is forwarded to the Registrar of Companies (and any company member on the payment of a designated fee):

1. special resolutions;
2. resolutions agreed by the members of the company which in the absence of such agreement would have required a special resolution;
3. resolutions agreed by the members of the company which in the absence of such agreement would have required a particular majority;

4. all resolutions or agreements which effectively bind all the members of any class of shareholders though not agreed to by all those members;
5. resolutions increasing the share capital of the company;
6. resolutions for the voluntary winding up of the company;
7. resolutions attaching rights or restrictions to any share;
8. resolutions varying any such rights or restrictions;
9. resolutions classifying any unclassified share;
10. resolutions converting classes of shares;
11. resolutions of directors of the company that an old public limited company be re-registered as a plc or canceling shares in a plc pursuant to section 43(3) of the Companies (Amendment) Act 1983.

Failure to comply with these obligations under section 143 of the Companies Act 1963 will render the company and every officer in default liable to a fine. It is expressly stated in section 143(7) that, in this case, a liquidator of the company shall be deemed to be an officer of the company.

13.3.8 Voting

In order to vote, the member must be registered in the register of members. There is no obligation on the chairman to adjourn the meeting pending the registration of share transfers. In *Kinsella v. Alliance and Dublin Gas Consumer's Company* (1982) the court held that only members appearing on the register could vote and that the chairman had no power to adjourn the meeting to enable registration in defiance of the wishes of the meeting.

There are two methods of voting, namely a show of hands and a poll. Unless the articles of the company provide otherwise, all questions should be first decided on a show of hands according to *Re Horbury Bridge Co.* (1879). Every member of a company has one vote irrespective of the number of shares held. A member may not have that vote where he holds shares that are expressed to be non-voting.

Under section 137 of the Companies Act 1963 the members of the company have the right to demand a poll on a matter before the general meeting, and in section 137(1) it is clarified that the right to demand a poll is extended to proxies. Any provision in the articles of the company restricting the right to demand a poll in the following manner is void:

1. excluding the right of members to demand a poll (save in the case of the election of the chairman or the adjournment of a meeting);
2. requiring a demand to be made by more than five members with a right to vote at the meeting;
3. requiring a demand to be made by voting member or members representing not less than one-tenth of all the members having the right to vote at the meeting;
4. requiring a demand to be made by member or members holding shares paid up to at least one-tenth of the total shares paid up that confer a right to vote.

Where a contentious issue is being decided or where the outcome of a show of hands is unclear, the chairman may wish to call for a poll in accordance with model article 59 of Table A. This article provides for a poll to be validly demanded by the chairman or at least three members present in person or by proxy. Model article 63 of Table A states that every member or proxy present has one vote only on a show of hands, but if a poll is demanded, every member has a vote for every share held. Section 138 of the Companies Act 1963 allows a member to use his votes in different ways. Model article 60 of Table A states that when a poll is demanded, the poll shall take place in the manner directed by the chairman. Model article 62 states that a poll on the election of the chairman or on the adjournment shall take place immediately. On any other matter, the poll shall take place at such time as the chairman directs. A poll is invalidated where a member who is entitled to vote is excluded (see *R v. Lambeth* (1839)).

13.3.9 Minutes of a general meeting

Section 145 of the Companies Act 1963 requires that a company maintain minutes of all proceedings at general meetings and they are prima facie evidence of the proceedings when they are signed by the chairman of the meeting. When minutes are made in accordance with this section, the meeting shall be presumed to have been duly held and convened, and all proceedings of the meeting are presumed to have been duly had. Further, all appointments of directors and liquidators shall be presumed valid. This is a rebuttable presumption, as the section allows for the contrary to be proved. Section 145(3A) (as amended by section

19 of the Company Law Enforcement Act 2001) provides that the company shall produce the books of the minutes to the Director of Corporate Enforcement, and inspection and copying facilities must also be provided to the Director where requested.

Where the company fails to maintain such minutes or comply with its obligations under section 145(3A), the company and every officer in default is liable to a fine. Section 146 provides that the books of the minutes must be kept at the registered office of the company and be open to the inspection of any member. Any member may also request a copy of any minutes within seven days of a request and the payment of a fee. Failure to allow an inspection or supply a duly requested copy may result in the company and every officer in default being liable to a fine. It is open to the court under section 146(4) to make an order compelling an inspection or directing that copies of minutes be provided.

14. SHAREHOLDERS' REMEDIES

Where shareholders can prove that a special fiduciary relationship exists between the shareholders and the directors of the company, they may now bring an action against the directors for a breach of directors' duties (see Chapter 7). A shareholder also has *locus standi* to apply to the court to seek the winding up of the company, and the grounds for making such an application are set out at Chapter 22.

Shareholders always have the right to bring an action to vindicate their own personal rights arising from the articles and memorandum of association; these are the section 25 contract rights discussed at Chapter 4. However, where a wrong has been committed against the company entity itself, the rule in *Foss v. Harbottle,* discussed below, prevents the shareholders from seeking redress. There are, however, limited circumstances where a shareholder may commence a derivative action on behalf of the company to vindicate the company's interests.

Further, a special statutory shareholder remedy was introduced by section 205 of the Companies Act 1963, and shareholders can now seek relief from the court where the members' interests are being oppressed or disregarded.

14.1 The rule in *Foss v. Harbottle*

As discussed in the early chapters, the shareholders may be the investors in the company, but the company is a separate entity managed by the board of directors. That separate entity can take legal actions in its own name and it can also be sued. Therefore, where a wrong is committed against the company it would be incorrect for a shareholder to presume that he can take action against the wrongdoer. This is because it is the general rule that where a wrong is committed against a company, it is the company who should sue for redress. The rationale behind this rule is three-fold:

1. it is loyal to the separate corporate personality principle;
2. it is loyal to the majority rules principle, as it prevents a shareholder taking an action where the majority of shareholders could legitimately ratify the "wrong" under the articles of association;
3. it avoids a scenario of multiple shareholder actions.

In *Prudential Assurance Co. v. Newman Industries Ltd (No. 2)* (1982) the Court of Appeal stated that the rule "is not merely a tiresome procedural obstacle placed in the path of a shareholder by a legalistic judiciary" but that it is a consequence of the fact that a corporation is a separate legal entity.

This general rule is commonly called the rule in *Foss v. Harbottle* deriving from a case by that name in 1843. In this case a number of promoters purchased land before the company was incorporated. On incorporation the land was sold to the company and the promoters became the company directors. Two shareholders of the company alleged that the land had been sold to the company at an exorbitant price. They also alleged that the directors had raised money through mortgaging the land, which was not allowed by the objects of the company. The action was dismissed by the court as it was held by Wigram L.J. that the company was the proper vehicle for the bringing of an action where the company suffers the wrong.

In *Prudential Assurance Co. v. Newman Industries Ltd (No. 2)* (1982) the Court of Appeal summarised the rule as follows:

1. the proper plaintiff where wrong is done to the company is, prima facie, the company; and
2. where the relevant transaction can be confirmed by a simple majority of the members and thus rendered binding on the company, no individual member can sue.

14.1.1 Exceptions to Foss v. Harbottle

The rule in *Foss v. Harbottle* will not prevent a shareholder from taking an action on one or more of the following grounds:

1. where the action by the company is *ultra vires* or illegal;
2. where the action by the company is in breach of the articles of association;
3. where the action by the company was incorrectly ratified by the shareholders (*i.e.* a special resolution and not an ordinary resolution was required in the circumstances);
4. where the action by the company was a fraud on the minority by those in control of the company;
5. where the justice of the case requires that an action may be taken.

14.1.2 Ultra vires actions

There is considerable support for the view that the shareholder has a personal right of action in the case of a company acting *ultra vires.*

In *Simpson v. Westminster Palace Hotel Co.* (1860) a single shareholder was allowed to seek an injunction to restrain the company from taking an *ultra vires* action. This right is now set out in the Companies Acts where section 8(2) of the Companies Act 1963 permits a member of the company to apply to the court for an order restraining the company from doing any act or thing which the company has no power to do. This is supported by *Prudential Assurance Co. v. Newman Industries Ltd (No. 2)* (1982) where it was held that if the transaction is *ultra vires* the company, it is not open to the majority to confirm it and, therefore, the rule in *Foss v. Harbottle* is inapplicable.

In *Hennessy & Ors v. National Agricultural and Industrial Development Association & Ors* (1947) it was held that where an *ultra vires* action had taken place, a member of the company can apply for a declaration that the action is *ultra vires*. However, it appears to be established by case law that where the shareholder seeks to recover compensation in the name of the company for the *ultra vires* action that has occurred, the rule in *Foss v. Harbottle* would apply and the prevent the action (see *Smith v. Croft (No. 2)* (1988)). The reason given is that the company should decide whether or not to seek compensation and it may decide not to pursue the damages due to possible adverse publicity. This line of reasoning has been heavily criticised.

14.1.3 Illegal actions

There is also support for the view that the shareholder has a personal right of action in the case of a company acting illegally.

Where the insiders of the company have acted illegally, the rule in *Foss v. Harbottle* does not prevent a shareholder or shareholders from taking an action for redress according to the case of *Cockburn v. Newbridge Sanitary Steam Laundry Ltd* (1915). In this case two members of the company sued the managing director, seeking an order requiring him to re-pay bribes for company contracts that he had paid out of the company's funds. The other shareholders did not support the action, and the managing director's defence was that the action should be brought in the name of the company. This defence was rejected by the court on the ground that *Foss v. Harbottle* does not protect acts "of a fraudulent character."

14.1.4 The majority principle and breach of the articles

The rule in *Foss v. Harbottle* does not prevent a dissenting member from personally attacking an action of the company that is passed by a bare majority when it in fact should have been passed by a special resolution. A member can also bring an action when the majority purports to act in contravention of the memorandum or articles, or purports to ratify a breach.

Initially, the court incorrectly found that the rule in *Foss v. Harbottle* prevented these actions. In *MacDougall v. Gardiner* (1875) the articles of the company provided that a poll could be demanded by five members in certain circumstances. A poll was duly demanded and the chairman refused to accept it. One of the shareholders issued proceedings against the company and the directors on his own behalf and on behalf of all the other shareholders seeking a declaration that the chairman's conduct was illegal and improper. The court refused to allow the action on the basis that it infringed the rule in *Foss v. Harbottle.*

However, in *Pender v. Lushington* (1877) the articles of the company provided that the votes of nominee shareholders would count at general meetings. The chairman refused to count the nominees of a shareholder, and the shareholder took an action to restrain the directors from proceeding. Jessel M.R. held that the right to have a vote recorded is granted by the articles of association, the breach of which has nothing to do with the rule in *Foss v. Harbottle*. This line of reasoning was supported and explained in *Edwards v. Haliwell* (1950). In this case the subscriptions required from members of a trade union were set out in the articles of association. These contributions could only be varied by a members' ballot. The subscriptions were increased by a meeting of the trade union delegates, and no members' ballot was held. The members sought a declaration that the change was invalid, and the action was opposed on the basis of the rule in *Foss v. Harbottle.* Jenkins L.J. found that the personal rights of the members had been infringed as a result of the breach of the articles of association and, therefore, the rule in *Foss v. Harbottle* did not apply. He stated that the rule had no application because the members of the union were suing for their individual rights *qua* members and not because of a wrong done to the company. This was followed in *Byng v. London Life Association Ltd* (1990), where a shareholder successfully sought a declaration that a meeting and a special resolution were void as the procedure for adjourning the meeting had not been followed.

Therefore, the directors and the majority shareholders must abide by the articles or alter them. If the alteration is not bona fide and in the interests of the company as a whole, then the minority can bring an action on their own behalf to challenge the alteration.

14.1.5 Fraud on the minority

Where a fraud is committed on the minority of the members of the company by the majority in control, then the former can bring an action seeking relief for the company. Fraud on the minority cases usually relate to expropriation or appropriation of the company's property, *i.e.* the diversion of property by the majority who are in control.

However, the fraud on the minority exception can be distinguished from the other exceptions mentioned above. As this action seeks relief for the company it cannot be constituted as a personal action by shareholders. The action must be commenced by way of a derivative action, *i.e.* commenced by the shareholder on behalf of the company and it is the company who is the beneficiary of any judgment of the court.

(1) Fraud

The minority shareholder must establish the existence of a fraud. In *Menier v. Hooper's Telegraph Works Ltd* (1874) James L.J. stated that the majority shareholders essentially divided the assets of a company between themselves to the exclusion of the minority. He stated that where "the majority have put something in their pockets at the expense of the minority", then they have a right of derivative action. In *Cook v. Deeks* (1916) the directors of a company diverted a lucrative contract away from the company to themselves, in breach of their fiduciary duty. They then caused a resolution to be passed approving this action as they were majority shareholders. The minority shareholder successfully brought a derivative action. The Privy Council stated that the resolution herein should be disregarded as it "would amount to forfeiting the interests and property of the minority of shareholders in favour of the majority" by votes of the potential beneficiaries.

In *Estmanco (Kilner House) Ltd v. GLC* (1982) a controlling shareholder used its control to discontinue an action taken by the company for a breach of contract. A minority shareholder then successfully sought to take over the action discontinued by the company. It was held that the majority shareholder could not selfishly exercise its voting rights "with impunity" and "injure his voteless fellow shareholders." A fraud is also committed where the majority of the shareholders support a breach of directors' duties or the mala fide use of the directors' powers.

(2) Control

The fraud must be committed by the majority in "control" of the company. Control is commonly proved by showing that those committing the fraud hold fifty-one per cent or more of the voting shares in the company. Alternatively, where simple voting control cannot be established, it is open to the minority shareholder to prove that (a) the company was requested but refused to commence the action on its own behalf or (b) as the wrongdoer was in control, it would be idle to apply to the company (see *Fisher v. St John's Opera House Co.* (1937)).

(3) A prima facie case

In order to bring a derivative action the shareholder must establish a prima facie case that:

1. the company is entitled to the relief claimed; and
2. the action falls within the proper boundaries of the exceptions to *Foss v. Harbottle.*

In *Smith v. Croft (No. 3)* (1987) Knox J. applied the two-step test and introduced a further step in that the attitude of the disinterested shareholders is relevant when allowing a derivative action to proceed. He considered that perhaps a majority of the minority shareholders should support the action. Some commentators have argued that this third step is bad law and should be disregarded.

The shareholder must prove that if the derivative action is not permitted, the wrong committed against the company will go unredressed. In *Wallersteiner v. Moir (No. 2)* (1975) Denning M.R. stated that in the context of the rule in *Foss v. Harbottle* the company has a remedy against wrongs done by outsiders, but not against insiders if they are in a majority. He held that without the derivative action "an injustice would be done without redress". The shareholder must also come within one of the exceptions to the rule. In *Horgan v. Murray and Milton* (1998) the plaintiff and defendants agreed to go into business together. The relationship between the plaintiff and the defendants broke down, and the plaintiff claimed that the defendants engaged in a course of action intended to exclude the plaintiff from the company and that the company had been damaged as a result of these actions. O'Sullivan J. held that it was for the company to pursue this action due to the rule in *Foss v. Harbottle.* As the plaintiff had failed to bring himself within one of the exceptions to *Foss v. Harbottle,* the proceedings were dismissed as showing no reasonable cause of action and as an abuse of the process of the court.

In *Wallersteiner v. Moir (No.2)* (1975) Denning M.R. held that the costs of the derivative action should be borne by the company.

14.1.6 Justice of the case

This exception to the rule in *Foss v. Harbottle* is not firmly established in this jurisdiction. In *Heything v. Dupont* (1964) Harmond L.J. stated that exceptions to the rule in *Foss v. Harbottle* may be made "where the justice of the case demands". This was quoted with approval in *Moylan v. Irish Whiting Manufacturers Ltd* (1980), but Irish legal commentators have advised a cautionary approach to this case as the comments relating to this exception were *obiter.* In *Prudential Assurance v.* Newman (1982) at first instance Vinelott J. allowed the derivative action on the basis that "the interests of justice require that a minority action should be permitted'. The Court of Appeal declined to deal with it except to state that it was an impractical test to adopt.

In *O'Neill v. Ryan & Ors* (1993) Blayney J. referred to the "justice of the case" exception but declined to dismiss or endorse it as he felt it was not relevant to the matters before him.

14.1.7 Diminution of share value

In *Prudential Assurance v. Newman Industries (No. 2)* (1982) the plaintiff was a minority shareholder in the defendant company. The plaintiff brought a derivative action and a personal action against the defendant and two of its directors, alleging that the actions of the directors had reduced the value of the plaintiff's shares. The Court of Appeal stated that this was "misconceived". While directors have a fiduciary duty to the shareholders, this does not extend to the company's losing value and the subsequent loss in value of shares being actionable against the director. That loss is the loss of the company, and the shares of the member are merely "a right of participation in the company on the terms of the articles of association", and this right is not reflected by the diminution in value. This is cited with approval by Blayney J. in *O'Neill v. Ryan Ors* (1993), where it was held that members could not sue for the diminution in the value of their shareholding. In *Flanagan v. Kelly* (1999) O' Sullivan J. endorsed the fundamental principle of company law that a shareholder cannot sue for a diminution in the value of his shareholding resulting from damage suffered by the company. He held that the alleged losses were those of the company.

14.1.8 Shareholders' actions

It is necessary to analyse the wrong that has occurred and the persons or entities affected thereby:

1. some wrongs are seen as being committed against the company as an entity in itself and in this case it is only the company who has the *locus standi* to bring an action for redress;
2. even where the wrong is committed in respect of the company itself, where that wrong is a fraud on the company and the minority shareholders, it is open to those minority shareholders to commence a "derivative action" in respect of the same if they satisfy certain conditions;
3. there are cases where the wrongs in question are considered as committed against the shareholders in their capacity as members of the company. In such a situation a shareholder can bring an action in his own name against the wrongdoer to vindicate his own rights.

14.2 Section 205 of the Companies Act 1963

A commonly used shareholder remedy is an action under section 205 of the Companies Act 1963. Section 205 provides a remedy to any member of a company who complains that the affairs of the company are being conducted or that the powers of the directors of the company are being exercised in a manner oppressive to him or any of the members (including himself), or in disregard of his or their interests as members.

14.2.1 Section 205 applications

The persons with *locus standi* to make an application under section 205 are the company members. As discussed in Chapter 13, a person does not become a member of a company until that person is entered on the register of members (section 31 of the Companies Act 1963). Section

205(6) of the Companies Act 1963 extends the benefit of section 205 to the personal representatives of members and any trustee of shares or any person beneficially entitled to shares under a will or on the intestate death of a member of the company. In *Re Via Net Works Ltd* (2002) the Supreme Court confirmed that persons who have voluntarily transferred their shares and yet remain on the register of members, are not entitled to maintain a section 205 action. It was held that the legislature could not have envisaged "that persons without any interest in the company but who, for whatever reason, remained on the register as members would be entitled to present a petition grounded on alleged oppression of them as members". According to Kenny J. in *Re Westwinds Holdings Ltd* (1974) the applicant member does not have to be in a minority.

It is open to the members to claim one or more of the following under section 205(1):

1. the affairs of the company are being conducted in a manner oppressive to him;

2. the affairs of the company are being conducted in disregard of his interests;

3. the powers of the directors are being exercised in a manner oppressive to him;

4. the powers of the directors are being exercised in disregard of his interests.

The English cases dealing with a similar section in the English legislation initially held that where a member took an action on the grounds of oppression, it could not succeed unless he was oppressed in his capacity as a member of the company (*Re Bellador Silk Ltd* (1965)). It appears that there is no such limitation on a section 205 action in this jurisdiction; in *Re Murphs Restaurants Ltd* (1979) the member-director took an action under section 205 claiming *inter alia* that he was oppressed as a result of his removal from the office of company director. However, where the action is commenced under the second limb of section 205 and based on the disregard of the member's interests, the damage complained of must be *qua* member.

In either case the application under section 205 must be presented for the genuine purpose of obtaining the relief claimed. A petition presented for a collateral purpose will be considered an abuse of the process of the court (*Re Bellador Silk Ltd* (1965)).

It is not open to the member in a section 205 application to complain about the conduct of the affairs of the company while it was under the protection of the court (*i.e.* in examinership). Section 5(4) of the Companies (Amendment) Act 1990 sets out that an order for relief under section 205 cannot be made on the grounds of such conduct. This section does not prevent a member from complaining that the powers of the directors were exercised oppressively or in disregard of a member's interest during this time.

14.2.2 Section 205 hearings

Where an application is made under section 205, there is provision for the hearing of all or part of the proceedings *in camera* under section 205(7) of the Companies Act 1963. An *in camera* hearing will be permitted where "in the opinion of the court, the hearing of proceedings under this section would involve the disclosure of information the publication of which would be seriously prejudicial to the legitimate interests of the company". However, in *Re R Ltd* (1989) it was stated by the Supreme Court that only in the most exceptional of circumstances should the court agree to hear the application *in camera.* It was held that the applicant for a private hearing has to prove both the probability of serious prejudice to the interests of the company and that the case was one in which justice could be done only in a private hearing.

In *Irish Press plc v. Ingersoll Irish Publications (No. 1)* (1994) Finlay C.J. considered the decision in *Re R Ltd* (1989) and stated that the person applying for a private hearing would have to establish the following to the satisfaction of the court:

1. if the complaining member or members are seeking a private hearing, it must be established that a public hearing would damage his or their shareholdings to such an extent that court would be incapable of ordering a just remedy under section 205(3);

2. if the shareholder or shareholders who are the subject of the complaint are seeking a private hearing, it must be established that a public hearing would damage his or their shareholding to such an extent that even the dismissal of the action and an award of costs in his or their favour would not be a just remedy;

3. in either case, it must be established that the damage to the shareholding as a result of a public hearing would so outweigh the advantage of succeeding in the application that a party to the action would refrain from tendering evidence which would proba-

bly influence the resolution of the issues and the achieving of a just result.

14.2.3 Section 205 remedies

One of the advantages of pursuing relief under section 205 is that the court has an extensive choice as to the relief that may be granted to the shareholder. Under section 205(3) the court has the power to make whatever order it thinks fit "with a view to bringing to an end the matters complained of."

The court may make orders:

1. directing or prohibiting any act by the company;
2. canceling or varying any transaction of the company;
3. regulating the conduct of the company's future affairs;
4. directing an alteration of memorandum and/or articles to safeguard the members' rights;
5. directing the purchase of shares of other members of the company by the company members; and/or
6. directing the purchase of the shares of other members of the company by the company itself and the reduction of the company's capital as a result.

In *Scottish Co-op Wholesale Society v. Meyer* (1959) the oppressive co-operative was ordered to purchase the complaining member's shares. In *Re NEW-AD Advertising Company Ltd* (1997) the court ordered the oppressing shareholder to purchase the shares of the minority at the value they would have been but for the oppressive conduct. In *Profinance Trust SA v. Gladstone* (2001) the English Court of Appeal held that the date for valuing shares ordered to be purchased by the majority shareholder would generally be the date of the court order. This was, however, subject to certain considerations based on fairness.

Alternatively as occurred in *Irish Press plc v. Ingersoll Irish Publications Ltd* (1994) it is open to the court to order the oppressor to sell his shares to the complaining member. It is not open to the court to award damages to the complaining member as according to the Supreme Court in *Irish Press plc v. Ingersoll Irish Publications Ltd* (1995) an award of damages would not achieve the objective of section 205 which is to bring an end to the matters complained of. Further, it was emphasised that section 205(3) makes no provision for such a remedy.

The court may be of the opinion that any of the above remedies would not end the matters complained of. In such a case it is open to the court to make an order winding up the company under section 213(f) (just and equitable grounds) or section 213(g) (oppression grounds) of the Companies Act 1963. In *Re Murph's Restaurants Ltd* (1979) Gannon J. stated that an order under section 205 would be insufficient to "end the matters complained of" where the parties involved in the company were in a close relationship of trust and confidence that had disintegrated. In the circumstances of the case, the court ordered that the company should be wound up on just and equitable grounds under section 213(f) of the Companies Act 1963 (see Chapter 22).

14.2.4 Oppression

The meaning of oppression was first considered by the English cases. In the Irish case of *Re Greenore Trading Company* (1980) Keane J. adopted the definition of Viscount Simonds in *Scottish Co-operative Wholesale Society Ltd v. Meyer* (1959) who considered that oppressive conduct was something "burdensome, harsh and wrongful". In *Re Greenore Trading* there were three shareholders, each with an equal shareholding of 8,000 shares. One of the shareholders, V, later purchased shares from shareholder B for the sum of £22,500. V paid the sum of £8,000 and the remaining consideration for the shares was paid by the company. V claimed the company's payment was compensation for loss of office. The now remaining minority shareholder brought an action under section 205 and sought the winding up of the company or an order that the shareholders had acted oppressively. Keane J. held that if the payment was for loss of office, it was unlawful as it was not approved by a general meeting of the company. If it was not a payment for loss of office, it constituted financial assistance by the company for the purchase of its own shares and was in breach of section 60 of the Companies Act 1963. He held that the payment was "a patent misapplication of the company's monies" for the purpose of giving the shareholder a dominant position. He described this conduct as "burdensome, harsh and wrongful" and ordered V to purchase the minority member's shares.

A continuous pattern of oppression is not required by the court, and a single isolated act can be the basis for a finding of oppression (*Re*

Westwinds Holdings Co. Ltd (1974) and *Re Williams Group Tullamore Ltd* (1985)).

Unlawful or fraudulent conduct clearly constitutes oppression. In *Re Westwinds Holdings Co. Ltd* (1974) there were two director-shareholders of the company. Land owned by the company was sold to a company in which one director-shareholder was the major shareholder. The signature of the other director-shareholder was forged on the transfer deed. Kenny J. found that the sale of the lands was at a "gross undervalue" and was a "fraud on the other member of the company" which alone would have justified an order under section 205(3). The same director-shareholder also caused the company to guarantee an overdraft of another company indirectly owned by him on the basis of forged meeting minutes and equitable mortgage documents. Again, Kenny J. found that this conduct was oppressive. Kenny J. ordered him to purchase the oppressed member's shares to be valued on the basis of the land still being in the name of the company and without regard to the restrictions on the transfer of shares. It is important to note that according to O'Hanlon J. in *Re Clubman Shirts Ltd* (1983), conduct does not need to be unlawful to be oppressive.

Mere incompetence or mismanagement of the company is not sufficient to ground an action for oppression, according to the English case of *Re Five Minute Car Wash Services Ltd* (1966). Buckley J. dismissed an application on the grounds of oppressive conduct as while the managing director might have been unwise, inefficient and careless, there was nothing to point to unscrupulous or unfair behavior, or anything which could be harsh, burdensome or wrongful towards any member.

However, oppressive management can result in a remedy under section 205. In *Re Harmer* (1958) a father and his sons were the shareholders of a family company. The actions of the father in running the business without regard for the other shareholders (his sons) and ignoring the company resolutions and board decisions were held to constitute oppression of the other shareholders. The court ordered that the father be excluded from the management of the business. In *Irish Press plc v. Ingersol Irish Publications Ltd (No. 1)* (1994) Barron J. stated that "where a deliberate plan to damage the interests of a company is carried out by a shareholder in the manner by which it exercises its power to conduct the affairs of the company, such behavior is oppression." Here a failure by the respondent shareholder to operate a management agreement was a repudiation of that agreement and this was central to the finding of oppression.

According to *Re Murph's Restaurants Ltd* (1979) exclusion of a director from management can amount to oppression. Non-consultation of directors with shareholders can amount to oppression, usually in quasi-partnership companies. In *Re Clubman Shirts Ltd* (1986) it was held that a minority shareholder was entitled to have an unusual and important transaction, completed without his knowledge or consent, subjected to the closest scrutiny.

14.2.5 Disregard of members' interests

The second limb of section 205 permits an action based on the disregard of members' interests. It appears from the case law that the level of proof required for such an action is less onerous than that of proving oppression. Further, the use of the word "interests" is very wide ranging and opens this part of section 205 to considerable case law development.

In *Re Williams Group Tullamore Ltd* (1985) the preference shareholders of the company received a fixed dividend and they did not participate in the profits distributed to the ordinary shareholders. Acting within their powers under the articles of association, they passed a resolution creating a new class of shares. This new class of shares would be issued to both ordinary and preference shareholders, but the shares would enable the preference shareholders to participate in a distribution of the company profits over and above their fixed dividend. The court found that the preference shareholders were not acting in a burdensome, harsh, wrongful manner, or a manner which lacked probity and that, therefore, their conduct was not oppressive. Barrington J. then considered the alternative ground and whether those actions were carried out "in disregard of the interests of some member or members." He found that that the resolutions were in disregard of the interests of the ordinary shareholders as the preference shareholders benefited to the detriment of the ordinary shareholders.

15. CAPITAL MAINTENANCE RULES

Companies raise capital by the issuing of shares and this share capital should remain permanently invested in the company as a comfort to the company's creditors. Jessel M.R. stated in *Re Exchange Banking Co.* (1982) that a creditor "gives credit to the company on the faith of the representation that the capital shall be applied only for the purposes of the business."

A private company is not required to have a minimum capital base save in the case where a restricted director proposes to join that private company (see Chapters 2 and 8). Therefore the share capital of a private company may be as little as €2. However, where a company is incorporated as a plc, it cannot commence business until the Registrar of Companies has certified that the nominal value of its allotted share capital is not less than €38,100 (section 19 of the Companies (Amendment) Act 1983). At least twenty-five per cent of that capital must be paid up in money or money's worth. The Companies (Amendment) Act 1983 also introduced a series of capital maintenance rules for plcs and some of those rules are extended to private companies also. The capital maintenance rules range from restrictions on the issuing of redeemable shares to an obligation to call an extraordinary general meeting when the company incurs serious capital loss.

15.1 Redemption of shares

Both private and public companies may issue redeemable shares pursuant to section 207 of the Companies Act 1990. A redeemable share is defined in section 206 of that Act as one which the company may buy back from the shareholder at the option of the company or the shareholder. Section 64 of the Companies Act 1963 allowed a company to issue redeemable preference shares. This section was repealed by the Companies Act 1990, and the power to issue redeemable shares was extended to all classes of shares. The power to issue such shares and the terms and conditions of any such share issue should be set out in the articles of association. If a company does not have the power to issue redeemable shares and it wishes to do so, it is necessary to amend the articles of association by way of a special resolution.

15.1.1 Conditions attached to redeemable shares

Section 207(2) of the Companies Act 1990 sets out that the issue and redemption of shares is subject to the following conditions:

1. the nominal value of issued share capital of the company which is not redeemable constitutes ten per cent or more of the nominal value of the total issued share capital of the company;
2. the shares cannot be redeemed unless they are fully paid up by the shareholder;
3. the terms of redemption must provide for payment on redemption.
4. the redemption must be funded from profits of the company that are available for distribution;
5. where the company proposes to cancel the redeemed shares (see paragraph 15.1.2 below) the redemption may be funded by the proceeds of a fresh issue of shares where that issue was made for the purposes of the redemption;
6. any premium payable by the company on the redemption must be funded from profits of the company that are available for distribution;
7. where the company proposes to cancel the redeemed shares (see paragraph 15.1.2 below) any premium payable on the redemption may be funded by the proceeds of a fresh issue of shares where that issue was made for the purposes of the redemption. In this case the company may pay a premium up to an amount which is equal to the aggregate of the premiums originally received by the company on the issue of the redeemable shares, or the current amount of the company's share premium account, whichever is less. The company's share premium account shall be reduced by an amount corresponding to the amount of any premium paid out of the proceeds of the new issue.

15.1.2 Cancellation under section 208 of the Companies Act 1990

Where shares are redeemed, it is open to the company to cancel those shares and reduce the issued share capital accordingly. The authorised share capital which is set out in the company's memorandum of association is not reduced.

Where the redemption is funded wholly or partly by the company's profits, the company is required to form a Capital Redemption Reserve Fund and a sum equal to the nominal amount of the shares redeemed should be paid into this fund (this is essentially the sum by which the issued share capital is reduced). Where it is proposed to fund the redemption by a fresh issue of shares discussed above and the amount obtained from the issue is less than the amount required to redeem the shares, a sum representing the shortfall must be paid into the fund. The purpose of the fund is to maintain the capital structure of the company. The fund is treated like issued share capital and can only be reduced in the same manner. Pursuant to section 208(e) of the Companies Act 1990 , the Capital Redemption Reserve Fund may be used by the company to fund an issue of bonus shares to members which bonus shares are to be treated as fully paid up.

15.1.3 Treasury shares under section 209 of the Companies Act 1990

It is open to the company to retain the shares upon redeeming them and these are called treasury shares. As the company does not intend to cancel the shares, the redemption and any premium payable on redemption must be funded only by the distributable profits of the company. Section 209(2)(a) of the Companies Act 1990 provides that the nominal value of the treasury shares may not exceed ten per cent of the nominal value of the company's issued share capital value.

In theory, these shares carry voting rights and a right to a dividend, but the company cannot exercise them. Section 209(3) of the Companies Act 1990 states that any purported exercise of such voting rights is void. Further, no payment or dividend may be paid in respect of those shares. Under section 209(4) it is open to the company to cancel the treasury shares. That section also permits the company to re-issue these shares. Under section 209(5) the issued share capital of the company is not increased by a re-issue. Section 209(6) states that the "re-issue price range" must be determined by a special resolution at a general meeting of the company shareholders (this prerequisite is not applicable where the re-issue is by a public company on a recognised stock exchange). The re-issue must take place within eighteen months of the resolution or during such shorter period as the resolution may fix.

15.1.4 Conversion

Section 210 of the Companies Act 1990 allows a company to convert existing shares into redeemable shares subject to the rules in the Companies Acts dealing with the variation of rights attached to different classes of shares. The power to convert shares must be set out in the company's articles of association. Prior to such a conversion it is open to the holder of the shares to notify the company of his unwillingness to have his shares converted. The conversion should therefore not apply to these shares, and if it does so, it is open to the shareholder to apply to the court for relief. Further, a conversion cannot be carried out by the company where the nominal value of the issued share capital that is not redeemable is less than ten per cent of the total issued share capital of the company.

15.1.5 Old redeemable preference shares

As noted above, the old section 64 of the Companies Act 1963, which permitted redeemable preference, was repealed by the Companies Act 1990. However, section 220 of the Companies Act 1990 sets out that redeemable shares issued pursuant to that section and before the operation of the Companies Act 1990 shall be redeemable in accordance with the new sections save that any premium payable on the redemption must be paid out of the share premium account and not out of profits. It is, however, open to the company to pay the premium partly out of this account and partly out of profits. The share premium account is opened by the company where shares are issued at a price that is greater than the nominal value of the shares. The surplus is called a premium and it is placed in the share premium account, which may only be used by the company for limited purposes.

15.1.6 Failure to redeem shares

According to section 219 of the Companies Act 1990 a company shall not be liable to pay damages where it fails to redeem shares. The court will not order the company to redeem the shares (an order for specific performance) where the company can show that it is unable to meet the cost of redeeming the shares out of the profits available for distribution.

Where the company goes into liquidation the shareholder has a right to enforce the redemption and these shares are then cancelled. The other debts and liabilities of the company must be paid first together with any preferred rights as to capital or income attaching to other shares (section 219(6)). The right to enforce a redemption in these circumstances will not be available to a shareholder where the date set for redemption is after the commencement of the winding up or where the company could not lawfully have paid the redemption price during a period commencing with the date fixed for redemption and the commencement of the winding up.

15.2 Acquisition by a company of its own shares

A fundamental rule of capital maintenance is that a company is prohibited from purchasing its own shares. In *Guinness v. Land Corporation of Ireland* (1882) it was noted that the only liability of a shareholder on winding up is whatever remains unpaid on their shareholding. Further, the capital of the company is the fund from which the creditors will be paid and whatever capital had been paid by a member cannot be returned to him "so as to take away from the fund to which creditors have a right to look as that out of which they have a right to be paid." In *Trevor v. Whitworth* (1887) the company's purchase of its own shares was found to be repugnant to the law and Watson L.J. stated that rules to prevent the reduction of share capital were to protect creditors who "are entitled to assume that no part of the capital which has been paid into the coffers of the company has been subsequently paid out, except in the legitimate course of its business."

This old rule is found in section 72(1) of the Companies Act 1963 and it was re-stated in section 41 of the Companies (Amendment) Act 1983 (as amended by section 232 of the Companies Act 1990). According to section 41(1) the prohibition only applies to companies limited by shares or limited by guarantees, *i.e.* unlimited companies remain free to purchase their own shares. There are harsh consequences for a company that acts in contravention of the prohibition, as section 41(3) of the Companies (Amendment) Act 1983 states that the company and every officer in default shall be guilty of an offence and that the purported acquisition is void.

Section 42 of the Companies (Amendment) Act 1983 prevents a company circumventing this prohibition by the acquisition of its shares by a nominee of the company. If shares are purchased by a nominee of the company, they will be treated as held by the nominee on its own account and the company shall be regarded as having no beneficial interest in them. If the nominee fails to pay what is due on the shares within twenty-one days of the purchase, the directors of the company are jointly and severally liable to pay that amount. It is open to the directors to seek relief from this liability where they can prove to the court that they acted honestly and responsibly and having regard to all the circumstances they should fairly be excused from liability.

15.2.1 Exceptions to the prohibition

Section 41(2) of the Companies (Amendment) Act 1983 states that the prohibition does not apply to a company limited by shares where the acquisition was not for valuable consideration, *i.e.* the company is acting as a trustee of the shares.

Under section 41(4) the prohibition does not applying in the following circumstances:

1. where the company redeems preference shares under section 65 of the Companies Act 1963;
2. where the company redeems or purchases shares under Part XI of the Companies Act 1990 (see paragraphs 15.1.1 and 15.2.2);
3. where the company acquires the shares in a duly authorised capital reduction (see paragraph 15.4.1);
4. where the company acquires the shares pursuant to a court order (see paragraph 15.4.2);
5. where the company forfeits shares or where shares are surrendered to the company because the member has failed to pay a sum in respect of his shares (see paragraph 15.4.3).

15.2.2 Permitted purchases

The Companies Act 1990 reconstructed the law in this area. Section 211 of the Companies Act 1990 permits a company to purchase its own shares in certain defined situations. The provisions governing the purchase differentiate between a "market purchase" and an "off-market purchase".

A market purchase is defined in section 212(1)(b) of the Companies Act 1990 as a purchase on a recognised stock exchange where the shares are subject to a marketing arrangement, *i.e.* they are listed on that stock exchange or the company has been afforded general dealing facilities for those shares on that stock exchange and there is no time limit on those facilities. If it is the latter case, *i.e.* dealing facilities in the shares are provided to the company, the company is obliged to notify the stock exchange of the purchase and the stock exchange may publish this information. It is an offence for the company and every officer in default to fail to comply with this requirement (section 229 of the Companies Act 1990). Where the stock exchange believes that this requirement has not been complied with, the Director of Corporate Enforcement must be notified according to section 230 of the Companies Act 1990 (as amended by section 39 of the Company Law Enforcement Act 2001).

An off-market purchase is defined in section 212(1)(a) of the Companies Act 1990 as purchase otherwise than on a recognised stock exchange. The definition also captures a purchase on a recognised stock exchange where the shares are not subject to a marketing arrangement.

Under section 213 of the Companies Act 1990 a company cannot make an off-market purchase its own shares unless all the following conditions are satisfied (called the section 213 contract):

1. the purchase must be permitted by the company's articles;
2. the purchase is made by way of a contract;
3. the members must pass a special resolution authorising the terms of the proposed contract (this authority may be varied, revoked or renewed by a special resolution);
4. the special resolution must be passed before the contract is entered into;
5. the special resolution shall not be valid if the member whose shares are being purchased votes on the special resolution and the resolution would not have been passed without his vote;
6. any member of the company may demand a poll on this special resolution;
7. prior to the meeting proposing to pass the special resolution, the contract must be available for inspection by the members at the registered office of the company for twenty-one days before the meeting and at the meeting itself;
8. the contract must contain the names of those whose shares are being purchased;

9. the company may agree to vary an existing purchase contract only where the alteration is first approved by a special resolution of the members;

10. where the company is a plc, the authority to make the purchase shall expire not later than eighteen months from the date of the special resolution.

It is open to the company to enter into a contingent contract to buy its own shares under section 214 of the Companies Act 1990 (called the section 214 contract). These contracts do not amount to a contract to purchase shares, but under these contracts the company may become entitled or obliged to purchase its own shares. The conditions regarding the contract and the authorising special resolution as set out in section 213 also apply to contingent contracts. Where the company is a plc, the authority to make the purchase shall expire not later than eighteen months from the date of the special resolution.

Section 215 of the Companies Act 1990 deals with market purchases (called the section 15 contract). Such a purchase must be authorised by the company in a general meeting and that authority may be varied, revoked or renewed by the company in general meeting. Where the company is a plc, that authority must specify the maximum number of shares that may be acquired together with the maximum and minimum prices which may be paid for those shares, and the authority to make the purchase shall expire not later than eighteen months from the date of the resolution.

The following provisions are applicable to all three of the above contracts:

1. sections 207(2), 208 and 209 apply to the purchase by a company of its own shares (section 211(2)), *i.e.* the payment for the purchase must be made from distributable profits and the shares may be cancelled or retained as treasury shares;

2. a company cannot purchase its own shares if as a result of the purchase, the nominal value of the issued share capital which is not redeemable would be less than ten per cent of the total issued share capital of the company (section 211(3));

3. the company can *only* use distributable profits for acquiring the option to purchase shares under a section 214 contract, and a breach of this provision renders the purchase unlawful (section 218(1)(a));

4. the company can *only* use distributable profits in consideration of a variation of a section 213 or section 214 contract, and a breach of this provision renders the purchase unlawful (section 218(1)(b));

5. the company can *only* use distributable profits in consideration for a release of its obligations under a section 213, 214, or 215 contract, and a breach of this provision renders the release void (section 218(1)(c));

6. the provisions of section 219 of the Companies Act 1990 set out at paragraph 15.1.6 above also apply in the case of a company failing to purchase its own shares under a section 213, 214 or 215 contract;

7. a company cannot assign its rights under a section 213, 214 or 215 contract and any attempt to do so is void (section 217(1));

8. a company may release its right under any of the above contracts but in the case of a release under a section 213 or section 214 contract, the release must be authorised by a special resolution of the company.

15.2.3 Disclosure of the purchase

The Companies Act 1990 requires public disclosure of the particulars of these permitted contracts.

Section 222 of the Companies Act 1990 provides that copies of the contract must be kept in the company's registered office for 10 years after the transaction is completed. Those copies may be inspected by the company members and, in the case of a plc, they may be inspected by any person. If the company fails to comply with these requirements, the company and every officer in default is guilty of an offence. It is open to the court to compel an inspection under section 222(4) of the Companies Act 1990.

Section 226 of the Companies Act 1990 requires that the company forward a form indicating the nature and details of the transaction to the Companies Registration Office within twenty-eight days of the purchase. In the case of a plc, the return should state the aggregate amount paid by the company for the shares and the maximum and minimum prices paid for the shares in respect of each class. Failure to comply with this requirement is an offence committed by the company and every officer in default.

Section 228 of the Companies Act 1990 empowers the Minister to make regulations for any such purchase of shares and any sale of treasury shares. The regulations may relate to the class or description of shares to be sold or not sold, the price, the timing or the method of sale or purchase and the volume of trading in the shares which may be carried out by companies.

15.3 Assisting the purchase of a company's own shares

Section 60(1) of the Companies Act 1963 prohibits a company from assisting in the purchase of its own shares. It states that a company cannot "give, whether directly or indirectly and whether by means of a loan, guarantee, the provision of security or otherwise, any financial assistance" for the purpose of, or in connection with, the purchase of its own shares and if the company is a subsidiary it cannot give such financial assistance for the purchase of shares in its holding company. The giving of any such financial assistance is unlawful.

15.3.1 Financial assistance

The definition of financial assistance in section 60(1) of the Companies Act 1963 is very broad. In the English case, *Charterhouse Investment Trust Limited v. Tempest Diesels Ltd* (1986) it was stated that:

> "the words have no technical meaning and their frame of reference is, in my judgment, the language of ordinary commerce. One must examine the commercial realities of the transaction and decide whether it can properly be described as the giving of financial assistance by the company, bearing in mind that the section is a penal one and should not be strained to cover transactions which are not fairly within it."

In *Wallersteiner v. Moir* (1974) Lord Denning M.R. stated: "[Y]ou look to the company's money and see what has become of it. You look to the company's shares and see into whose hands they have got. You will soon see if the company's money has been used to finance the purchase.

Despite the above guidelines, what constitutes financial assistance is not always clear. It is commonly the case that a company is a party to a share purchase agreement. In those agreements the company makes a series of representations and warranties to the prospective new shareholder. According to the Supreme Court of New South Wales in *Burton v. Palmer* (1980) this does not fall into the trap of financial assistance. In this case the giving of warranties by a company to the purchaser of its shares was held not to breach the New South Wales equivalent of section 60(1). Mahoney J.A. commented:

> "[T]he fact that a company facilitates a proposal for such a transfer will not involve it necessarily in a contravention of Section [60]. Thus, a company may answer requests for information relevant to the proposed transfer knowing that it does so in circumstances such that it will be liable for damages if, for lack of care, the information is incorrect ... but, by answering such requests, the company does not thereby give financial assistance."

In *McGill and anor v. Bogue et al* (2000) the Supreme Court considered a share purchase agreement whereby the plaintiff could purchase forty-nine per cent of the shares of a company. It was also agreed that the company would provide, by way of security for the plaintiff's borrowings to fund the purchase, security over part of an asset. The plaintiff sought to enforce the agreement and the defendant argued that the agreement was in breach of section 60(1) of the Companies Act 1963. The High Court dismissed this argument and the defendant unsuccessfully appealed to the Supreme Court. Keane C.J. dismissed the appeal on two grounds: (a) it could be said that the company was not a party to the share purchase agreement, and (b) even if it were implicated in the agreement, that agreement itself does not provide any financial assistance for the purchase of the shares. This was because it could be argued that the purchase of the shares and the granting of the security were two separate transactions and it was possible for the company to carry out the Section 60(2) (see paragraph 15.3.2 below) procedure prior to the granting of the security.

Where a company undertakes to pay money which would otherwise be payable by the existing shareholders or the purchaser of shares such as the payment of costs, charges and expenses payable upon the issue of new shares, there would be a breach of section 60(1).

However, costs and expenses which are properly incurred by the company in the subscription of its shares, such as their own legal costs and similar costs, seem to be generally accepted to be outside the prohibition in section 60(1) because they do not have the effect of relieving a prospective purchaser of any expense which the purchaser would otherwise incur.

15.3.2 Valid financial assistance under section 60(2)

Private companies may avoid the prohibition in section 60(1) by following the procedure outlined in section 60(2) of the Companies Act 1963. This procedure has been referred to as the "whitewash" procedure. Section 60(2) (as amended by section 89 of the Company Law Enforcement Act 2001) allows private companies to financially assist in the purchase of their shares where a special resolution of the company authorises the assistance and the directors swear a statutory declaration in accordance with section 60(4) of the Companies Act 1963. It is not open to a plc to use this procedure (section 60(15)(A) of the Companies Act 1963).

Under section 60(4) of the Companies Act 1963 the directors of the company must swear a statutory declaration (sworn by at least two directors or a majority of directors if there are more than two) stating the person to whom the assistance is to be given, the purpose of the assistance, and the form the assistance will take. It must also state that the company is solvent, *i.e.* that they have made a full inquiry into the affairs of the company and that having done so, they have formed the opinion that the company, having given the assistance, will be able to pay its debts in full as they fall due. The meeting of the directors at which this declaration is sworn must take place not more than twenty-four days before the special resolution of the company.

A copy of that declaration must be attached to the notice of the extraordinary general meeting at which the special resolution is proposed. Every member of the company must receive notice of the meeting. These resolutions may be passed informally as, according to section 60(6) of the Companies Act 1963, they may be passed in accordance with section 141(8) of the same Act (passed in writing and without the necessity of a formal general meeting, see Chapter 13). The financial assistance must be given within twelve months of the passing of the special resolution (section 60(2)(a)), and the Registrar of Companies must receive a copy of the directors' statutory declaration within twenty-one days of the giving of the assistance (section 60(2)(b)).

Where the special resolution is not unanimously carried by the members, the assistance must not be provided for thirty days or until any application made to court under section 60(8) of the Companies Act 1963 is disposed of. Section 60(8) gives the right to a dissenting member to apply to the court for the cancellation of the special resolution. The member or members must hold at least ten per cent in nominal value of the company's issued share capital and must not have consented to or voted in favour of the special resolution. The application must be made within twenty-eight days of the passing of the resolution.

The directors must exercise caution when swearing the statutory declaration, as under section 60(5) of the Companies Act 1963 the directors are liable to a criminal sanction if the declaration is incorrect. Where a director makes a declaration without having reasonable grounds for the opinion that the company will be able to pay its debts when due after the assistance is provided by the company, the director is liable to a term of imprisonment and/or a fine. Where the company is liquidated within twelve months after the statutory declaration is made and the company's debts are not paid within twelve months of the commencement of the winding up, it will be presumed, unless the contrary is shown, that the director did not have reasonable grounds for his opinion.

In order to avail of the section 60(2) exception to the prohibition, it appears that strict compliance with the "whitewash" procedure is required. In *Re Northside Motor Co. Ltd; Eddison v. Allied Irish Banks Ltd* (1985) financial assistance in the manner of a guarantee was given in violation of section 60(1) of the Companies Act 1963. When the defendant bank became aware that the "whitewash" procedure in section 60(2) had not been followed, it demanded that the company pass the necessary resolution and make the statutory declaration. Costello J. found that the company could not retrospectively validate the transaction and said that such a retrospective resolution and declaration would be "materially inaccurate and misleading". Such a resolution and declaration would not be sufficient compliance with section 60(2) of the Companies Act 1963.

In *Lombard & Ulster Banking Ltd v. Bank of Ireland* (1987) Costello J. re-stated that where reliance is placed on the exception to section 60(1), "strict compliance with the procedures is necessary". In the English case of *Re SH & Co. (Realisations) 1990 Ltd* (1993) Mummery J. stressed the need for strict compliance with the equivalent English statutory procedure.

A minor error in the section 60(2) procedure may not invalidate the special resolution and declaration. In *Re NL Electrical Ltd* (1994) a company provided financial assistance in connection with the purchase of its own shares, but the directors used an old form for their declaration. Further, a copy of the declaration was not delivered in time to the

Companies Registration Office. Harman J. held these defects insufficient to render the financial assistance voidable.

If the financial assistance proposes to assist "directors" to purchase the shares in the company, then the matter should also be discussed under section 31 of the Companies Act 1990 (see Chapter 7).

15.3.3 Exceptions to the prohibition

Section 60(12) of the Companies Act 1963 provides that the prohibition in section 60(1) will not prevent the payment of a dividend properly declared or the discharge of a liability lawfully incurred by the company.

Section 60(13) of the Companies Act 1963 provides that the general prohibition on financial assistance shall not prohibit the following transactions:

1. the lending of money in the ordinary course of business where the lending of money is part of the ordinary business of the company;
2. the provision of money by a company for the purchase of shares in the company or its holding company in the context of a properly constituted and approved employee benefit scheme; and
3. the making of loans to employees (other than directors) who are bona fide in the employment of the company or any subsidiary of the company with a view to enabling those employees to purchase fully paid shares in the company or its holding company which are to be held by them as beneficial owners.

According to section 60(15B) of the Companies Act 1963 a plc can only provide financial assistance in connection with any of these truncations where the company's net assets (the aggregate of the company's assets less the aggregate of the company's liabilities) would not be reduced as a result. If the net assets of the company would be reduced, it is open to the plc to pay the financial assistance out of the profits that are available for dividends.

15.3.4 Consequences of contravening section 60

Where there is a breach of section 60(1) of the Companies Act 1963, the transaction is voidable at the instance of the company against anyone (whether party to the transaction or not) who had notice of the breach or notice of the facts which constitute the breach (section

60(14) of the Companies Act 1963). In *Lombard and Ulster Banking Ltd v. Bank of Ireland* (1987) it was upheld that such a transaction is voidable and not void *ab initio*. It is then for the company providing the financial assistance for the purchase to seek to avoid the contract. It is commonly a liquidator of the company who seeks to avoid these contracts of financial assistance as he wants to swell the company assets for the creditors.

In order to avoid the contract, the company (or its liquidator) must prove that the other party had notice of the breach or of the facts constituting the breach. This has been held to mean "actual notice" in the case of *Bank of Ireland Finance Ltd v. Rockfield Ltd* (1979). Kenny J. refused to extend the doctrine of constructive notice to section 60(14). In this case the plaintiff bank agreed to advance money to a company and took security over the company's principal asset. The borrowed money was actually used to purchase shares in the company. Kenny J. stated that the onus of proof that the money was advanced for the purpose of purchase of shares in the company is on the person who alleges it. It must be proved that the plaintiff bank had notice, when lending the money, that it was to be used for the purchase of shares in the company. The knowledge of the purpose of the loan must be at the time of the loan, and subsequent knowledge is not sufficient. Here the bank did not have actual notice of the beach although they would have discovered it on making enquiries. Kenny J. held that the transaction was not voidable against the bank as they did not have actual notice.

In *Lombard and Ulster Banking Ltd v. Bank of Ireland* (1987) individuals came together to purchase a school-house by purchasing shares in the company that owned it. The bank agreed to finance the purchase on the basis of a charge over the building. The bank was assured that the section 60(2) procedure was followed at the time. It later transpired that this was not the case. Costello J. found a breach of section 60(1) and found that the contract was voidable against persons with notice of the breach. Costello J. stated that it was necessary to show that the bank actually knew of the breach and it was not sufficient to show that they knew that a contravention of section 60(1) was proposed. This actual notice must be established as a matter of probability. If the company cannot show that someone in the bank knew, the charge will be enforceable against them.

Where there is a breach of section 60(1) of the Companies Act 1963 section 60(15) of the Companies Act 1963 provides for criminal sanction in respect of any officer of the company who is in default.

15.4 Capital reduction

15.4.1 Court sanctioned capital reduction

An increase of a company's share capital is usually uncontroversial provided the power to do so is set out in the company's articles and a special resolution authorises the increase. The reduction of a company's share capital is more closely monitored and the sanction of the court is required under section 72 of the Companies Act 1963.

Section 72(1) of the Companies Act 1963 states that it is unlawful for a company limited by shares or a company limited by guarantee and having a share capital to reduce its share capital in any way. However, under section 72(2) of the Companies Act 1963 such a company may reduce its share capital in limited circumstances where such a reduction is authorised by the company's articles and a special resolution is passed by the members. The permitted reductions are as follows:

1. where the company extinguishes or reduces the liability in respect of shares that are not fully paid up by the shareholders (section 72(2)(a));
2. where the company cancels any paid-up share capital which is lost or unrepresented by available assets (section 72(2)(b)); and
3. where the company pays off any paid-up share capital which is in excess of the wants of the company (section 72(2)(c)).

The company must apply to the court for confirmation of the proposed reduction. Where the company proposes to reduce its share capital pursuant to sections 72(2)(a) or (b), every creditor of the company whose debt would be admissible to proof in a winding up (see Chapter 22) is entitled to object to the reduction (section 73 of the Companies Act 1963). The court will settle the list of such creditors and where a creditor objects to the reduction it is open to the court to dispense with the consent subject to the company discharging that creditor's debt. It is open to the court to direct that the creditors are not entitled to exercise their rights to object to the reduction having regard to the special circumstances of the case (section 73(3)). Any officer of the company who wilfully conceals the name of any creditor entitled to object to the reduction or who wilfully misrepresents the nature or amount of the debt of any creditor shall be liable on summary conviction to a fine (section 77 of the Companies Act 1963).

Pursuant to section 75 of the Companies Act 1963, the order of the court confirming the reduction must be sent to the Registrar of Companies who will register the order. The resolution of the company reducing the share capital only takes effect when the court order is registered. Notice of the registration must be published in such a manner as the court directs.

The reduction of the share capital must be bona fide and according to *Re John Power & Sons Ltd* (1934) the court must be satisfied that the statutory requirements are followed, that the reduction is reasonable and that the majority who are in favour of the reduction are acting bona fide. The reduction must also be equitable amongst the various classes of shareholders involved according to *Re Holders Investment Trust* (1971). Further, where the reduction involves a variation of class rights the consent of the class must be obtained (see *Re Old Silkstone Collieries* (1954)).

15.4.2 Court ordered capital reduction

The court may order the company to reduce its issued share capital as follows:

1. where the company is ordered to purchase its shares pursuant to an order under section 205 of the Companies Act 1963, *i.e.* in the case of a member's action for oppression;

2. where the company is ordered to purchase its shares pursuant to an order under section 15 of the Companies (Amendment) Act 1983, *i.e.* where a member objects to the conversion of a plc to a private limited company and applies to the court for relief;

3. where the company is ordered to purchase its shares pursuant to an order under section 10 of the Companies Act 1963, *i.e.* where a member objects to the alteration of the company's memorandum of association and applies to the court for relief.

15.4.3 Forfeiture of shares

The company's issued share capital may be reduced where the company forfeits shares because the member has failed to pay a sum in respect of his shares. The articles of association must permit such forfeiture and the model articles 33-39 of Table A expressly permit a forfeiture. This is not regarded as a capital reduction that requires the sanction of the court. The forfeiture of shares for any other reason is treated as a capital reduction and it is unlawful.

A member may surrender his shares in anticipation of a forfeiture arising from the non-payment of a call (see Chapter 12 for definition of a call). According to *Trevor v. Whitworth* (1887) this is considered a reduction in capital which requires the sanction of the court.

15.5 Serious capital loss

While trading losses may be a feature of business, directors are now placed under a positive obligation to deal with serious problems faced by the company. Directors are obliged under section 40 of the Companies (Amendment) Act 1983 to call an extraordinary general meeting when the company suffers a serious loss of capital. The meeting must be called not later than twenty-eight days from the earliest day when this fact is known to the directors. The meeting must be take place within fifty-six days of this day. A serious loss of capital is defined as when the "net assets of a company are half or less of the amount of the company's called-up share capital".

The purpose of the general meeting is to consider whether any, and if so what, measures should be taken to deal with the situation. Where there is a failure to convene this meeting, an offence is committed by the directors of the company. Under section 40(2) of the Companies (Amendment) Act 1983 any director who knowingly and willingly authorises or permits that failure or, after the expiry of the period during which the meeting should have been convened, knowingly and willingly authorises or permits that failure to continue, is guilty of an offence. The CLRG recommended that section 40 of the Companies (Amendment) Act 1983 should not apply to private companies (see paragraph 1.5.9(2)).

16. COMPANY BORROWING AND SECURITY

In most companies loan capital is a vital source of cash flow. Each company may have its own conditions and restrictions on borrowing and in some cases a company cannot borrow in the absence of a certificate from the Registrar of Companies.

The capacity of the company to borrow is invariably set out in the objects clause of the memorandum of association. In the case of companies established as lending or investment institutions, the power to borrow is treated as an express object. However, most companies do not have borrowing as their main business, and the power to borrow is interpreted as an express ancillary power (see Chapter 4). It may be the case that the power to borrow is not enumerated in the memorandum at all, and in this situation the power to borrow will be implied where the purpose of borrowing is reasonable and incidental to the company's main objects. If the company is a non-trading company, the power will only be implied where there is something in the memorandum or articles to indicate that it was intended to give such a power to the company.

The company's borrowing powers must be exercised in accordance with the memorandum and articles of association. If there are limits on the amount of loan capital or a procedure is to be followed, the requirements must be strictly observed. It is open to the company to amend these requirements by special resolution. In the case of a plc, it cannot borrow without first obtaining a certificate from the Registrar of Companies under section 6 of the Companies (Amendment) Act 1983 certifying that the plc is entitled to do business and exercise its borrowing powers.

It is usual for the articles of association to confer the authority to exercise this power on the directors of the company. Model article 79 of Table A is commonly adopted by companies, and it provides express authority for directors to borrow and secure a debt. Where model article 79 of Table A is adopted, the directors are not subject to any monetary limits. In line with the decision in *Rolled Steel Products (Holdings) Limited v. British Steel Corp. et al* (1985) (see Chapter 6), borrowing in circumstances that are not in accordance with the constitution of the company may be an abuse of the directors powers rather than *ultra vires* the company.

16.1 Security for loan capital

It may be that the power to give security for any borrowings is expressly set out in the company's constitution. In any case, the power to give such security will be implied as incidental to the power to borrow. Every company has a number of options when issuing security for a loan, some more acceptable to the lender than others.

It is always open to the company to grant a mortgage over any freehold or leasehold property that it may have. This mortgage may be a legal or an equitable mortgage, the latter involving the simple deposit of the title deeds with the lender. A legal mortgage involves giving the lender title to the property with the company retaining the "equity of redemption", *i.e.* the right to get the property back as free as the company gave it on the payment of loan capital and interest to the lender.

The company may choose to issue a debenture document that records the lending transaction and is evidence of the debt. Debenture stock, as explained below, is preferred by lenders and therefore more commonly used by companies. The debenture document or the debenture stock is usually secured by a charge over the company's assets, which may be fixed or floating in nature. The charge holder does not obtain any title to these assets and merely has the right to resort to the assets in defined circumstances in order to satisfy the debt.

Costello J. in *Re Clare Textiles Ltd* (1993) stated that "there is nothing special about the term 'charge'. It relates to a contract under the terms of which certain property is available as security to meet the performance of a liability, usually the payment of money. Its creation is dependent upon contract."

Certain types of charges are void unless they are registered with the Registrar of Companies within twenty-one days of their creation (see Chapter 17).

One category of security is a guarantee issued by the company for a debt. Guarantees in respect of loans given to directors and inter-company guarantees must be considered in the light of section 31 of the Companies Act 1990 as they may be voidable under section 38 of that Act (see Chapter 7).

16.2 Debentures

A debenture may be either one single document or a series of similar documents given to different lenders. These lenders are called debenture holders. They are not members of the company and they cannot attend company meetings. An influential debenture holder may be granted the right by the company to appoint a nominee director who can keep an eye on company affairs.

Common features of a debenture document are as follows:

1. it acknowledges a debt due and owing by the company to the debenture holder;
2 it contains an obligation to repay that debt;
3. it sets out the terms of repayment, usually with interest;
4. it usually grants security for the debt by way of a charge over the company assets;
5. it grants the debenture holder various options to enforce that security in the event of a default in repayment.

In *Levy* v. *Abercorris Company* (1887) Chitty J. stated:

> "[I]n my opinion, a debenture means a document which either creates a debt or acknowledges it, and any document which fulfills either of these conditions is a 'debenture'. I cannot find any precise legal definition of the term, it is not either in law or commerce a strictly technical term, or what is called a term of art."

16.2.1 Series of debentures

It is open to the company to issue a series of debentures. These debentures incorporate standard conditions and are issued for different amounts to each individual lender. These will state that each debenture will rank *parri passu, i.e.* equally with each other. The standard conditions include *inter alia* the events, on the happening of which, immediate repayment of the loan by the company will be triggered. Where there is a default in repayment and the affected debenture holder takes any action against the company, the Rules of the Superior Courts 1986 require that the debenture holder takes the action on behalf of all the debenture holders and must get the consent of the majority before proceeding.

16.2.2 Debenture stock

Debentures should not be confused with debenture stock where the company creates a loan fund and issues stock certificates to each debenture holder. The stock certificates will set out the debenture holders' share of the fund, *e.g.* €1,000 divided into 100 units. Debenture stock is very similar to shareholding as it is open to the debenture holder to sell some or all of his stock units in a similar manner to a shareholder selling his shares. The company will put in place a trustee to protect the interests of all the debenture stockholders and the repayment of the debt, just like a normal debenture, is usually secured by a fixed or floating charge.

16.2.3 Procedure

It is not unusual for the articles of association to detail procedure that must be followed when a company wishes to issue debentures. The court may have the discretion to validate debentures created in breach of this procedure, as occurred in the English case of *Re Torvale Group Ltd* (1999). In this case the articles of association required the sanction of the holders of the preferred ordinary shares to create a charge over the assets of the company. The company created three debentures and there was no record of such a sanction being obtained. Further, there was no evidence before the court that all the shareholders were present at the meeting that proposed the debentures and therefore agreed to the debenture issue (the *Duomatic* principle in *Re Duomatic Ltd* (1969)). However, although the debentures exceeded the directors' powers, the court exercised its discretion and validated the debentures.

16.2.4 Transfer of a debenture

The right to transfer and the transfer procedure are usually set out in the debenture document itself. However, the transferability of a debenture is governed by section 81 of the Companies Act 1963, which states that it is not lawful for a company to register a transfer of a debenture unless a proper instrument of transfer is delivered to the company.

In the case of bearer debentures, these can be transferred by delivery in the same manner as bearer share certificates.

In *Re Brown & Gregory Ltd* (1904) it was held that the transferee of the debenture takes the debenture subject to any equities (*i.e.* rights enjoyed by third parties) which affect the interest of the transferor, even if the transferee acquired the interest in good faith, for consideration and without notice of any equities. The case of *Hilger Analytical Ltd v. Rank Precision Industries Ltd et al* (1984) distinguished this authority where it was held that the debenture may be transferred free from any equities which the company (as opposed to a third party) may have, where the debenture itself provides for such conditions of transfer.

16.2.5 Remedies of the debenture holder

In the case of an unsecured debenture the debenture holder can sue for the debt or petition to wind up the company where the company defaults in repayment. Where the debenture is secured by a fixed or floating charge, it is commonly a term of the debenture that the debenture holder can appoint a person called a *receiver* over the assets covered by the charge (see Chapter 18).

16.3 Fixed charges

A debenture is commonly secured by a fixed or floating charge over the assets of the company. Holders of a fixed charge have a claim to identifiable property and they have a legal interest in that property from the date that the debenture is executed. Fixed charges are also known as specific or ascertained charges. MacNaughton L.J. in *Illingworth v. Houldsworth* (1904) stated that "a specific charge, I think, is one that without more fastens on ascertained or definite property or property capable of being ascertained or defined."

A fixed charge holder can enforce his security through an order for possession and/or sale of the property or the appointment of a receiver to the company. As discussed in Chapter 23, the fixed charge holder occupies a privileged position in the event that the company goes into liquidation. The fixed charge holder can opt to rely on his security and remain outside the winding up. This effectively means that he ranks above all the other creditors of the company. The holder of a fixed charge over book debts (discussed below) may however be subordinated to the Revenue Commissioners in certain circumstances (see Chapter 23).

Further, as discussed in Chapter 23, a floating charge may be vulnerable where a company goes into liquidation within twelve months of the charge being created as section 288 of the Companies Act 1963 may render that charge void. A fixed charge is not subject to a similar statutory sanction.

One of the primary disadvantages of a fixed charge from the perspective of the company is the "freezing" effect of the fixed charge as the company cannot deal with or replace the assets covered by the charge for the duration of the security without the consent of the debenture holder.

16.4 Floating charges

A floating charge holder is also a secured creditor, but the nature of the security is very different to that of a fixed charge. The floating charge covers an asset or class of assets which by their nature fluctuate and change in the day-to-day business of the company. According to MacNaughton L.J. in *Illingworth v. Houldsworth* (1904) "a floating charge is ambulatory and shifting in its nature, hovering over and so to speak floating with the property which it is intended to affect".

In *Re Old Bushmills Distillery Co.; ex. p. Brett* (1879) Walker L.J. stated that the assets may be "withdrawn by sale and the proceeds then take their place, or other assets may be substituted or additional assets added by trading; but the floating security follows the concern, reduced or added to, through every form of its trading existence".

Romer L.J. in *Re Yorkshire Woolcomber's Association Ltd* (1903) identified what he believed were three most important characteristics of a floating charge:

1. it is a charge on a class of assets of a company present and future;
2. that class is one, which in the ordinary course of the business of the company, would be changing from time to time;
3. it is contemplated that, until some future step is taken by or on behalf of those interested in the charge, the company may carry on its business in the ordinary way so far as concerns that particular class of assets.

However, a floating charge may exist where, in reality, the company does not dispose of the assets in the ordinary course of business. In *Welch v. Bowmaker (Ireland) Ltd* (1980) a debenture created a fixed charge over three pieces of land owned by the company and a floating charge on the company's undertaking and all its assets and property, present and future. The company owned a fourth property which was not specified in the fixed charge, and the issue was whether this property was subject to a fixed or a floating charge. As it was specifically stated that three properties were subject to a fixed charge, the Supreme Court found that the fourth was merely subject to a floating charge. The floating charge was found to exist even though the company does not dispose of the class of assets in the ordinary course of business.

A floating charge has therefore been described as dormant and the debenture holder has no power to interfere with the company's use of the assets until the charge become payable. When the floating charge becomes payable, it is said to crystallise and fasten onto the charged property or class of property, becoming a quasi-fixed charge. The ability of the company to continue dealing with the charged assets is the most advantageous feature of the floating charge.

The disadvantages of a floating charge from the creditor's perspective are as follows:

1. it may be invalidated under section 288 of the Companies Act 1963 where it was created within twelve months of a winding up (see Chapter 23);
2. the floating charge holder will be paid after preferential creditors in a winding up (see Chapter 23);
3. the assets captured by the charge on crystallisation may be insufficient to satisfy the debt and the floating charge holder may have to pursue the company for the shortfall;
4. it is not possible to identify assets covered by the floating charge until "crystallisation" discussed at paragraph 16.4.2.
5. section 98 of the Companies Act 1963 requires a receiver appointed under a floating charge to pay preferential creditors from the proceeds of the sale of the charged asset before paying the floating charge holder (see Chapter 18).

16.4.1 Present property interest

Given the dormant nature of the floating charge, it was initially thought the secured creditor had no real rights in the charged assets until the moment of crystallisation. MacNaughton in *Illingworth v. Houldsworth* (1904) said that the floating charge would "hover" over the property until crystallisation caused it to "settle" on the property, which implied that there was no interest in the asset until this event. This was unsettling news for the creditor who could now be trumped by the company granting a third party rights over those assets in the interim.

However, in *Evans v. Rival Granite Quarries Ltd* (1910) Buckley L.J. stated that "a floating charge is not a future security; it is a present security, which presently affects all the assets of the company expressed to be included in it". This was accepted in the Irish case of *Re Tullow Engineering (Holding) Ltd* (1990) where a floating charge which was created over shares in another company was held to be a present security and therefore unaffected by an option granted to a third party to buy those shares. In *Foamcrete (UK) Ltd v. Thrust Engineering Ltd* [2002] the Court of Appeal confirmed that that the holder of a floating charge had an immediate beneficial interest in the property covered by the charge but the court stated that this charge was subject to (and came after) any prior equitable charges that had been created by the company.

16.4.2 Crystallisation of floating charges

The concept of crystallisation only applies to floating charges. Crystallisation is triggered by certain "events" in the company's trading life which put an end to the company's ability to deal with the assts covered by the floating charge. Until the moment of crystallisation, no specific asset can be identified as covered by a floating charge. When crystallisation occurs, the floating charge becomes a quasi-fixed charge and settles onto the class of assets which it affects.

These crystallisation events are set out in the debenture document and case law and include the following:

1. The appointment of a *receiver* by the debenture holder or by order of the court will cause the floating charge to crystallise. It is not sufficient to take steps to appoint a receiver, the receiver must be actually appointed. The appointment will cause all floating charges created by the company to crystallise.

2. The *winding up* of the company, whether voluntary or compulsory, will cause crystallisation. In *Re Crompton & Co. Ltd* (1914) Warrington J. stated that "there can be no question at all that according to ordinary principles the winding up puts an end to the period of suspension; and the reason that it does is that the effect of the winding up is to put an end to the floating nature of the security".

3. Where a company *ceases to trade* all floating charges created by the company will crystallise according to the English case of *Re Woodruffes (Musical Instruments) Ltd* (1986). Nourse J., while admitting that automatic crystallisation was undesirable, held that there was no case in which the assumption that a charge crystallises upon the cessation of business was questioned and concluded that the "cessation of business necessarily puts an end to a company's dealings with its assets".

4. It is open to the parties to set out in the debenture document that the giving of *notice by the debenture holder* can cause crystallisation. In the English case of *Re Brightlife Ltd* (1987) the debenture holder gave notice of crystallisation to the company immediately before the company went into liquidation. This was challenged by the preferential creditors, but Hoffman L.J. held that it was not open to the courts to restrict the contractual freedom of parties to a floating charge, and that it was inappropriate for the courts to impose additional restrictive rules on the ground of public policy. He held that there was no reason the debenture holder should not be capable of crystallising the charge by the giving of notice. The Irish case of *Re Wogan's Drogheda Ltd* (1993) is authority for the giving of notice as a crystallising event in this jurisdiction.

5. It is open to the parties to agree that the charge will *crystallise automatically*, upon the occurrence of some specified event such as an attempt by the company to create a subsequent charge on the class of assets, an attempt by another creditor to levy execution against the company or the non-payment of a loan installment.

   A floating charge that has crystallised may decrystallise on the happening of certain events. In *Re Holidair* (1994) a floating charge which had crystallised on the appointment of a receiver, decrystallised and reverted to a floating charge on the appointment of an examiner under the Companies (Amendment) Act 1990.

16.4.3 Negative pledge clauses

A negative pledge clause usually forms part of debentures secured by a floating charge. It restricts the company from creating subsequent charges over the class of assets already charged save with the consent of the floating charge holder. It is a contractual promise and the company is in breach of contract if a subsequent charge is created over the assets. If the company later creates a fixed charge over the assets, the fixed charge holder will have priority over the prior chargee as, even though the fixed charge holder is deemed to have notice of the prior charge, he is not deemed to have notice of the actual contents of the prior charge, *i.e.* the negative pledge clause (see *Wilson v. Kelland* (1910)).

According to *English & Scottish Mercantile Investment Co. Ltd* (1892) it must be proved to the court that the subsequent fixed charge holder had actual notice of the negative pledge. In *Welch v. Bowmaker (Ireland) Ltd* (1980) an equitable mortgage was created over a parcel of land in respect of which there was already a floating charge containing a negative pledge clause. Henchy J. found that the later mortgagees had notice of the existence of the debentures, but not of their terms. It was submitted that constructive notice of the terms should be sufficient, and that a failure to inquire whether there was a negative pledge clause should cause the second charge to lose priority. However, Henchy J. rejected this submission, stating that "actual or express notice of the prohibition must be shown before the subsequent mortgage can be said to be deprived of priority" and that "it is settled law that there is no duty on a bank in a situation such as this to seek out the precise terms of the debenture."

Therefore, the doctrine of constructive notice does not apply and the subsequent chargee will not be deemed to have constructive notice of the clause. But many subsequent chargees will have actual or express notice as they invariably conduct a search at the Companies Registration Office where the terms of the clause are commonly set out in the particulars of the charge, which are registered with the Registrar of Companies.

16.5 Fixed charges over book debts

Book debts are a valuable company asset and they comprise a record of monies due and owing to the company at any point in time. New book debts are created and old book debts are discharged almost every day in a busy trading company. As a result, book debts are a fluctuating asset and when used by the company as security for borrowings, they are more suitable to a floating charge. However, as the following case law shows, it now seems to be accepted that a fixed charge may be created over present and future company book debts.

16.5.1 The issue of control

It was the English case of *Siebe Gorman & Co. Ltd v. Barclay's Bank Ltd* (1979) which first recognised a fixed charge over book debts. The company executed a debenture in favour of a bank "by way of a first fixed charge over all book debts and other debts now and from time to time due and owing to the company."

A specific account was set up with the bank for all the debts of the company and, according to the debenture, the company had no power to charge or assign that account without the consent of the bank. The company went into liquidation and the task before the court was to decide whether or not the bank held a valid fixed charge. Slade L.J. considered the characteristics of both a floating and fixed charge, holding it was the restriction on the company's ability to deal with assets that formed the corner stone of a fixed charge. Slade L.J. stated:

> "[I]t is perfectly possible in law for a mortgagor, by way of continuing security for future advances, to grant to a mortgagee a charge on future book debts in a form which creates in equity a specific charge on the proceeds of such debts as soon as they are received and consequently prevents the mortgagor from disposing of an unencumbered title to the subject matter of such charge without the mortgagee's consent."

He held that this was the effect of the debenture in this case and that there was no reason the courts should not give effect to the intention of the parties to create a fixed charge. On the facts of the case, the bank held a fixed charge over the future book debts of the company.

The crucial point in *Siebe Gorman* was that the company was restricted in its use of the charged asset. In *Re Armagh Shoes Ltd* (1982) there were no such restrictions in the charge over book debts and it was deemed a floating charge. In *Re Brightlife Ltd* (1987) the company created a first fixed charge over all the book debts and a floating charge over all of the undertakings of the company, present and future. The company was free to collect its debts and lodge them into its account where they remained at the free disposal of the company. According to Hoffman J. this freedom to deal with the asset in question was the badge of a floating charge and was inconsistent with a fixed charge.

The Irish courts had an opportunity to examine such a charge in *Re Keenan Bros Ltd* (1985). The company created a fixed charge over all of the company's book debts and other debts, present and future, in favour of Allied Irish Banks. The debenture document provided for a special bank account to be opened for the company's book debts and for all withdrawals, transfers and payments to be approved by the bank. The liquidator of the company applied to the court for directions as to whether the charge was fixed or floating. Keane J. in the High Court held that the charge was a floating charge because the company retained the power to collect the debts itself. The company could also deal with the asset in the course of its business, though its power to do so was restricted.

On appeal to the Supreme Court it was held that the debenture in fact created a fixed charge. It was considered significant that a new account was opened one month before the company went into liquidation, in respect of which no withdrawals or transfers could be made without the signature of the bank manager. The restrictions in this case were incompatible with a floating charge as the charged assets were segregated into a separate account and rendered frozen and virtually unusable. Therefore, far from being dormant or hovering, the charge had settled on the assets to such an extent that they were unusable in the ordinary course of business.

McCarthy J. stated that if it were a floating charge, the payment into such an account would be entirely inappropriate and would conflict with the ambulatory nature of the floating charge.

In *Re Wogan's (Drogheda) Ltd* (1993) a debenture contained a fixed charge over book debts and other debts, present and future. A clause in the debenture provided that the company would not be entitled to deal with the book debts or other debts and it required the company to pay the proceeds into designated accounts. It was specifically provided that all dealings in relation to these accounts would be subject to the prior consent in writing of the lender. This separate bank account was never established. In the High Court, Denham J. held that these provisions created a floating charge as the account had not been opened. On appeal to the Supreme Court it was stated that subsequent conduct was inadmissible as an aid to the construction of an agreement and the clause in the contract had all the essential characteristics of a fixed charge.

This decision attracted much criticism as the reality of the security arrangement was that the company remained in complete control of the book debts and free to continue to deal with its assets in the ordinary course of business. As the bank account was never opened, that bank did not have "meaningful control" over the book debts, an essential characteristic of a fixed charge.

The decision of *Re Holidair Ltd* (1994) attempted to remedy the situation. The debenture created fixed charges over the book debts with a provision for the establishment of special bank accounts. There was no prohibition on withdrawals by the company from the account. The bank accounts were never opened and the proceeds were used in the ordinary course of business. Costello J. in the High Court held that the security was a fixed charge based on a construction of the debenture itself, which provided for a separate account. On appeal to the Supreme Court, the court held that a floating charge had been created as there was no restriction in the debenture on the ability of the company to withdraw money from the account, and they were free to use the proceeds for the carrying on of their business.

In the English case of *Re ASRS Establishment Ltd (in administration) receivership and Liquidation)* (2000) a debenture purported to create a fixed charge over the book debts of the company and required the company to pay the proceeds into a designated bank account. Park J. held that as the account was never opened, the charge constituted a floating charge, because, on a true construction, the company was free to deal in the course of business with the charged debts.

Therefore, it appears that to create a valid fixed charge over book debts, the company must be restricted in its dealings with, and the lender must exercise real control over, the book debts. This control must be exercised in the capacity of lender according to *Re Double S Printers Ltd (In Liquidation)* (1999) where Parker J. refused to find a fixed charge where the control over the book debts related to the lender's role as a director of the company and not his role as debenture holder.

The court will also take into account the intentions of the lender and the company. In *Re Lakeglen Construction Co. Ltd* (1980) Costello J. stated that "if it was intended that the charge was to remain dormant until some future date and that the company was permitted to go on receiving the book debts and using them until then, the security would contain the true element of a floating charge". In *Chalk v. Kahn and anor* (2000) Hart J. held that a charge which purported to be a fixed charge on book debts was in reality a floating charge since the intention of the parties was that the company would be free to deal as it chose with the proceeds of the book debts paid into its account.

16.5.2 Divisible book debts

It was therefore firmly established by case law that a fixed charge over book debts could be safely used by lenders once it was carefully structured. Lenders, however, began to develop this category of security and in 1994 the English Court of Appeal had to consider the validity of a charge which provided that it was to be a fixed charge for as long as the book debts were uncollected but once the book debts were collected they became the subject of a floating charge.

In *Re New Bullas Trading Ltd* (1994) the validity of such a charge was upheld. Nourse J. considered that the parties were free to contract as they saw fit and that there appeared to be no public policy consideration preventing this type of clause. This case appeared to establish that book debts were divisible, there was a "collected" and an "uncollected" form. This new departure was of great benefit to the company which was free to deal with the books debts when collected in their ordinary course of business.

It was, however, treated with caution by legal commentators. If book debts were a single asset, the absence of control over that asset in its collected form would be fatal, in the light of existing case law, to the fixed charge. This caution now appears justified.

The New Zealand Court of Appeal examined the validity of such a clause in *Re Brumark Investments Ltd* (2001). The Court of Appeal held that the clause created a floating charge. It was stated that no matter how comprehensively drafted the restrictions on dealing with uncollected book debts might be, the power of the chargor to collect the debts and dispose of them for its own account was, on its own, sufficient to rob the charge of its fixed character. The Privy Council upheld this decision and held that *New Bullas* was wrongly decided.

Whether or not the Irish courts will follow *Re Brumark* remains to be seen. It appears that in past Irish cases, the parties proceeded on the basis that the book debts and their proceeds were a single indivisible asset encompassed by the charge. Further, in *Re Holidair* (1994) the Supreme Court took the view that where the lender as at liberty to use the proceeds of the book debts, the charge was a floating charge irrespective of how the parties described it.

It has been suggested by commentators that there is no conceptual prohibition on viewing them as separate assets, recognising that uncollected book debts can transform into a distinct form of asset when collected, and drafting the charge clause accordingly. This appears to be in line with Nourse J.'s belief in the freedom of contract between the parties.

16.6 Retention of title charges

The charge holder may be a secured creditor and someone who escapes the plight of unsecured creditors in a company liquidation, but he is vulnerable to the clever creditor who has supplied goods to the company on the basis of a reservation of title clause. These clauses are often referred to as "Romapla" clauses based on the English case of

Aluminum Industrie Vaasem BV v. Romalpa Aluminum Ltd (1976), which recognised their validity in that jurisdiction. The clause, if carefully drafted, may mean that the company has no legal title to the goods, or the proceeds of their sale, and, on liquidation, those goods/proceeds must be returned directly to the supplier.

There are three main categories of retention of title clauses:

1. simple retention of title clauses, which retain the legal title in the goods supplied, in their original state, until payment has been received;
2. aggregated retention of title clauses, which seek to retain legal title in the goods supplied, after they have been incorporated into a manufactured product, until payment has been received; and
3. proceeds of sale clauses, which claim legal title to the money received by the company from the sale of any such manufactured product or from the sale of the goods in the state supplied, until payment has been received.

16.6.1 Charges

It may be that the retention of title clause is in reality a charge over the company's assets which requires registration within twenty-one days under section 99(1) of the Companies Act 1963. Failing to register the charge will render that charge void as against the liquidator and any creditor of the company (see Chapter 17).

Simple retention of title clauses have been held not to constitute charges, as it is open to the vendor to retain legal title to the property in its original state (see *Clough Mill Ltd v. Martin* (1984) below).

Aggregate retention of title and proceeds of sale clauses are more problematic. The courts have held that in certain circumstances they in fact create a registrable charge. Such a charge arises where legal ownership of the goods/proceeds has, in reality, passed to the company and the supplier is deemed to hold only a charge over the good/proceeds.

16.6.2 Aggregated retention of title clauses

An examination of the case law on aggregate clauses appears to suggest two general rules:

1. If the supplied goods remain readily identifiable in the manufactured product, legal title has been successfully reserved and no charge is created.

2. If the supplied goods are irreversibly mixed in the manufactured product, a charge has been created and the title to the goods supplied has been extinguished.

In *Re Bond Worth Ltd* (1980) suppliers of yarn to a carpet manufacturer purported to reserve the "equitable and beneficial ownership" of the yarn. The court held that this had the effect of transferring the legal ownership to the manufacturer who then granted a charge back to the supplier. The court found that the charge was a floating charge as the manufacturer could sell the yarn or convert it into carpets. Slade L.J. held that the charge was void as it was unregistered.

In *Borden (UK) v. Scottish Timber Products Ltd* (1981) the contract for the supply of resin for chipboard manufacture retained title in the chipboard until all the goods supplied were paid for in full. The company went into receivership and the plaintiffs tried to claim legal title to any chipboard manufactured with the resin, or any proceeds of sale of such. Bridge L.J. found that once the resin was converted into chipboard, the resin disappeared and any rights to the title of the resin ceased to exist.

In *Clough Mill Ltd v. Martin* (1984) the supplier of yarn sought to retain (a) "ownership" of the material supplied and (b) "property" in the whole of the goods manufactured from the yarn. The first clause was held not to be a charge, but the second provision was deemed to be a charge and it was void for want of registration.

Therefore, if the goods supplied are still in their original state or still identifiable, the court will uphold the retention of title clause.

In *Hendy Lennox Ltd v. Grahame Puttick Ltd* (1984) the vendors supplied diesel engines for incorporation into generating sets, where the engines would be left unaltered in substance, and the contract contained a retention of title clause. When the company went into receivership, the vendors successfully claimed title to the engines. Staughton L.J. distinguished some of the above cases stating that, in this case, "it was a question of doing up bolts and other connections which could later be undone." He clarified the law in stating:

> "[T]he proprietary rights of the sellers in the engines were not affected when the engines were wholly or partly incorporated into generator sets. They were not like the fibre in *Re Bond Worth Ltd* which became yarn and then carpet, or the resin which became chip-

> board in *Borden*...they just remained engines, albeit connected to other things."

In *Somers v. James Allen (Ireland) Ltd* (1984) a firm supplied ingredients to a company manufacturing and selling animal feeding compounds. The Romalpa clause provided that title would not transfer until the supplier was paid in full. A receiver was appointed to the company and the supplier claimed ownership of the goods. The receiver claimed that an unregistered charge had been created. The ingredients were still identifiable and Carroll J. held that the goods should be returned to the supplier as it was perfectly within the competence of the parties to agree that the legal and beneficial ownership of the goods should remain with the supplier until payment was received.

16.6.3 Proceeds of sale

Similar difficulties arise for suppliers where goods are supplied subject to the condition that any proceeds from the sale of the goods, either in their original state or as part of a manufactured product, are to be held in trust for the supplier.

An examination of the case law on proceeds of sale clauses appears to suggest the following general rules:

1. where the proceeds are segregated from the company's other funds *and* represent only the value of the goods supplied *and* it is clear that the company was holding the funds on trust for the supplier, a retention of title clause can be upheld;

2. where the proceeds are mixed with other funds, a charge is created.

In *Aluminum Industrie Vaasem BV v. Romalpa Aluminum Ltd* (1976) the contract, which contained a retention of title clause, was for the supply of aluminum foil to the defendants, some of which the defendants sold on. The clause covered both proceeds of sale and the manufactured goods. The contractual terms regarding the foil were quite detailed. The material was to be stored in such a way as to indicate clearly that it was the property of the plaintiff. and the defendants were described as fiduciary owners and given the power to re-sell to third parties in the ordinary course of their business. The defendants went into liquidation. There was an amount representing the proceeds of sale of the aluminum in a bank account in the plaintiff-supplier's name. The legal ownership of the vendors was upheld as the clause contained "unusual and fairly elaborate provisions departing substantially from the debtor/creditor relationship" showing the intention to create a fiduciary relationship, *i.e.* the defendants were to hold the proceeds on trust for the supplier.

In *Sugar Distributors Ltd v. Monaghan Cash & Carry Ltd* (1982) the contract related to the supply of sugar and retained legal title in the sugar until the full purchase price was paid. The vendors claimed title to the sugar and the proceeds of sale of what had been sold. Carroll J. held that the proceeds of the sale were held in trust for the vendors under a simple retention of title clause, even though the contract contained no express term on ownership of proceeds or their segregation. As will be seen, later Irish cases appear to require more.

In *Re Andrabell Ltd* (1984) goods held subject to a retention of title clause were sold in the ordinary course of business, and the proceeds were paid into the general bank account of the company and were mixed with other monies of the company. Peter Gibson J. examined whether there was a fiduciary relationship, as, without such a relationship, only a charge could exist, and it would be void for want of registration. He compared that proceeds of sale clause with that in *Aluminum Industrie Vaasem BV v. Romalpa Aluminum Ltd* (1976) and found that in the matter before him:

1. there was no obligation on the company to store the goods separately in manifestation of the vendor's ownership;
2. there was no express acknowledgment of a "fiduciary relationship";
3. there was no suggestion that the company was acting as agent for the vendor on a re-sale and was therefore accountable for the proceeds;
4. there was no obligation to keep the proceeds separate, and the credit period granted to the company meant the company was free to use the proceeds within that period;
5. there were no detailed provisions in the contract for re-payment, and the court will not imply a term unless it is necessary to do so.

Peter Gibson J. concluded that there was no fiduciary relationship in this case and that the vendor had a charge over the proceeds which was void for want of registration.

In *Re W. J. Hickey Ltd* (1988) the words "to be held in trust" were used and the purchaser was bound to keep a separate account. The court held that it was a valid proceeds of sale clause.

In *Carroll Group Distributors Ltd v. G. & J.F. Bourke Ltd et al* (1990) the clause provided that proceeds from sub-sales should be held in trust for the supplier in a separate bank account.

However, the contract also provided that all risk passed to the purchaser and that the purchaser was not an agent for the vendors. No separate bank account was in fact ever opened, and the vendors took no steps to rectify this omission. Murphy J. said found that if the account had been opened, it would have contained monies representing the company's profit margin on the sales, and the vendor/supplier would not have been entitled to the entire account. As a result the court held that the fund would possess all the characteristics of a charge as "the substance of the transaction as ascertained from the words used by the parties and the context in which the document was executed was to confer a charge over the proceeds on the seller".

In *Hendy Lennox Ltd v. Grahame Puttick Ltd* (1984) the supplier also claimed the right to trace his title into the proceeds of sale of the engines. Staughton J. examined the relationship between the parties to see whether it was of a fiduciary nature. Like Peter Gibson J. in *Re Andrabell Ltd* (1984), he compared that proceeds of sale clause with that in *Aluminum Industrie Vaasem BV v. Romalpa Aluminum Ltd* (1976) and found that in the matter before him:

1. there was no express obligation on the company to store the goods in such a way as to indicate they belonged to the supplier;
2. there was no mention of a fiduciary relationship in the contract;
3. the clause appeared to capture the proceeds of sale of the generator sets, which comprised more than just the goods supplied under the contract, whereas the Romalpa clause dealt solely with the proceeds of sale of the actual goods supplied under the contract;
4. the one-month credit period granted to the company was not "easy to reconcile with an obligation to keep the proceeds of re-sale in a separate account."

Staughton J. found that the company was under no fiduciary obligation and the suppliers therefore had no claim for the proceeds of re-sale.

In *Associated Alloys Pty Ltd v. Metropolitan Engineering & Fabrication Ltd* (2000) the trial judge considered a proceeds of sale/aggregation clause and held that it created a registrable charge that was void for want of registration. This decision was upheld in the Supreme Court of New South Wales. The matter was appealed to the Australian High Court and in a surprising decision it was held that the clause did not create a registrable charge. The court referred to the legislation which defined the criterion for a registrable "charge" and it held that to treat the proceeds of sale/aggregation clause as falling under this criterion would be to "rewrite the statute".

17. REGISTRATION OF COMPANY CHARGES

Section 99(1) of the Companies Act 1963 (as amended by section 122 of the Companies Act 1990) imposes registration obligations on a company when granting certain categories of security to creditors. In the absence of such registration, the creditor who is the beneficiary of that security will be unable to rely on his security in priority over other creditors and, in particular, be unable to rely on his security in a winding up.

The rationale behind the requirement for registration is to afford protection to the other company creditors by providing them with a means of discovering whether, and to what extent, a company has secured creditors.

17.1 Particulars of the charge

Section 99(1) of the Companies Act 1963 requires that "the prescribed particulars of the charge, verified in the prescribed manner, are delivered to or received by the registrar of companies for registration in a manner required by this Act."

The prescribed particulars include the following:

1. the date and description of the charge;
2. the amount secured;
3. short particulars of the property charged; and
4. the names, addresses and occupations of the owners of the charge;

Under section 103 of the Companies Act 1963 the Registrar of Companies must keep, in relation to each company, a register of charges detailing the following:

1. the date of creation of the charge;
2. if the charge is a judgment mortgage, the date of creation of the judgment mortgage;
3. the amount secured by the charge;
4. short particulars of the property charged;

5. the person entitled to the charge; and

6. the date of the purchase of property, where the company has purchased property that is subject to a charge.

Section 91 of the Companies Act 1963 requires every company to keep a register of the holders of debentures. The section applies only to debentures issued as part of a series of debentures where each debenture in that series ranks *pari passu.* The company must generally keep the register at the registered office of the company and it must be available for inspection. Where it is kept other than at the registered office of the company, the Registrar of Companies must be notified of the location. Failure to comply with these requirements is an offence.

Further to sections 109 and 110 of the Companies Act 1963 the company is required to keep a copy of every instrument creating a registrable charge at its registered office and it must be open to inspection by any creditor or member of the company.

17.2 Registrable charges

17.2.1 Created by the company

According to section 99(1), the registration requirements apply only to charges created by the company. Therefore, charges arising by operation of law, such as an unpaid vendor's lien (see *Bank of Ireland Finance Ltd v. DJ Daly Ltd (in liquidation)* (1978)), do not, fall under the ambit of the section. The word "company" includes a foreign registered company who has an established place of business in Ireland and creates a charge over Irish assets. The categories of charges that must be registered are set out at section 99(2) of the Companies Act 1963.

17.2.2 Charge securing debentures – section 99(2)(a)

It appears to be the case that a charge securing a single debenture is not captured by this section. Therefore, a charge securing a series of debentures must be registered.

17.2.3 Charge on uncalled share capital – section 99(2)(b)

Uncalled share capital is discussed at Chapter 12. Any charge created by the company over this uncalled asset is registrable.

17.2.4 Charge created or evidenced by an instrument, which if executed by an individual, would require registration as a Bill of Sale – section 99(2)(c)

A bill of sale is a form of security granted over personal (moveable) assets by an unincorporated entity. Not every transaction entered into by a company (which, if executed by an individual, would require registration as a bill of sale) must be registered by a company as only those transactions where the repayment of money is secured must be registered.

17.2.5 Charge on land – section 99(2)(d)

There are two registration aspects where a charge is created over land: registration of the charge with the Registrar of Companies under section 99(1) of the Companies Act 1963 and registration in the Land Registry/Registry of Deeds.

A charge is defined in section 99(10) of the Companies Act 1963 as including a mortgage which, as noted in Chapter 16, involves a conveyance of title in the land to the lender with the company retaining the "equity of redemption". Every company will own freehold and/or leasehold property, which is a valuable asset commonly used to secure borrowings. Any mortgage issued by a company in respect of that land must be registered under section 99(1). The obligation to register covers both legal and equitable mortgages, the latter involving the deposit of the title deeds to the property with the lender for the duration of the loan. A deposit of title deeds may not be reflected in any written document but that does not affect the obligation to register the security with the Registrar of Companies.

However, where the land owned by the company is registered in the Land Registry under the Registration of Title Act 1964 (usually rural land), the company must be careful to register the mortgage with the Land Registry as a burden on the title. Failure to register the mortgage will result in the creditor losing priority to a subsequent creditor who registers a burden on the land. Where the land is unregistered land (registered in the Registry of Deeds and is usually urban land), the mortgage deed should also be registered. An unregistered creditor will also lose priority to a subsequent secured creditor save where the subsequent creditor had notice of the earlier mortgage.

17.2.6 Charge on company book debts – section 99(2)(e)

The court will examine the agreement between the creditor and the company, and if it is clear that the parties intended to assign the book debts to the creditor by way of security, then it is a registrable charge covered by this section. As noted in Chapter 16, companies may grant fixed charges over book debts and may in the future be in a position to grant a fixed charge over uncollected book debts and a floating charge over collected book debts.

17.2.7 Floating charges – section 99(2)(f)

A floating charge, as discussed in Chapter 16, is a registrable charge. In the case of registered land, the floating charge is usually registered as a caution or inhibition on the land in the Land Registry under the Registration of Title Act 1964. These cautions or inhibitions warn others dealing with the property that there is a floating charge on the property. Some of the cases dealing with failed retention of title clauses have held that the charge created is a floating charge which is captured by the obligation to register in this section (see Chapter 16 and *Re Bond Worth Ltd* (1980)).

17.2.8 Charge on calls made but unpaid – section 99(2)(g)

It is open to the company to use money owed to the company by shareholders as an asset which can be offered as security in exchange for borrowings.

17.2.9 Charge on a ship or aircraft – section 99(2)(h)

This section also covers any charge on a share of a ship or aircraft.

17.2.10 Charge on goodwill, patent or trademark – section 99(2)(I)

Charges executed over patents or trademarks must be registered under section 99(1) and they must also be notified to the Patents Office.

17.2.11 The Minister

According to section 99(2A) and (2B) of the Companies Act 1963 (as inserted by section 122 of the Companies Act 1990), the Minister may make a regulation amending the above list, adding further categories of charges that require registration.

17.2.12 Charges over purchased property

Section 101 of the Companies Act 1963 deals with property acquired by the company which is burdened by a charge at the date of purchase. If the charge falls within one of the categories enumerated in section 99(2), the company has twenty-one days from the date of the completion of the acquisition to deliver particulars of the charge to the Registrar of Companies. This strict time frame does not apply where the company has purchased such property outside the State.

17.3 Responsibility for compliance

According to section 100 of the Companies Act 1963 the company and "any person interested" in the matter may deliver the particulars of the charge to the Registrar of Companies. Where an interested person delivers the particulars, they are entitled to recover the registration fees from the company. Such interested parties commonly comprise lenders and suppliers. Where the company fails to deliver the particulars, and no interested party has done so, the company and every officer in default shall be liable to a fine under section 100(3) of the Companies Act 1963.

17.4 Time frame for compliance

Pursuant to section 99(1) of the Companies Act 1963, the particulars must be delivered to the Registrar of Companies within twenty-one days of the date of the creation of the charge. It should be noted that the date of the creation of the mortgage or charge is the date when that instrument was executed and it is not the date that any cash was subsequently advanced.

17.5 Certificate of registration and errors in registration

Section 104 of the Companies Act 1963 states that when a charge is duly registered under section 99, the Registrar of Companies shall issue a certificate of registration stating the amount secured by the charge. Section 104 goes on to state that the certificate of registration is conclusive evidence that the requirements of the Companies Act 1963 have been complied with. This complements the whole process of registration as not only can creditors investigate what security has been granted by the company, they can also rely on the results of the investigation.

In *Lombard & Ulster Banking Ltd v. Amurec Ltd* (1978) the liquidator of Amurec Ltd contended that the bank's charge was void because it had not been registered within twenty-one days of its creation as required by section 99(1). After it was executed the mortgage was not registered for some time and it was undated. The bank eventually dated the mortgage and registered the charge within twenty-one days. It was held by Hamilton J. that the charge was valid because the certificate of registration was conclusive evidence that the requirements of the Companies Act 1963 had been complied with and, in particular, that that the charge had been registered within the requisite twenty-one-day period. He based his decision on the fact that the wording of section 104 "is clear and unambiguous".

In the English case of *R v. Registrar of Companies, ex parte Central Bank of India* (1986) the court appeared to leave open the possibility of challenging the certificate where there is an error on the face of the certificate or where the certificate was obtained by fraud. It appears, however, to be settled that an error in the particulars of the charge and therefore the certificate of registration as to the amount secured by the charge will not invalidate the certificate (see *Re Mechanisations Eaglecliffe Ltd* (1964)). Further, in *Re Shannonside Holdings Ltd* (1993) Costello J. stated that while the certificate of registration will be conclusive evidence that particulars of the charge were delivered in accordance with the requirements of the Companies Act 1963, the actual terms of the debenture itself will always have precedence over the particulars.

In *Grove v Advantage Healthcare (T 10) Ltd* (1999) there was an error as to the registered number of the company and the error appeared on the certificate of charge. Lightman J. stated that the charge was still to be considered validly registered.

17.6 Effect of non-compliance

The failure to deliver the particulars of the charge to the Registrar within twenty-one days will render the charge void as against a liquidator of the company and the other company creditors, *i.e.* the creditor cannot rely on the charge as security in a winding up and, further, he cannot claim priority over the other company creditors. In *Smith (Administrator of Cosslett (Contractors) Ltd) v. Bridgend County Borough Council* (2002) the House of Lords held that an unregistered floating charge was void as against the company in administration, *i.e.* it was void as against the company when acting through its administrator. This reversed the Court of Appeal finding that the charge was void only as against the administrator of the company and not against the company.

A registrable charge, which is not registered, will be void (*i.e.* cannot be claimed against a subsequent creditor) against a subsequent creditor even where that creditor is aware of the prior unregistered charge. In *Re Monolithic Building Company* (1915) a subsequent secured creditor who registered his charge, notwithstanding his knowledge of the existence of a prior unregistered mortgage, was held to have priority by the Court of Appeal (see a possible exception to this rule in the case of mortgage over unregistered land at paragraph 17.2.5).

It is important to remember that failure to register the charge does not affect the obligation of the company to repay the debt secured. Section 99(1) states that when a charge is void for non-registration the sum secured by the charge will become immediately payable by the company.

17.7 Late registration

Section 106(1) of the Companies Act 1963 gives the court jurisdiction to extend the time for the registration of a charge or the rectification of any error or mis-statement of any particular submitted to the Registrar. The application may be made by the company or any interested person such as the creditor holding the charge. According to the section, the court will extend the time to register or rectify where it is satisfied that

1. the failure to register/rectify was accidental, due to inadvertence or some other sufficient cause; or

2. the failure to register/rectify is not of a nature to prejudice the position of the creditors or shareholders of the company; or

3. it is just and equitable for the court to grant relief.

The order for late registration or late rectification may include such terms and conditions that the court deems expedient but section 106(2) makes it very clear that an order for late registration will not relieve the company or the company officers from the liability for late registration imposed by section 100(3) of the Companies Act 1963. It is common for an order for late registration to include a proviso that the registration is without prejudice to those creditors who have acquired a secured interest in the company in the interim period. Therefore, unsecured creditors are not protected. In *Re Telematic Ltd* (1994) the court stated that the creditor must disclose all matters that will influence the court's discretion. In this case the creditor omitted to mention that the company had been dissolved.

An order for late registration will not be granted by the court where a company is in liquidation (see *Re Resinoid & Mica Products Ltd* (1983) and *Victoria Housing Estates Ltd v. Ashpurton Estates Ltd* (1983)). The position is less clear where the winding up of a company appears imminent. In *Re MIG Trust Ltd* (1933) it was stated that the court was not concerned with the imminence of a winding up. However, later cases have clearly taken a different view, with some cases categorically stating that an order for late registration should not be made where a winding up is imminent (see *Re Resinoid & Mica Products Ltd* (1983) and *Victoria Housing Estates Ltd v. Ashpurton Estates Ltd* (1983).

There are cases permitting late registration where a winding up order is on the horizon but they have required an undertaking from the creditor that in the event of the company going into liquidation within one month of the order, he will abide by the court's jurisdiction to set the order for late registration aside (see *Re Telford Motors Limited* (1978). The latter course of action appears to be the preferred option and it was adopted by *Barclays Bank Plc v. Stuart Landon Ltd & anor* (2001). In this case the bank failed through inadvertence to deliver particulars of a charge to the English Companies House within the prescribed twenty-one days. The company had created two charges, one in favour of the bank and the other in favour of a vendor of property it had acquired at the same time. It was expressly agreed that the vendor's charge would rank after the bank's charge. When the winding up of the company was imminent, the bank applied for late registration of the charge subject to the usual proviso that it would be without prejudice to the rights of shareholders and creditors rights acquired prior to the permitted late registration. Further, it was accepted that if the company went into liquidation, the liquidator could apply to have the order for late registration discharged. The District Court held that as the winding up of the company appeared inevitable, there was little benefit to the bank in an order for late registration. The Court of Appeal overturned the decision, as it had not been proved that an application to set aside the order for late registration would succeed. The court confirmed the order for late registration subject to the above provisos.

18. RECEIVERSHIP

A secured creditor (also called a debenture holder or chargee) has a variety of options available to enforce the payment of an outstanding debt. In the event that a company defaults in repayment or breaches another aspect of the loan, the secured creditor may *inter alia* issue a petition to wind up the company, seek a court order for the possession and sale of the secured property, or issue court proceedings to enforce the repayment. There may be further options open to the secured creditor which are negotiated with the company and are set out in a debenture document. A common negotiated option is the right to appoint a receiver over one or more of the company assets which have been mortgaged or charged as security for the debt.

The principal task of the receiver is to realise those assets and distribute the proceeds to the debenture holder in accordance with the provisions of the Companies Acts. In some cases the receiver may have the right to manage the affairs of the company if it will facilitate the repayment of the debt.

A receiver can be distinguished from both an examiner and a liquidator. Examinership provides the company with a breathing space from creditors by way of court protection to enable the company to get back on its feet. The examiner puts in place a framework of survival in the interests of both the shareholders and the creditors. A liquidation occurs where no such survival is feasible and the liquidator comes in to wind up the company affairs and eventually dissolve the company. The liquidator collects all the company assets in the interests of all the company creditors.

18.1 Appointment of a receiver

A receiver is appointed by a debenture holder on foot of a debenture document or by the court on an application by a creditor to enforce the repayment of a debt.

18.1.1 Appointment under the debenture

The debenture document will detail "default events" and if a default event occurs, the right to appoint a receiver will be triggered. Common default events include the failure to repay the loan principal and /or interest for a specified period of time, the passing of a resolution to wind up the company, the appointment of a receiver by another creditor, or the company ceasing, or threatening to cease, to carry on business.

Where the appointment is made by the debenture holder, there is no special duty to consider the effect of the appointment on the prospects of the company. The debenture holder acts to protect its own interests, and, according to *Re Potters Oil Ltd (No 2)* (1986), the potential loss to the company or its secured creditors does not mean that the debenture holder should refrain from making the appointment.

However, according to the decision of the Supreme Court of Canada in *Royal Bank of Canada v. W. Got & Associates Electric Ltd* (2000), the debenture holder must give the debtor company reasonable notice of intention to enforce the security and reasonable time to pay thereafter. In that case the bank intentionally avoided telling the company that it would be calling in the debenture and would be seeking to appoint a receiver. The court held that the length of notice would vary with the facts of each case but that in the instant case the bank has not given any reason to explain the absence of notice.

It may be the case that the debenture may permit a number of named creditors to appoint a receiver to the company. This may result in multiple receivers. In *Gwembe Valley Development Co. Ltd (in receivership) v. Koshy et al* (2000) Rimer J. examined such a debenture clause and held that the individual power to appoint a receiver was not exhausted by the appointment of a receiver by one of the other creditors. He dismissed the claim that multiple receivers were a recipe for chaos and stated that a regime could be put in place whereby the receivers divided their duties.

18.1.2 The agency relationship

When the receiver is appointed by the debenture holder, it follows logically that the receiver is an agent of the debenture holder. However, it is common for the debenture document to state that the receiver is an agent of the company, thus making the company liable for the agent's acts, omissions, and remuneration. In *Bula Ltd et al v. Crowley et al* (2002) Barr J. referred to the two distinct relationships, the first between the appointing mortagee/creditor and the receiver, and the second between the receiver and third parties such as the company. In the opinion of Barr J., "there was no inconsistency between the foregoing relationships which represent long established commercial good sense".

As in the case of a standard agency agreement, the receiver is a fiduciary and owes the usual fiduciary duties to his principal. However, this "agency" relationship with the company is an unusual one. Unlike standard agency relationships, the receiver is personally liable on contracts entered into on behalf of the company and his primary duty is to realise the security and act in the best interests of the debenture holder not the company.

The unorthodox nature of the receiver's relationship with the company was highlighted by the Australian High Court decision of *Sheehan v. Carrier Air Conditioning Pty Ltd* (1997). To encourage the completion of works, the receiver paid sub-contractors of the company from the sale proceeds of the debenture assets. It was the opinion of the receiver that the completion was in the debenture holder's best interest. When the company went into liquidation, the payments were challenged as a fraudulent preference by the company.

It was held that it would be "absurd" to say that the payments were made by the receiver as agent for the company and were, therefore, a fraudulent preference, as he had exercised his own discretion to make the payments. The decision had regard to the commercial dynamics of the course of action that the receiver took, but its effect was to render nugatory the standard agency clause purporting to make the receiver the agent of the company.

18.1.3 Appointment by the court

A receiver may be appointed by order of the court. The application for the appointment of a receiver by the court usually arises where the debenture document does not give adequate power to the debenture holder to appoint a receiver.

The Companies Acts do not enumerate the grounds for a court appointment of a receiver. The court will take into account whether or not the creditors' security is jeopardised or in arrears and, further, whether the company is winding up or about to wind up. The court, however, has complete discretion on the matter as Kenny J. in *Angelis v. Algemene Bank Nederland (Ireland) Ltd* (1974) referred to the court's inherent equitable jurisdiction to appoint a receiver. He stated that it was not necessary to cite authority for the proposition that a debenture holder may immediately appoint a receiver when assets which are the subject matter of the charge are in danger. In *Alexander*

Hull & Company Ltd v. O' Carroll Kent & Company Ltd (1955) the court appointed a receiver at the request of a lender who had advanced money to the company where there was only an agreement to execute a charge in place.

A court appointed receiver is an officer of the court who must take into account the interests of all creditors and cannot act solely in the interests of the secured creditor who procured his appointment. The receiver is not deemed to be an agent of the debenture holder or the court but the receiver is regarded as having a fiduciary relationship with the debenture holder according to *Re Gent, Gent-Davis v. Harris* (1889).

18.1.4 Effect of examinership

As a result of the Companies (Amendment) Act 1990, the position of a receiver is always vulnerable to the appointment of an examiner (see Chapter 20). A petition to appoint an examiner may be presented to the court even if a receiver is already in place, provided that the receiver stands appointed for less than three continuous days. If the petition is successful, it is often the case that the receiver has to cede his place to the examiner or act only in relation to certain specified assets.

Section 6 of the Companies (Amendment) Act 1990 (as amended by section 16 of the Companies (Amendment) (No. 2) Act 1999) gives the court a wide discretion to make whatever orders it thinks fit on the application to appoint an examiner. Such orders may include any or all of the following:

1. that the receiver shall cease to act;
2. that the receiver shall, from a specified date, act only in respect of certain assets;
3. that the receiver shall deliver the company's books, papers, and records to the examiner; and/or
4. that the receiver shall give the examiner details of all his dealings with the company's property and undertaking.

18.1.5 Effect of winding up and dissolution

When a receiver is appointed, it may adversely affect the solvency of the company and result in a winding up. *Gosling v. Gaskell* (1897) stated that the authority of an agent to act is terminated on the winding up of the company. To avoid this termination of authority, most debenture documents grant the receiver an irrevocable power of attorney to act on behalf of a company. Commentators have, however, doubted whether such a power of attorney can be irrevocable and survive a winding up. Under section 322B of the Companies Act 1963 it is open to the liquidator to apply to the court to have the receivership limited or determined.

The receiver cannot be appointed or continue to act if the company has been struck off the company register, as an agent cannot act if the principal has ceased to exist (see *Salton v. New Boston Cycle Co.* (1900)). It is open to the debenture holder to make an application to have the company restored to the register see Chapter 22).

18.1.6 The receiver-manager

It may be the case that the security for the debt is a charge over all the assets and undertakings of the company. A common term in such a debenture is one permitting the receiver to manage the affairs of the company. According to *Kernohan Estates Ltd v. Boyd* (1967) it is open to the receiver to resolve not to continue the company business if it could not be in the best interests of the debenture holder. A receiver-manager would commonly have the power to borrow money for the company, employ and dismiss employees, and negotiate with the creditors to compromise their debts. In *Medforth v. Blake et al* (1999) the English Court of Appeal held that in exercising management powers a receiver owes a duty to manage the property with due diligence subject to his primary duty of attempting to repay the interest and principal of the secured amount. The court also confirmed that a receiver is not obliged to manage a business but due diligence requires a receiver to take reasonable steps to manage it profitably if a receiver elects to continue the business.

18.1.7 Notification of receivership

The following notification obligations must be strictly complied with by the receiver:

1. section 107(1) of the Companies Act 1963 requires that the debenture holder publish notice of the appointment within seven days in *Iris Oifigiuil* and at least one daily newspaper circulating in the area of the company's registered office;

2. section 107(2) of the Companies Act 1963 requires that the Registrar of Companies be served with notice of the appointment;
3. the receiver must immediately notify the subject company of his appointment (section 319 of the Companies Act 1963);
4. every invoice issued by or on behalf of the company must contain a statement that a receiver has been appointed. Failure to comply with this requirement is an offence.

18.1.8 Statement of affairs

On receiving the notice of appointment, the company in receivership (the subject company) has fourteen days to submit a statement of affairs to the receiver (section 319(1)(b) of the Companies Act 1963). The statement is made by the company directors and secretary or by may be made by such others as are specified by the receiver, including the following:

1. present and former officers of the subject company;
2. those who took part in the formation of the subject company within the preceding year;
3. present and former employees of the subject company who the receiver thinks may be capable of giving the required information;
4. present or former officers of a company, where that company was an officer of the subject company.

The statement must show particulars of the company's assets, debts and liabilities, the names and addresses of creditors, and details of securities granted by the company (section 320(1) of the Companies Act 1963).

Failure to comply with this obligation is an offence, but it is a defence to prove that it was not possible to comply with these requirements (section 320(5) of the Companies Act 1963). It is open to the receiver and/or a creditor to apply to the court for an order of compliance under section 320A of the Companies Act 1963 as inserted by section 174 of the Companies Act 1990.

Section 319 (2) of the Companies Act 1963 requires the receiver to furnish the Registrar of Companies with an abstract within seven months of his appointment. The abstract must contain details of the assets taken into his possession and their estimated value, the proceeds of the sale of any such assets, and his receipts and payments since his appointment. This abstract must be submitted every six months thereafter and one month after he ceases to act.

18.2 Effect of receivership

The company, the creditors, and the directors are all affected by the appointment of a receiver.

18.2.1 Floating charges

All floating charges crystallise and become fixed on the asset or assets over which debt was secured (*Nelson & Co. v. Faber & Co.* (1903)). The company is prevented from dealing with those assets unless the consent of the receiver is obtained according to *Cripps (RA) & Son Ltd v. Wickenden* (1973).

18.2.2 The company and directors

On the appointment of a receiver, the directors of the company remain in place. However, the powers of the company and the authority of the directors cease in respect of the assets which are covered by the security. The company and/or the directors may only act in relation to those assets with the consent of the receiver. Where the receiver has been appointed as a receiver-manager, the powers of the directors are further curtailed as the receiver can run the business of the company. According to *Lascomme Ltd v. United Dominions Trust (Ireland) Ltd* (1994), the powers of the directors will continue only to the extent that they are not inconsistent with the duties of the receiver.

18.2.3 Company contracts

The effect of receivership on company contracts depends on the nature of the contract.

(1) Pre-receivership contracts

Contracts entered into by the company prior to receivership remain binding on the company but they do not bind the receiver (*Ardmore Studios (Ireland) Ltd v. Lynch* (1965), *Re Johnson (B) & Co. (Builders) Ltd* (1955), *Airlines Airspares Ltd v. Handley Page Ltd* (1970)).

According to *Newdigate Colliery Ltd* (1912), the receiver incurs no personal liability on the performance of these contracts save where the receiver expressly assumes personal responsibility. It may be the case that it is in the best interests of the debenture holder to carry on the existing contracts particularly if they affect the goodwill of the business.

(2) Post-receivership contracts

The receiver will be personally liable on any contract entered into by him in the performance of his functions pursuant to section 316(2) of the Companies Act 1963. It is open to the receiver to negotiate a term of the contract that he shall not be personally liable or that he shall be indemnified by the company assets in the event of personal liability arising.

(3) Employment contracts

It was the position that the appointment of a receiver by the court had the effect of terminating employment contracts. It now appears to be the case that contracts of employment remain valid and binding on the company as *Jowett (Angus) & Co. v. Tailors' and Garment Western Union* (1985) held that the European Communities (Safeguarding of Employees Rights on the Transfer of Undertakings) Regulations 1980 applies to receiverships. This regulation sets out that employment contracts continue on the transfer of an undertaking.

Where the receiver is appointed by a debenture holder, the employee contracts are not terminated according to *Griffiths v. Secretary of State for Social Services* (1974). *Nicoll v. Cutts* (1985) makes it clear that where the receiver does not terminate an employment contract (and the receiver has the discretion to do so), the receiver is not personally liable for the payment of employee wages.

18.3 Duties of a receiver

Much case law has queried and examined the duties owed by the receiver not simply to the debenture holder who made the appointment, but also the duties owed to the company, the directors, the shareholders, and even the company employees.

18.3.1 Duty to provide information to the company

In *Irish Oil & Cake Mills Ltd v.* Donnelly (1983) Costello J. stated that the receiver does not owe a *general duty* to keep the board of the directors apprised of how the business of the company is going. Costello J. accepted that there may be special circumstances where, to ensure the best price is obtained for the company assets, that trading information should be provided to the directors. Costello J. made it clear that his decision did not mean that there was no duty at all to account to the company. He stated that the extent of any such duty would depend on the facts of each separate case.

In *D Kinsella v. B Somers* (1999) Budd J. once again discussed the duty of the receiver to provide information. In this case a receiver was appointed to the Dublin Gas Company in 1986 and sold its assets to the debenture holder in 1987. The plaintiff was a shareholder and director of the receivership company and claimed that he had been provided with insufficient information about the company accounts, the background to the sale of the assets including particulars of the valuations and advices obtained, and the length of time taken to bring the receivership to a conclusion. He sought a direction from the High Court requiring the receiver to furnish information under section 316 of the Companies Act 1963.

Budd J. held that *Irish Oil and Cake Mills Ltd* (1984) dealt with the receiver's duty to provide information to the company, and not with the duty to give information to individual directors or shareholders. Section 316(1)(1A) of the Companies Act 1963 limits the circumstances in which an application for information may be made. Save where the receiver is the applicant, the application must be supported by such evidence as the court may require, showing that the applicant is being unfairly prejudiced by any actual or proposed action or omission of the receiver. It was held that the applicant had not proved that the information sought was required for any specific purpose and there was no evidence that the receiver had acted unreasonably in refusing to give further information to the applicant in his capacity as director and shareholder. Budd J. stated that different consideraiton might apply if the applicant were to prove that the refusal to give further information was activated by bad faith on the receiver's part.

18.3.2 Duty to exercise care in disposing of the assets of the company

It is established law that a receiver owes a duty to take reasonable care to companies to obtain the best price possible for the assets of the company. Originally this duty was enshrined in case law. In *Holohan v. Friends Provident and Century Life Office* (1966), *Cuckmere Brick Co. Ltd v. Mutual Finance Company Ltd* (1971), *Standard Charter Bank v. Walker* (1982), and *Irish Oil and Cake Mills Ltd v. Donnelly* (1983) the court interpreted the duty of the receiver as being one of exercising reasonable care to obtain the true market value of the asset at the time of sale.

Section 316A(1) of the Companies Act 1963 (as inserted by section 172 of the Companies Act 1990 Act) now imposes a statutory duty to exercise "all reasonable care to obtain the best price reasonably obtainable for the property at the time of sale". It is not a defence to plead that the receiver was acting as an agent of the company or pursuant to a power of attorney. Further, pursuant to section 316A(2)(b), a receiver who breaches this duty of care is not entitled to be compensated or indemnified by the company for any liability that may be incurred. Laffoy J. in *Edenfell Holdings Ltd* (1997) and McCracken J. in *Ruby Property Company Ltd et al v. Kilty and anor* (1999) held that section 316A(1) was a simple statutory acknowledgement of the position at common law.

(1) Burden of proof

It is the receiver who has the burden of proving that the best price possible for the assets was obtained. Laffoy J. in *Edenfell Holdings Ltd* (1997) placed a positive onus on the receiver to show that he considered whether the transaction, taking into account all its significant commercial elements, resulted in the company obtaining the best price reasonably obtainable at the time of sale.

(2) Operative date for the test

When considering whether or not the best price possible was obtained, the test must be applied at the date of the contract according to Kenny J. in *Casey v. Intercontinental Bank Ltd* (1979). In this case the receiver accepted an offer of £111,000 which at the time was the best price available. A later offer of £190,000 was rejected due to the prior contract. The court held that the receiver was not in breach of his duty to obtain the best price as he is not obliged to wait for an upturn in the market.

(3) Standard to be applied

The standard of care required is higher than simply acting in good faith. In *Holohan v. Friends Provident and Century Life Office* (1966) it was held that the receiver should have tried to sell the property with vacant possession, as he would have obtained a higher price for the building. The receiver had breached his duty of care as he had failed to consider the alternatives.

(4) Advice and representations

The receiver should take into account the advice of experts of the most efficient and valuable method of sale. In *Lambert Jones Estate Ltd v. Donnelly* (1982) the court found that expert advice on how best to dispose of the assets of receivership could be disregarded by the receiver in certain circumstances. In this case the receiver rejected the advice as it would involve costly and protracted planning applications while the interest was mounting against the company. The court found that in these circumstances the receiver had not breached his duty of care.

In *Ruby Property Company Ltd et al v. Kilty and anor* (1999) the court considered whether or not the receiver was under an obligation to take into account representations by the company as to the method of sale. The plaintiff companies argued that the receiver should have advertised the property to the public. The receiver contended that he had received lengthy and detailed advice from planning consultants and had acted on the advice of a competent and well-known firm of estate agents. McCracken J. found that the sale may in fact have been at an undervalue. The first plaintiff was a solvent company and the receiver would have been aware that the sale would create a considerable surplus which would be an asset of the company. It was stated *obiter* that in these circumstances a receiver may have an obligation to consider representations made to him by the company as to how to conduct the sale, provided the receiver is satisfied that in any event the sale will realise enough to discharge the debenture holder in full.

18.3.4 Duty in applying the proceeds of sale

Where a receiver realises the assets which are the subject of a fixed charge or a legal mortgage, his only obligation is to use the proceeds to discharge the amount owing to the debenture holder. Any surplus realised should be paid directly to the company.

If the security for the debt is a floating charge, then the receiver is obliged to take preferential creditors into account. Section 98 of the Companies Act 1963 requires the receiver to pay preferential creditors from the proceeds of the sale prior to making any payments of principal or interest to the debenture holders. The case of *United Bars Ltd et al v. Revenue Commissioners* (1991) examined the application of section 98 where the assets sold were subject to both a fixed and floating charge. The receiver realised these assets and paid the debenture holder.

The point of contention was whether or not the surplus should be paid to the company or to the preferential creditors. Murphy J. directed that the surplus should be paid to the company as the section applied only where the asset was subject to a floating charge.

18.3.5 Duty to guarantors

A guarantor may be called upon to pay out on his guarantee where the receiver has realised the charged assets and there is a shortfall in the amount owed to the debenture holder. As a result, the receiver has a duty of care to guarantors to ensure that the best price possible is obtained for the assets. This duty of care was confirmed in *Standard Chartered Bank v. Walker* (1982).

This point was confirmed in *McGowan v. Gannon* (1983) where Carroll J. stated that a guarantor could sue a receiver in negligence as there was sufficient proximity between the receiver and the guarantor for a duty of care to be owed to the guarantor.

18.4 Removal and resignation of a receiver

18.4.1 Removal

The receiver can be removed in the following ways:

1. the debenture holder may remove the receiver in accordance with the terms of the debenture document;

2. the court may remove the receiver "upon cause being shown" under section 322A(1) of the Companies Act 1963. The court may remove the receiver for misconduct or simply where it is in the best interests of creditors;

3. as set out at paragraph 18.1.5, the receiver may be removed on an application by the company liquidator;

4. as set out at paragraph 18.1.4, the receiver may be removed on an application by the company examiner.

18.4.2 Resignation

Under section 322C of the Companies Act 1963 the receiver, if appointed by a debenture holder, must give one month's notice of his resignation to the holders of fixed and floating charges, the company, and the liquidator of the company (if any). If he was appointed by the court, the court must consent to his resignation. Failure to obtain the consent of the court may lead to a fine under section 322C(3) of the Companies Act 1963.

If the receiver becomes disqualified, he must vacate the position or he will be guilty of an offence. Notice of his disqualification must be served on the company and either the debenture holder or the court.

The following are disqualified from acting as a receiver under sections 314 and 315 of the Companies Act 1963:

1. a body corporate;

2. an undischarged bankrupt;

3. a person/officer who was an officer of the company in receivership within the previous twelve months;

4. a parent, spouse, brother or sister of an officer of the subject company; and

5. a partner or employee of an officer of the subject company.

19. COMPANY INVESTIGATIONS

The procedure for conducting a company investigation has been available in Ireland since 1908. In particular, sections 165 to 173 of the Companies Act 1963 set out the provisions enabling the Minister for Industry and Commerce to appoint inspectors to investigate the affairs of companies. For several years the procedure was rarely used. The legislation was found to be too narrow and it was believed that successive Ministers were reluctant to order investigations. The company legislation introduced in 1990 radically amended much of the Companies Act 1963 and began what was to become a greater emphasis on company transparency. Sections 7 to 24 of the Companies Act 1990 breathed much needed life into the old investigation provisions. The powers of the Minister were significantly extended, and, for the first time, the power to order an investigation was vested in the High Court.

The Company Law Enforcement Act 2001 has again amended the preceding legislation by transferring the Minister's role in company investigations to the Office of the Director of Corporate Enforcement (the "Director"). Section 12 of the Company Law Enforcement Act 2001 sets out *inter alia* that the functions of the Director are to include encouraging compliance with the Companies Acts, investigating incidences of suspected offences under the Companies Acts and the referral of cases to the Director of Public Prosecutions for prosecution on indictment. An application to the court to appoint an inspector (see paragraph 19.2), an investigation of company membership (see paragraph 19.3), a preliminary investigation (see paragraph 19.4), and a direction to a company to produce documents (see paragaph 19.6) shall now be carried out by the Director of Corporate Enforcement and not the Minister.

19.1 Categories of investigations

The investigations that can proceed under current legislation are as follows:

1. a court ordered investigation where an inspector is appointed and the applicant requesting the investigation is the company, a company director, one or more of the members, and/or one or more of the creditors (section 7 of the Companies Act 1990, as amended);

2. a court ordered investigation where an inspector is appointed and the applicant requesting the investigation is the Director (section 8 of the Companies Act 1990, as amended);
3. a Director ordered investigation where an inspector is appointed to investigate the membership of a company (section 14 of the Companies Act 1990, as amended);
4. a preliminary investigation by the Director to determine if a formal investigation of membership is necessary (section 15 of the Companies Act 1990, as amended);
5. a notice by the Director to a company to produce books/documents (section 19 of the Companies Act 1990, as amended).

19.2 Court investigations

19.2.1 Section 7 investigations

Section 7 of the Companies Act 1990 (as amended by section 20 of the Company Law Enforcement Act 2001) empowers the High Court to appoint "one or more competent inspectors" to investigate matters specified by the court. The application may be made by the following categories:

1. in the case of a company having a share capital, by not less than one hundred members or a member or members holding not less than one-tenth of the paid-up share capital; or
2. in the case of a company not having a share capital, by not less than one-fifth in number of the persons in the company's register of members; or
3. in any case, by the company or a director of the company or a creditor of the company.

It is open to the court, under section 7(3) of the Companies Act 1990, to require that the applicant or applicants provide security for the costs of the investigation of not less than € 6,350 and not more than €317,500. This will have the effect of discouraging frivolous applications.

The application must be supported by such evidence as the court may require. The circumstances which must exist before an order can be made under section 7 of the Companies Act 1990 are not set out and each application must be determined on its own merits. Given that the attendant publicity and expense may have an adverse effect on the standing of the company and affect its market value if listed, it is safe to presume that the applicant would be required to show at least prima facie evidence of irregularity. However, it cannot be presumed that the court will over-indulge a company who has such concerns. Laffoy J. in *Dunnes Stores Ireland Co. v. Moloney* (1999) held that even though public knowledge of the appointment of an authorised officer under section 19 of the Companies Act 1990 could adversely affect the reputation of the subject companies, it was a legitimate statutory imposition which was incidental to obtaining the benefits of incorporation as limited liability companies.

The court has the discretion to give such directions to the inspector as the court considers are required in order to ensure that the investigation is carried out as quickly and as inexpensively as possible.

It is clear form the section that the court has no power to order investigations on its own. The categories of applicant also exclude a liquidator, a receiver or an examiner. It is, however, open to one of the above applicants to apply to the court under section 7 of the Companies Act 1990 during a winding up.

19.2.2 Section 8 investigations

Section 8 of the Companies Act 1990 (as amended by sections 14 and 21 of the Company Law Enforcement Act 2001) also empowers the court to order investigations into the affairs of the company on the application of the Director. The court may appoint one or more competent inspectors, who may be, or may include, an officer of the Director.

In contrast to section 7 of the Companies Act 1990 the Director is given guidance as to the onus of proof that must be satisfied. The power of appointment may be exercised where the court is satisfied that there are circumstances suggesting any of the following:

1. that the company's affairs are being, or have been, conducted with the intent to defraud its creditors or the creditors of any other person, or generally for a fraudulent or unlawful purpose, or in a manner which is unfairly prejudicial to some part of its members (which includes persons to whom shares have been transferred or transmitted but are not yet registered members), or that any act or proposed act or omission of the company is, or would be, so prejudicial, or that it was formed for any fraudulent or unlawful purpose; or

2. that persons connected with its formation or the management of its affairs have been guilty of fraud, misfeasance or other misconduct towards it or towards its members; or

3. that its members have not being given all the information relating to its affairs that they might reasonably expect.

One significant difference between section 7 of the Companies Act 1990 and section 8 of the Companies Act 1990 is that the power to make an order under section 8 extends to companies incorporated outside Ireland, and which carry on, or have at any time carried on, business in Ireland (section 17 of the Companies Act 1990). Section 7 is solely confined to companies incorporated in Ireland.

19.2.3 The investigation

An order under section 7 or section 8 enables an investigation of "the affairs of a company" to be carried out. This phrase has been interpreted in England in *R v. Board of Trade, ex. p. St Martin's Preserving Co. Ltd* (1965) as including the company's goodwill, its profits or losses, its contracts and assets including its shareholding in, and ability to control the affairs of, a subsidiary and even a sub-subsidiary. In that case the Board of Trade refused to appoint an inspector on the ground that the proposed investigation related solely to the conduct of a receiver appointed by debenture holders. The court reversed this decision and unanimously held that the activities of a receiver are an "affair" of the company in respect of which he is appointed.

The inspector must follow the principles of natural and constitutional justice. Laffoy J. in *Dunnes Stores Ireland Co. v. Moloney* (1999) made it clear that persons affected by a section 19 order (see paragraph 19.6) were entitled to fair procedures.

19.2.4 The expenses of the investigation

Under section 13(1) of the Companies Act 1990 (as amended by section 25 of the Company Law Enforcement Act 2001), the expenses of the investigation are to be borne initially by the relevant Minister. The court may, however, direct that a body corporate dealt with in the investigation report or the applicant or applicants for the investigation repay a sum to the relevant Minister, provided the amount directed does not exceed €317,500. The investigation report may, and shall if the court so requests, include recommendations as to whether such directions should be made.

Further, under section 13(2) of the Companies Act 1990, where proceedings are issued as a result of the investigation and a person is convicted on indictment, or is ordered to pay damages or restore property, or is awarded damages or restored property, the court may order in those same proceedings that some or all of the expenses of the investigation are repaid to the relevant Minister or to a person who was ordered to pay money under section 13(1). The court cannot make an order for payment which exceeds one-tenth of the value of damages or property, and the order can only be executed when the damages have been received or the property has been restored.

19.2.5 Powers of the inspectors

(1) Related companies

Section 9 of the Companies Act 1990 (as amended by section 22 of the Company Law Enforcement Act 2001) enables the inspector, with the court's approval, to extend the investigation to a body corporate which is a related company. Related companies are defined by section 140 of the Companies Act 1990 and include *inter alia* a subsidiary or holding company of the company under investigation. The definition now includes a body corporate that has a commercial relationship with the company under investigation. That commercial relationship is broadly defined and exists where goods/services are sold or given by one party to another.

In *Chestvale Properties Ltd v. Glackin* (1993) and *Lyons v. Curran* (1993) the High Court held that the inspector was not limited to inquiring into the affairs of the company named in the order and "related companies" as this would restrict investigation where there was a corporate shareholder of the company in the order/related company. In *Probets v. Glackin* (1993) McCarthy J. stated that this would make the section "intolerable".

(2) Books, documents and assistance

Section 10(1) of the Companies Act 1990 (as amended by section 23 of the Company Law Enforcement Act 2001) provides that the officers and agents of the company under investigation, and the officers and agents of any other body corporate whose affairs are being investigated, are under a duty to produce to the inspector all books and documents of, or relating to, the company in question which are in their custody and power. The officers and agents may be required to produce such books or documents by the inspector.

In *Glackin v. Trustee Savings Bank* (1993) a bank could not refuse to give the inspector information on the ground that it would breach their confidential relationship with their customers. The Companies Act 1990, as amended, does not, however, require that a company surrender information covered by a legal professional privilege. Section 23(2) of the Companies Act 1990 (as amended by section 32 of the Company Law Enforcement Act 2001) now provides that the Director shall not require a company carrying on the business of banking to produce any customer documents save where it is necessary to investigate the affairs of that company or customer.

These officers and agents are also under a duty to give to the inspectors all reasonable assistance in connection with the investigation, and may be required to do so by the inspectors. If the inspector considers that a person other than the above officers or agents is in possession of information concerning the affairs of the company or related body corporate, the inspector may require the production of books and documents relating to the company/body corporate, and that person is under a duty to comply. That person must also give all reasonable assistance in connection with the investigation.

(3) Bank accounts

Section 10(3) of the Companies Act 1990 gives the inspector the right to examine documents in the possession, or under the control of, a director of the company under investigation or a related body corporate, which relate to a bank account, whether in the State or elsewhere, into or out of which the following has been paid:

1. any money which has resulted from or been used in the financing of any transaction, arrangement or agreement and particulars of which were not disclosed in the company accounts or the register of transactions, or where there was an amount outstanding from the transaction, arrangement or agreement, the particulars of which were not disclosed in the company accounts; or

2. any money which has been in any way connected with any act or omission, or series of acts or omissions, which on the part of the director constituted misconduct towards that company or body corporate or its members.

The reference to director includes a present or past director, any person connected with such a director and any present or past shadow director.

(4) Examination on oath

Section 10(4) of the Companies Act 1990 provides that the inspectors may require the officers and agents of the relevant companies, and any other person whom they consider may be in possession of relevant information, to attend before them for the purpose of being examined on oath by the inspector in relation to the company's affairs. In this context, the inspectors must be careful to comply with the rules of natural or constitutional justice (see *Re Haughey* (1971)).

(5) Failure to cooperate

Section 10(5) of the Companies Act 1990 (as amended by section 23 of the Company Law Enforcement Act 2001) provides that where an officer or agent of the company or body corporate or any other person as mentioned above, refuses or fails within a reasonable time, to produce books or documents, or to attend before the inspector or answer questions put to them, the inspector may certify such refusal to the High Court. The High Court may then, after inquiring into the circumstances and hearing any relevant witnesses, make any order or direction it thinks fit. The constitutionality of section 10(5) of the Companies Act 1990 was challenged in *Desmond v. Glackin (No. 2)* (1993) on the ground that the part of the sub-section which allowed the High Court to punish the offender was unconstitutional. The court held that the part which permitted the court to produce books or documents or answer questions was severable and constitutional.

Under section 10(6) of the Companies Act 1990 (as amended by section 23 of the Company Law Enforcement Act 2001) the court may order that the person at issue attend before the inspector or answer questions or produce documents.

Section 18 of the Companies Act 1990 (as amended by section 28 of the Company Law Enforcement Act 2001) states that answers given under section 10 may be used in evidence against that individual in any proceedings.

19.2.6 The inspector's report

The inspector may present interim reports to the court during the course of the investigation. It is open to the court to direct that these reports be presented. Under section 11(1) of the Companies Act 1990, the inspector must make a final report to the court when the investigation is completed. Under section 11(2) the inspector may inform the court at any time of any matters arising from the investigation which tend to show that an offence has been committed.

A copy of all final reports must be furnished to the Director under section 11(3) of the Companies Act 1990 (as amended by section 24 of the Company Law Enforcement Act 2001), and the court may, if it thinks fit, furnish a copy on request to the following:

1. any member of a company or other body corporate which is the subject of the report;
2. any person whose conduct is referred to in the report;
3. the auditors of the company or the body corporate;
4. the applicant for the investigation;
5. any other person, including employees and creditors, whose financial interests appear to the court to be affected by any matter dealt with in the report;
6. the Central Bank, if the report relates wholly or partly to the affairs of a licensed bank.

It is also a matter for the court whether or not a copy of the report should be forwarded to the company's registered office. Before releasing the report to any of these persons or bodies, the court may direct that part of the report may be deleted, under section 11(4) of the Companies Act 1990, in order to safeguard the financial or other interests of a company or individual.

Section 12(1) of the Companies Act 1990 provides the court with very wide powers on receipt of the report. The court may make such order as it deems fit in relation to matters arising from the report. On examining the report, it is open to the court to order the winding up of the company. The Director may also take an active role in the winding up, as it is open to the Director to petition for the winding up of the company after an investigation where the court thinks that it is just and equitable to do so (section 12(2) of the Companies Act 1990 as amended by section 14 of the Company Law Enforcement Act 2001, see paragraph 22.1.4).

The type of orders the court might make are as follows:

1. the disqualification/restriction of a person from acting as an officer of the company;
2. the sending of the relevant papers to the Director of Public Prosecutions for the purpose of considering whether criminal charges should be instituted (the court could not, merely upon receipt of the report, find a person guilty of a criminal offence without affording him the protection of a criminal trial in accordance with the normal legal procedures);
3. the restitution of company property;
4. an award of damages.

19.3 Formal investigations of company membership

19.3.1 Section 14 investigations

Section 14 of the Companies Act 1990 (as amended by section 19 of the Company Law Enforcement Act 2001) enables the Director to order one or more inspectors to investigate and report to him on the membership of a company with a view to determining "the true persons who are or have been financially interested in the success or failure (real or apparent) of the company or able to control or materially to influence the policy of the company".

The purpose of a section 14 investigation is, therefore, to go behind the separate legal personality of the company to discover whether directors or other officers of a company have hidden behind another company when acting in breach of their duties to the company. The investigation can extend to the identification of those persons legally interested in the success and control of the company and also to those who are "in practice" so interested. Section 14(3) of the Companies Act 1990 provides that the investigation may be limited to matters or time frames and, in particular, may be limited to certain classes of shares or debentures.

Before ordering such an investigation, the Director must be of the opinion that there are circumstances present which justify such an investigation. These circumstances are as follows:

1. the investigation is necessary for the effective administration of company law;
2. the investigation is necessary for the effective discharge by him of his functions under any statute; or
3. The investigation is necessary in the public interest.

19.3.2 Powers of the inspector

During the investigation the inspectors have all the powers of a court-appointed investigation save the power to examine directors' documents relating to bank accounts. The duty to produce books and documents, provide assistance and attend before the inspector shall apply to all persons who are, or who have been (or whom the inspector has reasonable cause to believe to be or have been), financially interested in the success or failure, or the apparent success or failure, of the company or other related body corporate whose membership is investigated or who are able to control or materially to influence the policy of the company or body corporate.

This duty stretches to those who are concerned on behalf of others and any persons whom the inspector reasonably believes to possess relevant information.

It is open to the Director under section 14(5)(b) of the Companies Act 1990 to disclose the report compiled under section 14 and to omit a part where the Director has "good reason" for not divulging that part. Similar provisions also apply in the context of the presentation of interim and final reports to the Director and the privileged nature of the report. The inspector can investigate companies not set out in the warrant of appointment without further approval of the Director. The inspector should get approval with regard to related companies where he thinks, but does not know, that such an investigation is necessary.

19.3.3 Expenses

Under section 14(6) of the Companies Act 1990 (as inserted by section 26 of the Company Law Enforcement Act 2001), the Director may apply to the court for an order that the company who is the subject of the investigation pay the costs of the investigation. Section 14(7) of the Companies Act 1990 (as inserted by section 26 of the Company Law Enforcement Act 2001) states that a person who has been convicted on indictment, or ordered to pay damages, or ordered to restore property to the company as a result of the investigation may be also ordered in the same proceedings to pay the Director all or part of the expenses of the investigation. In the case of a person awarded damages or property, the court cannot make an order for payment of expenses which exceeds one-tenth of the value of damages or property restored, and the order can only be executed when the damages have been received or the property has been restored.

19.4 Informal investigations by the Director of Corporate Enforcement

19.4.1 Section 15 inquiry

Section 15 of the Companies Act 1990 (as amended by section 14 of the Company Law Enforcement Act 2001) provides that where it appears to the Director that an investigation of the ownership of shares or debentures of a company is necessary, he can conduct the inquiry himself without formally appointing an inspector.

Before commencing this inquiry the Director must be of the opinion that there are circumstances present which justify such an inquiry. These mirror the circumstances required before a section 14 investigation can be commenced and they are as follows:

1. the investigation is necessary for the effective administration of company law;
2. the investigation is necessary for the effective discharge by him of his functions under any statute; or
3. the investigation is necessary in the public interest.

The Director can use his powers under this section to require any person to give him information whom he has reasonable cause to believe has or is able to obtain information as to present or past interests in the shares or debentures and the names and addresses of interested persons. He may also require the identity of persons who have acted on behalf of interested persons. A person is deemed to have an interest in a share or debenture under section 15(2) of the Companies Act 1990 if:

1. he has the right to acquire or dispose of the share or debenture or any interest in that share or debenture;

2. he has the right to vote in respect of the share or debenture or any interest in that share or debenture;
3. his consent is necessary for the exercise of any rights of other persons interested therein;
4. other persons interested in the share or debenture are required to exercise, or are accustomed to exercising, their rights in accordance with his instructions.

Any person who fails to give the required information, or knowingly or recklessly gives materially false information, is guilty of an offence (section 15(3) of the Companies Act 1990).

19.5 Section 16 restrictions

Where, in connection with an inquiry into the company membership under section 15 or an inspector investigation into company membership under section 14, it appears to the Director that there is difficulty in finding the relevant facts about any shares or debentures, the Director may make an order under section 16 of the Companies Act 1990 (as amended by sections 14 and 27 of the Company Law Enforcement Act 2001) imposing restrictions on those shares. According to section 16(17) of the Companies Act 1990 the provisions of the section also apply to debentures.

This section is designed to deal with the situation where a possible membership inquiry could be frustrated by the sale or transfer of the relevant shares. Where the Director indicates in writing that the sale or transfer of such shares is restricted, the following consequences apply under section 16(7) of the Companies Act 1990:

1. any transfer of the restricted shares is void;
2. no voting rights are exercisable in respect of those shares;
3. no rights issue can be made to the holders of those shares; and
4. no payment can be made to the shareholders by the company of any sum due on the shares.

The Director may exercise his own discretion to lift the restrictions under section 16(6)(b) of the Companies Act 1990 (as amended by section 27 of the Company Law Enforcement Act 2001) where he is satisfied that the relevant facts have been disclosed. Where the restrictions are imposed and the Director refuses to lift the same, it is open to any aggrieved person to apply to the court for an order that the restrictions shall cease. The court will only lift the restrictions where it is satisfied that the relevant facts have been disclosed to the Director or otherwise that it is equitable to lift the restrictions.

It is open to the court to order that the restricted shares be sold and the proceeds of the sale less the cost of the sale be paid into court for the benefit of any person who is beneficially interested in the shares (section 16(9) of the Companies Act 1990). The latter person can then apply to the court for the proceeds, or part of the proceeds, to be released to him, depending on the extent of his interest. The person who made the application for the court sale may apply to the court to have the costs of the application paid out of the proceeds.

Section 16(14) of the Companies Act 1990 states that any person who breaches the restrictions, including any person who attempts to deal in such shares when he knows that their transfer is restricted, will be guilty of an offence. Further, where shares in any company are issued in contravention of the said restrictions, the company and every officer who is in default shall be guilty of an offence.

An order under section 16 of the Companies Act 1990 can also be made where the Director has ordered a formal investigation into the company membership under section 14.

19.6 Production of documents

19.6.1 Section 19 searches

These are designed to enable the Director to decide whether a formal section 8 or section 14 investigation is necessary.

Section 19 of the Companies Act 1990 (as repealed and substituted by section 29 of the Company Law Enforcement Act 2001) empowers the Director to direct a company, including a company not incorporated in the State but carrying on business in the State, to produce books or documents. According to section 19(2) of the Companies Act 1990 such directions may be made if there are circumstances suggesting:

1. that it is necessary to examine the books and documents of the company with a view to determining whether an inspector should be appointed to conduct an investigation of the company;
2. that the affairs of the company are being, or have been, conducted with intent to defraud its creditors, the creditors of another person, or its members;

3. that the company's affairs have been conducted for any other fraudulent purpose;
4. that the company's affairs are being conducted in a manner which is unfairly prejudicial to some of its members;
5. that any actual or proposed acts or omissions on the part of the company are, or would be, unfairly prejudicial to some of its members;
6. that any actual or proposed acts or omissions on the part of the company or by a company officer are likely to be unlawful;
7. that the company was formed for any fraudulent or unlawful purpose.

The Director or any officer authorised by him may also (under section 19(3) and (4) of the Companies Act 1990) give a similar direction to any third party who appears to be in possession of such books or documents or copies of those books and documents. The Directors may also direct any third party to produce other books or documents which may relate to the books and documents of the company but only where the Director has reasonable grounds for believing that they are so related and notifies the person in advance of those grounds. The obligation to notify the third party in advance is waived where the Director is of the opinion that the notification would result in the concealment, falsification, destruction or disposal of books or documents.

In *Dunnes Stores Ireland Co. v. Ryan* (1999) Kinlen J. stated that "section 19 enquiries are very restricted" and the right to demand books and documents cannot be made in general terms as that right is restricted to specific documents. The authorised officer can then make copies and, if necessary, seek explanations of the documents. Kinlen J. stated this is the limit of section 19 and that the authorised officer must strictly follow that order.

19.6.2 Cooperation

According to section 19(5) of the Companies Act 1990 (as amended by section 29 of the Company Law Enforcement Act 2001) the power to require a person to produce books and documents includes the power to copy those documents and to require that person (or any other person who is a present or past officer of the company, or who is or was employed by the company) to explain the books and documents and further, to explain any omission from them. Where the books and documents are not available the person requested to produce them may be required to state where they are. This section also makes it clear that the person ordered to produce books and documents must give all reasonable assistance to the Director as he is reasonably able to give in connection with the examination of the books and documents.

Under section 19(6) of the Companies Act 1990 (as amended by section 29 of the Company Law Enforcement Act 2001), failure by the company or other third party to comply with a order of production or to provide a requested explanation is an offence. It is a defence to prove that the books or documents were not in his possession or under his control and it was not reasonably practicable to comply with the requirement. This new section is similar to the old section 19(5) of the Companies Act which was held to be constitutional by Kearns J. in *Dunnes Stores (Ireland) Co & Heffernan v. Ryan* (2002).

Section 19(8) of the Companies Act 1990 states that any person who knowingly gives a false or misleading statement under section 19 is guilty of an offence.

A statement made or an explanation provided under section 19 of the Companies Act 1990 may be used in evidence against that person in any proceedings, save in criminal proceedings against that person (section 19(7) of the Companies Act 1990 as amended by section 29 of the Company Law Enforcement Act 2001). The exception for criminal proceedings does not apply to offences committed under section 19(6) or section 19(8) above. The old section 19(6) of the Companies Act 1990 simply provided that "a statement made by a person in compliance with a requirement imposed by virtue of this section may used in evidence against him". That old section was held to be unconstitutional by Kearns J. in *Dunnes Stores (Ireland) Co & Heffernan v. Ryan* (2002) as that section did not "immunise" the answers given from later criminal proceedings.

Under section 19(9) of the Companies Act 1990 it is an offence to destroy, alter, conceal or mutilate a document that is subject to a direction.

Section 19A of the Companies Act 1990 was inserted by section 29 of the Company Law Enforcement Act 2001 and the provision clearly confers personal responsibility on the officers and even personnel of a company for failure to co-operate with a production direction. Any person is guilty of an offence where he knows or suspects that the Director is investigating an offence under the Companies Act and either directly or indirectly falsifies, conceals, destroys or disposes of a document or record which he knows or suspects would be relevant.

Further, under section 19A(2) of the Companies Act 1990 a person is guilty of an offence who either directly or indirectly falsifies, conceals, destroys or disposes of a document or record in circumstances where it is reasonable to conclude that he knew or suspected there was such an investigation and the document would be relevant.

19.6.3 Expenses

The Director may apply to the court for an order that the company who is the subject of the direction pay the Director the costs incidental to the examination of the documentation under section 19(10) of the Companies Act 1990. Any person who has been indicted, or ordered to pay damages, or ordered to restore property to the company as a result of the direction to produce may also be ordered in the same proceedings to discharge the expenses of the examination. A person who has been awarded damages or restored property may also be ordered to pay the expenses under section 19(10) but these cannot exceed one-tenth of the amount of damages awarded or property restored.

19.6.4 Duty of the Director under section 19

In *Dunnes Stores (Ireland) Co. v. Moloney* (1999) the Minister appointer an authorised officer, George Moloney, to Dunnes Stores Ireland Company and Dunnes Stores (Ilac Centre) Limited for the purpose of obtaining information under section 19 of the Companies Act 1990. Both companies together with a director (the applicants) requested the Minister to give reasons as to why it was necessary to appoint an "authorised officer". The Minister argued that, having regard to the provisions of section 21 of the Companies Act 1990 (see paragraph 19.8 below), it was not possible to disclose the information upon which the Minister's opinion was based.

The matter came before Laffoy J. in the High Court by way of judicial review. Laffoy J. held as follows:

1. the power of appointment under section 19 was amenable to judicial review as the Minister was under a duty to ensure that anyone affected by the power received fair procedures;

2. the applicants were entitled to be informed of the reasons which formed the basis of the Minister's decision to appoint an "authorised officer" as they bona fide believed that the Minister had mis-

used her powers and, in the absence of reasons, they could not properly pursue redress by judicial review;

3. the authorised officer's demand for documents was both excessive and unreasonable as the inclusion of general categories gave the demand as a whole the "hallmark of a trawl".

The matter again came before the court with *Dunnes Stores (Ireland) Co. v. Ryan* (1999) (the defendant, Mr. Gerard Ryan, had replaced Mr. Moloney as authorised officer). The applicants were not satisfied with the reasons produced on behalf of the Minister. It was alleged *inter alia* that the reasons identified fell far outside the matters for which the Minister had statutory responsibility and that their ambiguous form continued to stymie the applicants' questioning of the Minister's decision. It was also alleged that the decision to appoint the authorised officer was irrational or prompted by an improper motive, and that the demand made for documents was unreasonable both in its extent and the time allowed for compliance.

Kinlen J. in the High Court held as follows:

1. the Minister had to make her decision because there were circumstances "suggesting" various matters which are unsatisfactory in relation to the administration of the applicant companies and it would be "unreasonable to put parameters to the ambit of their Inquiry as the books and other documents produced may suggest the need for clarification or explanation of directors or employees past or present";

2. the Minister must act at the time of the making of the appointment on circumstances and facts known to her. The court is only enquiring into her state of mind at that time. The Minister had strictly complied with the requirements of section 19(2) of the Companies Act 1990. He went on to say that a company may feel harassed and suspect hidden agendas but the section 19 procedure is "an essential administrative and fact-finding mechanism by which the Minister may exercise her role as statutory regulator to use her power to give directions to a company to produce specified records and she is of the opinion that there are circumstances addressing the various matters set out in section 19(2)";

3. the appointment of the authorised officer was satisfactory but he had acted *ultra vires* his powers as the demand issued was not sufficiently specific, there was insufficient time allowed for compliance, and a director and other officers of the companies were

required to attend a meeting and answer questions before the books and documents were produced.

On appeal to the Supreme Court in *Dunnes Stores (Ireland) Co. & Heffernan v. Ryan* (2000) the applicants claimed *inter alia* that having determined that the appointment was satisfactory under the Companies Act 1990, the High Court should have gone on to determine the constitutionality of section 19. The appeal was allowed by Keane C.J. and the matter was remitted to the High Court.

Butler J. in *Dunnes Stores (Ireland) Co. & Heffernan v. Ryan* (2000) agreed that the applicants' submission turned upon one essential issue: "do the reasons ultimately furnished by the Minister sustain the decision to appoint an authorised officer".

1. the first reason, that there was substantial cause for concern as to the standards of corporate governance operating in the company and that it was necessary to examine the books and documents to determine whether an inspector should be appointed, was rejected;

2. the second reason, that there were circumstances suggesting that the affairs of the applicant were being conducted with intent to defraud the Revenue Commissioners, was unsustainable as the Revenue Commissioners were not a "competent authority" to which the report under section 19 could be disclosed;

3. the third reason, that there were circumstances suggesting that the affairs of the applicant were being conducted with intent to defraud the members, was dismissed as "stretching credulity too far";

4. the reason of suspected illegality was dismissed as section 19(2)(f) of the Companies Act 1990 uses the present and future tense and does not encompass illegalities of the historical kind.

The court held that the Minister's decision to appoint an authorised officer "if based on the reasons summarised … is unsustainable and irrational in that it plainly and unambiguously flies in the face of fundamental reason and common sense and that the same is ultra vires". He did not find any evidence of mala fides on the part of the Minister.

When the matter came back before the Supreme Court *in Dunnes Stores (Ireland) Co & Heffernan v. Ryan* (2002) Keane C.J. held that the inquiry was justified in terms of section 19 of the Companies Act where *inter alia* there were circumstances suggesting that the affairs of the body had been conducted in a manner which was unfairly prejudicial to some part of its members. The court further held that the range of documents sought was not unduly extensive, having regard to the scale of misuse of the companies assets which had been identified.

The issue of the constitutionality of section 19 was remitted to the High Court and the matter came before Kearns J., whose judgment is discussed at paragraph 19.6.2 above.

19.7 Search warrants

Section 20 of the Companies Act 1990 (as amended by section 30 of the Company Law Enforcement Act 2001) empowers the District Court to grant a search warrant where the District Justice is satisfied on sworn information that there are reasonable grounds for suspecting that there is material information on the premises.

The warrant is issued to a member of the Garda Siochana, and any other person named in it, and entitles them to enter prescribed premises using such force as is reasonably necessary. A search of the premises may then be undertaken, and any books or documents, the subject matter of a requisition, may be seized and retained for a period of six months or such longer period as the District Judge may allow. Any person who obstructs an officer during the investigation is guilty of an offence (section 20(4) of the Companies Act 1990).

Material information includes books or documents required under section 14, 15 or 19 of the Act and which have not been produced in compliance with those sections. It also includes documents which the Garda officer has reasonable grounds to believe may provide evidence as to the commission of an offence under the Companies Acts.

19.8 Security of reports

Under 21 of the Companies Act 1990 (as amended by section 31 of the Company Law Enforcement Act 2001), no information, book or document relating to a company, which has been obtained under section 19 or 20, shall be published or disclosed without the written consent of the company. The Director may disclose or publish information to a competent authority which includes *inter alia* the Minister, a court of competent jurisdiction, the Central Bank or a body outside the State exercising similar investigative functions. This disclosure may only occur where the Director is of the opinion that it is required *inter alia* for the investigation or prosecution of an offence under the Companies Act or for the purposes of assisting a tribunal, the tax authority, the Government or the Competition Authority. Any person who publishes or discloses any information, book or document in contravention of this section is guilty of an offence.

Under section 22 of the Companies Act 1990 the report of an inspector acting under sections 7, 8, and 14 is admissible as evidence in civil proceedings. According to Laffoy J. in *Countyglen Ltd v. Carway* (1996) the inspectors report could be adduced in the proceedings as prima facie proof of the facts found therein. The burden of disputing the facts is on the challenger. It will not be enough to say that the rules of evidence were breached. The challenger will have to adduce evidence to contradict the report's findings.

Section 23(1) of the Companies Act 1990 provides that any person will not be compelled to disclose any information which he would, in the opinion of the court, be entitled to refuse to produce on the grounds of legal professional privilege. Under section 23(3), as amended, the publication of any report under these sections is privileged, *i.e.* any person affected by the contents of the report will be unable to bring any action for defamation.

The Director can now provide assistance to overseas regulatory or supervisory company law authorities under section 23A of the Companies Act 1990 (as inserted by section 33 of the Company Law Enforcement Act 2001) where he is of the opinion that it would assist them with their own inquiries. He may resist this request where the foreign company law authority will not contribute to the costs of complying with the same.

20. EXAMINERSHIP

The Companies (Amendment) Act 1990 (the "1990 Amendment Act") introduced into Irish company law the notion of nursing a failing company back to health. It implemented a survival framework whereby the company was granted temporary protection from hungry creditors and placed under the professional guidance of a court-appointed examiner. Prior to 1990 an ailing company was a prime target for receivership. The examiner provided a welcome alternative and according to *Re Atlantic Magnetics Ltd (in receivership)* (1993) it took the fate of the company and those who depend on it out of the hands of large creditors.

The examinership concept was not entirely novel; it was already available in the United Kingdom under the Companies Act 1985 and Chapter 11 in the United States. However, the model introduced into Ireland in 1990 was flawed in some respects. The primary criticism of the legislation being that the petitioner/applicant only had to prove to the court that the company, and the whole or any part of its undertaking, had "some prospect of survival". Creditors, both secured and unsecured, were heavily critical of the changes, as their debts were effectively frozen and new creditors coming on line during the examinership period could overtake them in priority of payment afterwards.

The Company Law Review Group reviewed the legislation in its report of December 1994. While identifying that examinership was a useful mechanism available in Irish company law, the Group recognised that two main areas were in need of reform: the onus on the applicant to prove that the company was a suitable candidate for examinership should be increased and the exposure of existing company creditors should be reduced.

Part 11 of the Companies (Amendment) (No.2) Act 1999 set about upgrading the examinership procedure in line with those recommendations. It raised the threshold for the appointment of an examiner as the petitioner now has to prove that the company, and the whole or any part of its undertaking, has a "reasonable prospect of survival" in order to qualify for examinership. The Companies (Amendment) (No. 2) Act 1999 now requires that the majority of the investigative work must be completed before the examiner is appointed, as the petitioner is required to submit a report by an independent accountant with the petition. It also increased creditor protection, in particular the protection of existing secured creditors.

20.1 Petition

An application to appoint an examiner to a company should be commenced by way of a petition in the High Court. Every petition for the appointment of an examiner must be verified by an affidavit which in most cases is sworn by the petitioner.

Under section 3(9) of the Companies (Amendment) Act 1990, the High Court may, on making such interim orders or such other orders as the court thinks fit, remit the matter to the Circuit Court where the liabilities of the company do not exceed €317,500.

Under section 3 of the Companies (Amendment) Act 1990 (as amended by section 6 of the Companies (Amendment) (No. 2) Act 1999), the petitioner must come within one of the following categories:

1. the company;
2. the directors;
3. the creditors (including prospective, contingent and employee creditors who must furnish such security for costs as the court considers reasonable);
4. the members (holding at least ten per cent or more of the paid-up share capital of the company);
5. the Central Bank is the only petitioner with locus standi in respect of certain companies, such as where the company is licensed by the Central Bank.

Under Section 3(3) of the Companies (Amendment) Act 1990 the petition that is presented to the court must set out the name of the person nominated to act as examiner and under section 3(4) a signed consent to their appointment as examiner must be attached. The petition must also be accompanied by a report of an independent accountant discussed at paragraph 20.2 below.

The procedure to be followed in the High Court in relation to the appointment of an examiner is set out in Order 75A of the Rules of the Superior Court 1986.

20.1.1 Uberrima fides

The presentation of the petition to the High Court is an *uberrima fides* application, meaning that the utmost good faith is required on the part of the petitioner. A lack of good faith will be penalised by the court as in *Re Wogan's (Drogheda) Ltd (No.2)* (1992) where the court refused to approve the scheme of arrangement (the survival plan) as the directors knowingly failed to disclose large revenue debts in the balance sheet put before the court. Costello J. criticised the petition as an abuse of process.

In *Re Selukwe Ltd* (1991) Costello J. found a lack of good faith but did not dismiss the petition as there were thirty jobs depending on the survival of the company.

This emphasis on good faith was given statutory endorsement under section 4A of the Companies (Amendment) Act 1990 (as inserted by section 13 of the Companies (Amendment) (No. 2) Act 1999). Section 4A states that the court "may" decline to hear a petition if it appears to the court that in the preparation or presentation of the petition, or in the preparation or presentation of the independent report (as discussed below at paragraph 20.2), the petitioner or the accountant has failed to disclose any information available to him which is material to the court's exercising of its powers under this Act, or has in any other way failed to exercise utmost good faith.

In *Re Tuskar Resources plc* (2001) McCracken J. considered the effect of the new section 4A. Here a creditor sought to have Tuskar Resources Plc wound up on the ground it was owed in excess of US$11,000,000. Tuskar Resources plc sought the protection of the court under the Companies (Amendment) Act 1990 as amended. The creditor complained that the original affidavit and the independent accountant's report were misleading and failed to disclose material matters to the court. McCracken J. found that in the light of subsequent evidence, both the petition and the accountant's report were "overly optimistic" about the future of the company. He did not, however, think that over-optimism was sufficient to show bad faith. He further emphasised that the use of the word "may" in section 4A of the Companies (Amendment) Act 1990 left the court with a wide discretion on the matter. Tuskar Resources plc also claimed that the creditor was acting in bad faith in opposing the petition for court protection. McCracken J. however felt that the creditor was attempting to protect its own commercial interests which was not a ground for ruling out the opposition on the part of the creditor.

20.2 Accountant's report

Under section 3(3A) of the Companies (Amendment) Act 1990 (as inserted by section 7 of the Companies (Amendment) (No. 2) Act 1999), the petition must be accompanied at the time of presentation to the court by a report of an independent accountant who is either an auditor or a person qualified to be appointed an examiner of the company.

Under section 3(3B) of the Companies (Amendment) Act 1990 (as inserted by section 7 of the Companies (Amendment) (No. 2) Act 1999) the report must contain *inter alia:*

1. the names and addresses of the officers of the company and the names of those in accordance with whose directions/instructions the directors of the company are accustomed to act ("shadow directors");
2. a statement as to the affairs of the company showing the assets, liabilities, creditors and details of their security;
3. an opinion as to whether the assets and liabilities of the company have been satisfactorily accounted for or whether there is evidence of substantial disappearance of property;
4. an opinion as to whether the formulation, acceptance and confirmation of proposals would offer such a reasonable prospect;
5. an opinion as to whether an attempt to continue the whole or any part of its undertaking would be likely to be more advantageous to the members as a whole and the creditors as a whole than a winding up of the company;
6. an opinion as to whether any action should be taken in relation to fraudulent and/or reckless trading;
7. detail as to how the company is to be funded during the protection period; and
8. recommendations as to what pre-petition liabilities should be paid by the examiner.

Crucially, the report must set out an "opinion" as to whether the company and the whole or any part of its undertaking has a reasonable prospect of survival, and conditions which are considered essential to ensure that survival. It must also state an opinion as to whether or not examinership is recommended as the next step for the ailing company.

In *Re Tuskar Resources plc* (2001) McCracken J. emphasised that this was a preliminary opinion as to whether the company and the whole or any part of its undertaking has a reasonable prospect of survival, and conditions which are considered essential to ensure that survival. He stated that the legislation does not require the accountant to detail the evidence that led to that opinion.

Section 3C(1) of the Companies (Amendment) Act 1990 (as inserted by section 11 of the Companies (Amendment) (No. 2) Act 1999) provides that a copy of this report shall be furnished to the company and any interested party where a written application is made to the accountant. Where court directions are sought in relation to its release, it is open to the court to order that material is first deleted prior to the disclosure.

The court may in particular direct that any information which would be likely to prejudice the survival of the company or the whole or any part of its undertaking as a going concern be omitted.

20.2.1 Unavailable reports

Section 3A(1) of the Companies (Amendment) Act 1990 (as inserted by section 9 of the Companies (Amendment) (No. 2) Act 1999) provides for the situation where a report is not available in court at the time of the presentation of the petition. The court may place the company under interim court protection for a period not exceeding ten days pending the production of the report. The court must be satisfied that the report is unavailable due to exceptional circumstances outside the control of the petitioner and that the petitioner could not reasonably have anticipated those circumstances.

Where the report is submitted prior to the expiry of the ten days, then the court will proceed to consider the petition and the report. A fresh petition will be required in the event that the report only becomes available after the interim protection has expired.

It is not open to the interim examiner to certify liabilities incurred during this interim protection period for the purposes of giving those liabilities priority over other creditors (see pararaph 20.6.6).

The "exceptional circumstances" anticipated by the section are not defined; however, it should only be availed of in rare circumstances. It is clarified by section 3A(3) of the Companies (Amendment) Act 1990 that the fact that a receiver has been appointed to the whole or any part of the undertaking of the company at the time of the presentation of a petition is not considered, in itself, an exceptional circumstance outside the control of the petitioner.

Where the petitioner is a creditor or a member of the company, section 3A(4) of the Companies (Amendment) Act 1990 stipulates that the directors must cooperate in the preparation of the report. In the event that the directors fail to cooperate, the petitioner may apply to the court for an order directing such compliance.

20.2.2 Irregularities disclosed

Under section 13A(1) of the Companies (Amendment) Act 1990 (as inserted by section 21 of the Companies (Amendment) (No. 2) Act 1999), the court may hold a hearing to consider a substantial disappearance of property or other serious irregularities in the conduct of a company's affairs that are disclosed in the independent accountant's report or otherwise.

The court may direct the examiner to prepare a report on such matters, which shall be distributed to the company and, subject to appropriate omissions, any interested party who applies in writing for the report. The parties that can be heard at the court hearing include the company, the examiner, an interested party, a person referred to in the independent accountant's report, and the independent accountant (section 13A(8) of the Companies (Amendment) Act 1990). The court may make such an order as it thinks fit, including the order of a trial of any issue relating to the matter in question, such as reckless or fraudulent trading (section 13A(9)).

20.3 Examiner

Under section 2(1) of the Companies (Amendment) Act 1990 (as amended by section 5 of the Companies (Amendment) (No. 2) Act 1999) and subject to section 2(2) (see paragraph 20.3.1 below), the court may proceed with the appointment of an examiner where it appears to the court that the following three conditions are met:

1. the company is, or is likely to be, unable to pay its debts; and
2. no resolution subsists for the winding up of the company; and
3. no order has been made for the winding up of the company.

Under section 2(3) of the Companies (Amendment) Act 1990 a company is unable to pay its debts if:

1. the company is unable to pay its debts as they fall due; or
2. the value of its assets is less than its liabilities, taking into account contingent and prospective liabilities; or
3. section 214(a) or (b) of the Companies Act 1963 applies to the company (a creditor who is owed €1,270 or more has served a demand letter threatening winding up proceedings within twenty-one days, or an execution of a decree, judgment or order of court has been returned by the sheriff unsatisfied in full or in part).

20.3.1 The new test

Under section 2(2) of the Companies (Amendment) Act 1990 (as amended by section 5 of the Companies (Amendment) (No. 2) Act 1999), the court shall not make an order appointing an examiner under section 2(1) above unless it is satisfied on the evidence before it that there is a "*reasonable prospect*" of the survival of the company and the whole or any part of its undertaking as a going concern.

The old position under the Companies (Amendment) Act 1990 allowed the court to appoint an examiner if it considered that the appointment would be *likely* to facilitate the survival of the company and the whole or any part of the undertaking as a going concern.

In *Re Atlantic Magnetics Ltd (in receivership)* (1993) Lardner J. in the High Court stated that where the evidence of survival was unclear, the court should look for a real prospect of survival. The Supreme Court felt that the court had a wider discretion and stated that "some prospect of survival" was sufficient. Finlay C.J. considered that the petition stage involved an evaluation of the chances of the company surviving and no more than that.

He stated that in unclear cases the standard was as follows: "does the evidence lead to the conclusion that in all the circumstances it appears worthwhile to order an investigation by the examiner into the company's affairs and see can it survive, there being some prospect of survival?" McCarthy J. rejected the "real prospect" test outright and stated that it would be difficult to come to any firm conclusion on the matter of survival until the examiner had carried out his preliminary three-week investigation.

This test was further refined and explained by Keane J. in the High Court in *Re Butlers Engineering Ltd* (1996). It was made clear that the petitioners should adduce evidence supporting the contention that there was an identifiable possibility of survival. *Westport Construction Co.*

Ltd (1996) followed the test laid down in *Re Atlantic Magnetics Ltd (in receivership)* (1993) and as expressed by Keane J. in *Re Butler Engineering Ltd* (1996).

This level of poof was criticised as too "soft" given that a number of companies placed under court protection were eventually wound up by the court. Reporting in 1994, and before the judgment of *Re Butler Engineering Ltd* (1996), and the Company Law Review Group recommended that the court should have to be satisfied that there is a reasonable prospect of the survival of the company and the whole or part of its undertaking.

In *Re Tuskar Resources Plc* (2001) McCracken J. interpreted the amendment of section 2(2) as bringing the law into line with the comments of Lardner J. in *Re Atlantic Magnetics Ltd (in receivership)* (1993). He stated that the amendment together with the introduction of the requirement of an independent accountant's report indicated that the "legislature clearly disagreed with McCarthy J. that no real decision can be reached until the examiner has been put in place for some weeks" and that the independent accountant's report clearly meant that the decision must be made at the initial stages of the application.

McCracken J. also felt that the new section 2(2) prohibited the court from appointing an examiner unless it was "satisfied" that there was a reasonable prospect of survival: "If the court is to be 'satisfied', it must be satisfied on the evidence before it, which is in the first instance the evidence of the petitioner".

He interpreted this as placing an onus of proof on the petitioner at the initial stage to satisfy the court that there is a reasonable prospect of survival. This is the usual burden of proof in civil proceedings and it is a clear divergence to the position prior to the Companies (Amendment) (No. 2) Act 1999 where Finlay C.J. in *Re Atlantic Magnetics Ltd (in receivership)* (1993) stated that there cannot be an onus of proof on a petitioner to establish as a matter of probability that the company is capable of surviving as a going concern.

20.3.2 Related companies

Section 4(2) of the Companies (Amendment) Act 1990 (as amended by section 12 of the Companies (Amendment) (No. 2) Act 1999) applies the new test to applications seeking to extend the examinership to related companies (see paragraph 23.6.1 for a definition of a related company). The court will now place that related company under protection only where there is a reasonable prospect of the survival of the related company as a going concern. In *Re Tuskar Resources Plc* (2001) McCracken J. stated that the definition of a "related company" under section 4(5) of the Companies (Amendment) Act 1990 did not include a company registered outside the jurisdiction, as that section sets out the conditions in which " a company is related to another company" and the word "company" is defined in the Companies Act 1963 as one formed and registered under that Act.

20.4 Hearing of the petition

Under section 3(7) of the Companies (Amendment) Act 1990, the court may make the following orders:

1. appoint an examiner;
2. dismiss the petition;
3. adjourn the petition;
4. make an interim order such as the appointment of an interim examiner;
5. make whatever other orders it thinks fit in the circumstances.

An interim order made under that sub-section may restrict the exercise of powers by the directors of the company.

It was common practice for the court to adjourn the matter and order the service and advertisement of the petition to ensure that all interested parties have an opportunity to be heard. Now under section 3B(1) of the Companies (Amendment) Act 1990 (as inserted by section 10 of the Companies (Amendment) (No. 2) Act 1999), the court shall not make an order dismissing the petition or appointing an examiner to a company without hearing every creditor who has indicated a desire to make a submission to the court on the matter. This will effectively result in an adjournment and order for advertisement of the petition in every case. Section 3B(2) of the Companies (Amendment) Act 1990 clarifies that this does not prevent the court from making an interim order.

The court will not appoint an examiner where *inter alia* the person nominated to act as examiner is disqualified from so acting. Under section 3(6) of the Companies (Amendment) Act 1990 the court will not appoint an examiner where the company has been in receivership for more than three continuous days before the petition was presented.

In *Re Tuskar Resources Plc* (2001) McCracken J. clarified that the law does not prohibit the court from appointing the independent accountant as the company examiner. He further accepted that there was merit in the argument that considerable expense would be incurred by requiring two accountants to separately investigate the prospects of the company. He went on to say, however, he could see cases where it would be "undesirable" to do so and referred to *Re Wogans (Drogheda) Ltd (No 3)* (1993) where Costello J. stated the court would be slow to appoint an accountant previously associated with the company as examiner, as his impartiality could be questioned.

Section 31 of the Companies (Amendment) Act 1990 makes provision for the hearing of the petition *in camera*. According to *Re R Ltd* (1989) the court would have to be satisfied that a public hearing would disclose sensitive commercial information and be financially damaging for those interested in the company.

20.5 Protection period

"The Act is to provide a breathing space albeit at the expense of some creditor or creditors" (McCarthy J. in *Re Atlantic Magnetics Ltd, (in receivership)* (1993) on the Companies (Amendment) Act 1990).

Under section 5(1) of the Companies (Amendment) Act 1990 (as amended by section 14 of the Companies (Amendment) (No. 2) Act 1999), the company is protected from any action that may be taken by the creditors for a period of 70 days from the date of the presentation of the petition (subject to the exceptional circumstances in section 3A discussed at paragraph 20.2.1 above). The period may be extended by one additional 30 day period where the examiner or the court requires more time to consider the matter. Prior to the Companies (Amendment) (No. 2) Act 1999 the protection period was three months.

This moratorium on actions against the company extends to the following:

1. no winding up proceedings can be issued;
2. no receiver can be appointed;
3. no attachment of or execution against assets of the company can be enforced without the consent of the examiner;
4. no re-possession of goods under a hire-purchase agreement or a retention of title agreement is permitted;

5. a secured creditor cannot take any steps to realise his security without the consent of the examiner;

6. no proceedings can be taken against a person liable for the company's debts, such as a guarantor. Further, no attachment, distress, sequestration, or enforcement in respect of the company's debts can be put in force against the latter's property;

7. proceedings under section 205 of the Companies Act 1963 in respect of complaints as to the conduct of the affairs of the company or the exercise of the powers of the directors prior to the presentation of the petition cannot be taken in respect of the protection period.

Any other type of proceedings may only be commenced with the leave of the court (section 5(3) of the Companies (Amendment) Act 1990).

20.5.1 Effect of protection on ordinary creditors

These creditors are restricted from instituting actions against the company. They have, however, a right to be heard in court at the hearing of the petition.

20.5.2 Effect of protection on secured creditors

The secured creditors cannot proceed to enforce their security save with the consent of the examiner. In *Re Holidair Ltd* (1994) the creditor bank had a charge over the book debts of the company and the company was required to lodge the book debts in a special bank account. The court refused to allow the bank to exercise its rights under the debenture regarding the bank account after the protection commenced.

Where a secured creditor appoints a receiver over all or part of the company's assets and that receiver is in place for less than three continuous days, a petition to appoint an examiner to the company may be presented to the court. Section 6 of the Companies (Amendment) Act 1990 (as amended by section 16 of the Companies (Amendment) (No. 2) Act 1999) gives the court the discretion to make such orders as it thinks fit including any or all of the following:

1. that the receiver shall cease to act;

2. that the receiver shall, from a specified date, act only in respect of certain assets;

3. that the receiver shall deliver the company's books, papers, and records to the examiner; and/or

4. that the receiver shall give the examiner details of all his dealings with the company's property and undertaking.

The court will make such orders only where the company, or part or all of its undertaking, has a reasonable prospect of survival as a going concern.

Further, under section 6A of the Companies (Amendment) Act 1990 (as inserted by section 17 of the Companies (Amendment) (No. 2) Act 1999), where an examiner has been, or is about to be, appointed to a company and a receiver stands appointed under a floating charge, the court may order that the receiver is not under an obligation to discharge debts due to preferential creditors out of secured assets prior to paying the charge-holder under section 98 of the Companies Act 1963 (see paragraph 18.3.4). Floating charges that crystallised on the appointment of the receiver (see Chapter 16) will decrystallise if an examiner is appointed according to *Re Holidair Limited* (1994), where a floating charge over book debts decrystallised on the appointment of an examiner.

A negative pledge clause requires the borrower to get the consent of the existing lender/debenture holder before creating any other charge over the charged property. Such clauses can be disregarded by the examiner under section 7(5B) and (5C) of the Companies (Amendment) Act 1990 (as inserted by the section 18 of the Companies (Amendment) (No. 2) Act 1999). Under those sections a provision in a pre-petition contract restricting the borrowing of monies or the creation of a mortgage, lien, charge, or encumbrance on the company property can now be disregarded by the examiner where a notice is served on the party to the contract. Such notice must state that enforcement of the negative pledge provision would be likely to prejudice the survival of the company and the whole or part of its undertaking as a going concern.

20.5.3 Effect of protection on guarantors

Under section 5(2)(f) of the Companies (Amendment) Act 1990, guarantees cannot be enforced while the company is under court protection as no proceedings can be taken against a person liable for the company's debts, such as a guarantor. Further, no attachment, distress, sequestration, or enforcement in respect of the company's debts can be put in force against the latter's property.

Despite criticism of this provision the position was not amended in 1999. The 1999 Act did, however, set out how the issue of guarantees was to be treated by creditors who vote on the scheme of arrangement. Where it is proposed in any scheme of arrangement to reduce a debt, a creditor intending subsequently to proceed against a guarantor of that debt for the full amount is required to follow the procedure set out in section 25A of the Companies (Amendment) Act 1990 (as inserted by section 25 of the Companies (Amendment) (No. 2) Act 1999). The creditor must give the guarantor notice of the meeting at which the examiner's proposals will be considered and offer to transfer his vote to the guarantor. If the guarantor accepts and attends the meeting, the guarantor may exercise the creditor's vote. In the event that the creditor fails to serve the notice within the required period, the guarantee may not later be enforced.

20.5.4 Effect of protection on directors

Unless the court has directed otherwise, the directors continue as normal. The court may order the curtailment of any or all of the director's powers and transfer them to the examiner under section 3(8) of the Companies (Amendment) Act 1990.

20.5.5 Effect of protection on provisional liquidators

Under section 6 of the Companies (Amendment) Act 1990 (as amended by section 16 of the Companies (Amendment) (No. 2) Act 1999), the court can make such orders as it thinks fit where, at the date of presentation of a petition, a provisional liquidator stands appointed over the company or part or all of its undertaking.

The court may order the following:

1. that the provisional liquidator shall act as examiner;
2. that some other person shall be appointed as examiner;
3. that the provisional liquidator shall cease to act;
4. that the provisional liquidator shall deliver the company's books, papers, and records to the examiner; and/or
5. that the provisional liquidator shall give the examiner details of all his dealings with the company's property and undertaking.

The court will make such orders only where the company, or part or all of its undertaking, has a reasonable prospect of survival as a going concern.

20.6 Powers of the examiner

20.6.1 Management

The examiner is entitled to supervise the management of the company or enter into contracts with third parties. If he does enter such contracts, he is personally liable under the same unless the contract states otherwise. He can, however, seek to be indemnified out of the company assets. He can convene and attend board meetings (section 7 of the Companies (Amendment) Act 1990).

20.6.2 Information and assistance

The directors of the company must deliver a statement of affairs of the company assets and liabilities to the examiner within seven days of his appointment. The officers and agents must deliver books and records to him and attend before the examiner if required. Under section 8(5) and section 8(5A) of the Companies (Amendment) Act 1990 (as amended by section 19 of the Companies (Amendment) (No. 2) Act 1999), where an officer or an agent refuses to produce documents, or refuses to attend before the examiner, or refuses to answer questions, the examiner may certify that refusal to the court, and the court may make any order it thinks fit, including direction that the officer is to give the documents or information, or the court may relieve the officer from having to do so.

20.6.3 Court assistance

Under section 7(6) of the Companies (Amendment) Act 1990, the examiner may apply to the court for directions on any matter.

20.6.4 Directors' powers

Where it is just and equitable to do so, the court may order that the powers of the directors should be transferred to the examiner under section 9 of the Companies (Amendment) Act 1990. It will be just and equitable where *inter alia* the affairs of the company are being, or are likely to be, conducted in a manner likely to prejudice the interests of the creditors or the members as a whole, or it is necessary in order to preserve the assets or safeguard the interests of the creditors or the members as a whole, or the company/directors have resolved that the powers are transferred to the examiner. Where the court makes such an order, the examiner is given the same powers as a court-appointed liquidator (see Chapter 22).

20.6.5 Contracts

The examiner may enter contracts in the name of the company or his own name. Section 13(6) of the Companies (Amendment) Act 1990 states that the examiner is personally liable in respect of such contracts unless the contract states that he is not to be personally liable. The examiner is entitled to an indemnity in respect of the liability from the company.

Under section 7(5) of the Companies (Amendment) Act 1990, the examiner has the power to "halt, prevent or rectify" the effects of any act, omission, course of conduct, decision, or contract by the company, its officers, employees, members, or creditors which in the opinion of the examiner is, or is likely to be, to the detriment of the company. This was interpreted as the power to repudiate contracts that the company had entered into. Now, under section 7(5A) of the Companies (Amendment) Act 1990 (as inserted by section 18 of the Companies (Amendment) (No. 2) Act 1999), an examiner may not repudiate contracts made by the company prior to the protection period. As mentioned in paragraph 20.5.2 above, section 7(5B) and section 7(5C) of the Companies (Amendment) Act 1990 give the examiner the power to disregard negative pledge provisions in pre-petition contracts in certain cases.

20.6.6 Costs, remuneration and expenses

Section 10 of the Companies (Amendment) Act 1990 provides that liabilities incurred by the company during the protection period may be certified by the examiner as incurred in order to avoid seriously prejudicing the survival of the company as a going concern during the protection period. These "expenses" are then brought within section 29(3) of the Companies (Amendment) Act 1990 and given priority over pre-petition creditors.

Section 29(3) of the Companies (Amendment) Act 1990 (as amended by section 28 of the Companies (Amendment) (No. 2) Act 1999) provides:

> "The remuneration, costs and expenses of an examiner which have been sanctioned by order of the court (other than the expenses referred to in Section 29(3A)) shall be paid in full and shall be paid before any other claim, secured or unsecured, under any compromise or scheme of arrangement or in any receivership or winding up of the company to which he has been appointed."

This was aimed at giving the examiner access to much needed cash flow, as many creditors were reluctant to fund a company that required court protection. It was the combined effect of these provisions that caused much of the already mentioned creditor criticism and opposition to the Companies (Amendment) Act 1990.

In *Re Edenpark Construction Ltd* (1994) Murphy J. stated that to qualify for certification, the expenses must be incurred in circumstances where the survival of the company as a going concern would otherwise be seriously prejudiced, that the prejudice must be foreseen as occurring during the examination period, and that the certification by the examiner must take place at the time when the expense occurred.

In *Re Don Bluth Entertainment* (1994) the court held that the examiner should exercise great care and professional expertise with regard to section 10 and confirmed that the court can refuse *ab initio* to sanction all expenses where the examiner was attempting to prefer creditors.

The effect of the above two provisions was that a fixed chargeholder lost priority rights (see Chapter 23) and ranked below the "expenses" certified by the examiner. In *Re Holidair Ltd* (1994) Finlay C.J. stated that:

> "the true interpretation of s.29(3) is that the remuneration, costs and expenses as defined in that section of an examiner which had been sanctioned by order of the court shall be paid in actual priority to the claims of any secured or unsecured creditor and that under the provisions of s. 29(2) the court may if necessary and must if it has sanctioned such remuneration, costs and expenses in a case where unsecured assets are insufficient to pay the total of the amounts involved direct their payment out of secured assets".

The criticisms of the secured creditors were taken on board by the Company Law Review Group which recommended that creditors with fixed security should have priority over these "certified expenses". Now, under section 29(3A) of the Companies (Amendment) Act 1990 (as inserted by section 28 of the Companies (Amendment) (No. 2) Act 1999), the liabilities under section 29 shall be paid in full before all other claims (including a claim secured by a floating charge), but after any claim secured by a mortgage, charge, lien, or encumbrance of a fixed nature. The fixed charge-holder has been reinstated in his prioritised position.

Section 29(3B) of the Companies (Amendment) Act 1990 (as inserted by section 28 of the Companies (Amendment) (No. 2) Act 1999) states all references to a "claim" in section 29 shall include the costs, charges, and expenses of that winding up, including the remuneration of the liquidator. The effect of the amendment was to clarify that the costs, remuneration, and expenses of an examiner will be paid in priority to the costs, remuneration, and expenses of a liquidator in the event that the company under court protection is later wound up. This amendment was to reverse the effect of the decision in *Re Springline Ltd* (1997) where a company in examinership was later liquidated as there was no prospect of the company surviving. Shanley J. was asked to determine whether the word "claim" in section 29 included the remuneration, costs, and expenses of the liquidator appointed by the court in a winding up. Shanley J. held that it did not and, therefore, the costs, remuneration, and expenses of a liquidator were given priority over the examiner's costs.

20.6.7 Pre-petition debts

In *Re Don Bluth Entertainment Ltd* (1994) and in *Re Edenpark Construction Ltd* (1994) it was held that an examiner could not certify prepetition debts under section 10 of the Companies (Amendment) Act 1990 and give those debts priority of payment. It was stated that only liability incurred during the protection period could be certified. Section 5A of the Companies (Amendment) Act 1990 (as inserted by section 15 of the Companies (Amendment) (No. 2) Act 1999) amends this prohibition and permits the payment of pre-petition debts only where the independent accountant's report recommends they should be paid or, alternatively, where the court decides that a failure to pay the liability would considerably reduce the survival prospects of the company. This is in line with the recommendations of the Company Law Review Group which advocated that the matter of pre-petition debts should be controlled such that the directors could not decide unilaterally to prefer a pre-petition creditor.

20.6.8 Set-off

Section 5(2)(h) of the Companies (Amendment) Act 1990 prohibited the right of set-off by creditor banks without the consent of the examiner. Section 14(b)(ii) of the Companies (Amendment) (No. 2) Act 1999 removes this prohibition and restores the right of set-off as between bank accounts.

20.6.9 Secured property

Under section 11 of the Companies (Amendment) Act 1990 the examiner can deal with secured property. This can only be done with the sanction of the court. In the case of property covered by a floating charge, the examiner can dispose of it where the disposal would be likely to facilitate the survival of the whole or any part of the company.

Under section 11(3) of the Companies (Amendment) Act 1990 the floating charge-holder will have the same priority in respect of any property of the company directly or indirectly representing the property sold. Therefore, the charge moves to the proceeds of the sale.

In the case of a fixed charged, the creditor is more protected. The examiner may deal with assets subject to fixed security only with the sanction of the court and the proceeds must be used to pay the charge-holder. According to section 11(4) Companies (Amendment) Act 1990, where the proceeds are less than the market value of the asset as determined by the court, the deficiency must be paid to the secured creditor by the company.

20.7 Examiner's report

20.7.1 The old reports

The primary duty of the examiner is to report to the court. The old reporting procedure under the Companies (Amendment) Act 1990 consisted of two reports. The first was produced within twenty-one days of his appointment, and if the report was favourable, the examiner would draft proposals for rescuing the company. These proposals would be put before creditors' and members' meetings where creditors and members had the opportunity to vote on the proposed plan. The proposals were then set out before the court in a second report. The court would sanction the rescue plan if

1. it had secured a reasonable level of support from creditors and members; and
2. it was "just and equitable" to the parties; and
3. it was not "unfairly prejudicial" to any class of creditors or shareholders.

20.7.2 The new report

The Companies (Amendment) (No. 2) Act 1999 now requires one report only. Section 18 of the Companies (Amendment) Act 1990 (as amended by section 22 of the Companies (Amendment) (No. 2) Act 1999) provides that the examiner shall formulate proposals called a "scheme of arrangement" as soon as practicable after he is appointed. This is effectively a proposed compromise of the debts of the creditors. The examiner must then hold meetings with the creditors and members and disclose the scheme of arrangement.

The examiner must report to the court on the proposals and the outcome of the meetings within thirty-five days of appointment or such longer period as the court may allow. If the examiner cannot complete the report within the seventy-day protection period, an application may be made to the court for an extension, which cannot, however, exceed thirty days (section 18(3) of the Companies (Amendment) Act 1990. The examiner may appoint a committee of creditors to assist him in the exercise of his functions under section 21 of the Companies (Amendment) Act 1990.

20.7.3 The scheme of arrangement

Section 22 of the Companies (Amendment) Act 1990 sets out in detail the contents of the proposals which must *inter alia*

1. specify each class of members and creditors of the company;
2. specify any class of creditors and members whose claims or interests will not be impaired and such classes which will be impaired;
3. treat each person within a particular class equally unless there is an agreement to unequal treatment;
4. provide for the implementation of the proposals;

5. specify whatever changes should be made in relation to the management or direction of the company;

6. specify whatever changes should be made in the memorandum or articles of the company as regards the management or the direction of the company or otherwise;

7. include such matters as the examiner deems appropriate.

According to section 22(5) of the Companies (Amendment) Act 1990 the claims of a creditor will be impaired if the full amount of the claim will not be paid under the proposals.

Section 22(6) of the Companies (Amendment) Act 1990 provides that the interests of a member will be impaired where *inter alia* the nominal value of the member's shareholding in the company will be reduced or where the member is entitled to a fixed dividend in respect of his shareholding and that dividend is reduced or where the member is deprived of any or all of the rights attached to the shares.

A copy of the scheme of arrangement must be delivered to the company and to any interested party who applies to the examiner in writing. The court may order that material is omitted prior to such release, particularly material likely to prejudice the survival of the company or the whole or any part of its undertaking as a going concern.

20.7.4 Creditors and members

Under section 23 of the Companies (Amendment) Act 1990 (as amended by section 23 of the Companies (Amendment) (No. 2) Act 1999), the proposals must be put before the creditors and shareholders. The creditors shall be deemed to have accepted such proposals if a majority in number representing a majority in value of the claims represented at that meeting vote in favour of the proposals. The failure to vote or an abstention from voting cannot be counted as a vote against the proposals under section 23(4A) of the Companies (Amendment) Act 1990 (as inserted by section 23 of the Companies (Amendment) (No. 2) Act 1999). It was recommended by the Company Law Review Group that the requirement of creditor approval should be abolished. However, this was one recommendation that was not implemented by the Companies (Amendment) (No. 2) Act 1999.

Meetings of members held to discuss proposals are informative only and a member vote in favour of the proposals is no longer required. Proper notice of the meetings must be served and a statement of the assets and the liabilities must be attached to the notice.

20.7.5 Court examination

The proposals are then considered by the court under section 24 of the Companies (Amendment) Act 1990. The company, the examiner, any creditor or member whose interests or claims would be impaired by the proposals, and, in certain cases, the Central Bank may appear and make submissions in relation to the report. According to section 24(4)(a) of the Companies (Amendment) Act 1990 (as amended by section 24 of the Companies (Amendment) (No. 2) Act 1999), the court cannot confirm the proposals unless at least one class of creditors whose interests would be impaired have accepted the proposals.

The requirement under the Companies (Amendment) Act 1990 that at least one class of members whose interests would be impaired must also accept the proposals has now been abolished. Members may, however, object under section 24(4)(c) of the Companies (Amendment) Act 1990 on the grounds that the proposals are not fair and equitable to them as a class, or that the proposals are unfairly prejudicial to them individually.

Under section 24(4A) of the Companies (Amendment) Act 1990 (as inserted by section 24 of the Companies (Amendment) (No. 2) Act 1999), the court cannot confirm a scheme if the proposals would have the effect of impairing the interests of the creditors of the company in such a manner as to favour the interests of the creditors or members of a related company which is also under court protection.

Under section 25(1) of the Companies (Amendment) Act 1990 any member or creditor whose interests would be impaired by the implementation of the scheme of arrangement is entitled to object on one or more of the following grounds:

1. that there was some material irregularity at one of the members' or creditors' meetings;
2. the acceptance of the proposals was obtained by some improper means;
3. the proposals were put forward for some improper purpose;
4. the proposals unfairly prejudice the interests of the objector.

In *Re Castleholding Investment Co. Ltd* (2001) McCracken J. refused to accept the submission of the creditor bank that it was being unfairly prejudiced under the scheme. Under the scheme all creditors were to receive the full amount due at the date of the petition but these payments were to be deferred. The bank opposed the scheme on the basis that it was not proposed to pay interest accruing during the deferred period. McCracken J. felt that the bank was not being unfairly prejudiced given the benefits they were receiving under the scheme.

Section 25 makes it clear that a person who voted in favour of the proposals is not entitled to later object unless acceptance of the proposals was obtained by some improper means or he later became aware that they were put forward for some improper purpose.

In *Re Wogans (Drogheda) Ltd (No 2)* (1992) the court refused to confirm the proposals, as a Revenue debt had been deliberately concealed in the petition, tax clearance certificates essential to the success of the scheme were not forthcoming from the Revenue, and the proposed investor under the scheme could unilaterally withdraw at any time creating uncertainty that the scheme could proceed.

If the court suggests that the proposals should be modified and these modifications are a fundamental alteration, the creditors and members should be given the opportunity to consider the altered scheme (see *Re Goodman International* (1991)). In *Re Castleholding Investment Co. Ltd* (2001) McCracken J. cautioned that while the court could make modifications it could not re-write the scheme.

If the court confirms the proposals, they are binding on all the parties involved with the company according to section 24(5) of the Companies (Amendment) Act 1990. Court protection ceases when the scheme of arrangement becomes effective. The court may revoke that confirmation within 180 days on the application of the company or any interested party under section 27 of the Companies (Amendment) Act 1990 where the court is satisfied that it was obtained by fraud.

If the examiner is not in able to formulate the proposals or reach necessary agreements with interested parties, then he can apply to the court for directions. The court may order a winding up of the company if it is just and equitable to do so (section 24(11) of the Companies (Amendment) Act 1990.

21. VOLUNTARY WINDING UP

Liquidation involves the winding up of the affairs of a company including *inter alia* gathering the company assets, completing or terminating the company contracts, discharging the company debts, and distributing the company assets. When the liquidation process is complete the company is dissolved (struck off the company register). Some liquidations are supervised by the court and these are called an involuntary, compulsory or official winding up (see Chapter 22).

It is open to the company shareholders to resolve to wind up the affairs of the company on a voluntary basis, *i.e.* without the supervision of the court. There are two categories of voluntary winding up, one where the company shareholders retain control of certain matters (a members' voluntary winding up) and the other where the company creditors exercise that control (a creditors' voluntary winding up). An application may, however, be made to the court in the course of the liquidation in relation to a contentious matter.

Section 251 of the Companies Act 1963 sets out three situations where the members may resolve to wind up the company voluntarily:

1. where the company is permitted to terminate naturally under the articles of association (*e.g.* at the end of a fixed period or on the happening of a stated event) and an *ordinary resolution* is passed to wind up voluntarily (section 251(1)(a)).

2. where a *special resolution* is passed to wind up the company voluntarily (section 251(1)(b)).

3. where the company can no longer continue its business by reason of its liabilities and an *ordinary resolution* is passed to wind up the company voluntarily (section 251(1)(c)).

In order to proceed as a members' voluntary winding up, the company must be solvent at the time the resolution is passed, *i.e.* able to pay its debts as they fall due. A members' voluntary winding up will, therefore, commence under either section 251(1)(a) or (b). If the company is insolvent at the time of the decision to wind up voluntarily, a resolution should be passed in accordance with section 251(1)(c), and the liquidation should proceed as a creditors' voluntary winding up.

21.1 Members' voluntary winding up

A members' voluntary winding up most commonly arises where a special resolution is passed by the members to wind up the company voluntarily (section 251(1)(b)).

The company must comply with the following procedure:

1. A resolution to wind-up the company must be passed by the shareholders.
2. A declaration of solvency must be sworn by the directors.
3. A report of an independent person must be prepared.

21.1.1 Resolution of shareholders

As noted above, this shareholder resolution will be either ordinary (section 251(1)(a)) or special (section 251(1)(b)). It is open to a shareholder and/or a creditor to object to the passing of the resolution and, as held by Carroll J. in *Re Oakthorpe Holdings Ltd* (1988), the courts have the power to annul a resolution to wind up.

Once the resolution is passed, the company must advertise a notice of the passing of the resolution in *Iris Oifigiuil* within fourteen days. Failure to publish this notice will render the company directors and every officer in default liable to a fine pursuant to section 252 of the Companies Act 1963, as amended.

Section 253 of the Companies Act 1963 states that the voluntary winding up is deemed to commence at the time of the passing of the resolution. According to *Re West Cumberland Iron and Steel Company Ltd* (1889) and *Re Norditrack (UK) Ltd* (1999) the court has no power to alter the date of commencement.

21.1.2 Declaration of solvency

Section 256 of the Companies Act 1963 requires the directors to swear a declaration that the company is solvent. The declaration should be sworn by two directors or by a majority of directors if there are more than two.

The declaration must state that they have made a full enquiry into the affairs of the company and have formed the opinion that the company will be able to pay its liabilities in full within a specified period. This "specified period" cannot exceed twelve months from the date of the commencement of the winding up. Further, the declaration must include a statement of the assets and liabilities of the company as they stand at a date that is not more than three months prior to the declaration.

Under section 256(2) of the Companies Act 1963, this declaration of solvency will have no effect unless it is made within twenty-eight days prior to the resolution and delivered to the Registrar of Companies not later than fifteen days after the passing of the winding up resolution.

The directors must exercise caution when swearing the declaration of solvency as section 256(8) of the Companies Act 1963 imposes personal liability on the directors where the declaration of solvency is sworn and the company is found to be insolvent. An application to court under this section is commonly made by a liquidator or a creditor of the company.

The court will impose liability where it believes that the directors had no reasonable grounds for their opinion that the company was solvent. If the company's debts have not been paid within twelve months of the commencement of the winding up, there is a presumption under section 256(9) of the Companies Act 1963 that the director did not have reasonable grounds for making the declaration. This presumption can be rebutted by the directors.

Timetable for the declaration

Statement of assets and liabilities	Declaration	Resolution	Registrar of Companies
The statement of assets and liabilities must be as up-to-date as possible when the declaration is sworn.	The declaration must be sworn by the directors within at least three months of the date of the statement.	The shareholders must pass the resolution to wind up within at least twenty-eight days of the declaration.	A copy of the declaration must be delivered to the Registrar of Companies within fourteen days of the resolution.

21.1.3 Report of the independent person

To protect creditors from inaccurate, misleading, or overly optimistic declarations of solvency, the section 128 of the Companies Act 1990 amended section 256 of the Companies Act 1963 and the amendment requires that a report by an independent person must be attached to the declaration of solvency (section 256(2)(c) of the Companies Act 1963).

Under section 256(4) of the Companies Act 1963 an independent person must state an opinion, based on the information available, as to whether the directors' declaration of solvency and the statement of affairs are reasonable.

This independent person must be someone qualified at the time of the report to be auditor of the company (section 256(3) of the Companies Act 1963), and, further, the independent person must have issued a consent to release the declaration with his report attached (section 256(2)(d) of the Companies Act 1963).

21.1.4 Appointment and remuneration of the liquidator

There is no comprehensive list setting out the required qualifications of a liquidator. Section 300 of the Companies Act 1963 prohibits a body corporate from acting as such, and section 300A goes on to disqualify any person who was an employee or officer of the company within the previous twelve months, a close relative or employee of an employee or officer, or someone who would be so disqualified regarding the company's holding or subsidiary company. To act while disqualified is an offence.

In a members' voluntary liquidation, the liquidator is appointed in a general meeting and is commonly named in the proposed resolution. It is open to the members to appoint more than one liquidator. The person appointed to act as liquidator must give prior written consent to his appointment (section 276A of the Companies Act 1963).

Pursuant to section 258(2) of the Companies Act 1963, the powers of the directors cease save where the members or the liquidator agree that they may continue to act.

The members will also fix the remuneration of the liquidator at this point, and in the event that the members do not do so, or fail to fix the remuneration, it is open to the court to settle the sum (see *Amalgamated Syndicates Ltd* (1901)).

Where the members' winding up exceeds one year, the liquidator has a duty to call a general meeting of the company within three months of the end of that year and each succeeding year (section 262 of the Companies Act 1963).

21.2 Creditors' voluntary winding up

A creditors' voluntary winding up arises in two circumstances:

1. where the company is insolvent and an ordinary resolution is passed under section 256(1)(c); or

2. where a members' winding up is converted to a creditors' winding up.

As noted when discussing the duties of the directors of a company, there is a statutory obligation on all directors to call an extraordinary general meeting where the company is suffering a serious capital loss (section 40 of the Companies (Amendment) Act 1983). A director who fails to convene the meeting and knowingly or willingly permits such a failure is guilty of an offence. Therefore, it is common for the directors to determine that the company should liquidate on the grounds of insolvency under section 251(1)(c) of the Companies Act 1963 and call an extraordinary general meeting to pass the necessary resolution.

21.2.1 Members' meeting

Section 251(1)(c) of the Companies Act 1963 enables the shareholders to pass an *ordinary resolution* winding up the company on the grounds that the company cannot by reason of its liabilities continue its business.

Unless the articles provide for longer, the shareholders must be given seven days' notice in writing of this meeting. The members can, and usually do, nominate a liquidator at this meeting.

The resolution to wind up on the grounds of insolvency must be bona fide, and it can be attacked by the suspicious creditor.

In *Re Shannonside Holdings Ltd* (1993) the members' resolution to wind up the company was challenged by secured creditors who argued that it was not bona fide. It was submitted that the winding up was for the purpose of avoiding their judgment mortgage which would be ineffective if the company was wound up within three months of its creation. Costello J. found that once the company was insolvent and the duty to wind up was established, the fact that the winding up was to the directors' advantage was immaterial.

21.2.2 Creditors' meeting

The directors are obliged by section 266(1) of the Companies Act 1963 to convene a creditors' meeting.

(1) The procedure

The meeting must be held on the same day or the day following the members' meeting and the creditors must be given at least ten days' notice of the creditors' meeting.

An advertisement must be placed in two daily newspapers which circulate in the area of the registered office of the company or where the principal place of business of the company is situated (section 266(2) of the Companies Act 1963).

(2) Duty of directors

A director of the company must attend the meeting and present to the creditors a statement of the company's affairs together with a full list of creditors detailing the extent of their debts. Section 266(6) of the Companies Act 1963, as amended by section 15 of the Companies (Amendment) Act 1982, imposes a fine on the directors who fail to comply with these requirements.

(3) Appointment of a liquidator

It is open to the creditors to retain or replace the liquidator who may have already been appointed/proposed by the members. Where the creditors propose their own liquidator, that liquidator should be at the meeting of creditors. In the event that he is not present, the chairperson must notify him within seven days so as to give consent to the appointment. The liquidator, as mentioned in the case of a members' voluntary winding up, must give his prior written consent to his appointment (section 276A of the Companies Act 1963).

Under section 267(2) of the Companies Act 1963, it remains open to a director, a creditor, or a member to apply to court for an order retaining the members' choice of liquidator or directing that both the members' nominated liquidator and the creditors' nominated liquidator act jointly.

If a creditor has a connection with the proposed liquidator, it must be disclosed at the meeting, and failure to do so may result in a fine (section 310A of the Companies Act 1963, as inserted by section 147 of the Companies Act 1990).

The court can appoint a voluntary liquidator where no liquidator is acting or can remove the liquidator and appoint another where cause is shown.

(4) Committee of inspection

It is also open to the creditors, but not mandatory, to appoint a committee of inspection comprising of up to five creditors to oversee the liquidator in the liquidation. The five creditors can be joined by up to three persons nominated by the members of the company (section 268(1) of the Companies Act 1963). The creditors have the power to object to these nominated individuals and they can be disqualified save where the court objects to such a disqualification.

As well as generally overseeing the liquidation, the other main powers of the committee are set out in section 269 of the Companies Act 1963 and include the determination of the remuneration of the liquidator, the determination as to whether the liquidator should continue the business of the company, and the determination as to whether the powers of the directors should continue. Where no committee of inspection is appointed, the creditors, by way of majority in number and value, exercise these powers.

(5) Power to vote

Creditors can and do vote on matters at a creditors' meeting, and a resolution is deemed passed when a majority in number and value vote in its favour. A creditor can only vote if that creditor has an ascertained debt.

Secured creditors can vote at a creditors' meeting but only by rendering their debt unsecured, or voting to the value of their debt minus the value of their security. If the secured creditor votes to the value of his whole debt, he will be deemed to have surrendered his security and will become an unsecured creditor. As a result, many secured creditors will not exercise their right to vote and will rely on their security.

(6) Meetings

Every voluntary liquidator must call a meeting of the creditors and the company at the end of the first year of the winding up, and each successive year (section 272 of the Companies Act 1963). At every such meeting the liquidator must give an account of the conduct of the wind-up. A copy of this account must be sent to the Companies Registration Office.

21.3 Conversion: A members' winding up to a creditors' winding up

A members' winding up may be converted to a creditors' voluntary winding up in the situations discussed below.

21.3.1 Conversion under section 256(5) of the Companies Act 1963

It is open to a creditor to apply to the court within twenty-eight days of the advertisement that a resolution has been passed placing the company in a members' voluntary liquidation. The applicant creditor, plus any creditors supporting him, must represent one fifth in numbers or value of all the creditors of the company.

If the court is of the opinion that it is unlikely that the company will be able to pay its debts within the "specified period" (see paragraph 21.1.2.3 above), the court may order that the liquidation proceed as a creditors' voluntary liquidation.

21.3.2 Conversion under section 261 of the Companies Act 1963

Where a liquidator is appointed in a members' voluntary winding up and he forms the opinion that the company cannot meet its debts within the "specified period", the liquidator is obliged by statute to call a meeting of the company creditors within fourteen days of forming this opinion.

The notice must state that the liquidator has a duty to call the meeting as a result of the above opinion. The liquidator must post a notice of the meeting to all known creditors at least seven days before the meeting and advertise in the meeting in two national newspapers and Iris Oifigiuil at least ten days before the meeting. Where a creditor reasonably requests further information the liquidator is under a duty to provide it.

At this meeting, the liquidator must present a statement of affairs of the company, attend, and preside over the meeting. According to section 131(3) of the Companies Act 1990 the liquidation becomes a creditors' voluntary winding up from the time of the meeting. It is open to the creditors to replace the members' liquidator if a majority in number and value support such a change.

21.3.3 Conversion under section 131(5) of the Companies Act 1990

A company is in breach of section 256 of the Companies Act 1963 where the report of an independent person is not attached to the declaration of solvency in a members' voluntary winding up. The liquidator has seven days to apply to the court for directions. According to *Re Favon Investments Co. Ltd* (1993) the court does not have the discretion to extend the time for the report and, as a result, there is an automatic conversion to a creditors' voluntary winding up.

21.4 Conversion: A voluntary winding up to a court winding up

Prior to the completion of a voluntary winding up, a company creditor, contributory (defined in section 207 of the Companies Act 1963 as any person liable to contribute to the assets of the company in the event of a winding up and includes past and present members), or member may apply to the court under section 213 of the Companies Act 1963 for an order directing that the liquidation proceed under the supervision of the court.

Section 213 of the Companies Act 1963 (see Chapter 22) sets out the grounds under which the court may order a compulsory /court winding up; the burden is on the petitioner to plead one of these grounds and establish why the company should be placed in a court monitored liquidation. The court will take into account the position of the other creditors and may refuse to convert the winding up where a majority in number and value of creditors object to such a conversion.

The court will require compelling reasons to justify the application. In *Re Gilt Construction Ltd* (1994) O'Hanlon J. stated that the courts must be slow to overturn the appointment of the majority in number and value in a voluntary liquidation, and turn it into a court liquidation. Such compelling reasons may include the failure of the voluntary liquidator to swell the company assets or investigate questionable directors' behaviour.

Further, in *Re Oakthorpe Holdings Ltd* (1988) Carroll J. stated *obiter* that a situation where the members commenced a winding up but refused to put in place the declaration of solvency or call a creditors' meeting was one whereby the court might intervene, at the petition of the creditors and convert the voluntary winding up.

21.5 Duties of a voluntary liquidator

The primary function of the voluntary liquidator is to swell the assets of the company and distribute the assets to those entitled in accordance with the Company Acts (see Chapter 23 for the priorities on distribution). Further, as an agent of the company, the liquidator is subject to the usual fiduciary duties.

The liquidator assumes the management of the company, but any pre-existing deal with the existing creditors will remain in place if supported by a special resolution of members, or three quarters of the creditors. This may be appealed to the court by a creditor or contributory.

The duty of the voluntary liquidator to call meetings in various circumstances is detailed at paragraphs 21.1.4, 21.2.1, 21.2.2 and 21.3.2 above.

21.6 Powers of a voluntary liquidator

It is the general rule of voluntary liquidations that the powers of the directors cease and are vested in the liquidator. This is subject to the proviso that a certain amount of control is vested in the members of the company (in the case of a members' winding up) or in the committee of inspection/creditors (in the case of a creditors' winding up).

21.6.1 Fettered powers

According to section 276(1)(a) of the Companies Act 1963 certain powers may be exercised by the voluntary liquidator only where that exercise is sanctioned by a members' special resolution (in the case of a member's winding up) or by the committee of inspection/creditors (in the case of a creditors' winding up).

These fettered powers are as follows:

1. the payment of a class of creditor in full;
2. any arrangement or compromise with creditors or persons claiming to be creditors of the company;
3. any compromise of calls, liabilities to calls, debts and claims between the company and a contributory or other debtors or possible debtors.

21.6.2 Unfettered powers

According to section 276(1)(b) of the Companies Act 1963, the voluntary liquidator may exercise all the powers vested in a court /official liquidator. The powers vested in the latter are enumerated in section 231 of the Companies Act 1963 and include *inter alia* the power

1. to bring or defend any action or other legal proceeding in the name of and on behalf of the company;
2. to carry on the business of the company so far as necessary for a beneficial winding up;
3. to appoint a solicitor;
4. to sell the real and personal property of the company;
5. to execute all deeds and other documents in the name of the company;
6. to borrow money and use the corporate assets as security;
7. to appoint an agent;
8. to give security for costs in any proceedings commenced by the company or commenced by the liquidator in the name of the company;
9. to do whatever is necessary for the winding up of the company and the distribution of the company assets.

Other unfettered powers include the power to exercise the power of the court in settling a list of contributories (section 276(1)(c)), to exercise the power of the court in making calls on shares (section 276(1)(d)), to summon a general meeting of the company (section 276(1)(e)), and to disclaim onerous or unsaleable property with the leave of the court (section 290 of the Companies Act 1963; see Chapter 23).

21.6.3 Unfettered powers and a creditors' winding up

Prior to the Companies Act 1990, in the case of a creditors' winding up there was a danger that a member nominated liquidator could exercise the above "unfettered" powers prior to the holding of the creditors' meeting where, as noted above, the creditors could replace the liquidator with their own nominee. The case of *Re Centrebind Ltd* (1966) established that a voluntary liquidator could exercise his powers which were held to be unfettered until the creditors' meeting was held.

In order to avoid a possible detriment to the creditors, section 131(2) of the Companies Act 1990 prohibits the exercise of the "unfettered" powers, save where there is the sanction of the court, before a creditors' meeting is held. Section 131(3) of the Companies Act 1990 provides that the prohibition does apply in three situations:

1. where the liquidator takes control/custody of the company property;
2. where the liquidator disposes of perishable goods or goods whose value will diminish if not disposed of immediately;
3. where the liquidator acts to protect the company's assets.

21.6.4 Court directions

Section 280 of the Companies Act 1963 allows a voluntary liquidator to apply to court for directions as to any matter arising during the winding up. The application may consist of the liquidator requesting the court to exercise a power that the court would have the discretion to exercise in a court/compulsory winding up. The court will accede to the application only where the exercise of the power is "just and beneficial".

A common application under this section is an application to stay proceedings against the company as a voluntary liquidation, and unlike a court liquidation, it does not automatically stay such proceedings.

This facility is also available to a creditor or contributory of the company. In *Re Comet Food Machinery Co. Ltd (in liquidation)* (1999) an application under section 280 was made by the creditor of the company who believed that assets had been diverted to another company. The creditor requested that the owners of the company be examined by the court. Both the High Court and the Supreme Court on appeal granted the application as the creditor had discharged the onus of proof that the examination would probably result in some benefit accruing to him, *i.e.* the grounds for a action requiring the return of improperly transferred assets may be uncovered.

21.6.5 Consideration for company property

Section 260 of the Companies Act 1963 permits a voluntary liquidator in a members' voluntary winding up to accept shares in another company, in consideration for the sale of property of the company being wound up. The members must consent to this arrangement by way of a special resolution. This option is also available in a creditors' voluntary winding up but only with the sanction of the committee of inspection or the court where no such committee has been appointed.

21.6.6 Sale of non-cash assets

Section 124 of the Companies Act 1990 prevents the voluntary liquidator from selling a non-cash asset for requisite value to an individual who was an officer of the company within three years prior to the liquidation save where fourteen days' notice is given to all the company creditors.

A "non-cash" asset means any property other than cash, and "requisite value" is defined under section 29 of the Companies Act 1990 as meaning not less than €1,270 and not exceed €63,500 or ten per cent of the company's relevant assets. An "officer" includes a person connected with a director of the company and a shadow director.

21.7 Liability of a liquidator

The liquidator must comply with both the statutory obligations and, as agent of the company, fiduciary obligations. In *Re Home and Colonial Insurance Company Ltd* (1930) it was held that "a high standard of care and diligence" is required from a liquidator in a winding up. Under section 298 of the Companies Act 1963 (as amended by the Companies Act 1990 and the Company Law Enforcement Act 2001), a liquidator who has "misapplied or retained or become liable or accountable for any money or property of the company, or has been guilty of misfeasance or other breach of duty or trust in relation to the company" may be compelled to repay or restore the money or property or pay compensation to the company.

In the English case of *Pioneer Seafood Ltd v. The Braer Corporation* (2000) the liquidator who allowed an insolvent company to continue to trade after his appointment (without the sanction of the court) and who failed to realise the assets quickly after his appointment, was found liable in misfeasance.

Under section 277 of the Companies Act 1963 the Court has the power to remove and replace a voluntary liquidator "on cause shown" to the court.

21.8 Company dissolution

When the affairs of the company are fully wound up in a members' voluntary winding up, section 263(1) of the Companies Act 1963 requires an account of the liquidation to be presented to the members at an extraordinary general meeting. The account should set out how the liquidation was conducted and detail how the assets were realised and distributed. The meeting must be advertised in two daily newspapers at least twenty-eight days prior to the meeting (section 263(2)). A copy of the account must be sent to the Companies Registration Office within a week of the date of the general meeting (section 263(3)) The company is deemed to be dissolved within three months of the date of that registration (section 263(4)).

The same procedure applies in the case of a creditors' winding up, save that the account is presented to a general meeting of members and a meeting of creditors (section 273 of the Companies Act 1963).

An application may be made to the court within two years of the date of the dissolution to have the dissolution declared void (section 310 of the Companies Act 1963).

22. INVOLUNTARY WINDING UP

An involuntary winding up proceeds under the supervision of the High Court, and the liquidator is deemed an officer of the court for the duration of the liquidation. The applicant for a court winding up is called a petitioner and the document presented to the High Court is a petition.

An involuntary winding up is also referred to as an official, compulsory, or court liquidation.

22.1 Petitioners

The persons with the *locus standi* to present the petition to the High Court are discussed below.

22.1.1 Company – section 215 of the Companies Act 1963

It is open to the company shareholders to resolve to wind up the company under the supervision of the court. In *Re Galway and Salthill Tramways Co.* (1918) it was established that model article 80 of Table A (see Chapter 4) does not give the directors the power to decide to bring a winding up petition on behalf of the company. The articles of association may extend the directors' powers and give the directors an express power to petition the court for a winding up order.

22.1.2 Creditors – section 215 of the Companies Act 1963

An application to the court to wind up a company may be presented by the company creditors. The term "creditors" includes contingent or prospective creditors. Section 215(c) of the Companies Act 1963 states that the court will not hear the petition of a contingent or prospective creditor until the petitioner has established a *prima facie* case for a winding up and has given such security for the costs of the application as the court thinks reasonable.

In the English case of *JSF Finance and Currency Exchange Co. Ltd v. Akma Solutions Inc* (2001) Park J. held that a contingent creditor whose debt had not yet materialised (as the contingency had not yet happened) could not bring a petition to have the company wound up.

A creditor's petition is open to attack from other creditors, and it may also be challenged on the basis that the creditor's debt is disputed and the application is therefore an abuse of process.

(1) Opposition from other creditors

Other creditors of the company may be opposed to the petition. In *Re RW Sharman Ltd* (1957) the court exercised its discretion to refuse a winding up petition as the majority of the creditors opposed it.

In the English case of *Re Demaglass Holdings Ltd* (2001) Neuberger J. set out the following principles that would apply where a petition was opposed by other creditors:

1. The court has a discretion to accede to, or refuse, the application.
2. The petitioning creditor has to establish the possibility of some benefit accruing form the winding up.
3. An unpaid creditor is entitled to a winding up virtually as of right.
4. Where some creditors are in favour and others against, an order would be made if the majority supported it and would only be refused if the majority opposed it.
5. The fact that the majority of creditors oppose the making of the order is insufficient, *per se*, to refuse the making of the order and the court has to be satisfied that there is sufficient reason to refuse to make the order.
6. The views of independent creditors are particularly important and normally the secured creditors' views would be given little weight.
7. The court would balance the rights where satisfied that the supporting and opposing creditors have justified positions.

In *Re Lummus Agricultural Services Ltd* (1999) there were a number of creditors opposed to the petition, but Park J. discounted those views as they were not independent but were in fact associated with the respondent company and the directors. In *Re Huon Foam Pty Ltd* (2000) the Tasmanian court held that creditors of an insolvent company were entitled as of right to a winding up order, notwithstanding that certain of its creditors were willing to allow the company an opportunity to implement a strategy to satisfy the debts.

In *Re WMG (Toughening) Ltd* (2001) Murphy J. dismissed the creditor's petition where the court was not satisfied that the petition was being presented for the benefit of the members and creditors.

(2) Disputed debt/abuse of process

Where a creditor presents a petition to the court, the creditor must have a present and liquidated debt due and owing to him. The debt must be undisputed as a winding up petition is not a legitimate means of seeking to enforce payment of a debt which is bona fide disputed.

The English cases of *Mann v. Goldstein* (1968) and *Stonegate Securities Ltd v. Gregory* (1980) and in this jurisdiction *Re Pageboy Couriers Ltd* (1983) support the proposition that if it is clear that a company in good faith and on substantial grounds disputes any liability in respect of the alleged debt, the petition will be dismissed, or if the matter is brought before the court before the petition is issued, its presentation will be restrained.

In *Re Millhouse Taverns Ltd* (2000) Finnegan J. confirmed that a petition to wind up a company will not be granted where the petitioner is aware that the company has a substantial and reasonable defence to the claim it wishes to plead and on which it proposes to rely to defeat the entire claim brought against it. The cases of *Stonegate Securities* and *Pageboy Couriers* were followed.

Presenting a winding up in these circumstances has been termed an abuse of process. The burden of proving an abuse of process is on the party opposing the petition who must establish a *prima facie* case of abuse of process. In *Bryanston Finance Ltd v. Devires (No. 2)* (1976) Buckley J. confirmed that the principles used to restrain an abuse of the process of the court were applicable to a winding up petition. In *Truck and Machinery Sales Ltd v. Marubeni Komatsu Ltd* (1996) Keane J. held that in order to establish an abuse of process the company must show (a) that the entire debt is bona fide disputed on substantial grounds or (b) that all of the debt with the exception of £1,000 is disputed. He went on to say that the court would still have discretion to order a winding up where there is evidence to show that the company would in any event be insolvent. Further, where the petition was presented for a collateral purpose or with an ulterior motive, the court could restrain the petition.

An abuse of court process was found in *Re Bula Ltd* (1988) where several banks attempted to wind up the company in order to prevent another creditor from registering his judgment as a mortgage and thus ranking with the banks as secured creditors.

22.1.3 Contributories – section 215 of the Companies Act 1963

Section 208 of the Companies Act 1963 defines a contributory as one "liable to contribute to the assets of a company in the event of its being wound up", and according to section 207 of the Companies Acts 1963, the term includes present and past members of the company. A contributory can issue a petition where the number of members in a public company has reduced below seven or where (a) the shares were originally allotted to him; or (b) the shares were held by him and registered in his name for six of the last eighteen months; or (c) the shares were inherited by him on the death of a former holder.

22.1.4 Director of Corporate Enforcement – section 12(2) of the Companies Act 1990, as amended by section 14 of the Company Law Enforcement Act 2001

The Director of Corporate Enforcement may present a winding up petition to the court where it appears from any of the following that a petition should be presented:

1. an inspectors' report issued pursuant to an investigation under sections 8 of the Companies Act 1990;

2. a report made by inspectors appointed by the Director; or

3. any information or document obtained by the Director as a result of an investigation.

The court must be satisfied that it is just and equitable that the company be placed in compulsory liquidation. An application can be made under section 124A of the English Companies Act 1985 to wind up the company in the public interest in the aftermath of a company investigation.

In the English case of *Secretary of State for Trade and Industry v. Travel Time (UK) Ltd et al* (2000) Park J. held that that the court should reach its decision on the totality of the evidence before it. He stated that it was essential that some intentional and dishonest deceit of the public be alleged and that even if there was a deliberate misstatement or omission, it had to be of some significance for the severe sanction of a compulsory winding up. Section 12(2) of the Companies Act 1990 is a similar provision.

Further, in the case of the *Secretary of State for Trade and Industry v Aurum Marketing Ltd et al* (2000) the court held that the sole director and shareholder of the company could be ordered to pay the costs of such a petition and that the costs should not be paid out of the company assets until all creditors had been paid. In *Re North West Holdings plc* (2001) it was held that if the company directors had a bona fide defence, their company had an arguable defence to the petition, and if it was in the company's interests to advance that defence, then, save in special circumstances, it would not be appropriate to order its directors to pay the costs of the petition.

22.1.5 Registrar of Companies – section 215 of the Companies Act 1963

The Registrar of Companies may petition for the winding up a company under the supervision of the court.

22.1.6 Members – section 215 of the Companies Act 1963

Any person with the *locus standi* to present a petition pursuant to section 205 of the Companies Act 1963 (*i.e.* the company shareholders) may petition the court for the winding up of the company (see Chapter 14 for a discussion of shareholders' remedies and section 205).

22.2 Grounds for a court winding up

One or more of the following grounds enumerated in section 213 of the Companies Act 1963 must be set out in the petition presented to the court seeking the winding up of a company:

22.2.1 Special resolution

Section 213 (a); The company members have passed a special resolution that the company be wound up by the court.

22.2.2 Failure to commence business

Section 213 (c); The company has failed to commence business within one year of incorporation or has suspended its business for a whole year.

22.2.3 Minimum membership

Section 213 (d); The number of members has fallen below two in the case of a private company and seven in the case of any other company. This does not apply to a private company limited by shares or by guarantees who can have just one member (see Chapter 2).

22.2.4 Inability to pay company debts

Section 213(e); The company is unable to pay its debts as they fall due. This is the most commonly used ground under section 213 of the Companies Act 1963 and it essentially means that the company should be wound up because it is insolvent. Once a creditor has established that a company is insolvent, he is entitled as of right to an order for the winding up of the company.

Section 214 of the Companies Act 1963 sets out three methods that can be used by the petitioner to prove that a company is insolvent:

1. Section 214(a); a creditor owed the sum €1,270 or more has served a written demand by registered post on the registered office of the company requesting the payment of the debt and after the expiration of three weeks from the date of the letter the debt remains due and owing to the creditor (in *Re WMG (Toughening) Ltd* (2001) Murphy J. held that the service of the demand has "to be done with exactitude" and that a facsimile was insufficient).

2. Section 214(b); a creditor has attempted to execute a decree, judgment or order of court and it has been returned unsatisfied by the sheriff.

3. Section 214(c); it is proved to the satisfaction of the court that the company is unable to pay its debts and the court will take contingent and prospective liabilities of the company into account.

In *Taylors Industrial Flooring Ltd v. M & H Plant Hire (Manchester) Ltd* (1990) it was held that where a debt owed by a company is not disputed, the proof of failure to pay is evidence of inability to pay.

If a company can only dispute a portion of the debt, it is obliged to pay off the rest immediately. (see paragraph 22.1.2.(2) in relation to disputed debts and abuse of process).

22.2.5 Just and Equitable

Section 213(f); The court finds that it is just and equitable that the company be wound up.

There are no defined limits to this ground and the following are examples of the instances where the court has found that it was just and equitable to wind up a company:

(1) Quasi-partnership

In many instances private companies are small family-run entities where the corporate decisions are made by all the members. The courts view these companies as quasi-partnerships, as a close relationship of "trust and confidence" commonly exists between the members.

According to the case of *Re Murph's Restaurants* (1979), it may be appropriate to wind up a company where this close relationship has disintegrated. That case involved a company established in 1972 by two brothers and friend to run two restaurants. The company was run informally and all three were directors and equal shareholders. The business relationship between the parties broke down and the brothers decided to remove the friend from his position as a director.

The friend sought to have the company wound up under section 213(f) and (g) of the Companies Act 1963. The petition was opposed by the brothers on the ground that a petition under section 205 of the Companies Act 1963 would be more appropriate. Gannon J. refused to accept this argument given the fundamental breakdown in the relationship between the parties.

Gannon J. in the High Court found that the action of the brothers was "a deliberate and calculated repudiation by both of them [the brothers] of that relationship of equality, mutuality, trust and confidence between the three of them which constituted the very essence of the company."

He referred to the case of *Ebrahimi v. Westbourne Galleries Ltd* (1973) where Lord Cross of Chelsea states at p.383:

> "[P]eople do not become partners unless they have confidence in one another and it is of the essence of the relationship that mutual confidence is maintained. If neither has any longer confidence in the other so that they cannot work together in the way originally contemplated then the relationship should be ended - unless, indeed, the party who wishes to end it has been solely responsible for the situation which has arisen."

Gannon J. ordered the winding up of the company under the just and equitable ground, as he stated, that the just and equitable provision comes to the assistance of the petitioner "if he can point to, and prove, some special underlying obligation of his fellow member(s) in good faith or confidence, that so long as the business continues he shall be entitled to management participation, an obligation so basic that, if broken, the conclusion must be that the association be dissolved".

In *McGilligan v. O'Grady* (1999) the court considered the above cases and stated *obiter* that if there was a relationship between shareholders in a company indicating a degree of mutual confidence and trust, the court might order the winding up of the company on the just and equitable ground where one or more of the shareholders and/or directors exercised their powers in a manner which was inconsistent with that relationship.

(2) Deadlock in corporate management

This occurs where the voting power evenly divided between two opposed blocks.

Re Yenidje Tobacco Co (1916) was an example of this, where the two directors would not speak to each other. The Irish cases of *Re Irish Tourist Promotions Ltd* (1974) and *Re Vehicle Buildings and Insulations Ltd* (1986) demonstrates this well.

In the latter case two equal shareholders were at loggerheads. Murphy J. spoke of the "complete unwillingness of each party to co-operate with the other" and spoke of the objective fact that "the shareholders/directors cannot legally or practically administer the company without the co-operation of each other"; the solvent business was wound up.

In *Re Tradalco Ltd; Bluzwedmetals Ltd v. Transworld Metals SA* (2001) Lavan J. granted a winding up petition where two quasi-partners in a joint venture company were in a deadlock which effectively paralysed the company's activities to the detriment of both members and creditors.

(3) Failure of substratum

There is failure of substratum where a company was formed for a purpose that is no longer pursued or where the company pursues a different venture to that originally envisaged. In *Re German Date Coffee Co* (1882) a contributory successfully petitioned for the winding up of a company where the sole purpose for which the company had been established, manufacturing coffee dates under a patent, could not be achieved due to the inability to secure that patent.

(4) Illegal or fraudulent objects

Where the company is found to have illegal objects, the court can wind up the company on just and equitable grounds. Where the company is being used as an instrument of fraud, the court will wind up the company. In *Re Shrinkpak Ltd* (1989) the liquidator of an insolvent company successfully petitioned to wind up Shrinkpak as it had been used to divert funds from the insolvent company.

22.2.6 Oppression

Section 213(g); The court is satisfied that the affairs of the company are being conducted, or the powers of the directors are being exercised, in a manner oppressive to any member or in disregard of his interests as a member and that a winding up would be justified in the general circumstance of the case. The court will dismiss such an application if proceedings under section 205 of the Companies Act 1963 would be more appropriate (see Chapter 14).

22.2.7 Old public companies

Section 213 (h); The court is satisfied that an old public company has not converted to a public limited company (a plc) at the end of the transitional period under the Companies (Amendment) Act 1983 (see Chapter 2).

22.2.8 Share capital

Section 213(i); The court is satisfied that a company has not complied with the share capital requirements at the end of the transitional period under section 12(9) of the Companies (Amendment) Act 1983.

22.3 Involuntary winding up procedure

22.3.1 The hearing

As stated above, the petition must set out the details of the company and the ground or grounds for the application under section 213 of the

Companies Act 1963. It is presented to the Central Office of the High Court where a date for the hearing of the petition is allocated.

The petition must be served on the registered office of the company which is the subject matter of the application. The Rules of the Superior Courts 1986 require that notice of the petition is advertised at least seven clear days before the hearing in *Iris Oifigiuil* and in two Dublin daily newspapers or such other papers as the court registrar directs.

At the hearing of the petition and pursuant to section 216 of the Companies Act 1963, the court may order that the company be wound up under section 213, dismiss the petition, adjourn the petition with or without conditions, or make any interim order "that it thinks fit". One such interim order that may be made is the appointment of a provisional liquidator under section 226 of the Companies Act 1963. The function of the provisional liquidator is to preserve the assets so that they can be orderly realised and distributed by the official liquidator.

Where the court makes an order to wind up the company, an official liquidator is appointed by the court and the winding up is deemed to have commenced on the date that the petition was first presented to the court (section 220(2) of the Companies Act 1963). Where the company was in voluntary liquidation and the court converts that liquidation to an involuntary winding up, the winding up is deemed to have commenced on the date of the initial resolution to wind up the company voluntarily.

A copy of the winding up order must be delivered to the Registrar of Companies, and any person responsible for failing to deliver the said order may be subject to a fine (section 221 of the Companies Act 1963).

22.3.2 Effect of the winding up order

Pursuant to section 218 of the Companies Act 1963 any disposition of the company property, any transfer of shares or any alteration of the status of members after the commencement of the winding up is void, save where the court otherwise orders (see Chapter 23).

Pursuant to section 219 of the Companies Act 1963, any attachment, sequestration, distress, or execution put in force against the company property after the commencement of the winding up is void.

Pursuant to section 222 of the Companies Act 1963, and unlike voluntary liquidations, no "actions or proceedings" against the company may proceed or be commenced, save with the leave of the court.

Pursuant to section 229 of the Companies Act 1963, the powers of the directors to deal with the company assets cease and are vested in the liquidator.

Pursuant to section 303 of the Companies Act 1963, every invoice, business letter, and order for goods which bears the name of the company must state that the company is in liquidation.

22.3.3 Statement of affairs

Pursuant to section 224 of the Companies Act 1963, where a winding up order has been made by the court or a provisional liquidator has been appointed, a statement of affairs of the company must be filed in court setting out the assets, debts, and liabilities, the names, residences, and occupations of its creditors, the securities held by the creditors, and the dates when those securities were executed.

The statement must contain such further information as the court may require. The statement must be made by the directors and secretary of the company at that time. The court may, however, require present or past company officers, or present or past company employees, or those who took part in the formation of the company within the previous year to file the statement.

The statement must be filed within twenty-one days of the winding up order/appointment of the provisional liquidator unless the court extends the time. Failure to file the statement, without reasonable excuse, is an offence under section 224(5) of the Companies Act 1963.

22.4 The liquidator

22.4.1 Qualifications

The qualifications of a compulsory liquidator are the same as those discussed at Chapter 21.1.4.

22.4.2 Committee of inspection

Pursuant to section 232 of the Companies Act 1963, the court may order the liquidator to summon a meeting of the creditors and contributories of the company in order to determine if a committee of inspection should be put in place and to determine the members of such a committee. The court may order separate meetings of the creditors and the contributories of the company.

Where the meeting(s) determine that a committee should be established to act in accordance with the liquidator, the court will duly make that appointment.

22.4.3 Duties

The primary duty of the liquidator is to take possession of and realise the value of the company's assets. The proceeds must be used to discharge the company debts in accordance with the Companies Acts and the liquidator must distribute any surplus (see Chapter 23).

Section 244A of the Companies Act 1963 grants the liquidator the right to possession of "any deed, instrument, or other document belonging to the company or the books of account, receipts, invoices or other papers of like nature relating to the accounts or trade dealings or business of the company". According to *Re Galeforce Pleating Co. Ltd* (1999) it was held that it was incumbent on a director to co-operate with the liquidator and to volunteer such information as that director has on the records and the transactions of the company.

22.4.4 Remuneration

According to section 228(d) of the Companies Act 1963, the liquidator "shall receive such salary or remuneration by way of percentage or otherwise as the court may direct". In *Re Car Replacements Ltd (*1999) Murphy J. held that section 228 granted the High Court a wide discretion as to what a liquidator shall receive in salary and remuneration. Murphy J. found that the practice of the High Court was to calculate the liquidator's remuneration on the basis of hours worked by the liquidator and his or her staff. Murphy J. pointed out that this practice was not without its deficiencies, as it did not encourage a liquidator to complete a winding up in an expeditious fashion. It is also the practice of the court to appoint a creditor from the general body of creditors to monitor, and if necessary make a submission on, the liquidator's charges.

22.4.5 Resignation and removal

Section 228(c) of the Companies Act 1963 allows a liquidator to resign or be removed by the court "on cause shown". Where this occurs, the liquidator must deliver all books papers, documents and accounts relating to company to the new liquidator. Under section 228(e) the vacancy is filled by the court.

22.4.6 Liability

The liability of an official liquidator is the same as that of a voluntary liquidator and it is discussed at Chapter 21.7.

22.5 Powers of the liquidator

The powers of the official liquidator are detailed below.

22.5.1 Section 231(1) of the Companies Act 1963

The exercise of the following powers by the official liquidator requires the sanction of the court or the committee of inspection where one is put in place:

1. to bring or defend any action or other legal proceeding in the name of and on behalf of the company (the court may order that the sanction of the court is not necessary);
2. to carry on the business of the company so far as necessary for a beneficial winding up (the court may order that the sanction of the court is not necessary);
3. to appoint a solicitor to assist him;
4. to pay a class of creditor in full;
5. to arrange or compromise with creditors or persons claiming to be creditors of the company;
6. to compromise calls, liabilities to calls, debts, and claims between the company and a contributory or other debtors or possible debtors.

22.5.2 Section 231(2) of the Companies Act 1963

No such sanction is required for the exercise of the following powers:

1. to sell the real and personal property of the company;
2. to execute all deeds and other documents in the name of the company;

3. to borrow money and use the corporate assets as security;

4. to appoint an agent;

5. to accept and make bills of exchange or promissory notes on the security of the assets;

6. to prove in the bankruptcy of any contributory;

7. to take out administration to the estate of a deceased contributory;

8. to give security for costs in any proceedings commenced by the company or commenced by the liquidator in the name of the company;

9. to do whatever is necessary for the winding up of the company and the distribution of the company assets.

22.5.3 Section 290 of the Companies Act 1963

The liquidator has the power to disclaim onerous or unsaleable company property (see Chapter 23).

22.6 Powers of the court

The Companies Act 1963 grants a comprehensive list of powers to the court that can be exercised in an involuntary winding up. These powers have been extended and improved by both the Companies Act 1990 and the Company Law Enforcement Act 2001 and they are as follows:

1. Section 234(1); the power to annul a winding up order;

2. Section 234(2); the power to stay the winding up;

3. Section 235; the power to settle the list of contributories;

4. Section 236; the power to order a contributory, officer, trustee, banker, receiver, or agent to deliver property to the company;

5. Section 237; the power to order the payment of debts due to the company by a contributory;

6. Section 238; the power to make calls on the contributories of the company;

7. Section 239; the power to order any contributory, purchaser, or other person to make payment of monies due to the company into a designated bank account;

8. Section 241; the power to fix a time or times within which a creditor must prove his debt or face exclusion from the distribution of assets;

9. Section 242; the power to adjust the rights of contributories;

10 Section 243; the power to make an order for the inspection of the books and papers of the company by the creditors/contributories of the company/Director of Corporate Enforcement (extended by the Company Law Enforcement Act 2001 Act);

11. Section 244; the power to order the payment of the costs of the winding up out of company assets;

12. Section 244A; no person can claim a lien on, and the liquidator has a right to possession of, "any deed, instrument, or other document belonging to the company or the books of account, receipts, invoices or other papers of like nature relating to the accounts or trade dealings or business of the company", save in the case of a mortgage, charge or pledge (inserted by the Companies Act 1990 Act);

13. Section 246; power to compel company officers to attend a meeting of creditors/contributories/committee of inspection for the purpose of giving information as to the trade or business of the company;

14. Section 247; power to cause a contributory, director, shadow director, secretary, or other officer of the company to be arrested where *inter alia* they threaten to abscond or remove company property (as replaced by the Company Law Enforcement Act 2001);

One of the most frequently exercised power of the court is the power under section 245 of the Companies Act 1963 to summon a person for examination.

After the appointment of a provisional liquidator or the making of a winding up order, the court may summon for examination, any officer of the company, or any person known or suspected to have in his possession any property of the company or supposed to be indebted to the company, or any person whom the court deems capable of giving information relating to the promotion, formation, trade, dealings, affairs or property of the company. The examination may be ordered by its own motion or, further to section 44 of the Company Law Enforcement act 2001, on the application of the Director of Corporate Enforcement.

Pursuant to section 245(5) of the Companies Act 1963, the costs of the examination shall be paid by the person examined where the court thinks it is just and equitable. The person under examination may not refuse to answer any question on the grounds that the answer may incriminate him, and the answer may be used as evidence in any proceedings save proceedings for an offence. Failure to attend, without reasonable excuse, is a contempt of court under section 245(7), and the court may order the arrest of that person under section 245(8).

In *Money Markets International Stock Brokers Ltd v. Fanning et al* (2000) the liquidator applied to the court to exercise the power of examination and compel two directors to reply to interrogatories. The liquidator claimed that the directors had transferred moneys from the company's account to their own benefit. O'Sullivan J. held that the liquidator had established a "special exigency" for compelling the replies.

Under section 245A(1) of the Companies Act 1963 (as amended by the Company Law Enforcement Act 2001), the court may order the person examined to pay money or deliver property to the company. This order may be made where the person examined is (a) indebted to the company; or (b) has in his possession or control any money, property, or books and papers of the company.

Pursuant to section 245A(2) of the Companies Act 1963 and on the application of the Director of Corporate Enforcement or the liquidator, the court may make an order permitting the applicant to enter and search the premises of the person who is the subject of an order under section 245A(1), and seize any money, property, or books and papers of the company found on the premises. To obstruct the entry, search, or seizure is an offence.

It is open to the liquidator to request the court to exercise one of the above powers.

22.7 Cross-border insolvency

The European Council Regulation on Insolvency Proceedings came into force on the May 31, 2002. The regulation radically reformed the position in relation to insolvency practice and established a regime for improved efficiency and effectiveness of the conduct of cross border insolvencies. It provides for the cross-border recognition and enforcement of basic orders such as the appointment of liquidators and other insolvency office holders and of the remedies typically invoked in insolvency proceedings. It also established a mechanism for the management of asset realisation and the processing of creditor claims in multi-jurisdictional cases.

22.8 Company dissolution

Pursuant to section 249(1) of the Companies Act 1963, where the affairs of the company have been completely wound up and the liquidator so applies, the court will make an order for the dissolution of the company from the date of the order. The liquidator is obliged to deliver a copy of that order to the Registrar of Companies within twenty-one days pursuant to section 249(2), and failure to do so constitutes an offence.

Within two years of the date of the dissolution and on the application of the liquidator or by any other person who appears to the court to be interested, the court may order the dissolution to have been void and proceedings may be taken against the company (section 310 of the Companies Act 1963). A copy of the order must be delivered to the Registrar of Companies within fourteen days.

22.9 Restoration to the company register

It has been noted that a company is struck off the register of companies when the affairs of the company are fully wound up and the Registrar of Companies is duly notified by the liquidator.

Sections 12 and 12A of the Companies (Amendment) Act 1982 and section 311 of the Companies Act 1963 provide further circumstances where a company can be struck off the register at the discretion of the Registrar of Companies.

22.9.1 Section 12 of the Companies (Amendment) Act 1982; annual returns

Section 12(1) of the Companies (Amendment) Act 1982 (as amended by section 46 of the Companies (Amendment) (No. 2) Act 1999) provides that where a company has not, for one or more years, made annual returns required by sections 125 and 126 of the Companies Act 1963, the Registrar of Companies may send a registered letter stating that unless all outstanding annual returns are delivered within one month of the date of the letter, a notice will be published in *Iris Oifigiuil* with a view to striking the company off the register.

Where the company confirms that it is not carrying on business or fails to deliver all annual returns within one month of the date of the letter, the Registrar of Companies shall publish the notice stating that within one month of the date of the notice the name of the company will be struck off the register unless all outstanding returns are delivered to the Registrar. The company is then struck off pursuant to section 12(3) and a notice published in *Iris Oifigiuil* to this effect.

22.9.2 Section 12A of the Companies (Amendment) Act 1982; revenue statement

Section 12A of the Companies (Amendment) Act 1982 (as inserted by section 46 of the Companies (Amendment) (No. 2) Act 1999) provides for the striking-off of a company for failing to deliver a statement (setting out *inter alia* the name of the company, the date it commenced business, the date to which the accounts of the business will be made up to) to the Revenue Commissioners under section 882(3) of the Taxes Consolidation Act 1997. The Revenue Commissioners must notify the Registrar of Companies in writing of the failure to deliver the statement. The Registrar of Companies may send a registered letter to the company stating that unless the company delivers the statement to the Revenue Commissioners within one month of the date of the letter, a notice will be published in *Iris Oifigiuil* with a view to striking the company off the register.

Where the company fails to deliver the statement to the Revenue Commissioners, the Registrar of Companies shall publish the notice stating that within one month of the date of the notice the name of the company will be struck off the register unless the said statement is delivered to the Revenue Commissioners. The Company is then struck off pursuant to section 12A(3) and a notice published in *Iris Oifigiuil* to this effect.

22.9.3 Section 311(1) of the Companies Act 1963; failure to carry on business

Section 311(1) of the Companies Act 1963 (as amended by section 11 of the Companies (Amendment) Act 1982) states that where the Registrar of Companies has reasonable cause to believe that a company is not carrying on business, he may send a registered letter to the company inquiring whether the company is carrying on business. The letter should make it clear that if no response is received within one month, a notice will be published in *Iris Oifigiuil* with a view to striking the company off the register.

Where the company confirms that it is not carrying on business or the company fails to respond within one month of the date of the letter, the Registrar of Companies shall publish the notice stating that within one month of the date of the notice the name of the company will be struck off the register unless cause is shown to the contrary. The company is then struck off pursuant to section 311(5) and a notice published in *Iris Oifigiuil* to this effect.

22.9.4 Section 311(3) of the Companies Act 1963; delayed liquidations

Section 311(3) of the Companies Act 1963 (as amended by section 11 of the Companies (Amendment) Act 1982) provides that where the Registrar of Companies has reasonable cause to believe either that no liquidator is acting or that the affairs of the company have been fully wound up and that the liquidator has failed to make annual returns for a period of six consecutive months, a notice shall be sent to the company and published in *Iris Oifigiuil* stating that, unless contrary cause is shown, the name of the company shall be struck off the register within one month of the date of the notice. At the expiration of one month and where no contrary cause is shown, the company is struck off the register pursuant to section 311(5) and a notice published in *Iris Oifigiuil* to this effect.

22.9.5 Section 43(15) of the Companies (Amendment (No 2) Act 1999

Where the Registrar of Companies has reasonable cause to believe that the company does not have at least one director resident in Ireland (nor has it lodged a bond in lieu thereof), he may send a registered letter to the company requesting the company to provide evidence that it is compliant with these requirements. The letter should make it clear that if no response is received within one month, a notice will be published in *Iris Oifigiuil* with a view to striking the company off the register. If his request is not complied with, the Registrar may publish a notice in

Iris Oifigiuil stating that the company will be struck off the register within one month of the date of the notice.

22.9.6 Effect of a strike-off

When the company is struck off the register, the company ceases to exist and all the company property, save property held on trust by the company, will vest in the State.

It is expressly provided in section 311(6) of the Companies Act 1963 (a section 311 striking-off) and section 12B(1) of the Companies (Amendment) Act 1982 (a section 12/12A striking-off) that the directors, officers or members of the company can still be pursued, as their liability continues notwithstanding the dissolution.

The fact that a company is dissolved will not affect the right of the courts to wind up the company, but the company should first be reinstated to the register (section 311(7) of the Companies Act 1963 and section 12B(2) of the Companies (Amendment) Act 1982).

22.9.7 Restoration of the company to the register

(1) Restoration within twenty years

Where a company is struck off under section 311 of the Companies Act 1963, a company, member or creditor who is aggrieved by a striking-off may apply to the court under section 311(8) for the restoration of the company to the register. The application is on notice to the Registrar of Companies and the court will restore the company to the register where it is satisfied that the company is carrying on business or where it is just to do so.

Where the company is struck off under section 12 or section 12A of the Companies (Amendment) Act 1982, a member, officer, or creditor who is aggrieved by a striking-off may apply to the court under section 12B(3) of the Companies (Amendment) Act 1982 (as inserted by section 46 of the Companies (Amendment) (No. 2) Act 1999) for the restoration of the company to the register. The application is on notice to the Registrar of Companies, the Revenue Commissioners, and the Minister for Finance. The court will restore the company to the register where it is satisfied that it is just to do so. Where the application is presented by a member or officer of the company, the order of restoration will not have effect unless all outstanding returns/statements are delivered within one month of the court order. Where the applicant is a creditor of the company, the court will nominate a member or officer of the company to deliver these documents.

Section 12B(7) of the Companies (Amendment) Act 1982 (as inserted by section 46 of the Companies (Amendment) (No. 2) Act 1999) allows the Registrar of Companies to apply to the court for the restoration of the company struck off pursuant to sections 12 and 12A.

Re Deauville Communications Worldwide Ltd (2002) Keane C.J. stated that an application for the restoration of a company to the register under section 12B of the Companies (Amendment) Act 1982 could be brought either in the High Court or the Circuit Court. This decision also clarified that a contingent creditor has the right to bring an application for the restoration of the company to the register.

Each application must be made within twenty years of the date of the published notice that the company was struck off. In all of the above cases, the company will be deemed to have continued in existence and the court will attempt to place the company and all other persons in the same position as if the company had never been struck off. It is open to the court to order that an officer of the company is liable for the debts incurred by the company while it was struck off the register (Section 311(8A) of the Companies Act 1963 and section 12B(4) of the Companies (Amendment) Act 1982).

In the Australian case of *Casali v. Crisp* (2001) the Supreme Court held that the mere fact that a person is a shareholder or a director of a dissolved company is insufficient to establish that that person is an aggrieved person.

(2) Restoration within twelve months

Where a company has been struck off the register under section 12, 12A, or 311, it is open to the an aggrieved company to apply to the Registrar of Companies, within twelve months of the publication of the notice striking off the company, for the restoration of the company to the register. The application is made pursuant to section 311A of the Companies Act 1963.

The Registrar of Companies may exercise his discretion to restore the company to the register where all outstanding annual returns are delivered. The company will be deemed to have continued in existence as if it had not been struck off, and all rights and liabilities incurred during the dissolution period are deemed to be binding on the company.

Section 12C of the Companies (Amendment) Act 1982 extends this facility to aggrieved members or officers of the company where the company has been struck off the register for failing to file a statement (section 12A(3)). The company will only be restored where the Registrar of Companies has received confirmation from the Revenue Commissioners that the outstanding statement has been delivered.

22.9.8 Case law

The English case of *Tyman's Ltd v. Craven* (1952) confirmed that where a company is deemed to continue in existence, all acts done in the name or on behalf of the company during the period between its dissolution and restoration of its name to the register are retrospectively validated.

In the English case of *Re Blenheim Leisure (Restaurants) Ltd (No. 2)* (1999) Neuberger J. held that court has the jurisdiction to impose certain requirements as a condition of restoration and in this case required the company to make payments to certain parties who were owed money pursuant to specified agreements. However, in *Re Blue Note Enterprises Ltd* (2001) the court held that preconditions to restoration would only be imposed in exceptional circumstances.

In *Top Creative Ltd & anor v. St Albans District Council* (1999) the English Court of Appeal held that an action for damages commenced by a company prior to being struck off the register was revived when the company was restored to the register. Further, the court applied the case of *Tyman's Ltd v. Craven* (1952) and held that it would be incorrect to say that the company had no existence of any kind during the period of dissolution, as the fact that the company had standing to apply for restoration implied that it had an existence at least for that purpose.

In the English case of *Re Blue Note Enterprises Ltd* (2001) the court held that all an applicant had to do was to cross a relatively low threshold in terms of showing some interest in the company's restoration. In Ireland the courts may not be so accommodating.

In *Re Amantiss Enterprises Ltd* (2000) the company was dissolved in May 1993 for failing to file annual returns. The company was unaware that it was struck off and it was placed in voluntary liquidation in April 1994. In 1996 the company instituted proceedings against several companies for anti-competitive practices. One of the defendants discovered that the company had been struck off the register and made an application to strike out the company's claim.

The company petitioned the court to have its name restored to the register. The company claimed that an order restoring its name to the register automatically validated all acts done by it between its dissolution and its restoration to the register, in particular the institution of proceedings in 1996.

O'Neill J. granted the petition to restore the company and confirmed that the restoration validated the company's actions during the dissolution period. He held that the power of the court under section 12 of the Companies (Amendment) Act 1982 was to be used to prevent the company and all others from being affected by the company's removal from the register, as far as this is possible.

He stated that the purpose of section 12 was to preserve the validity of transactions entered into during a period of dissolution where frequently that dissolution is unknown to either the company, the company's officer, or third parties dealing with the company. Business is conducted on the basis that the company enjoys lawful existence. The removal of validity from such transactions would in many cases work injustices and provide the opportunity for mischief. O'Neill J. found that while the failure to file the annual returns indicated a high degree of carelessness and dereliction of duty, the defendants to the proceedings were not able to point to any specific prejudice that they had suffered as a result of the company being struck off the register. He was impressed by the fact that the Registrar of Companies had no objection to the application for restoration.

22.9.9 The CLRG recommendations

See Chapter 1.5.16 on the changes to the restoration procedure recommended by the CLRG in its First Report.

23. DISPOSITION OF COMPANY ASSETS

One primary role played by the liquidator in both a voluntary and an involuntary liquidation is the investigation of the affairs of the company before and after the commencement of the winding up in order to realise the true assets of the company.

This is because it is the duty of the liquidator to maximise the company assets available for distribution to the creditors, contributories, and members. Some liquidators discover questionable and at times unscrupulous company transactions such as the siphoning-off of some or all of the company's assets either before or after the commencement of the winding up or the payment of certain creditors in preference to others.

It is only when the assets of the company are fully realised that the liquidator can proceed to distribute the company property in accordance with sections 283-285 of the Companies Act 1963 discussed below.

23.1 Realisation of company assets

23.1.1 Disclaimer of property under section 290 of the Companies Act 1963

It may be the case that in order to effect an efficient winding up and maximise the value of the company assets, it is necessary for the liquidator to rid the company of burdensome property or contracts.

Within twelve months of the commencement of the winding up, the liquidator may, in writing and with the approval of the court, disclaim the following property:

1. land of any tenure burdened with onerous covenants;
2. shares or stock in companies;
3. unprofitable contracts;
4. property that is unsaleable or not readily saleable because the possessor is bound to an onerous act or the payment of a sum of money.

If, within one month of the commencement of the liquidation, the liquidator was not aware that the company owned any of the aforesaid property, the liquidator has twelve months from the date of becoming aware of the property to exercise a disclaimer. (For the definition of commencement in a voluntary and involuntary winding up, see paragraphs 21.1.1 and 22.3.1.)

It is open to a creditor or any person interested in such property or contracts to apply to the liquidator in writing during the twelve months and request whether or not the liquidator intends to disclaim. The liquidator must respond within twenty-eight days unless the court allows a longer period.

Pursuant to section 290(3) of the Companies Act 1963 the disclaimer shall not have the effect of releasing the company from a liability owed by the company to any person in respect of that property. Further, the rights and liabilities of third parties also remain unaffected. In *Tempany v. Royal Liver Co.* (1984) the right of a landlord to recover rent from a guarantor in respect of a disclaimed lease was not affected by the disclaimer.

Pursuant to section 290(6) the court may order the payment by the company of damages for non-performance of any contract rescinded under section 290. The damages are payable to a person who was entitled to the benefit or subject to a burden of the contract made with the company.

Pursuant to section 290(9) any person damaged by a disclaimer under this section shall be deemed to be a creditor of the company to the amount of the damages and may prove that debt in the winding up.

Where the liquidator takes possession or remains in possession of property that is later disclaimed, the court will hold that the money owed by the company as a result of that possession is a "debt contracted for the purpose of the winding up and should be paid in full like any other debt or expense properly incurred by the liquidator for that purpose" according to Murphy J. in *Re GWI Ltd* (1988). In that case the liquidator sub-let leasehold property that was later disclaimed. The court held that rent was payable to the landlord by the company for the period of the sub-letting, and the court calculated the rent as the amount the company had received from the sub-tenant.

23.1.2 Invalid dispositions under section 218 of the Companies Act 1963

Section 218 of the Companies Act 1963 applies only in the case of an involuntary winding up by the court. As discussed at Chapter 22, there is a gap between the presentation and advertisement of the petition, and the hearing of the petition by the court. Further, it was noted that it was open to the court to adjourn the hearing of the petition to a later date. In the absence of an interim order putting in place a provisional liquidator, the company assets may be vulnerable to dissipation or removal by those involved with the company.

Section 218 of the Companies Act 1963 is designed to minimise the danger to the company assets and sets out that any disposition of the company property, including things in action, and any transfer of shares or alteration in the status of the members of the company, made after the commencement of the winding up, shall, unless the court otherwise orders, be void.

In *Re Industrial Services Company (Dublin) Ltd* (2001) Kearns J. stated that the objective of section 218 was to preserve the net value as of the date of the petition for the benefit of the general body of creditors.

(1) The operative date

The operative date for the application of section 218 is the date of the commencement of the winding up, *i.e.* the date of the presentation of the petition. In *Re PMPA Coaches Ltd* (1993) Murphy J. stated that "the debts and liabilities of a company in liquidation are ascertained as of the date of the presentation of the petition" and are distributed amongst the creditors "as of the operative date subject only to the particular preferences and priorities created by the legislation".

All dispositions after the "operative date" are void save where sanctioned by the court.

(2) The disposition

The section can be sweeping in its effect as it invalidates "any disposition of company property".

In *Re Ashmark Ltd (No. 2)* (1990) Blaney J. held that where a cheque was written before the operative date, and was paid from the company's account after the operative date, this constituted a disposition under section 218. In *Re Ashmark Ltd; Ashmark Ltd v. Allied Irish Banks plc*

(1994) the court also considered whether the charging of interest by the company's bank on a company bank account constituted a disposition for the purpose of section 218. Lardner J. held that this payment of interest was not a disposition as the account was in credit at the time the interest was charged. He stated that the credit balance on the overdraft account never actually belonged to the company because of the overall debit situation of the company with the bank.

Recently the courts have examined payments into and out of a company's bank account after the operative date. In the English case of *Re Gray's Inn Construction Co Ltd* (1980) it was held that any payment out of the company's bank account constituted a disposition, including any payment into an overdrawn account as, according to Buckley L.J., the company "discharges its indebtedness to the bank *pro tanto*".

The English case of *Hollicourt (Contracts) Ltd v. Bank of Ireland* (2001) concerned post-operative date payments out of a company's bank account and the restitution of the payments to the company. This case concerned section 127 of the English Insolvency Act 1986, which is the equivalent of section 218. Here the bank allowed a company, in respect of which a petition to wind up that company had been presented, to continue to operate a current account. Blackburne J. in the High Court held that the payments out of the account constituted dispositions under section 127 of the Insolvency Act 1986 and that the bank was liable to make restitution to the company.

The bank successfully appealed to the Court of Appeal. The Court of Appeal held that section 127 only invalidated dispositions of company property to payees of cheques and the liquidator was only entitled to recover the money from these payees. Mummary L.J. noted that in the recent case of *Coutts & Co. v. Stock* (2000) Lightman J. had held that the bank was not, in similar circumstances, liable.

Mummery L.J. stated that it was possible to fulfil the statutory purpose of preserving the assets of the company from spoliation without any need for the section to encroach upon the legal validity of intermediate steps, such as banking transactions, which merely facilitated the process whereby dispositions were made. The bank, in operating the company's account, was the agent of the company. Mummery L.J. referred to the judgment of Street C.J. in *Re Mal Bower's Macquarie Electrical Centre Pty Ltd* (1974) where Street C.J. said that "the intermediary functions fulfilled by the bank in respect of paying cheques drawn by a company in favour of and presented on behalf of a third party do not implicate the bank in the consequences of the statutory avoidance".

The court held that the effect of section 127 was aimed at the end result of that process called "the point of ultimate receipt" of the company's property. In examining the dispositions affected by section 127, the Court of Appeal looked at the "point of ultimate receipt" rather than the intermediate steps carried out by the bank in determining who should be liable to make restitution to the company. The "point of ultimate receipt" was the payees. Section 127 was not intended to impose restitutionary liability on a bank in respect of payments made by cheque in favour of creditors in addition to the liability of the payees.

In *Re Industrial Services Company (Dublin) Ltd* (2001) Kearns J. considered payments both into and out of a company's account after the presentation of the petition when the account was in credit. The liquidator sought a declaration that the payments were void under section 218. Kearns J. noted the judgment of *Hollicourt* where the court held that such payments were not "dispositions" as against the bank. He noted, however, that such payments were considered void "dispositions" by Costello J. in *Re Pat Ruth Ltd* (1981) where the bank had made payments to the company creditors (Costello J. based his decision on the Court of Appeal decision in *Re Gray's Inn Construction Company Ltd* (1980)). Kearns J. was not convinced that the reasoning of the Court of Appeal in *Hollicourt* was preferable to that in *Gray's Inn Construction Company Ltd* and he did not see that some "commercial interpretation advantageous to the bank" must be given to section 218. Kearns J. agreed that a bank acts as the company agent but the "true relationship" was of borrower and lender so that the bank could be both agent, creditor, and debtor. He held that section 218 invalidates the transaction both as regards third parties and the bank processing the particular account.

(3) Validation of the disposition

The case law establishes that a void disposition may be validated where the following applies:

1. it was made bona fide and in the ordinary course of business;
2. the recipient was unaware that the company was being wound up;
3. the disposition was to the benefit of the company or at least in the interests of the unsecured creditors.

Buckley J. stated in *Re Gray's Inn Construction Company Ltd* (1980) that a disposition "carried out in good faith in the ordinary course of business at a time when the parties are unaware that a petition has been presented may, it seems, normally be validated by the court". Cairns L.J. stated in *Re Wiltshire Iron Co* (1868) that if bona fide transactions in the ordinary course of its current trade were not to be validated by the court, "the result would be that the presentation of a petition, groundless or well-founded, would *ipso facto*, paralyse the trade of the company, and great injury, without any counter-balance of advantage, would be done to those interested in the assets of the company".

In *Ashmark Ltd (No. 1)* (1990) a payment made to a company solicitor after the operative date was void under section 218. The company sought the validation of the court on the grounds that the solicitor was unaware that the disposition was made after the wind-up, and the payments were made in the best interests of the company and were beneficial to the creditors. O'Hanlon J. accepted that these were grounds upon which a disposition could be justified, but declined to do so as the solicitor was aware of the petition under the doctrine of constructive notice. He could not validate a payment for services rendered prior to the winding up when "similar treatment could not be accorded to the general body of unsecured creditors".

In *Re McBirney and Co. Ltd* (1992) Murphy J. accepted the court may validate a disposition where it could be shown that it was to the benefit of the company or "at least desirable in the interests of the unsecured creditors as a body". In this case the court validated payments made by a receiver-manager appointed under the Insurance (No. 2) Act 1983, as innocent third parties believed that the receiver-manager was acting with the authority of the court. The payments made to employees were validated, as the payments did not prejudice unsecured creditors given that the employees already had preferential status.

In *Re Al Levy (Holdings) Ltd* (1963) the company sold a leasehold asset after the presentation of the petition to wind up the company. The lease was sold, as it was liable to be forfeited when the company was wound up. To obtain the landlord's consent to the sale, the company had to discharge arrears of rent. Both dispositions were validated by the court, as they were of benefit to the creditors given that the company received the proceeds for the sale of property which had been forfeited on the winding up.

23.1.3 Fraudulent preferences under section 286 of the Companies Act 1963

It may be the case that a voluntary or an official liquidator discovers a transaction relating to the company property in favour of one or more creditors and at the expense of others shortly before a company was liquidated.

It is open to the liquidator to apply to the court pursuant to section 286 of the Companies Act 1963 (as amended by section 135 of the Companies Act 1990) for an order declaring the transaction void as a fraudulent preference and seeking the restitution (return) of the company property.

The ambit of the section is very wide capturing any "conveyance, mortgage, delivery of goods, payment, execution or other act relating to property".

The burden is on the liquidator to prove the following:

1. the company was insolvent at the time of the winding up; and
2. the company was insolvent at the time of the transaction; and
3. the transaction occurred within six months of the winding up of the company; and
4. the transaction was in favour of a creditor (see *Parkes & Sons Ltd v. Hong Kong and Shanghai Banking Corp.* (1990)); and
5. the transaction constituted a preference of the creditor; and
6. at the time of the transaction, the company intended to prefer the creditor.

Where a fraudulent preference is established, the transaction is *void ab initio*. This does not affect the rights of a bona fide purchaser for valuable consideration who buys the company property from the preferenced creditor (section 286(4) of the Companies Act 1963). If that purchaser has any notice of the fraudulent preference, then he is no longer protected.

The section is for the benefit of all the company creditors and it cannot be invoked according to section 286(2) where to do so would only benefit a section of the creditors.

(1) Time frame

Section 286(1) requires that the alleged preference must have occurred within the six months preceding the liquidation. The burden of proving this is squarely on the liquidator. Section 135 of the Companies Act 1990 extends the time limit to two years in the case of a connected person who is defined in section 286(5) as:

1. a director or shadow director of the company;
2. a director's spouse, parent sibling or child;
3. a related company as defined in section 140(5) of the Companies Act 1990 (see paragraph 23.1.6 below); and
4. any trustee of, or surety or guarantor for a debt due to any of the above.

Section 286(3) creates a presumption that a transaction in favour of a connected person was made with a view to giving that person a preference over other creditors and is a fraudulent preference. The burden shifts to the connected person to prove that this is not the case.

(2) Proof of intention to prefer

The liquidator must be able to prove that the company had the intention to prefer the creditor at the time the transaction was made.

That intention must arise from the free volition of the company, which does not exist if the transaction results from creditor pressure. In *Re Daly & Co.* (1887-8) Porter M.R. stated:

> "Where pressure exists so as to overbear the volition of the debtor a payment is not made with a view to prefer the creditor exerting it, but because the debtor cannot help it. The view to prefer is absent; or at least is not the real view, or motive or reason actuating the debtor."

In *Assignees of Taylor* (1869-70) the fear of losing clients was held sufficient pressure. *In Parkes & Sons Ltd v. Hong Kong and Shanghai Banking Corp.* (1990) a company controller caused the company to give a guarantee and mortgage in respect of a third company. The controller was threatened by the bank with the imposition of a receiver and, as such, was held by Blayney J. to have had no option, as his dominant concern was to save the company. He further found that while the effect of the mortgage was to reduce his liability under his personal guarantees, this was not the dominant motive.

In *Corran Construction Company v. Bank of Ireland Finance Ltd* (1976-7) an equitable deposit of title deeds was made by the plaintiff, and the defendant omitted to register the charge. The bank realised this and made the company give a fresh deposit, which was registered; however, the company was wound-up within six months of this deposit. The liquidator sought to have this set aside as a fraudulent preference. McWilliam J. refused to find a fraudulent preference on the grounds that there was no intention to prefer. The member-director who ran the company had been overborne by the pressure that the defendant had put on him to rectify their defective charge.

The court can draw an inference of an intention to prefer from the circumstances of the case where there is no direct evidence of such an intention, according to Carroll J, in *Re Station Motors Ltd* (1985). In that case the controllers of the company had personal guarantees over the company bank account. Before placing the company into voluntary liquidation, they reduced the company's overdraft and therefore their personal liability.

Carroll J. found these to be fraudulent preferences on the basis that they had the direct effect of preferring the bank and the indirect effect of preferring the controllers. The intention to prefer must be the dominant motive behind the transaction.

Carroll J. based this decision on three important factors:

1. the personal liability of the controllers was significantly reduced;
2. the dispositions were made after the resolution to wind up; therefore, they were fully aware of the state of the company finances;
3. only cheques presented to the bank to pay off the overdraft were honoured.

According to *Re Kushler (M) Ltd* (1943) the liquidator will have failed to discharge the onus proving an intention to prefer if the circumstances of the case are equally consistent with guilt or innocence.

23.1.4 Fraudulent dispositions under section 139 of the Companies Act 1990

Section 139 of the Companies Act 1990 facilitates recovery of company property which has been disposed of in any way that defrauded the company, its creditors, or its members. The disposition can be by way of "conveyance, transfer, mortgage, security, loan, or in any way whatsoever whether by actor omission, direct or indirect".

The court may, if it is just and equitable, order the person who appears to have the use, control, or possession of such property (or the proceeds of the sale or development thereof) to deliver the property or pay an equivalent sum to the liquidator. According to section 139(3) the court will have regard to any rights of bona fide purchasers for value and without notice of the fraud.

An action can be brought by a creditor, contributory, or by the liquidator of the company, and proof of a fraudulent effect on the company, members, or creditors is essential. The section does not apply to transactions covered by section 286 of the Companies Act 1963, and section 139 is commonly used to recover company property or money transferred to persons other than creditors.

23.1.5 Invalidation of floating charges under section 288 of the Companies Act 1963

Section 288 renders any floating charge created within twelve months before a company is wound up, invalid, unless "it is proved that the company immediately after the creation of the charge was solvent".

In the case of a of a connected person, as defined at paragraph 23.1.3(1), the time limit has been extended from twelve months to two years.

The charge will, however, be saved where money was actually advanced or paid, or goods or services were sold or supplied to the company, at the time of or subsequent to the creation of the charge and, most importantly, in consideration of the charge.

In *Re Daniel Murphy Ltd* (1964) it was held that a delay of 35 days between the taking of the charge and the advancement of the money was not unreasonable, provided that there was no delay in the execution of the charge and there was no intention to deceive the creditors. In *Smurfit Paribas Bank Ltd v. AAB Export Finance Ltd (No. 2)* (1991) Barron J. held that a delay of two years in the execution of the charge could not be justified, and the floating charge was invalidated.

The onus is on the floating charge-holder to prove that the company was solvent at the time of the creation or that money or goods were advanced at the time of the creation.

If the floating charge crystallises before winding up commences, it cannot be invalidated under section 288 on a winding up. Such a charge may still be attacked as a fraudulent preference by the liquidator under section 286 of the Companies Act 1963.

The charge may be invalidated under section 288 but the debt itself is not. The creditor ranks as an unsecured creditor.

23.1.6 Pooling and contribution orders under sections 140 and 141 of the Companies Act 1990

Pursuant to section 140 of the Companies Act 1990, the liquidator may apply to the court for an order directing a related company to contribute to the assets of the company that is under liquidation. The court must be of the opinion that it is just and equitable to make such an order and it will take into account the following:

1. the extent to which the related company took part in the management of the company in liquidation;
2. the conduct of the related company towards the creditors of the company that is in liquidation; and
3. the effect that the order is likely to have on the creditors of the related company.

The court will not make the order unless it is satisfied that the circumstances that gave rise to the winding up of the company are attributable to the actions or omissions of the related company.

A related company is defined in Section 140(5) of the Companies Act 1990 and a company (hereinafter "A") is related to another company (hereinafter "B") if one of the following situations applies:

1. company B is A's holding company or A's subsidiary company;
2. more than half of the equity share capital of A is held by B or companies related to B;
3. more than half the equity share capital of A is held by members of B;
4. company B or companies related to B are entitled to exercise or control the exercise of more than one half of the voting power at any general meeting of A;
5. the business of both companies has been carried on so that the separate business of each company, or a substantial part thereof, is not readily identifiable;
6. there is another body corporate to which both A and B are related.

Where two or more related companies are in liquidation, the liquidator may apply to the court pursuant to section 141 of the Companies Act 1990 for an order directing that the assets of the companies be pooled between the creditors of both companies. The court will only make this order where it is just and equitable to do so and from the date of the order the companies shall be wound up as one company. The court will have particular regard to the interests of the members of the companies, and the rights of the secured creditors of either company shall not be affected. The unsecured debts of the companies rank equally among themselves. The court will take into account the following:

1. the extent to which any of the companies took part in the management of any of the other companies;
2. the conduct of any of the companies towards the creditors of any of the other companies;
3. the effect which the order is likely to have on the creditors of the related company;
4. the extent to which the circumstances that gave rise to the winding up of any of the companies are attributable to the actions or omissions of any of the other companies; and
5. the extent to which the businesses of the companies have been intermingled.

23.1.7 Misfeasance proceedings under section 298 of the Companies Act 1963

Section 298 of the Companies Act 1963 (as substituted by section 142 of the Companies Act 1990) may be used to recover money from promoters, directors, managers or other officers of the company which they have misapplied or wrongfully received or for which they are accountable to the company.

23.1.8 Personal liability for company debts

The liquidator may apply to the court for an order directing that a director, officer, or any other person is personally liable to contribute to the assets of the company that is in liquidation.

Such an application may be made on the following grounds:

1. breach of fiduciary obligations by directors (see Chapter 7);
2. breach of the duty of due care, skill and competence by the directors (see Chapter 7);
3. breach of the duty to maintain proper books of accounts under section 202 of the Companies Act 1963 (see Chapter 5);
4. breach of the duty to take care when making a declaration of solvency in connection with the giving of financial assistance for the purchase of the company shares under section 60(5) of the Companies Act 1963 (see Chapter 5);
5. breach of the duty to take care when making a declaration of solvency in connection with a member's voluntary liquidation under section 256(8) of the Companies Act 1963 (see Chapter 5);
6. fraudulent and/or reckless trading under sections 297 and 297A of the Companies Act 1963 (see Chapter 10).

23.2 Distribution of company assets

Once the assets of the company are fully realized, it is the function of the liquidator to distribute those assets in accordance with the provisions of the Companies Acts. In the case of an insolvent company, the rules governing the distribution of the assets are based on the law of bankruptcy according to section 284(1) of the Companies Act 1963. Bankruptcy rules are applicable to the following:

1. the rights of secured and unsecured creditors;
2. the proving of debts; and
3. the valuation of annuities and future and contingent liabilities.

23.2.1 Proving debts

The liquidator must ascertain the identity of the company creditors together with the nature and the extent of their debts. The Companies Acts and the Rules of the Superior Courts 1986 establish a procedure for the creditors to come to the liquidator and prove their claims. Section 283(1) of the Companies Act 1963 sets out that the following claims can be proved against a company in liquidation:

1. all debts payable on a contingency; and

2. all claims against the company, present or future, certain or contingent, whether ascertained or sounding only in damages.

According to section 283(2) of the Companies Act 1963, an unclaimed dividend which was declared in the six years preceding the winding up cannot be proved against the company save where the articles of association or the conditions of the declaration provide otherwise.

The liquidator must reject claims that are barred under the Statute of Limitations Act 1957 where the period of limitation expired before the commencement of the liquidation.

Section 214 of the Companies Act 1963 permits the court to fix a time or times for the creditors of the company to send particulars of their claims or face exclusion from any distribution. The Rules of the Superior Courts 1986 require the liquidator to advertise such times and the date that has been allocated for the adjudication of the claims. It falls on the liquidator to investigate the claims and notify the court Examiner (a Court Registrar or the Master of the High Court) of the claims, identifying those claims which appear valid and those which require further proof. The Examiner then adjudicates the claims and may, if necessary, request further proof. The liquidator then notifies the creditors whose claims have been allowed and those who must present further proof of their claims. The final adjudication must be certified by the court Examiner.

As noted in paragraph 23.2.2(5) a secured creditor has the option of not proving his debt in a winding up and simply relies on the security for the payment of the debt.

23.2.2 Matters settled before distribution

(1) Retention of title contracts

Retention of title contracts is discussed at Chapter 16. A contract with the company may contain a valid retention of title clause in respect of goods or the proceeds of the sale of goods. Such goods or proceeds do not form part of the company assets on the winding up, and the liquidator must honour the contract and return the goods/proceeds.

(2) Trust property and property subject to the equities

Property held on trust by the company for any persons must be returned by the liquidator. The beneficial owner of the property is entitled to the return of the property.

Property which is "subject to the equities" is property that is covered by a contractual obligation at the time of the winding up and the claimant is not seeking to prove a debt but to enforce his contractual rights.

(3) Set-off

One of the laws of bankruptcy that is applicable to a liquidation is the right of set-off between a company and a creditor where there are mutual debts between the company and the creditor. The creditor can opt to set off these debts against each other rather than proceed to prove his debt in a liquidation.

The debts must be "mutual", *i.e.* the debts must be between the parties and in the same right. In *McKinnon v. Armstrong* (1877) a trustee could not set off a debt owed to him personally against a debt owed to him in his capacity as trustee. Further, the debts must be "mutual" at the date of the resolution or the court order to wind up the company.

A creditor can also exercise a contractual right of set-off, *i.e.* where the contract with the company contains a set-off clause. According to *Dempsey v. Bank of Ireland* (1985) the liquidator remains bound by this clause when the company is wound up.

The option of set-off is not available to a secured creditor unless the secured creditor surrenders its security and opts to prove the debt in the liquidation.

(4) Costs of proving debts

The costs of proving a claim are borne by the creditor unless a liquidator requires a creditor to attend and prove a claim further. Where a creditor litigates during the liquidation to prove his debt, that creditor is entitled to receive his costs pursuant to Order 74 of the Rules of the Superior Courts 1986.

(5) Creditors by a fixed charge

Secured (fixed) creditors, who hold a mortgage, charge or a lien on the company property, are entitled to remain outside the winding up and rely on their security according to section 136(2) of the Bankruptcy Act 1988.

In any insolvent liquidation a secured creditor has three further options:

1. realise the security and, if it is insufficient, prove for any deficiency; or
2. value the security and prove for the deficiency; the liquidator has the option to accept the valuation; or
3. surrender the security and prove for the entire debt in the manner set out at paragraph 23.2.1.

In the majority of cases the secured creditor opts to remain outside the winding up and realise the security. Where there is a surplus on realisation, it must be paid to the liquidator.

Where the fixed charge is in the nature of a fixed charge over book debts, as discussed in Chapter 16, the fixed charge-holder will not enjoy preference over the Revenue Commissioners where the Revenue Commissioners serve notice of their debt on the secured creditor. This is as a result of section 115 of Finance Act 1986, as amended by section 174 of the Finance Act 1995 and now section 1001 of the Taxes Consolidation Act 1997, which allows the Revenue Commissioners to gain priority over certain fixed charge-holders.

(6) Execution creditors

An execution creditor is a creditor who obtained a court judgment against the company prior to the commencement of the winding up. Any such creditor who took no active steps to enforce his judgment/security prior to the commencement of the winding up is not entitled to be paid in priority to the secured creditor (see *Re Leinster Contract Corp* (1902).

(7) Costs and expense of the liquidator

The liquidator gets paid his costs and expenses before other debts in a voluntary winding up. Section 281 of the Companies Act 1963 states that in a voluntary liquidation the liquidator is entitled to be paid "costs, charges and expenses properly incurred in a winding up, including remuneration" in priority to all other claims.

The same rule applies in a court winding up but the costs and expenses must be approved by the court Examiner. Under section 244 of the Companies Act 1963, where the assets are insufficient to satisfy liabilities, the court may make an order for payment of such costs in such priority as the court thinks fit.

It must be noted that where a secured creditor opts to remain outside the winding up and relies on his security, his debt will be discharged in priority to a liquidator's fees, costs and expenses.

In the English case of *Lewis v. Inland Revenue Commissioners et al* (2000) the court of appeal held that a liquidator does not have the automatic right to recoup the costs of litigation, including any costs that he may be ordered to pay out of the assets of the company as an expense of litigation.

It may be the case that the company in liquidation was in examinership and under court protection prior to the winding up. For a number of years it was uncertain whether the costs and expenses of the liquidator would be paid in priority to those of the examiner. In Chapter 20, it was discussed that, pursuant to section 29(3B) of the Companies (Amendment) Act 1990 (as inserted by section 28 of the Companies (Amendment (No 2) Act 1999), the costs, remuneration and expenses of an examiner will be paid in priority to the costs, remuneration and expenses of a liquidator in the event that the company under court protection is later wound up.

23.2.3 Priority in distribution

When the assets of the company have been realised, as discussed in paragraph 23.1, the creditors' claims have been certified by the Examiner as detailed in paragraph 23.2.1 and the matters set out at paragraph 23.2.2 have been settled, the liquidator must proceed to distribute the assets among the general creditors. The order of priority is set out in the Companies Acts.

(1) Preferential creditors

Preferential creditors are paid first, and, according to section 285(7)(b) of the Companies Act 1963, they should be paid in priority to floating charge-holders.

Section 285(2) sets out the following as preferential debts in a winding up:

1. local rates due and payable within twelve months of the commencement date;

2. all assessed taxes not exceeding one year's assessment;

3. all wages and salaries of an employee of the company for services rendered to the company within four months prior to commencement of the winding up;
4. all accrued holiday pay due to an employee/ workman/labourer of the company;
5. social welfare contributions;
6. compensation and damages for uninsured accidents to employees;
7. sickness and superannuation payments;
8. claims for unfair dismissal;
9. claims for minimum notice payments; and
10. redundancy payments to employees.

These claims must be notified to the liquidator within six months of the advertisement for claims. The claims rank *pari passu*, and where the assets of the company are insufficient to pay all of the above in full, the claims abate in equal proportions.

(2) Floating charges

Floating charge-holders are secured creditors but they are not afforded the same protection as secured fixed charge-holders in a liquidation. The floating charge crystallises on the winding up and the debt is discharged only after the payment of the preferential creditors. If the assets of the company are insufficient to satisfy all the floating charge-holders, the priority of payment will be based on the date of the creation of the charge.

Where the floating charge has crystallised prior to the commencement of the winding up, the charge-holder belongs to the category of secured fixed charge-holders noted at paragraph 23.2.2(5).

(3) Unsecured creditors

Unsecured creditors are paid next in line. Where the assets of the company are insufficient to satisfy all their claims, they will rank *pari passu* amongst themselves.

(4) Members and contributories

Section 275 of the Companies Act 1963 states that any surplus assets remaining after the distribution to creditors shall be available for contributories (past and present members) of the company. They are called "deferred creditors" who are owed declared dividends and capital and who are paid only after all the creditors' debts have been discharged.

Contributories will first receive the amount (capital) paid up on their shares. Contributories who are owed declared but unpaid dividends are not deemed to be creditors of the company, but the sum will be taken into account when distributing the surplus. Any remaining amount is distributed in proportion to the nominal amount of the share capital held by each contributory.

In a court winding up, the court will fix a list of contributories and state how the assets are to be applied (see section 235 of the Companies Act 1963). In a voluntary winding up it is the duty of the liquidator to fix the rights of the contributories (see section 276 of the Companies Act 1963).

Under section 275 of the Companies Act 1963 every member shall, unless the articles provide otherwise, receive the surplus assets according to his rights and interests in the company. The articles and memorandum of association together with any shareholder agreements will have to be examined in order to determine those rights and interests.

INDEX

(*references are to paragraph numbers*)

Accounts, 9.1 *et seq*, *see also* **auditors**
- annual, *see* **annual accounts**
- audited, 1.2.5, *see also* **Auditors**
- books of, 9.1.1
- disclosure requirements, 1.2.3

Annual accounts, 1.3.1, 9.1.2
- audit of, 1.3.1, *see also* **Auditors**

Annual general meeting (AGM), 13.3.1, *see also* **Meetings**

Annual report, 1.3.1

Annual returns, 9.2.9 *et seq*
- contents of, 9.2.1
- date, 9.2.2
- late filing fee, 9.2.3

Articles of association, 4.2 *et seq*, *see also* **Memorandum of association**
- alteration, 4.2.2
- informal alteration, 4.2.3
- model, 4.2.1
- public documents as, 4.4
- section 25 contract, 4.3

Auditors, 9.2 *et seq*
- appointment of, 9.2.1
- competence of, 1.3.1
- education standards of, 1.3.1
- exemption to obligation to appoint, 9.2.8
- liability of, 9.2.7
- qualifications of, 9.2.4a
- removal, 9.2.3
- remuneration, 9.2.2

Auditors — *contd.*
- report of, 9.2.6
- resignation of, 9.2.4
- retirement of, 9.2.4
- rights of, 9.2.5

Borrowing, 16.1 *et seq*, *see also* **Charges**
- debentures, 16.2 *et seq*, *see* **Debentures**
- retention of title charges, 16.6
  - aggregated, 16.6.2
  - charges, 16.6.1
  - proceeds of sale, 16.6.3
- security for loan capital, 16.1

Capital, Maintenance of, 15.1 *et seq*, *see also* **Borrowing** and **Shares**
- Acquisition by company of own shares, 15.2 *et seq*
  - assisting purchase, 15.3 *et seq*
  - disclosure of purchase, 15.2.3
  - exceptions to prohibition, 15.2.1
  - permitted purchases, 15.2.2
- reduction of capital, 15.4 *et seq*
  - court ordered, 15.4.2
  - court sanctioned, 15.4.1
  - forfeiture of shares, 15.4.3
- redemption of shares, 15.1
  - cancellation, 15.1.2
  - conditions attached to redeemable shares, 15.1.1
  - conversion, 15.1.4

Capital, Maintenance of— *contd.*
redemption of shares — *contd.*
old redeemable preference shares, 15.1.5
treasury shares, 15.1.3, *see also* **shares**
serious capital loss, 15.5

Charges, 17.1 *et seq, see also* **Borrowing**
compliance, 17.3 *et seq*
non-compliance, 17.6
responsibility for, 17.3
timeframe for, 17.4
errors in registration, 17.5
late registration, 17.7
particulars of charge, 17.1
registration certificate, 17.5
registrable charges, 17.2 *et seq*
aircraft, 17.2.9
bills of sale, 17.2.4
calls made but unpaid, 17.2.8
company book debts on, 17.2.6, *see also* **Fixed charges**
created by company, 17.2.1
floating charges, 17.2.7, *see also* **Floating charges**
goodwill, 17.2.10
land charge, 17.2.5
minister, 17.2.11
patent, 17.2.10
purchased property, 71.2.12
securing debentures, 17.2.2, *see also* **Debentures**
ship, 17.2.9
trademark, 17.2.10
unshared capital, 17.2.3

Companies,
accounts, *see* **Accounts**
advantages of, 1.1
amending acts, 1.2.2 *et seq*
assets, disposition of, *see* **Disposition of assets**
character of, 5.5, *see also* **Corporate personalty**
conversion of, 2.3 *et seq*
corporate personality, 5.1 *et seq*, *see* **Corporate personality**
EU developments, 1.3 *et seq*
formation, 2.1 *et seq*, *see also* **Limited** and **Unlimited companies**
generally, 1.1
incorporation of , *see* **Incorporation**
legislation, 1.2.1 *et seq*
limited liability shield of, 1.1
membership of, *see* **Membership of a company**
plc, 1.2.1, 1.3.1
principal act, 1.2.1
strike off, effect of, 1.5.16

Company law enforcement, 1.2.7

Company Law Review Group, (CLRG) 1.2.7, 1.5 *et seq*, 22.9.9
composition of, 1.5.2
corporate governance, simplification of, 1.5.8
directors' meetings, 1.5.8, *see also* **Directors**
inspections, 1.5.8
meetings of members, 1.5.8
number of company members, 1.5.8
registers, 1.5.8

Company Law Review Group — *contd.*
creditor protection, 1.5.9
serious capital loss, 1.5.9
validation procedure for prohibited acts, 1.5.9
criminal acts, 1.5.11
criminal omissions, 1.5.11
directors duties, *see* directors
electronic transactions, 1.5.7
first report of, 1.5.4 *et seq*, 1.5.17
functions of, 1.5.1
insolvency and, 1.5.15, *see also* **Insolvency**
practice and procedure, 1.5.14
private company limited by shares, 1.5.5, 1.5.10, *see also* **Private limited companies**
reporting obligations of, 1.5.3
second work programme, 1.5.17
single companies act, 1.5.6
strike off, 1.5.16
ultra vires doctrine, *see* ***Ultra vires***

Company secretary, 1.5.13, 4.1.3, 5.3.5, 6.2, 6.3.2, 12.6.1

Contracts, 6.1 *et seq*, *see also* **Corporate personality** and **Receivership**
article 6(2) transactions, 6.1.2
breach of objects of company, 6.1
express ancillary powers of company, in breach of, 6.2
internal company rules, in breach of, 6.4
Turquand's case, rule in, 6.4.1 *et seq*

Contracts — *contd.*
section 8 contracts, 6.1.1
ultra vires, abolition of, *see* ***Ultra vires***
without company authority, 6.3
actual authority, 6.3.1
implied authority, 6.3.2
ostensible, 6.3.3
ratification of contract, 6.3.4

Corporate personality, 5.1 *et seq*, *see also* **Contracts**
concept of, 5.1 *et seq*
corporate veil,
effect of, 5.2
lifting of corporate veil by courts, 5.4 *et seq*
avoidance of legal duty, 5.4.1
implied agency, 5.4.2
single economic entity, 5.4.4
trusteeship, 5.4.3
lifting of corporate veil by statute, 5.3 *et seq*
capital requirements, 5.3.7
company name irregularities, personal liability for, 5.3.5
contribution upon winding up, 5.3.9
disqualification orders, breach of, 5.3.4
fraudulent trading, personal liability for, 5.3.3
numbers of members, personal liability for, 5.3.1
pooling orders upon winding up, 5.3.9
proper records, failure to keep, 5.3.6
reckless trading, personal liability for, 5.3.2

Corporate personality — *contd.*
lifting of corporate veil by statute — *contd.*
related examinerships, 5.3.10
restriction orders, breach of, 5.3.4
taxation, 5.3.11
unreasonable declaration of insolvency, 5.3.8

Debentures, 16.2 *et seq*, *see also* **Borrowing** and **Charges**
debenture stock, 16.2.2
fixed charge, 16.3, *see* **Fixed charges**
floating charges, 16.4 *et seq*, *see* **Floating charges**
holder, 16.2, 16.2.5
procedure, 16.2.3
rank pari passu, 16.2.1
remedies for debenture holder, 16.2.5
series of, 16.2.1
transfer of, 16.2.4

Directors, 7.1 *et seq*, *see also* **Officers**
appointment, 7.1.1
definition, 7
directorships, number of, 7.1.3
disqualification of, 7.1.5, 8.2 *et seq*
automatic, 8.2.1
breach of order for, 8.2.5
conduct resulting in, 8.2.6
court applicants, 8.2.4
court grounds for, 8.2.3
court-ordered, 8.2.2
duties, 1.5.13, 7.8 *et seq*
avoidance of conflicts on interest with company, 7.8.3

Directors — *contd.*
duties — *contd.*
beneficiaries of, 7.8.4
care, 7.8.2
creditors, 7.8.4
diligence of, 7.8.2
employees, 7.8.4
exercise powers bona fide, 7.8.1
interest of company in, 7.8.1
proper skill, 7.8.2
shareholders, 7.8.4
examinership and, 20.5.4, *see also* **Examinership**
interests, disclosure of, 7.4 *et seq*
contracts in, 7.4.1
debentures, 7.4.2
directorships, 7.4.3
payments, 7.4.4
shares, 7.4.2
loans by company to, 1.2.3
meetings of, 1.5.8, 7.3
misfeasance by, 7.8.6
powers of, 7.7
prohibited transactions by, 7.6 *et seq*
credit transactions, 7.6.2
loans, 7.6.2
quasi-loans, 7.6.2
share options, 7.6.1
property transactions (substantial) by, 7.5
register of, 7.2
receivership and, 18.2.2, *see also* **Receivership**
removal, 7.1.4
remuneration of, 7.1.6
resident, 7.1.2
restriction of, 8.1 *et seq*
acting under, 8.1.5
breach of, 8.1.5

Directors — *contd.*
restriction of — *contd.*
defences, 8.1.2
duration of, 8.1.3
lifting order of, 8.1.4
locus standi, 8.1.1
shares, *see* **Shares**
silent, 7.8.5
voluntary winding up and, *see* **Voluntary winding up**

Director of Corporate Enforcement, 1.2.6, 1.5.11, 19.1 *et seq*
acting, 1.4
functions of, 1.4, 1.4.1
information received by, 1.4.3
investigations by, 19.1 *et seq*, *see also* **Investigations**
informal, 19.4 *et seq*
section 15 inquiry by, 19.4.1
office of, 1.4
powers of, 1.4.4
removal of, 1.4
reporting obligations of, 1.4.2
tenure of office of, 1.4
involuntary liquidation and, 21.1.4

Disposition of company assets, 23.1 *et seq*, *see also* **Involuntary winding up**, **Liquidation** and **Voluntary winding up**
contribution orders, 23.1.6
distribution of assets, 23.2 *et seq*
costs of proving debts, 23.2.2
creditors by a fixed charge, 23.2.2, *see also* **Fixed charges**
execution creditors, 23.2.2
matters settled before, 23.2.2

Disposition of company assets — *contd.*
distribution of assets — *contd.*
proving debts, 23.2.1
retention of title contracts, 23.2.2
set-off, 23.2.2
trust property subject to equity, 23.2.2
fraudulent preferences, 23.1.3, 23.1.4
proof of intention to prefer, 23.1.3
time frame for, 23.1.3
invalid, 23.1.2
invalidation of floating charges, 23.1.5, *see also* **Floating charges**
misfeasance proceedings, 23.1.7
personal liability for company debts, 23.1.8
pooling orders, 23.1.6
priority in distribution, 23.2.3
contributors, 23.2.3
floating charges, 23.2.3, *see also* **Floating** charges
members, 23.2.3
preferential creditors, 23.2.3
unsecured creditors, 23.2.3
realisation of company assets, 23.1 *et seq*
disclaimer of property, 23.1.1
validation of, 23.1.2

Dividends, 12.2 *et seq*, *see* Shares

Examiner, 20.3 *et seq*, *see also* **Examinership**
appointment of, 20.3, 20.3.1
costs, 20.6.6
expenses of, 20.6.6

Examiner — *contd.*
powers of, 20.6 *et seq*
contracts and, 20.6.5
court assistance, 20.6.2
director's powers, 20.6.3, *see also* **Directors**
information and assistance, 20.6.2
management, 20.6.1
pre-petition debts and, 20.6.7
secured property and, 20.6.9
set-offs, 20.6.8
related companies and, 20.3.2
report of, 20.7 *et seq*
court examination, 20.7.5
creditors, 20.7.4
members, 20.7.4
new, 20.7.2
old, 20.7.1
scheme of arrangement, 20.7.3

Examinership, 1.2.2, 1.2.5, 5.3.10, 20.1 *et seq*, *see also* **Examiner**
accountant's report, 20.2
irregularities disclosed in, 20.2.2
unavailable reports, 20.2.1
petition for, 20.1
hearing of, 20.4
uberrimae fides, 20.1.1
protection period, 20.5
directors, 20.5.4, *see also* **Directors**
guarantors, 20.5.3
ordinary creditors and, 20.5.1
provisional liquidators, 20.5.6
secured creditors, 20.5.2
remuneration, 20.6.6

European Business Register, 1.3.1

European company, 1.3.3

European Economic Interest Groupings (EEIGS), 1.3.4

Extraordinary general meeting, 13.3.2, *see also* **Meetings**

Fixed charges, 16.3, *see* Borrowing and Charges
book debts and, 16.5
control, issue of, 16.5.1
divisible book debts, 16.5.2
creditors by, 23.2.2

Floating charges, 2.6.5, 16.4 *et seq*, 23.2.3, *see* Borrowing, Charges and Receivership
crystallisation, 16.4, 16.4.2
invalidation, 23.1.5
negative pledge clauses, 16.4.3
present property interests, 16.4.1

Foreign companies, formation of, 2.4

Fraudulent trading, 10.1, 10.3 *et seq*, *see also* **Reckless trading**
civil liability for, 10.3
criminal liability for, 10.3.2
intent to defraud, 10.3, 10.3.1
subjective test, 10.3

Incorporation, 2.5 *et seq*
carrying on activities in the State, 2.5.1
certificate of registration, 2.5.3
commencement of business, 2.5.5

Incorporation,— *contd.*
consequences of, 2.6 *et seq*
contract actions, 2.6.6
corporate manslaughter and, 2.6.6
corporate personalty, 2.6.1
criminal liability, 2.6.6
criminal proceedings, 2.6.6
floating charges, 2.6.5
limited liability, 2.6.2
party to legal proceedings, 2.6.6
perpetual succession, 2.6.4
tort actions, 2.6.6
transfer of interests, 2.6.3
documents required for registration, 2.5.2
obligations on registration, 2.5.4
registered office of company, 2.5.6

Insider dealing, 1.2.4, 11.1 *et seq*
civil liability for, 11.4
company's right to deal, 11.3
criminal liability for, 11.5
exempt transactions, 11.6
share price, stabilisation of, 11.8
stock exchange, role of and, 11.7
unlawful dealings by connected persons, 11.1 *et seq*
being 'connected,' 11.1.3
dealing, 11.1.2
extension to other companies, 11.1.4
securities, 11.1
unlawful dealings by unconnected persons, 11.2

Insolvency, 1.2.2, 1.5.15, *see also* **Liquidation** and **Winding up**
cross-border, 1.3.5, 22.7
regulator, 1.5.15

Inspectors, 19.3 *et seq*, *see also* **Investigations**
expenses of, 19.2.4
failure to co-operate with, 19.2.5
powers of, 19.2.5 *et seq*, 19.3.2
assisting, 19.2.5
bank accounts and, 19.2.65
books and, 19.2.5
documents for, 19.2.5
examination oath, 19.2.5
related companies, 19.2.5
report of, 19.2.6

Investigations, 19.1 *et seq*, *see also* **Director of Corporate** Enforcement *and* Inspectors
carrying out of, 19.2.3
categories of, 19.1
co-operation with, 19.6.2
court, 19.2
section 7 investigations, 19.2.1
section 8 investigations, 19.2.2
expenses of, 19.2.4, 19.3.3, 19.6.3
formal investigation of company membership, 19.3 *et seq*, 19.5
section 14 investigations, 19.3.1
expenses and, 19.3.3
powers of inspector in, 19.3.2
inspectors, *see* **Inspectors**
production of documents, 19.6 *et seq*

Investigations — *contd.*
search warrants, 19.7
security of reports, 19.8

Involuntary winding up, 22.1 *et seq*, *see also* **Disposition of company assets, Voluntary winding up** and **Winding up**
company dissolution, 22.8
company register, restoration to, 22.9 *et seq*, 22.9.7
court powers and, 22.6
court winding up, 22.2 *et seq*
deadlock in corporate management, 22.2.5
failure of substratum, 22.2.5
failure to commence business, 22.2.2
fraudulent objects, 22.2.5
illegal objects, 22.2.5
inability to pay company debts, 22.2.4
just and equitable to, 22.2.5
minimum membership, 22.2.3
old public companies, 22.2.7
oppression, 22.2.6
quasi-partnership, 22.2.5
share capital, 22.2.8
special resolution, 22.2.1
cross border insolvency, 22.7
liquidator, 22.4 *et seq*, *see also* **Liquidator**
petitioners, 22.1 *et seq*
abuse of process, 22.1.2
company, 22.1.1
contributories, 22.1.3
creditors, 22.1.2

Involuntary winding up — *contd.*
petitioners — *contd.*
director of corporate enforcement, 22.1.4, *see* **Director of Corporate Enforcement**
disputed debts, 22.1.2
members, 22.1.6
opposition from other creditors, 22.1.2
registrar of companies, 22.1.5
procedure for, 22.3 *et seq*
effect of order, 22.3.2
hearing, 22.3.1
statement of affairs, 22.3.3
strike-off, effect of, 22.9.6

Legal personality, 1.3.2, *see* Corporate personality
European perspective on, 1.3.2

Limited companies, 2.1 *et seq*, 2.6.2
company limited by guarantee, 2.1.1
share capital with, 2.1.1
company limited by shares, 2.1.1
conversion to unlimited, 2.3.4
limited liability, 2.1.1

Liquidation, 2.1.2, 20.5.6, 21.8, *see* Disposition of company assets, Involuntary winding up, Liquidator *and* Voluntary winding up

Liquidator, *see also* **Liquidation**
appointment of, 21.1.4, 21.2.2, 22.4 *et seq*
committee of inspection, 22.4.2
costs, 23.2.2

Liquidator — *contd.*
duties, 22.4.3
expenses, 23.2.2
liability, 21.7, 22.4.6
powers of (involuntary liquidation), 22..5 *et seq*
section 231(1), 22.5.1
section 231(2), 22.5.2
section 290, 22.5.3
qualifications of, 22.4.1
removal, 22.4.5
remuneration of, 21.1.4, 22.4.4
resignation, 22.4.5
voluntary, powers of, 21.6 *et seq*
consideration for company property, 21.6.5
court directions, 21.6.4
creditors winding up and, 21.6.3
fettered powers, 21.6.1
sale of non-cash assets, 21.6.6
unfettered powers, 21.6.2

Meetings, 13.3 *et seq*
annual general meeting, 13.3.1
chairman, 13.3.6
extraordinary general meeting, 13.3.2
minutes of a general meeting, 13.3.9
notice for, 13.3.3
proxies, 13.3.5
quorums, 13.3.4
resolutions at, 13.3.7
voting, 13.3.8

Membership of a company, 13.1 *et seq*
eligible members, 13.1.3
investigation of, 19.3 et seq, *see also* **Investigations**

Membership of a company— *contd.*
original subscribers, 13.1.1
register of, 13.1.4
registration of beneficial interests, 13.1.5
share transfer and, *see* **Shares**
share transmission, *see* **Shares**
shareholders' meetings, *see* **Shares**
subsequent members, 13.1.2
termination of, 13.1.6

Memorandum of association, 4.1 *et seq*, *see also* **Articles of association**
alteration in general of, 4.1.8
association clause, 4.1.7
compulsory clauses, 4.1.1
liability clause, 4.1.5
model, 4.1.1
name clause, 4.1.3
amendment of company name, 4.1.3
exemption for private limited company, 4.1.3, *see also* **Private limited company**
failure to display company name, 4.1.3
liability for using words 'Ltd' or 'Teo', 4.1.3
undesirable company names, 4.1.3
objects clause, 4.1.4
alteration, 4.1.4
bell houses clause, 4.1.4
express ancillary powers of company, 4.1.4
implied ancillary powers of a company, 4.1.4
independent, 4.1.4
objects of a company, 4.1.4
public documents as, 4.4

Memorandum of association — *contd.*
section 25 contract, 4.3
share capital clause, 4.1.6

Minority shareholders, *see also* **Shares**
fraud on, 14.1.5
control, 14.1.5
fraud, 14.1.5
prima facie case, 14.1.5
obligations of, 1.3.1
rights of, 1.3.1

Officers of a company, *see also* **Company Secretary and Directors**
disqualification orders for, 1.2.3, 8 8.2 *et seq*
automatic, 8.2.1
breach of order for, 8.2.5
conduct resulting in, 8.2.6
court applicants, 8.2.4
court grounds for, 8.2.3
court-ordered, 8.2.2
errant, 1.2.3
restriction of, 8 *et seq*
acting under, 8.1.5
breach of, 8.1.5
duration of, 8.1.3
lifting order of, 8.1.4
locus standi, 8.1.1

Partnership, 1.1
disadvantages of, 1.1

Promoters, 2.1, 3.1 *et seq*
damages, 3.2.2
definition, 3
disqualification of, 3.2.3
duties of, 3.1et seq
breach of, 3.2 *et seq*
disclosure, 3.1.1

Partnership — *contd.*
pre-incorporation contracts and, 3.3 *et seq*
personal liability and, 3.3.1
ratification, 3.3.2
rescission, 3.2.1
remuneration, 3.3.3

Private limited, 1.2.5, 1.3.1, 1.5.5, 2.2. , 2.2.1
conversion to public, 2.3.1
memorandum, 4.1.3, *see also* **Memorandum of association**
single member, 1.3.1, 2.2.2, 2.3.5
shares by, 1.5.5
disclosure requirements, 1.3.1, 12.6.7, *see also* **Shares**
incorporation procedure and, 1.5.10

Private unlimited, 2.2.1

Public limited, 1.2.11.3.1, 2.2.3
articles of association, 1.3.1
conversion to private, 2.3.2
discourse requirements, 1.3.1, 12.6.2, 12.6.3
division of, 1.3.1
formation of, 1.3.1
maintenance of capital of, 1.3.1
memorandum of, 1.3.1
merger of, 1.3.1
purchasing shares in, 1.3.1

Public unlimited, 2.2.3

Receiver, *see also* **Receivership**
appointment, 16.4.2, 18.1 *et seq*
agency relationship, 18.1.2
court, 18.1.1.3
debenture under, 18.1.1

Receiver — *contd.*
duties of receiver, 18.3 *et seq*
application of proceeds of sale, 18.3.3
exercise care in disposal of assets, 18.3.2
guarantors to, 18.3.4
provide information to the company, 18.3.1
standard of care to be applied, 18.3.2
notification obligations, 18.1.7
receiver/manager, 18.1.6
removal of, 18.4.1
resignation of, 18.4.2
statement of affairs of company, 18.1.8

Receivership, 18.1 *et seq*, *see also* **Receiver**
effect of, 18.1.4, 18.2 *et seq*
company and, 18.2.2
company contracts, 18.2.3, *see also* **Contracts**
directors and, 18.2.2, *see also* **Directors**
employment contracts, 18.2.3
floating charges, 18.2.1, *see also* **Floating charges**
post-receivership contacts, 18.2.3
pre-receivership contracts, 18.2.3
statement of affairs of company, 18.1.8

Reckless trading, 1.2.3, 10.1, 10.2 *et seq*, 10.2.4, *see also* **Fraudulent trading**
civil liability for, 10.2
subjective test for, 10.2.1
objective test and, 10.2.2
relief and, 10.2.3

Shares, 12.1 *et seq*, *see also* **capital**, maintenance of *and* **minority shareholders**
allotment of, , 12.5 *et seq*, 12.5.2
consideration for, 12.5.5
power to allot, 12.5.1
pre-emption rights, 12.5.4
public to, 12.5.3
shares issued at a premium, 12.5.7
shares issued at discount, 12.5.6
calls, 12.1.4
capital, 12.1.1
certificates, 12.1.2
classes of, 12.4 *et seq*
bonus, 12.4.4
deferred, 12.4.4
founders', 12.4.4
ordinary, 12.4.1
preference, 12.4.2
redeemable, 12.4.3
treasury, 12.4.4, 15.1.3
class rights,
variation of, 12.4.6
discount, issued at, 12.5.6
dividends, 12.2 *et seq*
declaration of, 12.2.2
declared but unpaid, 12.2.3
distributions, 12.2.1
fixed, 12.4.4
shareholder's right to, 12.3.1
unlawful, 12.2.4
interests in, disclosure of, 12.6 *et seq*
company secretary and, 12.6.1, *see also* **Company secretary**
directors and, 12.6.1, *see also* **Directors**
liens on, 12.4.5

Shares — *contd.*
interests in, disclosure of — *contd.*
penalties for non, 12.6.4
plc's, 12.6.2, 12.6.3, 12.6.6, *see also* **Public limited company**
private company, 12.6.7
register of, 12.6.5
nominal value, 12.1.1
par value, 12.1.1
shareholder's meetings, 13.3 *et seq*, *see* **Meetings**
shareholder's remedies, 14.1 *et seq*
disregard of members' interests, 14.2.5
fraud on the minority, *see* **Minority shareholders**
illegal actions, 14.1.3
justice of the case, 14.1.6
majority principle, 14.1.4
oppression, 14.2.4
rule in *Foss v. Harbottle*, 14.1, *et seq*, *see also* **Corporate personality**
section 205 remedy, 14.2 *et seq*
shareholder's actions, 14.1.7
ultra vires actions, 14.1.2, *see also* ***Ultra vires***
shareholder's rights,
dividends, 12.3.1
attend meetings, 12.3.2
participate in winding up, 12.3.3
personal, 12.3.5
statutory, 12.3.4
vote, 12.3.2

Shares — *contd.*
transfer of, 13.2, 13.2.1
pre-emption rights, 13.2.2
refusal to register, 13.2.4
registration of, 12.3.3
unregistered, 13.2.5
transmission of, 13.2
bankruptcy and, 13.2.6
death and, 13.2.6
warrants, 12.1.3

Tax,
liability, 5.5

Tribunal of inquiry, 1.2.6

Ultra vires,
abolition of doctrine of, 1.5.12, 6.1.3

Unlimited companies, 1.2, 2.1.2, *see also* **Public and Private companies**
actions, 14.1.2
conversion to limited,.2.3.3
unlimited liability, 2.1.2

Voluntary winding up, 16.4.2, 21.1 *et seq*, 21.4, *see* Disposition of company assets, Liquidator, Involuntary winding up *and* Winding up
creditor's, 21.2 *et seq*
committee of inspection, 21.2.2
creditors' meeting, 21.2.2
duty of directors, 21.2.2, *see also* **Directors**
liquidator, 21.2.2, *see also* **Liquidator**
meetings, 21.2.2
members' meeting, 21.2.1
power to vote, 21.2.2
members', 21.1 *et seq*

Voluntary winding up — *contd.*
conversion to creditors' winding up, 21.3 *et seq*
declaration of solvency, 21.1.2
liquidation, *see* **Liquidation**
liquidator, *see* **Liquidator**
report of the independent person, 21.1.3
shareholder's resolution, 21.1.1

Winding up,
compulsory, 16.4.2
court, 21.2 *et seq*, *see* **Involuntary winding up**
conversion to voluntary, 21.4
— *contd.*
effect of, 18.1.5
involuntary, *see* **Involuntary winding up**
voluntary, 16.4.2, 21.1 *et seq*, *see* **Voluntary winding up**